THE WINNING SIDE

Questions on Living the Culture of LIFE

Charles E. Rice

St. Brendan's Institute

Mishawaka, Indiana
1999

Cover by Michael Murphy Design, Mishawaka, Indiana

Cover photo used with permission of Archive Photos, New York, New York
© 1999 St. Brendan's Institute, Mishawaka, Indiana

ISBN 0-9674691-0-4

Library of Congress Card Number: 99-091104

Printed in the United States of America

THE WINNING SIDE:

QUESTIONS ON LIVING

THE CULTURE OF LIFE

DEDICATION

To my wife, Mary, our children and our grandchildren.

Acknowledgments

I gratefully acknowledge the incomparable assistance of Lois Plawecki in expertly preparing and managing the manuscript from start to finish; of Notre Dame Law School Librarians Carmela Kinslow and Dwight King, and their research staff in their prompt acquisition of often arcane materials; of Rev. Robert A. Connor, of the Prelature of Opus Dei, for his comments and suggestions; and especially of my daughters, Ellen and Patricia Rice, and of my wife, Mary, in reviewing and evaluating numerous drafts of the manuscript.

I acknowledge my special indebtedness to the late Professor Edward J. Murphy and the late Professor Frank E. Booker, both of Notre Dame Law School. Prof. Murphy, with the help of Prof. Booker, founded Cashel Institute to promote a reasoned understanding of the Faith. St. Brendan's Institute carries on that work. Both Prof. Murphy and Prof. Booker provided inspiration by example to me and to generations of Notre Dame Law School faculty and students. *Requiescant in pace.*

Quotations from the Second Vatican Council taken from the 1992 edition, Austin Flannery, O.P., ed. Quotations from the *Summa Theologica* taken from the Benzinger edition, 1947.

Excerpts from the English translation of the *Catechism of the Catholic Church* for use in the United States of America © 1994, United States Catholic Conference, Inc. — Libreria Editrice Vaticana. Used with permission.

TABLE OF CONTENTS

Introduction xiii

PART I: THE PROBLEM
A. Conflict and Choices
1. Can we really be unconditionally pro-life today? 3
2. Shouldn't we be tolerant? And nonjudgmental? 7

B. The Law on Abortion and Euthanasia
3. What did the Supreme Court do in *Roe v. Wade*? 11
4. But hasn't the Court retreated from its holding in *Roe*? . . 17
5. Hasn't the Supreme Court held that there is no "right to die"?
    Isn't that a pro-life victory? 23

PART II: WHY LAW AND POLITICS CANNOT SOLVE THE PROBLEM
A. The American Republic is No More
6. What constitutional changes prevent legal restoration
    of the right to life? 35
7. How did we end up with a centralized government
    of practically unlimited powers? 37
8. How did the Supreme Court become dominant? 47
9. Did Congress surrender to the Supreme Court? 57
10. How did secularism become the official religion of the nation?
    And what difference does it make? 61

B. Technology Has Made Murder a Private Matter
11. How did abortion become a private choice beyond the law? . . . 69
12. But isn't the claim that life begins at
    conception a "religious" position? 75
13. Euthanasia: How did we move toward
    a privatized duty to die? 81

C. The Problem is Spiritual and Cultural
14. What Enlightenment ideas corrupted our culture? 89

15. How does legal positivism separate law and morality? . . . 97

16. Why is contraception the decisive issue? 107

17. How does contraception put a dangerous
weapon in the hands of government? 119

PART III: THE SOLUTION

A. **The Culture of Life**

18. Wait a minute. First, what is the answer to the ideas of the
Enlightenment? 129

19. So what is the culture of life? 139

B. **Some Family Questions**

20. What is the family and how does it work? 145

21. How can the civil law help the family? 151

22. If we are going to live the culture of life, how should
we educate our kids?
Should we give up on the public schools? 159

23. But shouldn't the state provide vouchers or tax credits
for students in private schools? 167

24. What about "sex education"? 173

25. What happened to the Catholic universities?
Are any of them still Catholic? 183

26. When is it right to "pull the plug" on a family member? 199

27. Should I have a living will? 205

28. Is homosexuality a sin? 209

29. What should our attitude be on "gay rights"? 211

30. Should we make Sunday a special kind of day? 217

C. **The Right to Life: No Exception**

31. Why is abortion never morally or legally
justified in any case? 221

32. Can it ever be moral to pursue an incremental strategy,
proposing or supporting laws that would limit
abortion but allow it in some cases? 225

33. What principles govern the morality of cooperation with
abortion or other evils? 229

34. Although an incremental strategy of limiting abortion can
be morally justified, does it make practical sense? 233

35. What kinds of legislation should we promote
on the federal level? 243

36. What kinds of legislation should we
promote on the state level? 247

37. What about candidates?
    Should we ever vote for one who is pro-abortion? 257

38. Why not kill abortionists? 259

39. What tactics, at abortuaries and elsewhere, are legal and
    effective ways of saving lives? 267

D. **Related Issues**

40. Can we be pro-life and support capital punishment? . . . 275

41. If we are pro-life, don't we have to be opposed to war?
    Doesn't a Catholic have to be a pacifist? 287

42. Shouldn't the government recognize the right of
    conscientious objection to military service? 295

43. How does immigration affect the life issues
    and the family? 299

44. What is the economic foundation of the culture of life?. 307

45. What does "global free trade" have to do with all this?. . 315

46. Can we ever hope to restore morality in government? . . 323

E. **The Constitution: Is It Still There?**

47. Was there some deficiency in the Constitution which
    invited its collapse? 327

48. Should we give up on the Constitution? 335

49. Should the government of the United States affirm that
    the Declaration of Independence is true? 339

PART IV: THE FUTURE

50. Are we <u>really</u> on the winning side? 349

Index 355

xi

INTRODUCTION

This book began as a second edition of *No Exception: A Pro-Life Imperative*. In 1990, that book offered reasons for the pro-life movement to adopt uncompromising tactics to restore the right to life of the unborn. Over the past decade, however, the "culture of death," including euthanasia as well as abortion, has imbedded itself in American law beyond any prospect of correction by legal or political means. Nevertheless, abundant signs point to the growth of a new "culture of life" from the bottom up. Pope John Paul II has defined the way to build that "culture of life." The Pope is more than a teacher of law. Rather, he integrates the natural law into the teaching of Christ. But his insights, especially on the nature of truth and the dignity of the human person, make him the most effective writer of jurisprudence in the world today. This book, as a second edition, updates and amplifies the *No Exception* book.[1] But this is a new book in that it will examine the problem, and the solution, in light of the principles expounded by John Paul II.

There should be no exception to the legal protection of innocent life. But the pro-life effort is not reducible to law and politics. It is about living pro-life in every respect. A decade ago it was already apparent that "[i]n secular and political terms the pro-life cause is absolutely, utterly hopeless."[2] But it is true today as it was then, that "we need not fight in merely human terms" and that "we have every reason for confidence if, in addition to our work, we repent, trust God, and call on Him for guidance and help, particularly through the intercession of Mary, His mother."[3] The pro-life effort must be part of a larger enterprise: the voluntary reconversion of this nation, in freedom, to faith in God and total respect for His law. One step toward that reconversion is the recovery of the neglected principle that the human law can never validly tolerate the intentional killing of innocent human beings. The more important step

xiii

is for each of us to live the culture of life in the midst of a culture of death.

If we do so, one by one, a new culture of life will develop without our consciously trying to create it. This book will offer a few suggestions that may be useful in that effort.

---

[1] This book also draws, with permission, on the analysis in Charles E. Rice, "Abortion, Euthanasia, and the Need to Build a New 'Culture of Life,'" 12 *Notre Dame J. of Law, Ethics and Public Policy* 101 (1998); see Questions 1, 3, 4, 11, 13, 16, 34 and 50.

[2] Charles E. Rice, *No Exception: A Pro-life Imperative* (1990), 119.

[3] *Ibid.*

ABBREVIATIONS

In this book abbreviations are used in the footnotes for frequently cited sources. In all quotations in this book, all indicated emphases are in the original documents unless otherwise indicated.

CA   John Paul II, Encyclical Letter *Centisimus Annus* (1991)

CCC   *Catechism of the Catholic Church* (1992)

EA   John Paul II, Post-Synodal Apostolic Exhortation *Ecclesia in America* (1999)

EV   John Paul II, Encyclical Letter *Evangelium Vitae* (1995)

FR   John Paul II, Encyclical Letter *Fides et Ratio* (1998)

LF   John Paul II, Encyclical Letter *Letter to Families* (1994)

ST   St. Thomas Aquinas, *Summa Theologica*

TMHS   Pontifical Council for the Family, *The Truth and Meaning of Human Sexuality* (1995)

VS   John Paul II, Encyclical Letter *Veritatis Splendor* (1993)

PART I:

THE PROBLEM

A. Conflict and Choices

1. CAN WE REALLY BE UNCONDITIONALLY PRO-LIFE TODAY?

> We are facing an enormous and dramatic clash between good and evil, death and life, the "culture of death" and the "culture of life." We find ourselves not only "faced with" but necessarily "in the midst of" this conflict: we are all involved and we all share in it with the responsibility of *choosing to be unconditionally pro-life*. – *Evangelium Vitae*[1]

Is it possible to be unconditionally pro-life in the United States today? At World Youth Day in Denver, Pope John Paul described the twentieth century as "an era of massive attacks on life, an endless series of wars and a continual taking of innocent human life. False prophets and false teachers have had the greatest success."[2] "With time," he said, "the threats against life have not grown weaker. They are taking on vast proportions. They are not only threats coming from the outside, from the forces of nature or the 'Cains' who kill the 'Abels;' no, they are scientifically and systematically programmed threats."

Since *Roe v. Wade*, in 1973, legalized abortion has delivered a body count of at least 40 million,[3] not including deaths from uncountable abortions by pill, intrauterine device, etc. And we have legalized euthanasia, notwithstanding the false optimism generated by the Supreme Court's refusal to discover a "right to die" in the Constitution.

The immediate pro-life response to *Roe* was, properly, to undo that ruling by constitutional amendment or legislation. Those efforts have failed. And, in seeking incremental restrictions on abortion rather than its prohibition, the establishment pro-life movement has implicitly accepted the basic premise of *Roe*, that the unborn child is a nonperson whose execution can be legitimately tolerated by the state.[4] In any event, technology is moving abortion and euthanasia beyond effective reach of the law. They are truly becoming matters of private choice.

Legalized abortion and euthanasia, however, are symptoms. In a culture dominated by a relativist and utilitarian contraceptive ethic, it is predictable that man will make himself (or herself) the arbiter of the ending as well as the beginning of life. A national moral meltdown has

---

[1] *EV*, no. 28.
[2] Pope John Paul II, *Address*, Aug. 14, 1993; quoted in *EV*, no. 17.
[3] See National Right to Life Committee: *Abortion in the United States: Statistics and Trends* (1997), 1; see also *National Right to Life News*, Dec. 10, 1998, p. 14.
[4] See Question 34.

accelerated the dominance of the culture of death. With respect to the Constitution, legalized abortion and euthanasia are not aberrations in an otherwise healthy system. Rather they were facilitated, and protected against reversal, by the transformation of the Constitution into a warrant for a centralized government of open-ended legislative and administrative powers operating under judicial supremacy, liberated from God and practically impervious to popular control. And the executive branch, with the acquiescence of Congress and the courts, has ceded major elements of sovereignty to international agencies. In short, the electroencephalograph of the American Republic is a flat line. The Republic, as given to us by the Founders, was a marvelous construct of human wisdom and courage. But it died by the hands of its custodians. Although it is unrealistic to expect a formal restoration of the right to life, the law and the Constitution can still be used defensively to keep the government off the backs of those who are trying to live the culture of life.

"Choosing to be unconditionally pro-life" is difficult because of these cultural and constitutional developments. But the choice is inescapable. "With the approach of the millennium and the total or near collapse of many ideologies rooted in atheism — most notably Marxism, Freudianism, and Darwinism — there appears to be an increasing return to a radical choice for humanity, not unlike the one represented in the first centuries of the Christian era, that between a fixed credal, hierarchical Christianity, with its sacramental system and the message of the 'gift of self,' and a despairing hedonistic paganism with its corollaries in Gnostic and 'nature' religions, the modern forms of which are worship of progress and modern science."[5]

In a sense, we suffer from the scourge of having the 60s and 70s generations in power. But, like an oil slick on a river, this, too, will pass. One of John Paul's recurrent themes is that "God is preparing a great springtime for Christianity, and we can already see its first signs."[6] There may be confirmation of this idea in the large numbers of young people at the Pope's appearances and in the enthusiasm of their reaction:

> The youth of the 90s are not the youth of the 60s. The youth of the 90s have been forced to grow up with the mistakes and moral nightmares of the 60s generation: drugs, illicit sex widely condoned, addiction, abortion and the Culture of Death which flowed from this ill-conceived social revolution. Divorce deprived them of parents and stability. Contraception deprived them of brothers and sisters, often replaced by the toys and

---

[5] C. John McCloskey, "The Rise of Christianity," *Position Paper* 284/285 (Dublin, Ireland) Aug/Sept. 1997, 231.

[6] See *Redemptoris Missio* , *The Mission of the Redeemer* (1990), no. 86.

junk of materialism. Euthanasia and assisted suicide threaten to deprive them of the wisdom of age and reverence for suffering.

Where the 60s generation eschewed authority, the 90s generation *craves* and *recognizes legitimate* authority. Legitimate authority is the authority of love. God's love which John Paul II radiates. You can't kid kids. The youth of today love John Paul II *because* his message is difficult, not *despite* it. They know he loves them enough to tell them the truth. They know he is calling them to a love and beauty that does not come cheap and does not always make one popular, but which is worth it. They know well the pain and squalor of the alternative.

They also know that if they were born after 1973 their status is that of survivor. They could not be blamed for thinking, "Thirty-seven million others were aborted, why not me?" Children have been discarded in one way or another for the last 35 years, while their elders pursued vanity and the way of the Self. Children got in the way. In truth, the only thing wrong with the younger generation is that there are not enough of them.

Alternatively, John Paul II, the greatest figure on the world stage, throws his arms open to the youth and proclaims, "You are my hope!" And they have responded to him in kind for almost 20 years.[7]

This book is not a "Catholic tract." But it proceeds from the conviction that the answers to the problems discussed are found in the moral and social teachings of the Catholic Church. Those teachings merit consideration by everyone, and not just Catholics, as the foundation for a culture of life. They are discussed in this book in that spirit.

The culture of life, however, cannot be built merely on reasoning and abstractions. Rather, "[t]he Gospel of life is something concrete and personal, for it consists in the proclamation of *the very person of Jesus*. . . . Through the words, the actions and the very person of Jesus, man is given the possibility of 'knowing' the *complete truth* concerning the value of human life. From this source he receives. . . the capacity to 'accomplish' this truth perfectly. . . , that is to accept and fulfill completely the responsibility of loving and serving, of defending and promoting human life. In Christ, the *Gospel of life* is definitely proclaimed and fully given."[8] From Christ, man receives the capacity to "accomplish" the truth. "Human perfection," John Paul said in *Fides et Ratio*, "consists not simply in acquiring an abstract knowledge of the truth, but in a dynamic relationship of faithful self-giving with others."[9] We can, even today, be unconditionally pro-life through the gift of self, in faith, to God and to others.

---

[7] Editorial, *The Sooner Catholic* (Oklahoma City), July 27, 1997, p. 8.

[8] *EV,* no. 29.

[9] *FR,* no. 32.

2. Shouldn't We Be Tolerant? And Nonjudgmental?

We are concerned here with issues, not with the motivations of those who participate in abortion or euthanasia or who cause the law to tolerate those evils. To condemn the objective wrong of abortion and euthanasia is not to judge the subjective guilt of the perpetrators. The distinction between objective wrong and subjective culpability is familiar in law and morality. When John Hinckley shot President Reagan and three others, he committed an objective wrong. But he was not subjectively culpable and was therefore not subject to criminal punishment. He was found not guilty by reason of insanity and was committed to a mental hospital.[1]

To be morally culpable for committing a wrong, one must know it is wrong and yet choose to do it. In cases like Hinckley's, courts have a duty to judge culpability. But, as private citizens, we generally have neither the right nor the capacity to judge the moral culpability of anyone. Opponents of abortion should avoid criticizing its participants, including the mother and even the abortionist, in personal terms. They should seek the participants' conversion rather than their condemnation. Their subjective culpability may be reduced or eliminated by their circumstances. But that cannot change the objective wrongness of their act.

The Natural Law

While avoiding judgments as to culpability, we must also confront the more prevalent error that denies the reality of objective wrong. Some actions such as murder, blasphemy, perjury and adultery are always wrong regardless of the motive or purpose of the perpetrator. A good purpose does not justify the doing of an intrinsically evil act.[2]

Miseducation has caused many to be unable or unwilling to distinguish objective wrong from subjective culpability. Many seem to think that nothing is wrong "for you" unless you "feel" it is wrong. If we were to ask an average high-school student, Catholic or otherwise, even one who does not favor abortion, what he (or she) thinks about it, he would likely say that, while not personally approving of abortion, he cannot say it is always wrong for everyone else. Perhaps without realizing it, he would deny the reality of objective standards of good rooted in nature, a reality we all recognize in everyday actions. Suppose you see your friend, Freddy, with the hood of his car up, holding a can of oil in one hand and a can of molasses in the other, and you ask, "What are you doing?"

---

[1] *New York Times*, Aug. 10, 1982, p. 1.
[2] See *CCC*, no. 1756; see also no. 1750.

Freddy answers, "Trying to decide whether to put oil or molasses in my car." If you were a real friend of Freddy, how would you respond? Would you say, "Freddy, how do you *feel* about it?" No, what you would say is, "Freddy, you should do good by your car. And the good is that which is in accord with the nature of the thing. Oil is good for cars. Molasses isn't." "Yeah, but this is a Chevy." "Freddy, it doesn't make any difference. Cars are all the same." "Is that right? Well, who are you to tell me what to do with my car?" "If you don't believe me, Freddy, look in the glove compartment at the manufacturer's directions." (That is what the natural law and the Ten Commandments are — the Manufacturer's directions.) Freddy looks at the owner's manual and sees, in red letters on page 10, "Use oil — do not use molasses." Freddy says, "That's what it says, all right. But wait a minute. Whose car is this? It's my car. (It's my body, etc.) They can't push me around. I'll do what I want with my own car." So Freddy puts in the molasses. He is sincere. He is liberated. He is pro-choice. And he is a pedestrian. He violated the natural law of his car.[3]

Whether we are talking about automobiles, human beings or society, the natural law is the story of how things work.[4] The intentional killing of an innocent human being is always objectively wrong. It is contrary to natural justice, the revealed law of God and the common good of society, regardless of the motive or other subjective dispositions of the killer. We do no favor to the person contemplating abortion when we encourage her to decide according to her feelings. It is a lie to pretend that abortion can ever be anything but an objective evil. But we cannot condemn her, whatever she decides. The subjective guilt, if any, of those involved in abortion is for the judgment of God and, in the Sacrament of Penance, the confessor.

THE UNJUST LAW

The natural law dictates that human law can never legitimately tolerate the intentional killing of innocent human beings. This principle, which allows no exception, also implies the law's duty to protect all innocent life. Human law, St. Thomas Aquinas explained, is enacted "for the common good of all the citizens."[5] The purpose of that law "is to lead men to virtue, not suddenly but gradually."[6] Although the law should promote virtue, it should not prescribe every virtue or forbid ev-

---

[3] See Charles E. Rice, "Some Reasons for a Restoration of Natural Law Jurisprudence," 24 *Wake Forest L. Rev.* 539, 563 (1989).

[4] See Charles E. Rice, *50 Questions on the Natural Law* (2d ed.,1999).

[5] St. Thomas Aquinas, *ST,* I, II, Q. 96, art. 1

[6] *Ibid.*, at art. 2.

ery vice lest by its unenforceability the law be "despised" and "greater evils" result.[7] Murder, however, is one evil which the law is bound to forbid:

> Now human law is framed for a number of human beings, the majority of whom are not perfect in virtue. Wherefore human laws do not forbid all vices, from which the virtuous abstain, but only the more grievous vices, from which it is possible for the majority to abstain; and chiefly those that are to the hurt of others, without the prohibition of which human society could not be maintained; thus *human law prohibits murder*, theft and suchlike.[8]

If human laws are just, they bind in conscience. But if a human law "deflects from the law of nature," it is unjust "and is no longer a law but a perversion of law."[9] Laws authorizing the intentional killing of the innocent are unjust because they withdraw from the potential victim the even-handed protection of the law to which he is entitled. Aquinas, of course, knew nothing of the process of fertilization and gestation.[10] But he denied that there can be any right intentionally to kill the innocent in any case: "Therefore it is in no way lawful to slay the innocent."[11]

DISCUSS ISSUES, NOT MOTIVES

Confusion can also arise from a failure to distinguish the objective merits of pro-life legislative proposals from the motives of those who advocate them. Prominent leaders in the pro-life movement have spent at least two decades validating the pro-death premise that the law may legitimately allow the intentional killing of innocent human beings. They

---

[7] *Ibid.*

[8] *Ibid.* (emphasis added).

[9] *Ibid.*, I, II, Q. 95, art. 2; St. Thomas explains that a law may be unjust in two ways: [F]irst by being contrary to human good. . . either in respect of the end, as when an authority imposes on his subjects burdensome laws, conducive, not to the common good, but rather to his own cupidity or vainglory; or in respect of the author, as when a man makes a law that goes beyond the power committed to him; or in respect of the form, as when burdens are imposed unequally on the community, although with a view to the common good. The like are acts of violence rather than laws; because as Augustine says *(De Lib. Arb. i.5)*, a law that is not just, seems to be no law at all. Wherefore such laws do not bind in conscience, except perhaps in order to avoid scandal or disturbance, for which cause a man should even yield his right, according to Matth. v. 40, 41. . . .
Secondly, laws may be unjust through being opposed to the Divine good; such are the laws of tyrants inducing to idolatry, or to anything else contrary to the Divine law; and laws of this kind must nowise to observed, because, as stated in Acts v. 29, we ought to obey God rather than men. *Ibid.* at Q. 96, art 4. (emphasis added).

[10] See discussion in Question 12.

[11] *ST*, II, Q. 64, art. 6.

began by conceding the legality of abortion to save the life of the mother. They have ended by proposing only marginal restrictions on otherwise unlimited abortion. When the "pro-life" movement itself concedes that the intentional killing of the innocent is politically negotiable, how can we be surprised at the impotence of that movement in confronting euthanasia? The futility of the establishment pro-life movement arises basically from its refusal to condemn the objective wrong of contraception. In contraception man makes himself, rather than God, the arbiter of life's beginning. Why is anyone surprised when he makes himself the arbiter also of its end? The elimination of the unwanted at both ends of life will be a predictable response to the problems caused by an excess of old people and a shortage of workers to support them, a shortage directly resulting from contraception and abortion.

The pro-life movement has lost the war it chose to fight on the enemy's terms. Early abortifacient technology, however, signals a new war in which abortion and euthanasia will be a truly private choice. This war can be won only through a reconversion of the American people to respect for life as a gift of God. The pro-life movement can contribute to that reconversion only if it bears witness to the truth without compromise of principle. Some pro-life issues involve the prudential choice of permissible options. Others involve principles on which no compromise is possible. On nonessentials, we should strive for unity. But unity cannot be itself the object. We must recover some lost principles and stand for them, whatever the cost to unity within the movement. Pro-life discussion, however, ought to limit itself to the objective merits of the issues. Disagreement, whether on principle or tactics, must not degenerate into disparagement of the motives of those who disagree.

B.   The Law on Abortion and Euthanasia

3.   WHAT DID THE SUPREME COURT DO IN *ROE V. WADE?*

Amy Grossberg and Brian Peterson, age 19 and 20, were sentenced to 2-1/2 and 2 years, respectively, for manslaughter for killing their baby after Amy gave birth to him in 1996 at the Comfort Inn in Newark, Delaware.[1] The autopsy showed that the full-term, healthy boy died from "multiple fractures. . .with injury to the brain due to blunt force head trauma and shaking." Amy and Brian did not concede that they knew the baby was alive when they put him in a plastic bag which they put in a trash container in the hotel parking lot. It is unclear whether the injuries to the baby happened before or after he was put in the trash bin. After the birth, Amy and Brian returned to their colleges. The incident came to light when she was hospitalized for complications from the delivery.

Amy and Brian are criminals in the eyes of the law, not because they intentionally, or through indifference, killed an innocent human being, but because they waited ten minutes too long and used the wrong method. They would be in the clear if they had hired an abortionist to solve their problem, even during delivery, by a legal partial-birth abortion. The Supreme Court has decreed that abortion may not be banned, even in the ninth month, when it is sought to protect the mother's mental health, as could be claimed in a case such as this. Had Amy and Brian exercised their "right to choose" in this way, the abortionist would have dilated the entrance to the uterus sufficiently to deliver the baby's body, except for the head. He would have delivered the baby, feet first, except for the head. He then would have inserted scissors into the base of the baby's skull and opened the scissors to enlarge the hole. He would have inserted a suction catheter and sucked out the baby's brains. The head would have collapsed and the abortionist then would have removed and disposed of the body.[2] If they had chosen that course, Amy and Brian could have gone back to college, not as targets of a homicide prosecution, but as vindicators of the preferred constitutional "right to choose."

The attorneys for Amy and Brian chose not to use an insanity defense. In fact, Amy and Brian would seem to be more in touch with reality than are the Supreme Court of the United States and the State of Delaware. Their boy was no less a human being — and no less a person

---

[1]   *N.Y. Times*, Dec. 3, 1996, p. A1; *N.Y. Times*, Apr. 23, 1998, p. A1. *Washington Times*, July 10, 1998, p. A5; *N.Y. Times*, July 10, 1998, p. A1.
[2]   See testimony of Curtis R. Cook, M.D., 14 *Issues in Law & Medicine* 65, 66 (1998).

— during delivery, or at his conception, than he was when they killed him or put him in the trash bin. Yet the Court and the State would have mobilized the federal marshals to protect their right to kill him before birth and even during delivery. But because Amy and Brian waited for ten minutes and did not use an approved method of killing, the State charged them with murder and sought the death penalty. As columnist George Will put it: "Could Delaware choose to execute [Amy and Brian] by inserting scissors into the bases of their skulls, opening the scissors, inserting suction tubes and sucking out their brains? Of course not. The Constitution forbids choosing cruel and unusual punishments."[3] But Amy and Brian could have legally done just that to their baby. So who's crazy?

The killing of newborn babies who could have been legally and secretly aborted is not all that rare.[4] This case drew attention because Amy and Brian are children of wealth who could have easily had an abortion. But their case reminds us that legalized abortion will inevitably lead to infanticide and euthanasia. All three are founded on the denial of personhood to the victim. A "[r]eckless disregard for the value of human life has been transmitted through the culture for 25 years. The easy resort to abortion and the extremist rhetoric supporting the abortion regime have clearly cheapened the lives of babies. . . . There never was a clear dividing line between abortion and infanticide. . . . [I]t should not come as a huge surprise that young women from nice families don't quite see why prosecutors are knocking at their doors for performing very late abortions. Isn't it still a choice?"[5]

THE SUPREME COURT RULINGS

The Supreme Court's abortion rulings include four principal elements:

1. *The unborn child is a nonperson and therefore has no constitutional rights;*

2. *The right of his mother to kill that nonperson is a "liberty interest" protected by the due process clause of the Fourteenth Amendment;*

3. *The states may impose some marginal restrictions on abortion but are barred from effectively prohibiting abortion at any stage of pregnancy;*

4. *Efforts undertaken in the vicinity of an abortuary to dissuade women from abortion are subject to more stringent restrictions than are other forms of speech, assembly and association.*[6]

---

[3] *The Times-Picayune* (New Orleans, LA), Nov. 24, 1996, p. B7.
[4] See *N.Y. Times,* July 3, 1997, p. A10; *Philadelphia Inquirer,* Aug. 12, 1997, p. A1; *Wash. Post,* July 15, 1997, p. A12; Ellen Goodman, "'Prom Mom' Shame," *Boston Globe,* July 17, 1997, p. A15.
[5] Mona Charen, "Misguided Search for Answers," *Wash. Times,* June 16, 1997, p. A13.
[6] See Question 39.

A NONPERSON

The Fourteenth Amendment, adopted in 1868, protects the right of a "person" to life and to the equal protection of the laws. The framers of that amendment did not consider the status of the unborn child but they intended that, "in the eyes of the Constitution, every <u>human being</u> within its sphere. . .from the President to the slave, is a <u>person</u>."[7] This was in reaction to the *Dred Scott* case in 1857, in which the Supreme Court held that the free descendants of slaves were not citizens and said that slaves were property rather than persons.[8]

In any society where personhood determines the possession of legal rights, justice mandates an inseparable connection between humanity and personhood. If that connection is broken, where does one draw the line? Peter Singer carries to its logical conclusion the separation of humanity from personhood:

> We should reject the doctrine that places the lives of members of our species above the lives of members of other species. Some members of other species are persons; some members of our own species are not. No objective assessment can give greater value to the lives of members of our species who are not persons than to the lives of members of other species who are. On the contrary, as we have seen there are strong arguments for placing the lives of persons above the lives of non-persons. So it seems that killing, say a chimpanzee is worse than the killing of a gravely defective human who is not a person.[9]

Singer, an Australian ethicist, is the Ira W. DeCamp Professor of Bioethics at the Princeton University Center for Human Values,[10] which may tell us something about Princeton. "We can no longer base our ethics," says Singer, "on the idea that human beings are a special form of creation, made in the image of God, singled out from all other animals, and alone possessing an immortal soul."[11] Singer's views are a consistent application of mainstream positivist jurisprudence. "The right to life," Singer thinks, "is not a right of members of the species *Homo sapiens*; it is. . . a right that properly belongs to persons. Not all members of the species *Homo sapiens* are persons, and not all persons are members of the

---

[7] *Cong. Glob*, 37th Cong., 2d Sess. 1449 (1862) (Sen. Sumner) (first emphasis added). Brief, *Amicus Curiae*, Catholics United For Life, in *Webster v. Reproductive Health Services*, 492 U.S. 490 (1989), 14.

[8] *Scott v. Sandford*, 60 U.S. (19 How.) 393, 15 L. Ed. 691, 709, 720 (1857).

[9] Peter Singer, *Practical Ethics* (1979), 97. See also Helga Kuhse and Peter Singer, *Should the Baby Live?* (1985).

[10] See David S. Odenberg, "A Messenger of Death at Princeton," *Wash. Times*, June 30, 1998, p. A12; *N.Y. Times*, Apr. 10, 1999, p. A1.

[11] Peter Singer, "Sanctity of Life or Quality of Life?" *Pediatrics*, July 1986, 128, 128-29.

species *Homo sapiens.*"[12] Singer believes that while chimpanzees, whales, dolphins, dogs and cats can be persons, newborn infants and retarded humans are not. He even seems to think that chickens may be persons,[13] raising the prospect that the greatest mass murderer in history is not Ghengis Khan, Hitler or Stalin but Colonel Sanders.

If all human beings are not entitled to be treated as persons before the law, the criteria for inclusion and exclusion will be utilitarian, political and arbitrary. The denial of personhood was the technique by which the Nazis set the Jews on the road to the gas chambers. Under the Nuremberg Laws of 1935, the Nazis stripped Jews of their citizenship and political rights, effectively depriving them of personhood.[14] Hitler's euthanasia program, designed to achieve "the destruction of life devoid of value," would later deprive them of their lives as well.[15]

An innocent human being subject to execution at the discretion of another is, in that most important respect, a nonperson. If a human being can be defined as a nonperson at the beginning of his life and put to death at the discretion of others, the same thing can be done to his elder retarded brother or his grandmother. Abortion is merely prenatal euthanasia.

Before 1973, state and lower federal courts increasingly recognized the personhood rights of the unborn child with respect to his right to recover for prenatal injuries and wrongful death, to inherit property and to get a court to compel his mother to get a blood transfusion to save his life.[16] The precise question of the personhood of the unborn child, however, did not reach the Supreme Court until 1973. In *Roe v. Wade*[17] and *Doe v. Bolton,*[18] the unborn child's right to life was asserted against the mother's constitutional right to privacy, which the Court had discovered in 1965 in the "penumbras formed by emanations from" the Bill of Rights.[19] The Court acknowledged that the right to life is superior, indicating that if the unborn child were a person abortion would not be permitted even to save the life of his mother:

---

[12] Peter Singer, "Rethinking Life and Death: A New Ethical Approach," in Michael W. Uhlmann, *Last Rights? Assisted Suicide and Euthanasia Debated* (1998), 171, 187; see also Helga Kuhse and Peter Singer, *A Companion to Bioethics* (1998).

[13] Peter Singer, *Practical Ethics* (1979), 104.

[14] See Hannah Arendt, *Eichmann in Jerusalem* (1964), 39.

[15] See generally, Frederic Wertham, *A Sign for Cain* (1969), 153; William Brennan, *The Abortion Holocaust* (1983).

[16] See *Note*, "The Law and the Unborn Child: The Legal and Logical Inconsistencies," 46 *Notre Dame Lawyer* 349 (1972).

[17] 410 U.S. 113 (1973).

[18] 410 U.S. 179 (1973).

[19] *Griswold v. Conn.*, 381 U.S. 479, 484 (1965).

When Texas urges that a fetus is entitled to Fourteenth Amendment protection as a person, it faces a dilemma. Neither in Texas nor in any other state are all abortions prohibited. Despite broad proscription, an exception. . . for an abortion. . . for the purpose of saving the life of the mother, is typical. But if the fetus is a person who is not to be deprived of life without due process of law, and if the mother's condition is the sole determinant, does not the Texas exception appear to be out of line with the Amendment's command?[20]

The Court stated that if the personhood of the unborn child were established, the pro-abortion case "collapses, for the fetus' right to life is then guaranteed by the (Fourteenth) Amendment."[21]

After declining to decide whether an unborn child is a living human being, the Court ruled that he is not a person, since "the word 'person,' as used in the Fourteenth Amendment, does not include the unborn."[22] Regardless of whether he is a human being, he is not a person. This ruling is the same, in effect, as a ruling that an acknowledged human being is a nonperson. As a nonperson the unborn child has no more constitutional rights than does a goldfish or a turnip.

Once the Court ruled out the rights of the unborn nonperson, the only right remaining was the mother's right to privacy. While asserting that this right is not absolute, the Court defined it so as to permit, in effect, elective abortion at every stage of pregnancy up to the time of normal delivery. According to *Roe*, even after viability, when the state may regulate and even prohibit abortion, the state may not prohibit abortion "where it is necessary, in appropriate medical judgment, for the preservation of the life or health of the mother."[23] The health of the mother includes her psychological as well as physical well-being. And "the medical judgment may be exercised in the light of all factors — physical, emotional, psychological, familial, and the woman's age — relevant to the well-being of the mother."[24] This is equivalent to a sanction for permissive abortion at every stage of pregnancy.[25]

The *essential* holding of *Roe* is that the unborn child is not a "person" within the meaning of the Fourteenth Amendment, which protects the right to life of persons.

---

[20] 410 U.S. at 157, n. 54.

[21] 410 U.S. at 156-57.

[22] 410 U.S. at 158.

[23] *Doe v. Bolton,* 410 U.S. at 165.

[24] 410 U.S. at 192.

[25] See Charles E. Rice, "Implications of the Coming Retreat from *Roe v. Wade*," 4 *J. of Contemp. Health Law and Policy,* 1, 2-3 (1988).

4. BUT HASN'T THE COURT RETREATED FROM ITS HOLDING IN *ROE*?

Not really. Since 1973, the Court has upheld marginal restrictions on abortion, such as a requirement that abortions be performed by physicians.[1] In 1992, in *Planned Parenthood v. Casey*,[2] the Court upheld Pennsylvania requirements that the woman be given information about abortion 24 hours before the abortion; that a minor have the consent of at least one of her parents, or the approval of a judge, before she can have an abortion; and that abortion facilities comply with record keeping and reporting requirements. But the Court struck down a requirement that the woman notify her spouse before the abortion.

A "LIBERTY INTEREST"

The Court in *Casey* described the woman's right to an abortion as a "liberty interest" protected under the Fourteenth Amendment rather than as an exercise of the right to privacy.[3] "[L]iberty as conceived in *Casey* is broader than privacy as conceived in *Roe*. But the shift has significant substantive ramifications as well. . . . Abortion as privacy, for instance, means that women are protected against governmental intrusion but can make no claim to governmental assistance. Abortion as a liberty issue, on the other hand, permits a broader understanding of abortion that more accurately reflects the multiple meanings of reproductive rights. . . . By identifying abortion as part of a more general liberty interest, the Court raised the stature of the abortion decision."[4]

In the 1997 "right to die" case, the Court described its *Casey* ruling as follows: "There, the Court's opinion concluded that 'the essential holding of *Roe v. Wade* should be retained and once again reaffirmed.'[5] We held, first, that a woman has a right, before her fetus is viable, to an abortion, without undue interference from the State, second, that States may restrict postviability abortions, so long as exceptions are made to protect a woman's life and health; and third, that the State has legitimate interests throughout a pregnancy in protecting the health of the woman and the life of the unborn child."[6]

---

[1] *Conn. v. Menillo*, 423 U.S. 9 (1975); *Mazurek v. Armstrong*, 520 U.S. 968 (1997).
[2] 505 U.S. 833 (1992).
[3] 505 U.S. at 846-53.
[4] Erin Daly, "Reconsidering Abortion Law: Liberty, Equality, and the New Rhetoric of *Planned Parenthood v. Casey*," 45 *Am. U. L. Rev.* 77, 121-22 (1995).
[5] *Casey*, 505 U.S. at 846.
[6] *Washington v. Glucksberg*, 521 U.S. 702, 726 (1997).

No Effective Prohibition of Abortion

Although the Court allows marginal restrictions on abortion, the Court will not allow the states to enact any effective prohibition of abortion at any stage of pregnancy. The Court requires that the states allow abortion for emotional as well as physical health even up to the time of normal delivery. The Court has also imposed severe restrictions on pro-life activities at abortion sites.[7]

A Unanimous Court

Casey reaffirmed *Roe* by a 5-4 vote. That margin led some to conclude that we are only one vote away from overruling *Roe v. Wade*. That is not true. The *Casey* dissenters did say, in Chief Justice Rehnquist's words, that *Roe* "was wrongly decided and that it can and should be overruled."[8] However, when those dissenters (Rehnquist, White, Scalia, Thomas) say they want to overrule *Roe*, they mean they want to turn the issue back to the states to let them decide whether to allow or forbid abortion.

Such a states' rights solution would confirm, rather than overturn, the holding of *Roe* that the unborn child is a nonperson who has no constitutional rights and who can therefore be legally killed at the discretion of others. In his *Casey* opinion, Justice John Paul Stevens explained this basic holding of *Roe*:

> The Court in *Roe* carefully considered, and rejected, the State's argument "that the fetus is 'a person' within the language and meaning of the Fourteenth Amendment.". . . [T]he Court concluded that that word "has application only postnatally.". . . Accordingly, an abortion is not "the termination of life entitled to Fourteenth Amendment protection.". . . From this holding, there was no dissent,. . .indeed, no Member of the Court has ever questioned this fundamental proposition. Thus, as a matter of federal constitutional law, a developing organism that is not yet a "person" does not have what is sometimes described as a "right to life." This has been and, by the Court's holding today, remains a fundamental premise of our constitutional law governing reproductive autonomy.[9]

In his *Webster* opinion, in 1989, Justice Stevens had stressed that "(e)ven the dissenters in *Roe* implicitly endorsed that holding [of

---

[7] See *Madsen v. Women's Health Center*, 512 U.S. 753 (1994); *Schenck v. Pro-Choice Network of Western New York*, 519 U.S. 357 (1997). See Question 39.
[8] 505 U.S. at 944
[9] 505 U.S. at 913-14.

nonpersonhood] by arguing that state legislatures should decide whether to prohibit or to authorize abortions. . . . By characterizing the basic question as a 'political issue,'. . . Justice Scalia likewise implicitly accepts this holding."[10] In the *Thornburgh* case, in 1986, Justice Stevens said that, "unless the religious view that a fetus is a 'person' is adopted. . . there is a fundamental and well-recognized difference between a fetus and a human being; indeed, if there is not such a difference, the permissibility of terminating the life of a fetus could scarcely be left to the will of the state legislatures."[11]

When the *Casey* dissenters argue for a states' rights solution, they confirm the nonpersonhood of the unborn child. If an innocent human being is subject to execution at the decision of another whenever the legislature so decrees, he is a nonperson with no constitutional right to live. Justice Rehnquist's bottom line is that: "A woman's interest in having an abortion is a form of liberty protected by the Due Process Clause, but States may regulate abortion procedures in ways rationally related to a legitimate state interest."[12] Justice Scalia's bottom line is that: "The states may, if they wish, permit abortion-on-demand, but the Constitution does not *require* them to do so. The permissibility of abortion, and the limitations upon it, are to be resolved like most important questions in our democracy: by citizens trying to persuade one another and then voting. As the Court acknowledges, 'where reasonable people disagree the government can adopt one position or the other.'"[13]

The Supreme Court is unanimous in its endorsement of the proposition that the law can validly depersonalize innocent human beings so as to subject them to execution at the discretion of others.

WORSE THAN SLAVERY

The Thirteenth Amendment[14] was adopted to eliminate slavery, which, throughout history, has been based on a comparable denial of personhood. In the Roman Republic, "the slave had no rights respected by the law. . . . The slave was property, not a person. . . . The owner of a slave was free to whip him, jail him, or kill him, with or without reason.

---

[10] *Webster v. Reproductive Health Services*, 492 U.S. 490, 568, n. 13 (1989).

[11] *Thornburgh v. American College of Obstetricians and Gynecologists*, 476 U.S. 747, 879 (1986).

[12] 505 U.S. at 944.

[13] 505 U.S. at 979.

[14] "Section 1. Neither slavery nor involuntary servitude, except as a punishment for crime whereof the party shall have been duly convicted, shall exist within the United States, or any place subject to their jurisdiction. Section 2. Congress shall have power to enforce this article by appropriate legislation."

He could send his slaves to death against beasts or against men in the arena or put them out to die of starvation."[15] In the United States before the Civil War, "In the law's eye the slaves were chattels to be disposed of at their master's pleasure. The slave, therefore, had no political or civil rights. . . . If he was killed by a white the white would probably not be tried for murder."[16]

However, there were cases in which whites were convicted of murder for killing slaves in the pre-Civil War South.[17] In this light, *Roe v. Wade*, because it allows him to be killed with total impunity, inflicts on the unborn child a status worse than American chattel slavery.

In 1854, William Lloyd Garrison, leader of a radical antislavery movement, described the United States Constitution as "a covenant with death, and an agreement with hell."[18] A century and one-half later, the Supreme Court's conversion of murder of the innocent into a constitutional right has again merited for the Constitution that same evaluation.

TO RESTORE CONVICTION

Roe applies precisely the principle that underlay the Nazi extermination of the Jews, that an innocent human being can be declared a nonperson and subjected to death at the discretion of those who regard him as unfit or unwanted. The Justices who triggered the abortion avalanche by their own free decision are no more defensible than the Nazi judges, who acquiesced in the crimes of that regime, and the functionaries who administered its decrees at Auschwitz and similar places. At least in some cases, those who cooperated with the Nazi exterminations did so under the impression that they would be subjected to serious sanctions if they did not cooperate. The most that our depersonalizing justices have to fear is that a pro-life vote could cost them favor in the media and the academy. And Pontius Pilate, an operational positivist who executed the innocent for reasons of state and of his own convenience, would have found little to quarrel with in the philosophy of the Supreme Court.

The Court will allow states to enact marginal restrictions on surgical abortions, but those abortions are becoming obsolete because of early abortifacient drugs and devices. As Pope John Paul II said at the Capitol Mall in 1979, "No one ever has the authority to destroy unborn life."[19]

---

[15] Milton Meltzer, *Slavery I: From the Rise of Western Civilization to the Renaissance* (1971), 176-77.
[16] Milton Meltzer, *Slavery II: From the Renaissance to Today* (1972), 202.
[17] See *ibid.* at 206-07.
[18] Truman Nelson, ed., *Documents of Upheaval* (1966), 216.
[19] 9 *Origins* 277 (1979).

Until that conviction is restored among the American people, there will be no chance of enacting the licensing and other restrictions and prohibitions which will be the only possibly effective ways of preventing the use of early abortifacients. Nor will there be any chance of ending the legally sanctioned practice of euthanasia.

5.   Hasn't the Supreme Court held that there is no "right to die"? Isn't that a pro-life victory?

> I predict that the "right to die" — which really means that hospitals and doctors and other health care "providers" will be *required* to kill — will dwarf the abortion phenomenon in magnitude, in numbers, in horror. As mothers have become legalized agents of the deaths of their children, so children will become legalized agents of the deaths of their mothers — and fathers. Fathers will have no more legal right to defend themselves than they currently have to defend their unborn babies — a right the courts have restricted to mothers. "Right to die" laws will one day force a patient to prove that he or she has a right to live, just as we are now forced to prove that the unborn child has a right to live. — *John Cardinal O'Connor*[1]

A decade later, Cardinal O'Connor's prediction is nearing realization. Legalized abortion put the nation on a slippery slope to euthanasia, which is merely postnatal abortion. While the Supreme Court held in 1997 that there is no "right to die," this decision is pro-life only in a narrowly tactical sense. The "right to die" cases confirmed that the Supreme Court allows the states to permit the intentional killing of innocent persons.

The "Right to Die" Cases

In *Washington v. Glucksberg*,[2] the Court held that there is no constitutional "right to die" that would require the states to allow assisted suicide. The Washington statute punishing one who "knowingly causes or aids another person to attempt suicide" was upheld as "rationally related to legitimate government interests."[3] The Court noted that the recognition of a right to die would "to a great extent, place the matter outside the arena of public debate and legislative action."[4] The Court concluded: "Throughout the Nation, Americans are engaged in an earnest. . . debate about. . . physician-assisted suicide. Our holding permits this debate to continue as it should in a democratic society."[5] The Court did not say whether it would defer to the legislative judgment so as to uphold a state law allowing assisted suicide.

---

[1] John Cardinal O'Connor, "A Cardinal's Chilling Warning," *New Covenant,* May 1989, 23, 24.
[2] 521 U.S. 702 (1997).
[3] 521 U.S. at 707, 728.
[4] 521 U.S. at 720.
[5] 521 U.S. at 735.

Assisted suicide involves active participation by the physician in providing the patient with a prescription or other means by which the patient can kill himself. Assisted suicide is not merely the withholding of treatment by the physician. Nor does it involve active killing by the physician. In 1994, Oregon adopted, by a referendum margin of 51-49%, a "Death With Dignity Act," which legalized assisted-suicide for competent, terminally ill adults. In 1996, Oregon voters rejected, by a 60-40% margin, a proposal to repeal the 1994 Act.[6] The focus on assisted suicide, however, ought not to obscure the reality that the Supreme Court already allows the states to permit the intentional killing of innocent persons by other means than those included in the definition of "assisted suicide."

In *Vacco v. Quill*,[7] the other 1997 "right to die" case, the Supreme Court upheld the New York law which forbids assisted suicide. The Court of Appeals had held that the law unconstitutionally denied equal protection because "those in the final stages of terminal illness who are on life-support systems are allowed to hasten their deaths by directing the removal of such systems; but those who are similarly situated, except for the previous attachment of life-sustaining equipment, are not allowed to hasten death by self-administering prescribed drugs."[8] The Supreme Court upheld the New York statute on the ground that "the distinction between assisting suicide and withdrawing life-sustaining treatment. . . is certainly rational."[9]

In *Vacco*, the Supreme Court quoted its 1990 *Cruzan* decision,[10] for the conclusion that "This Court has also recognized, at least implicitly, the distinction between letting a patient die and making that patient die."[11] Nancy Beth Cruzan, 30 years old at the time of trial, "was rendered incompetent as a result of severe injuries sustained during an automobile accident." Her parents "sought a court order directing the withdrawal of their daughter's artificial feeding and hydration equipment after it became apparent that she had virtually no chance of recovering her cognitive faculties. The Supreme Court of Missouri held that because there was no clear and convincing evidence of Nancy's desire to have life-sustaining treatment withdrawn under such circumstances, her parents lacked authority to effectuate such a request."[12] The Supreme Court of

---

[6] *N.Y. Times*, Nov. 6, 1997, p. A31.
[7] 521 U.S. 793 (1997).
[8] *Koppell v. Quill*, 80 F.3d 716, 729 (2d Cir., 1996); see 521 U.S. at 798.
[9] 521 U.S. at 800-01.
[10] *Cruzan v. Director, Mo. Dept. Of Health*, 497 U.S. 261 (1990).
[11] 521 U.S. at 807.
[12] 497 U.S. at 265.

the United States held that Missouri could require proof of Nancy's intent by clear and convincing evidence. On rehearing, that evidence was found, the tube was removed, and twelve days later Nancy died.[13] The official cause of death was "shock due to dehydration due to traumatic brain injury."[14] *Cruzan* does not forbid the states to allow withdrawal of food and water on a lesser showing of the patient's intent or on the basis that withdrawal is in the incompetent patient's best interest in the absence of a showing of intent.[15]

PERMISSION FOR INTENTIONAL KILLING

It can be difficult to distinguish legitimate withholding or withdrawal of medical treatment, including termination of food and water that no longer sustains the life of a patient near death, from actions which are homicidal in intent. The law is a blunt instrument. It should not require that excessive treatment be given to impede the act of dying. There comes a time when a person has done all that is reasonably required to preserve his life, and nature should be allowed to take its course. He should then be allowed to die a natural and dignified death. But the rulings in *Cruzan*, and implicitly *Vacco*, can fairly be read as permission to the states to allow the intentional killing of at least some patients from whom "treatment" is withdrawn. Four factors distinguish the *Cruzan*-type case from the difficult cases of medical judgment from which the law should abstain:

1. *The patient in the* Cruzan-*type case is not dying or near death.* Nancy Cruzan, for example, had a life expectancy of 30 years. If she were near death, it still should be forbidden to kill her intentionally, as by shooting her, even with her consent. However, if she were in the final stages of dying, it would be extremely difficult to prove that the removal of a feeding tube was done with the intent to cause death rather than to accept the immediately inevitable outcome. But none of the patients in the *Cruzan*-type cases was dying.

2. *Cases of this type do not involve the withdrawal of medical treatment, including food and water provided by tube, that is burdensome, dangerous, extraordinary, or disproportionate to the expected outcome.* Nancy Cruzan was not in significant distress. The administration of food and water by tube was effective in sustaining her life. It was therefore not useless even though it obviously would not correct her underlying condition.

---

[13] See *N.Y. Times,* Dec. 29, 1990, p. 1.
[14] *News-Leader,* Springfield, Mo, Dec. 26, 1990, p. 1.
[15] See, for example, *Matter of Conroy,* 486 A.2d 1209 (N.J., 1985); *In re Jobes,* 529 A.2d 434 (N.J., 1987).

3. *Contrary to the Supreme Court's statement in* Vacco, *the removal of the feeding tube, in the usual case, causes death by starvation and dehydration and not by the "underlying fatal disease or pathology."* [16] Nancy Cruzan had no real prospect of recovery from her underlying condition. But she was not dying when her tube was withdrawn. She was stable and the nourishment she received through the tube kept her alive. When that tube was withdrawn, she starved and dehydrated to death. Interestingly, the petitioners in *Vacco*, who were attacking the ban on assisted suicide, implicitly conceded this point:

> "Patient-plaintiff Jane Doe, like some other terminal patients in the final stages of their illness, thus had lawfully available to her one method of physician assistance in ending her suffering. Because she required a feeding tube for nutrition and had had one surgically inserted, she could have asked to have it removed without running afoul of New York's assisted suicide laws. But while this would have permitted Jane Doe to die with her physician's assistance before her cancer ravaged her further, she would have been subject to what for her would have been the degrading process of death by starvation. See JA 86 (Grossman Dec.) (Describing 'starvation and dehydration' as 'an excruciating process that may continue for weeks'). She (and her family) would have been relegated to watching — perhaps only in glimpses as she was roused from a stupor brought on by malnutrition or medication or both — the degeneration of her body unto death."[17]

4. *In* Cruzan, *as in the typical such case, food and water are withdrawn with the specific intent to cause the death of the patient.*[18] The removal of Nancy Cruzan's tube was not intended to relieve pain or to terminate an administration of food and water that was ineffective to sustain bodily life. The tube was supposed to sustain Nancy's biological life and it did that. A permissible intention in removal, on the other hand, would be to ease excessive pain *caused by the medical treatment itself.* But Nancy was not in such pain and that was not the intent in the *Cruzan* case. The intent in removing her tube was to allow Nancy to starve and dehydrate to death. When the tube was removed, she did that. The purpose of the removal may have been to relieve the patient of a life considered burdensome or useless, but the specific intent was to achieve that purpose by means of intentionally killing the patient. The removal of the feeding tube in the usual case is not justified by the principle of the double effect since the "good" objective,

---

[16] 521 U.S. at 801.

[17] *Vacco v. Quill*, Respondent's brief in U.S. Supreme Court, Dec. 10, 1996, p. 16; 1996 WL 708912.

[18] See, e.g., *Guardianship of Jane Doe*, 583 N.E.2d 1263 (Mass., 1992); *Brophy v. New England Sinai Hospital*, 497 N.E.2d 626 (Mass., 1986); *In re Jobes*, 529 A.2d 434 (N.J., 1987); *In re Lawrance*, 579 N.E.2d 32 (Ind., 1991).

e.g., the relief of a burdensome life, is achieved by means of an intrinsically evil act, i.e., the intentional killing of the innocent.[19]

This analysis involves no reflection on the families in these difficult situations. The problem arises not from the families but rather from the Supreme Court, which authorizes the federal and state governments to permit intentional killing in such cases.

UNEQUAL PROTECTION

In the *Cruzan*-type case, the constitutional problem is one of equal protection of the laws. The Fourteenth Amendment provides: "No state shall. . . deny to *any person* the equal protection of the laws."[20] In "right to die" cases, the patients involved are all "persons" within the meaning of the Fourteenth Amendment. They are innocent non-aggressors. The state protects innocent, non-aggressor persons in general by forbidding them to be intentionally killed. Does it not deny equal protection of the laws for the state to exclude from that protection some such persons because they are terminally ill or because they have asked to be killed? When an innocent human being is thus excluded from the protection of the homicide laws, he is treated by the law as a nonperson.

In some cases, where a treatment or procedure is ineffective or where it is burdensome, dangerous, extraordinary or disproportionate to what it might achieve, the intent of the physician who removes or withholds that treatment or procedure might not be to kill the patient. But, in a case such as *Cruzan*, the intent appears to be to end the patient's life, that is, to kill. In *Cruzan*, the Missouri Supreme Court accurately said, "This is also a case in which euphemisms readily find their way to the fore, perhaps to soften the reality of what is really at stake. *But this is not a case in which we are asked to let someone die.* Nancy is not dead. Nor is she terminally ill. *This is a case in which we are asked to allow the medical profession to make Nancy die by starvation and dehydration.* The debate here is thus not between life and death; it is between quality of life and death. We are asked to hold that the cost of maintaining Nancy's present life is too great when weighed against the benefit that life conveys both to Nancy and her loved ones and that she must die."[21] As discussed in Question 13, the Supreme Court of the United States allows the states to decline even to try to distinguish in such cases between those who act with, and those who act without, the intent to kill.

---

[19] See Brief, American Life League, *Amicus Curiae, Vacco v. Quill,* 521 U.S. 793 (1997), 19- 20. For a discussion of the principle of the double effect, see Question 13.

[20] U.S. Constitution, Amend. XIV,§ 1 (emphasis added).

[21] *Cruzan v. Harmon,* 760 S.W.2d 408, 412 (Mo., 1988) (emphasis added).

A Functional Definition of Life and Personhood

"Right-to-die" issues are not as clear as those involved in abortion. In right-to-die cases, however, it should be kept in mind that the patients are not dying and that biological life is in itself a good; it is not a good only to the extent that it is useful for something else, e.g., pleasure. Justice Stevens, and perhaps others on the Court, appear to adopt a view that life is defined by its utility. Moreover, Stevens questioned whether the persistently vegetative Nancy Cruzan was even alive in constitutional terms:

> Missouri insists, without regard to Nancy Cruzan's own interests, upon equating her life with the biological persistence of her bodily functions. Nancy Cruzan. . . is not now simply incompetent. She is in a persistent vegetative state, and has been so for seven years. . . . [T]he Court errs insofar as it characterizes this case as involving "judgments about the 'quality' of life that a particular individual may enjoy". . . . Nancy Cruzan is obviously *"alive"* in a physiological sense. But for patients like Nancy Cruzan, who have no consciousness and no chance of recovery, there is a serious question as to whether the mere persistence of their bodies is *"life"* as that word is commonly understood, or as it is used in both the Constitution and the Declaration of Independence. The State's unflagging determination to perpetuate Nancy Cruzan's physical existence is comprehensible only as an effort to define life's meaning, not as an attempt to preserve its sanctity. [22]

Stevens' implication that the unconscious Nancy Cruzan is no longer alive parallels his observation in the *Webster* case on the beginning stages of life:

> As a secular matter, there is an obvious difference between the state interest in protecting the freshly fertilized egg and the state interest in protecting a nine-month-gestated, fully sentient fetus on the eve of birth. There can be no interest in protecting the newly fertilized egg from physical pain or mental anguish, because the capacity for such suffering does not yet exist; respecting a developed fetus, however, that interest is valid. . . . Contrary to the theological "finding" of the Missouri Legislature, a woman's constitutionally protected liberty encompasses the right to act on her own belief that. . . until a seed has acquired the powers of sensation and movement, the life of a human being has not yet begun. [23]

These references to "the powers of sensation and movement" and the "capacity" for "suffering" and to experience "physical pain or mental

---

[22] 497 U.S. at 344-45.
[23] *Webster v. Reproductive Health Services,* 492 U.S. at 569, 571 (1989).

anguish" are relevant to euthanasia. If the state interest in protecting human life does not begin until one has "the powers of sensation and movement," has that interest ended with respect to the adult patient who no longer has those powers? From his *Cruzan* opinion, Justice Stevens apparently thinks so. Interestingly, Justice Blackmun quoted Stevens in his *Webster* opinion:

> In answering the plurality's claim that the state's interest in the fetus is uniform and compelling throughout pregnancy, I cannot improve upon what Justice Stevens has written:
>
> "I should think it obvious that the state's interest in the protection of an embryo... increases progressively and dramatically as the organism's capacity to feel pain, to experience pleasure, to survive, and to react to its surroundings increases day by day. The development of a fetus — and pregnancy itself — are not static conditions, and the assertion that the government's interest is static simply ignores this reality."[24]

Justice Stevens' view raises the question whether the state's interest also *decreases* "progressively and dramatically" at the other end of life as the capacity to experience pleasure and pain and to react decreases.

The euthanasia movement employs a functional definition of personhood: a human being is entitled to treatment as a person only to the extent that he can perform in some useful way. Related to this is the concept of law as will: entitlement to personhood does not follow from one's nature as a human being. Instead, the legislature or courts can decree which innocent human beings may be treated as nonpersons so as to be intentionally killed.

THE DETERMINATION OF DEATH

A related issue involves the use of "brain death" criteria for determining death. A detailed discussion of this issue is beyond the scope of this book.[25] The widespread adoption of "brain death" is attributable in part to a desire to facilitate transplantation of vital organs. The soundness of any test employed to determine death should be measured by

---

[24] 492 U.S. 552, quoting from Justice Stevens' opinion in *Thornburgh v, ACOG,* 476 U.S. 757, 778-79 (1986).

[25] See Report of the Ad Hoc Committee of the Harvard Medical School, 205 *J. of Am. Med. Assn.* 337 (1968); Paul A. Byrne, M.D., Sean O'Reilly, M.D. and Paul M. Quay, S.J., "Brain Death — An Opposing Viewpoint," 242 *J. of Am. Med. Assn.* 1985 (1979); Report of the Medical Consultants to the President's Commission, 246 *J. of Am. Med. Assn.* 2184 (1981). For an argument in favor of using brain death criteria to determine death, contact National Federation of Catholic Physicians' Guilds, 850 Elm Grove Road, Elm Grove, WI 53127, (414) 784-3435, for the position paper drafted by Eugene F. Diamond, M.D.

whether it protects living people against being treated as dead.[26] In transplant cases, the brain death test can operate in the opposite direction, to prevent people from being regarded as alive rather than to prevent them from being regarded as dead.

In his address to a 1989 congress on the determination of the moment of death, John Paul II said, "Death . . . . occurs when the spiritual principle which ensures the unity of the individual can no longer exercise its functions in and upon the organism, whose elements, left to themselves, disintegrate. . . . The moment of this separation is not directly discernible, and the problem is to identify its signs. . . . In practice, there seems to arise a tragic dilemma. On the one hand there is the urgent need to find replacement organs for sick people who would otherwise die or at least would not recover . . . . [T]o escape certain and imminent death a patient may need to receive an organ which another patient. . . could provide, but about whose death there still remains some doubt. . . . [T]here arises the danger of terminating a human life. . . a real possibility that the life whose continuation is made unsustainable by the removal of a vital organ may be that of a living person, whereas the respect due to human life absolutely prohibits the direct. . . sacrifice of that life, even though it may be for the benefit of another human being. . . . Moralists, philosophers and theologians. . . must exercise. . . prudence, which presupposes moral rectitude and faithfulness to the good. . . . Scientific research and moral reflection must proceed side by side in a spirit of mutual help. We must never lose sight of the supreme dignity of the human person whose well-being research and reflection are called to serve, and in whom the believer recognizes nothing less than the image of God himself."[27]

THE NAZI MODEL

In his seminal analysis of the involvement of the German medical profession in the Nazi euthanasia program. Dr. Leo Alexander wrote:

[T]he German people were considered by their Nazi leaders more ready to accept the exterminations of the sick than those for political reasons. It was for that reason that the first exterminations of the latter group were carried out under the guise of sickness. . . .

Whatever proportions these crimes finally assumed,. . . they had started from . . . a subtle shift in. . . the basic attitude of the physicians. It started with the acceptance of the attitude, basic in the euthanasia movement, that there is such a thing as life not worthy to be

---

[26] See Monica Seeley, "Not Quite Dead?: The Case for Caution in the Definition of 'Brain Death,'" *Catholic World Report,* Feb. 1998, 48.

[27] *Address,* Dec. 14, 1989; 35 *The Pope Speaks* 207, 209-211 (1990).

lived. This attitude in its early stages concerned itself merely with the severely and chronically sick. Gradually the sphere. . . was enlarged to encompass the socially unproductive, the ideologically unwanted, the racially unwanted and finally all non-Germans. But. . . the infinitely small wedged-in lever from which this entire trend of mind received its impetus was the attitude toward the nonrehabilitable sick. . . .

The question. . . is whether. . . American physicians have also been infected with. . . cold-blooded, utilitarian philosophy and whether early traces of it can be detected in their medical thinking that may make them vulnerable to departures of the type that occurred in Germany. . . . Physicians have become dangerously close to being mere technicians of rehabilitation. . . . The patient with [an acute and chronic disease] carries an obvious stigma as the one less likely to be fully rehabilitable for social usefulness. In an increasingly utilitarian society these patients are being looked down upon. . . as unwanted ballast. A. . . contempt for the people who cannot be rehabilitated with present knowledge has developed. This is probably due to. . . unconscious hostility, because these people for whom there seem to be no effective remedies have become a threat to newly acquired delusions of omnipotence.

Hospitals like to limit themselves to the care of patients who can be fully rehabilitated, and the patient whose full rehabilitation is unlikely finds himself, at least in the best. . . centers of healing, as a second-class patient faced with a reluctance. . . to suggest and apply therapeutic procedures that are not likely to bring about immediately striking results in terms of recovery. I. . . emphasize that this point of view. . . was imposed by the shortage of funds available, both private and public. From the attitude of easing patients with chronic diseases away from the doors of the best types of treatment facilities available to the actual dispatching of such patients to killing centers is a long but nevertheless logical step. . . . There can be no doubt that in a subtle way the Hegelian premise of "what is useful is right" has infected society, including the medical portion. Physicians must return to the older premises, which were the emotional foundation and driving force of an amazingly successful quest to increase powers of healing and which are bound to carry them still farther if they are not held down to earth by the pernicious attitudes of an overdone practical realism.[28]

Dr. Alexander, shortly before his death, commented in 1984 on the American situation, "It is much like Germany in the 20's and 30's — the barriers against killing are being removed."[29]

---

[28] Leo Alexander, M.D., "Medical Science Under Dictatorship," 241 *New England J. of Med.* 39, 44-46 (1949).

[29] See Joseph R. Stanton, M.D., "The New Untermenschen," *Human Life Review,* Fall 1985, 77, 82.

PART II:

WHY LAW AND POLITICS
CANNOT SOLVE THE PROBLEM

A.   The American Republic is No More

6.   WHAT CONSTITUTIONAL CHANGES PREVENT LEGAL RESTORATION OF THE RIGHT TO LIFE?

The immediate pro-life reaction to *Roe v. Wade* was to challenge it as a violation of the letter and the spirit of the Constitution. The idea seemed to be that if we could reverse *Roe*, by constitutional amendment or legislation, all would be well with the Constitution again. We know better now. The old Constitution is not there any more. Three transformations in that Constitution have made it practically impossible to revive that document as a guarantor of the right to life:

1. *The collapse of the division of powers between the state and federal governments.* Instead of the limited federal government created by the Constitution, we have in Washington a centralized government of practically unlimited powers which is beyond effective control by the people or their representatives. That government is committed, beyond recall by legal or political means, to the institutionalization of an anti-life ethic.

2. *The collapse of the original balance of powers among the branches of the federal government.* Personal rights, including the right to life, are subject to the arbitrary dictates of an unelected Supreme Court liberated from adherence to constitutional intent and impervious to restraint by Congress or the executive branch.

3. *The implicit establishment by the Supreme Court, with the acquiescence of Congress and the executive branch, of secularism as the official national religion.* The right to live of the unborn and of other vulnerable classes of persons must be evaluated in secular terms without reference to the Divine law or any objective natural law. In that game, the potential victim is a guaranteed loser.

These transformations signal the demise of the Constitution. "When the Constitutional Convention adjourned in September, 1787, a woman hurried up to Benjamin Franklin and asked, 'Well, Doctor, what have we got? A republic or a monarchy?' Franklin answered, 'A republic — if you can keep it!'"[1] Today one can speak of the American Republic only in the past tense. Not coincidentally, the same is true of the constitutional right to life. The pro-life movement can use the law and the Constitution defensively to protect the ability to build a new culture of life independently of the state. But that movement must abandon the Fourth of July illusion that legal and political activism can induce the American Leviathan to restore effective legal protection to the right to life. The solution lies elsewhere.

---

[1] John Alexander Carroll and Odie B. Faulk, *Home of the Brave* (1976), 92.

7. HOW DID WE END UP WITH A CENTRALIZED GOVERN-
MENT OF PRACTICALLY UNLIMITED POWERS?

In 1997, the House of Representatives voted, 217 to 216, to eliminate the $99.5 million subsidy for the National Endowment for the
Arts. Instead of directly subsidizing artists, the House voted to give
block grants to the states for promotion of the arts. Like other efforts
against the NEA, this one ultimately failed.[1]

Article I, Section 8 of the Constitution lists the powers granted to
Congress, but the power to subsidize the arts is not among them. In the
House debate, Representative Gerald B.H. Solomon (R.-NY) said, "The
Founding Fathers designed a government with limited defined powers,
but that idea has been turned on its head. . . because instead of the Government doing only what the Constitution allows it to do, it does whatever the Constitution does not forbid it to do."[2] However, neither Mr.
Solomon nor any other member explicitly questioned whether the Constitution delegated to Congress the power to provide subsidies for the
arts at all, whether through the NEA or any other means. No one asked
because it would not have done any good. Very few care. Several Con-
gressmen have introduced a bill to require that "Each Act of Congress
shall contain a concise and definite statement of the constitutional authority relied upon for the enactment of each portion of that Act."[3] The
sponsors should not hold their breath waiting for favorable action.

In *National Endowment for the Arts v. Finley*,[4] the Supreme Court
upheld an advisory test for NEA grants which authorized "taking into
consideration general standards of decency and respect for the diverse
beliefs and values of the American public." The Court did not discuss
whether Congress has power to make such grants in the first place. So
how does Congress claim the authority to fund the Houston Ballet? By
what authority does $250,000 of federal money go every year to the
Manhattan Theater Club, which produced "Corpus Christi," "a play fea-
turing a gay Jesus-like figure who has sex with his apostles"?[5] The play
was aptly described as "part of the daily sewage of modernity."[6]And

---

[1] *N.Y. Times*, July 11, 1997, p. A13; *N.Y. Times*, July 12, 1997, p. 1. See also *N.Y.
Times*, June 19, 1998, p. A17; *N.Y. Times*, June 26, 1998, p. A17; *American Family
Assn. Journal*, Sept. 1998, p. 1.
[2] 143 Cong. Rec. H5049-01, H5051 (July 10, 1997).
[3] H.R. 292, 105th Cong., 1st Sess. (Jan. 7, 1997).
[4] 118 S.C. 2168 (1998).
[5] *N.Y. Times*, May 29, 1998, p. A1; *The Wanderer*, Oct. 8, 1998, p. 1.
[6] Patrick Buchanan, "Hate Crimes of the Cultural Elite," *Wash. Times*, Aug. 10, 1998,
p. A17.

where is Congress' delegated power to regulate the placement of foster children, to prescribe curricula in local public schools, to fund loans and grants for college students, and to mandate the distribution of athletic scholarships between males and females at the private colleges at which those federally aided students enroll? And so on. The lawyer's answer is that Congress has power to tax and spend for the general welfare; and when Congress subsidizes it has a power and duty to regulate the use of the subsidy. The general welfare clause and other provisions have been interpreted to create a centralized government of practically unlimited jurisdiction. This affects the right to life because that government has assumed the role of protector and promoter of the culture of death.

THE ORIGINAL PLAN

The United States Constitution reversed the course of history. Until then, the story of liberty had been one of struggle to curb the otherwise unlimited power of government. The Magna Carta, the Petition of Right of 1628 and the English Bill of Rights of 1689 merely imposed restrictions on the otherwise unlimited power of the Crown. And so it went. But, in 1789, the Constitution created a federal system of government, that is, one with divided powers. It created a limited government of the United States possessing only the powers delegated to it by the states. That government had implied powers which were limited to the implementation of the delegated powers. Under the division of powers, what has since come to be called "the federal government" was limited to its delegated powers and the states possessed all powers inherent in government except as limited by the Constitution. Within the federal government, power was separated among the legislative, executive and judicial branches, with checks and balances built in to prevent any one or two branches from dominating. The Constitution itself was a bill of rights, since the limitation of government was seen as the most effective safeguard of liberty. In 1791, the ten amendments of the Bill of Rights were added to emphasize the limited character of the new government. The first eight restricted the federal government — and not the states. For protection against their state governments the people relied on their state constitutions and state courts. The last two amendments in the Bill of Rights restated the obvious. The Ninth provided, "The enumeration, in the Constitution, of certain rights, shall not be construed to deny or disparage others retained by the people." And the Tenth stated: "The powers not delegated to the United States, are reserved to the States respectively, or to the people."

EROSION OF THE DIVISION OF POWERS

The centralization of power in Washington gained momentum during and after the Civil War. In the aftermath of the imperialist adventure of the Spanish-American War, the twentieth century brought centralizing pressure from World War I, Prohibition, the Depression, the New Deal, World War II, the Korean War, Vietnam and the Cold War. The Sixteenth and Seventeenth Amendments, both adopted in 1913, put the centralizing movement into high gear. In 1895, the Supreme Court had held that a federal income tax was a "direct" tax and was unconstitutional because it was not apportioned among the states in accordance with their populations, as required by Article I, Section 9, of the Constitution.[7] The Sixteenth Amendment provided: "The Congress shall have power to lay and collect taxes on incomes, from whatever source derived, without apportionment among the several States, and without regard to any census or enumeration." "On October 3, 1913, a tax 'accepted as a natural and inevitable culmination of the constitutional amendment' was approved. . . . [I]ts rates were graduated, reaching a top bracket of 7 percent on incomes over $500,000. To all but the very rich the levies were irrelevant — 98 percent of the people owed no income tax under the act of 1913 — but if ever there was an entering wedge this was it."[8]

Prior to 1913, United States Senators were chosen by state legislatures. The members of one House of Congress were thus dependent on the state governments as such. But the Seventeenth Amendment made Senators popularly elected. Before 1913, some Senators bought their elections by bribing state legislators. Now, with the Sixteenth Amendment's conferral of virtually unlimited power to tax incomes, members of both houses of Congress can buy their elections by bribing the people as a whole with the people's own money by means of federal subsidies.

"As a result of the Income Tax Amendment," said Dr. James McClellan, "the states have also lost their economic base of power and financial independence and are now dependent upon federal largess or subject to federal control in providing for. . . their citizens under their police powers. . . . [T]he few remaining powers they enjoy under the Tenth Amendment, such as education and local or intrastate commerce, have been usurped by the Federal Government through congressional statutes and Supreme Court decisions. . . . [T]he fifty states are little more than administrative units of the central government, and the

---

[7] *Pollock v. Farmers' Loan & Trust Co.*, 157 U.S. 429 (1895).
[8] Robert Higgs, *Crisis and Leviathan* (1987), 113.

United States is a federal system of government in name only."[9] The pervasive presence of the federal government can be seen also in the fact that it "owns about 650 million acres — almost 30% of the entire United States. That's an area roughly equal in size to Argentina. Most of the land is concentrated in 12 Western states."[10]

In the 1997 debate on the NEA, Representative Solomon said, "What our Founding Fathers could not even comprehend is the idea of paying more in taxes than they do for food and shelter. . . the idea of the American people working six months out of the year just to pay for the cost of government."[11] In 1997, Cost of Government Day (COGD) fell on July 3rd, the eve of Independence Day. "As measured by the Americans for Tax Reform Foundation,. . . COGD is the date by which the average American has earned enough in cumulative gross income to pay for all costs associated with government."[12] Tax Freedom Day, when the average taxpayer finishes paying his federal, state and local taxes, apart from other costs of government, was calculated by the Tax Foundation to fall in 1999 on May 11th.[13]

In his 1998 State of the Union address, President Clinton offered a shopping list of federal initiatives, including, on education, federal funding to "hire 100,000 new teachers [to] reduce class size in the first, second and third grades to an average of 18 students a class"; to "end social promotion in America's schools"; to "make college as universal as high school is today"; and so on. Neither President Clinton nor Republican Senator Trent Lott, in his response, said one word about the Constitution.[14] The Constitution was not mentioned because it is not there any more. There are no effective limitations on federal power beyond the pragmatic and the political.

---

[9] James M. McClellan, "Our Conservative Constitution," 4 *Benchmark* 361, 368 (1990). For information on the proposal to repeal the Sixteenth Amendment and replace the federal individual and corporate income tax with a national sales tax, contact Americans for Fair Taxation, P.O. Box 34527, Houston, TX 77234-9637, (713) 963-9023.

[10] Laura M. Litvan, "The Great Government Land Rush of '97," *Investor's Business Daily*, June 11, 1997, p. A1.

[11] 143 *Cong. Rec.* H5049, H5051 (July 10, 1997).

[12] Michael Kamburowski, "Happy Cost of Government Day," *Wash. Times,* July 3, 1997, p. A17.

[13] See Doug Bandow, "Working for Your Own Gain," *Wash. Times*, May 13, 1999, p. A18.

[14] See *N.Y. Times*, Jan. 28, 1998, p. A1. See, along similar lines, President Clinton's 1999 State of the Union address, in which he said, "Later this year, I will send Congress a plan that for the first time holds states and school districts responsible for progress and rewards them for results." *N.Y. Times*, Jan. 20, 1999, p. A22.

Within the federal government, the separation of powers among the branches was originally maintained by a system of checks and balances. Instead, we now have Congressional subordination, executive and judicial dominance in major respects, and pervasive regulation by administrative agencies. "It was with [President Franklin D. Roosevelt] that conversion to the planning state and a system of full-fledged 'presidential government' became decisive."[15] The process has accelerated in each of the later administrations, compounded by delegations of power by Congress to the "fourth branch of government," the administrative agencies who make "law" by fiat without effective control by Congress or the courts.[16] The long-term trend is toward executive aggrandizement. The 1999 war in Yugoslavia, in which the Congress acquiesced, confirmed the importation into the Constitution of the principle that the nation can be taken into war at the will of one man. That is precisely the evil the Constitution sought to avoid by lodging the ultimate war power in Congress.[17] In the Clinton impeachment, the House of Representatives roused itself to assert its prerogative. But the Senate, to its disgrace, could not summon the will to remove an impeached and certified perjurer from the Presidency.

These developments reflect an immunity of the federal government to restraint by the people and the states. The eclipse of the federal-state division of powers is evident in what former Attorney General Edwin Meese III called "the expanding federalization of crime":

> "We federalize everything that walks, talks, and moves," said Senator Joseph R. Biden, Jr. . . . . Unfortunately, this is not much of an exaggeration; there are well over 3,000 federal crimes today. And this number does not include the 10,000 regulatory requirements that carry criminal penalties. Few crimes, no matter how local in nature, are beyond the reach of the federal criminal jurisdiction. . . . [T]he following is a . . . sample of serious, but purely local, crimes that have been duplicated in the federal code: virtually all drug crimes, carjacking, blocking an abortion clinic, failure to pay child support, drive-by shootings, possession of a handgun near a school, possession of a handgun by a juvenile, embezzlement from an insurance company,

---

[15] M. Stanton Evans, *Clear and Present Dangers* (1975), 57-58.

[16] See Gary Lawson, "The Rise and Rise of the Administrative State," in "Symposium, Changing Images of the State," 107 *Harv. L. Rev.* 1231-54 (1994); Peter B. McCutchen, "Mistakes, Precedent and the Rise of the Administrative State: Toward a Constitutional Theory of the Second Best," 80 *Cornell L. Rev.* 1 (1994).

[17] See discussion in Douglas W. Kmiec and Stephen B. Presser, *The American Constitutional Order* (1998), 498-500; see also "War and Responsibility: A Symposium on Congress, the President and the Authority to Initiate Hostilities," 50 *Miami L. Rev.* 1 (1995).

and murder of a state official assisting a federal law enforcement agent. While most of these crimes pose real threats to public safety, they are outlawed by the states already and need not be duplicated in the federal criminal code.

The federalization of crime also includes trivial crimes. . . . The following is a sampling of actual federal crimes: damaging a livestock facility, unauthorized reproduction of the "Smokey the Bear" image, transporting artificial teeth into a state without permission, theft of a major artwork, writing checks for less than a dollar, and falsely impersonating a 4-H member. . . . The more crime is federalized, the more the potential exists for an oppressive and burdensome federal police state. . . .

[F]ederal law enforcement authorities are not as attuned to the. . . mores of local communities as state and local law enforcement. In the Ruby Ridge tragedy,. . . would the local Idaho authorities have tried to apprehend [Randy] Weaver in such an aggressive fashion? Would they have spent $10 million on a relatively minor case, as did the federal agencies?. . . [W]ould Idaho officials have even cared about two sawed-off shotguns? In the Waco disaster, would the local sheriff's department have stormed the compound as the BATF did or instead have waited for David Koresh to venture into town for supplies, which he frequently did, to arrest him? This is not meant to question the character or competency of federal agents. . . . But. . . both of these tragedies resulted in part from the federalization of state gun laws. If the regulation of firearms had remained with the states, where it was traditionally handled, these tragedies may never have occurred.

One of the most pernicious aspects of the federalization of crime is the opportunity it creates to circumvent our constitutional double jeopardy protections. . . . Federalization of criminal laws often creates concurrent state and federal jurisdiction over the same offense. This. . . grants both state and federal prosecutors the opportunity to prosecute the same case successively. [T]he rules of double jeopardy do not apply when state and federal courts, or different state courts, are involved because these courts represent different sovereign governments. Nevertheless, the spirit of double jeopardy is violated when a defendant can be acquitted in state court and retried for the exact same crime in federal court, or vice versa.[18]

---

[18] Edwin Meese III, "Big Brother on the Beat: The Expanding Federalization of Crime," 1 *Texas Review of Law and Politics* 1 (1997). See also Lynn N. Hughes, "Don't Make a Federal Case Out of It: The Constitution and the Nationalization of Crime," 25 *Am. J. Crim.* L. 150 (1997).

The constitutional division of powers has given way to dominance by the federal government. That government is assumed to have authority to do whatever is useful in the national interest. Regrettably, that government's vision of the national interest is hostile to the family and the right to life.

THE COMMERCE CLAUSE

Supreme Court interpretations of the Commerce Clause and the General Welfare Clause have expanded the power of the federal government and of the Court itself. Starting with the New Deal, the Supreme Court expansively interpreted Congress' power "[t]o regulate Commerce with foreign Nations, and among the several States, and with the Indian tribes."[19] That commerce power extends not only to "channels" or "instrumentalities" of interstate or foreign commerce, but also to "activities affecting commerce."[20] Ollie's Barbecue in Birmingham, Alabama, "purchased locally $150,000 worth of food . . . . 49% of which was meat that it had bought from a local supplier who had purchased it from outside the state."[21] Ollie's was held bound by the Civil Rights Act of 1964, which applies to restaurants "if they serve or offer to serve interstate travelers or if a substantial portion of the food which they serve or products which they sell have moved in [interstate] commerce." Under that standard, virtually every local business is subject to federal regulation, which is not at all what the framers of the Constitution had in mind.

In *Wickard v. Filburn*,[22] the Court held that a wheat grower who exceeded the acreage limit set by the Secretary of Agriculture could be penalized even though he consumed the excess 239 bushels on his own farm. The Court said that "Congress may properly have considered that wheat consumed on the farm where grown, if wholly outside the scheme of regulation, would have a substantial effect in. . . obstructing its purpose to stimulate trade therein at increased prices."[23] "That [Filburn's] own contribution to the demand for wheat may be trivial by itself is not enough to remove him from the scope of federal regulation where,. . . his contribution, taken together with that of many others similarly situated, is far from trivial."[24] Filburn was penalized, not because of something he did in interstate commerce, but precisely because he did *not* engage in commerce. Instead, he consumed his own wheat. Here again, the

---

[19] Art. I, Sec. 8.
[20] *Perez v. U.S.*, 402 U.S. 146 (1971).
[21] *Katzenbach v. McClung*, 379 U.S. 294, 296 (1964).
[22] 317 U.S. 111 (1942).
[23] 317 U.S. at 128-29.
[24] 317 U.S. at 127-28.

framers of the Constitution would have been surprised that the Commerce Clause gives Congress a blank check to impose such local regimentation whenever Congress thinks it appropriate to solve whatever national problem it has identified. In effect, the only realistic limitation on Congress' power to regulate "activities affecting commerce" is the self-restraint of Congress itself. Congress has limited the reach of some federal statutes, such as those prohibiting discrimination, but Congress' power is indeterminably more extensive than that which Congress has chosen to exercise.

The Supreme Court has recently begun to impose some restraint on the commerce power. In 1995, in *U.S. v. Lopez,* the Court held that the Gun-Free School Zones Act, which banned gun possession within 1,000 feet of a school, was unconstitutional because "the possession of a gun in a local school zone is in no sense an economic activity that might, through repetition elsewhere, substantially affect any sort of interstate commerce."[25] And in 1997, the Court held that the Brady Act, commanding state and local law-enforcement officers "to perform background checks on prospective handgun purchasers," is not justified under the Commerce Clause because it "violates the very principle of separate state sovereignty."[26] It is unlikely, however, that those rulings foreshadow any general rollback of Congress' power to regulate local activities that "substantially affect" interstate commerce. Congress, incidentally, reacted to the *Lopez* decision by re-enacting the Gun-Free School Zones Act with the mere addition of a requirement that the "firearm. . . has moved in or. . . otherwise affects interstate or foreign commerce."[27]

Whether or not the Court imposes some curbs on Congress' commerce power, the determination of the extent of that federal power has become a matter for exclusive decision by an agency of that federal government, the Supreme Court, according to indefinite criteria of the Court's own creation.

Under current interpretations of the Commerce Clause, if you grow tomatoes for your own consumption, Congress can tell you how many you may grow. If your ten year-old son sells lemonade to passers-by outside your house, Congress can regulate his prices and hours of work if the lemons or the cups were made in another state. The commerce power also is the primary basis on which Congress, and the regulators to whom it has delegated its powers, have imposed extensive restrictions on employment conditions:

---

[25] *U.S. v. Lopez,* 514 U.S. 549, 567 (1995).
[26] *Printz v. U.S.,* 117 S. Ct. 2365, 2383 (1977).
[27] 18 U.S.C., Sec. 922(q)(2)(A).

Since the mid-1960s the American workplace has been transformed by. . . powerful new laws. . . .[T]he new laws differ greatly from what came before.

[T]hey are vast in the scope of their ambition. They aim to regulate not just a few readily measured dimensions of working life — such as pay scales, hours worked, or the conditions under which employers must recognize unions — but a wide range of personal interactions that includes job assignments, employee evaluations, benefit packages, and working conditions. And the latter. . . includes the intangible elements of workplace life: what gets said in casual conversations, the tones in managers' voices and the looks on their faces, and other intimate details of daily interaction among workers. Unlike most previous laws, the new ones tend to avoid giving employers definite rules to obey but instead lay out sweeping if vague aspirations that are given the force of law. Thus employers are expected to refrain from "wrongful" firings, to give disabled workers "reasonable" accommodation, and to shelter employees from profanity or pointed criticism that reaches the point of creating a "hostile environment." No one really knows where these concepts begin and leave off; all employers know is that if they guess wrong some future jury or judge may decide that they have broken the law. Finally, and not least, the new laws draw their clout from a distinctive method of enforcement; individual workers can take their employers to court in lawsuits, often for very rich damages.[28]

As recently as 1919, the Eighteenth Amendment was adopted to prohibit "the manufacture, sale, or transportation of intoxicating liquors within, the importation thereof into, or the exportation thereof from the United States. . . for beverage purposes." In those days the Congress, as well as the people, took it for granted that a formal constitutional amendment would be necessary to confer such power on Congress. That attitude strikes us today as quaint. If Congress were of a mind to ban liquor, tobacco or anything else, it would do so under today's Commerce Clause without batting an eye. Today the Commerce Clause is interpreted to give Congress a virtual blank check. Keep that in mind the next time you take a shower or flush a toilet with the limited flow of water that federal law, enacted under the Commerce Clause, now permits you to use for those purposes.[29]

THE GENERAL WELFARE CLAUSE

The other clause that the Supreme Court has used to centralize power is the General Welfare Clause. Congress, under Article I, Sec. 8, Clause 1, has "Power to Lay and collect Taxes, Duties, Imposts and Excises, *to pay the Debts and provide for the common Defence and general*

---

[28] Walter Olson, *The Excuse Factory* (1997), 3.
[29] See 63 *Fed. Register* 13308 (March 18, 1998); 10 *CFR* Part 430.

Welfare of the United States."[30] The remaining clauses of Section 8 enumerate the specific powers delegated to Congress: to regulate commerce, declare war, provide for military forces, establish post offices, coin money and regulate its value, regulate naturalization of citizens, regulate bankruptcies, etc. Note, for example, that the Constitution gives Congress no power to regulate local schools. The Supreme Court, however, has interpreted the General Welfare Clause to give Congress the power to regulate schools and anything else Congress might choose to subsidize.

In 1936, the Supreme Court held that the General Welfare power to tax and to spend the money raised is not limited to the objects specified in the remaining clauses of Section 8.[31] The Court did say that the appropriations must be truly for the *general* welfare of the nation and not for the welfare of local or special interests, but this was not an enduring limitation. The Court has left it practically to Congress' discretion as to what purposes are for the "general" welfare. Although the Court does not give Congress a power to *regulate* for whatever purposes it believes to be for the general welfare, this, too, is an illusion. The power to appropriate carries with it the power to impose regulations to govern the use of the appropriation. "It is hardly lack of due process for the Government to regulate that which it subsidizes."[32] With federal money comes federal control. Always. In plain English, there is no such thing as a free lunch.

This is the basis for the grant-in-aid programs under which states and private persons accepting federal money are subject to federal regulation of the way the money is spent. Thus, a private college, even though it directly receives no federal money, will be considered a "recipient of federal financial assistance" and will be bound by the record-keeping and other restrictions of federal civil rights laws if it enrolls even one student who has a federally guaranteed student loan.[33]

THE ENABLING OF *ROE V. WADE*

Roe v. Wade could not have occurred without the prior assertion of open-ended powers by the federal government as a whole. The expansion of federal power facilitated the Court's decisions on abortion and euthanasia, and it has insulated those rulings against popular efforts to reverse them. Nor could *Roe* have occurred without the prior emergence of the Supreme Court as the unchallenged, final arbiter of the "living Constitution."

---

[30] Emphasis added.

[31] *U. S. v. Butler*, 297 U.S. 1 (1936).

[32] *Wickard v. Filburn*, 317 U.S. 111, 131 (1942).

[33] *Grove City College v. Bell*, 465 U.S. 455 (1984). See also P. Michael Villalobos, "The Civil Rights Restoration Act of 1987: Revitalization of Title IX," 1 *Marquette Sports L.J.*, 149, 162 (1990).

8.   HOW DID THE SUPREME COURT BECOME DOMINANT?

Viewing the carnage created by the Court, George Will referred to the
Justices as "our robed masters." When the VMI decision[1] [requiring
Virginia Military Institute to admit women] came down, my wife said
the Justices were behaving like a "band of outlaws." Neither of those
appellations is in the least bit extreme. The Justices are our masters in a
way that no President, congressman, governor, or other elected official
is. They order our lives and we have no recourse. . . They are indeed
robed masters. But "band of outlaws"? An outlaw is a person who co-
erces others without warrant in law. That is precisely what a majority
of the present Supreme Court does. That is, given the opportunity,
what the Supreme Court has always done. — *Robert H. Bork*[2]

The Supreme Court gained dominance through its misuse of the
Fourteenth Amendment. The Court "has perverted the Fourteenth
Amendment. . . . *First,* the Court has undermined the federal structure
by fastening the Bill of Rights upon the states through the fraudulent
doctrine of incorporation. It has further eroded state autonomy, *second,*
by interpreting provisions of the Bill of Rights as if their general language embodied detailed statutory schemes, thus depriving the states of
their traditional authority to define the incidents of those natural and
civil rights that are due every person. *Third,* the Court has given an un-
warranted imprimatur to egalitarian doctrines through. . . the equal protection clause, once again depriving the states of their traditional authority to make reasonable legislative classifications in support of legitimate
public policies."[3]

The post-Civil War constitutional amendments redefined the division of powers between the state and federal governments. The Thirteenth, adopted in 1865, prohibited slavery; private individuals as well
as the state and federal governments are bound by this prohibition. The
Fifteenth, adopted in 1870, provided that, "The right of citizens of the
United States to vote shall not be denied or abridged by the United
States or by any State on account of race, color, or previous condition of
servitude." Previously the states had entirely determined eligibility to
vote in federal elections.[4] However, it was the Fourteenth, adopted in
1868, which, as construed by the Supreme Court, so radically changed

---

[1]   *U.S. v. Virginia,* 518 U.S. 515 (1996).
[2]   Robert H. Bork, "Our Judicial Oligarchy," *First Things,* Nov. 1996, 21, 23.
[3]   James E. Bond, *No Easy Walk to Freedom* (1997), 252 (emphasis added).
[4]   "The House of Representatives shall be. . . chosen. . . by the people of the several
states, and the electors in each State shall have the qualifications requisite for electors of
the most numerous branch of the State legislature." U.S. Constitution, Art. I, Sec. 2.

the division of powers, that it is fairly described as the "second constitution." This change occurred through the "incorporation doctrine," a judicial invention by which the Court has applied the protections of the Bill of Rights against the states.

THE INCORPORATION DOCTRINE

The Bill of Rights, as decided by the Supreme Court in 1833, was intended to protect only against invasion of the specified rights by the federal government.[5] Federal courts had no jurisdiction to enforce any of the guarantees of the Bill of Rights against the states. For protection of those and other rights, the people looked primarily to their state constitutions and the state courts.

After the Civil War, the Confederate states generally enacted Black Codes which restricted the rights of blacks. The federal Civil Rights Act of 1866 outlawed the Black Codes by requiring that all persons "shall have the same right. . . as is enjoyed by white citizens" with respect to property, contracts, personal security and participation in legal proceedings.[6] There was doubt as to whether that 1866 Act was within the power of Congress even after the Thirteenth Amendment. The Fourteenth Amendment was intended in part to remove that doubt. Section 1 of the Fourteenth Amendment provides:

> No State shall. . . abridge the privileges or immunities of citizens of the United States; nor shall any State deprive any person of life, liberty, or property, without due process of law; nor deny to any person within its jurisdiction the equal protection of the laws.

The "privileges or immunities" clause was intended to confirm the constitutionality of the Civil Rights Act of 1866. "[T]he 'fundamental' rights which the framers were anxious to secure were those described by Blackstone — personal security, freedom to move about and to own property; . . . the incidental rights necessary for their protection were 'enumerated' in the Civil Rights Act of 1866; that enumeration marked the bounds of the grant;. . . those rights were embodied in the 'privileges or immunities' of the Fourteenth Amendment."[7] The "original design" of the Fourteenth Amendment "was to make the 'privileges or immunities' clause the pivotal provision. . . to shield the 'fundamental rights' enumerated in the Civil Rights Act from the Black Codes. . . . In lawyer's parlance, the privileges or immunities clause conferred *substan-*

---

[5] *Barron v. Baltimore*, 32 U.S. (7 Pet.) 243 (1833).
[6] Civil Rights Act of 1866, Ch. 31, 14 Stat. 27 (1866); 42 U.S.C. § 1982 (1978).
[7] Raoul Berger, *Government by Judiciary* (2d ed., 1997), 44.

tive rights which were to be secured through the medium of two *adjec-tive* rights: the equal protection clause outlawed statutory, the due process clause judicial, discrimination with respect to those substantive rights."[8]

The "privileges or immunities" clause was intended, therefore, to require the states to protect basic rights, including the rights to life, property, personal security and mobility. Under that clause, federal courts would have a limited power to declare state laws unconstitutional. In the *Slaughter-House Cases,*[9] in 1873 the Supreme Court held that the clause did not protect such basic rights but only a limited category of privileges and immunities derived from United States citizenship, such as the right of "a citizen of the United States [to] become a citizen of any state. . . by residence therein."[10] (The Court relied on this "right to travel" in holding, in 1999, that states may not restrict new residents to the welfare benefits they would have received in their home states.)[11] *Slaughter-House,* however, effectively nullified the "privileges or immunities" clause as a general protector of basic rights against the states.

By the turn of the century, however, the Court began to fill the vacuum by using the due process clause of the Fourteenth Amendment to impose substantive, rather than merely procedural, restrictions on the states.[12] A substantive restriction tells a state *what* it may do; a procedural restriction tells it *how* it must do something. The early twentieth century brought a trend toward nationalization, accelerated by the adoption of the Sixteenth and Seventeenth Amendments, and the centralizing impact of World War I.[13] Against the background of that nationalizing trend, it is understandable that the Supreme Court in the 1920s began to interpret the due process clause in a way that would give federal courts expanded control over the states. The Court did this by requiring the states to abide by the protections embodied in the Bill of Rights.[14] Over the past seven decades, the Supreme Court has held that virtually all the protections of the first eight amendments of the Bill of Rights are included in the "liberty" protected by due process clause and that therefore "[t]he Fourteenth Amendment has rendered the legislatures of the states as incompetent as Congress to enact" laws in violation of, for ex-

---

[8] *Ibid.,* 234-35.
[9] 83 U.S. (16 Wall.) 36 (1873).
[10] 83 U.S. at 80.
[11] *Saenz v. Roe* 119 S. Ct. 1518 (1999).
[12] See *Allgeyer v. Louisiana,* 165 U.S. 578 (1897); *Lochner v. N.Y.,* 198 U.S. 45 (1905).
[13] See Question 7.
[14] See *Gitlow v. N.Y.,* 268 U.S. 652, 666 (1925); *Stromberg v. California,* 283 U.S. 359, 368 (1931).

ample, the clause of the First Amendment which provides, "Congress shall make no law respecting an establishment of religion."[15]

Even if the Fourteenth Amendment had been intended to include the liberties covered by the Bill of Rights within the "liberty" protected by the due process clause, it should not have been held to include the Establishment Clause of the First Amendment within that "liberty."[16] Professor Edward S. Corwin accurately described the intent of the Establishment Clause: "That is, Congress should not prescribe a national faith, a possibility which those states [which themselves had officially established churches] — Massachusetts, New Hampshire, Connecticut, Maryland, and South Carolina — probably regarded with fully as much concern as those which had gotten rid of their establishments."[17] "[T]he principal importance of the [First] amendment," wrote Professor Corwin, "lay in the separation which it effected between the respective jurisdictions of state and nation regarding religion, rather than in its bearing on the question of the separation of church and state."[18] The Establishment Clause, unlike the other Bill of Rights protections of personal liberties, was merely a delineation of jurisdiction between federal and state governments, affirming that the subject of religion was reserved to the states. It is therefore unsound to claim that it was applied against the states by the Fourteenth Amendment's prohibition of state laws depriving a person of "liberty" without due process of law. The Supreme Court's "incorporation" of the Establishment Clause was actually a radical amendment of the Constitution, intruding the federal government, pursuant to the dictate of one branch of that government, into a substantive area from which the First Amendment had excluded it.[19] While the Establishment Clause was merely a definition of federal-state jurisdiction, the incorporation doctrine not only obliterated that arrangement but also fastened upon the federal government, as well as

---

[15] *Abington School District v. Schempp*, 374 U.S. 203, 215 (1963).

[16] See William K. Lietzau, "Rediscovering the Establishment Clause: Federalism and the Rollback of Incorporation," 39 *DePaul L. Rev.*, 1191 (1990); Notes, "Rethinking the Incorporation of the Establishment Clause: A Federalist View," 105 *Harv. L. Rev.* 1700 (1992); William P. Gray, Jr., "The Ten Commandments and the Ten Amendments: A Case Study in Religious Freedom in Alabama," 49 *Ala. L. Rev.* 509 (1998); Robert R. Baugh, "Applying the Bill of Rights to the States: A Response to William P. Gray, Jr.," 49 *Ala. L. Rev.* 551 (1998); William P. Gray, Jr., "'We the People' or 'We the Judges': A Reply to Robert R. Baugh's Response," 49 *Ala. L. Rev.* 607 (1998).

[17] Edward S. Corwin, "The Supreme Court as National School Board," 14 *Law and Contemp. Problems*, 3, 11-12 (1949).

[18] *Ibid.* at 14.

[19] See Steven D. Smith, *Foreordained Failure* (1995) 49-50; Steven D. Smith, "The Repeal of the Religion Clauses," *Liberty*, Mar.Apr.1998, 27.

upon the states, the Court's own conceptions of religious neutrality and religious liberty:

> [T]he religion clauses amounted to a decision by the national government not to address substantive questions concerning the proper relationship between religion and government. There would be no *national* law, theory, or principle — and, consequently, no *constitutional* law, theory or principle — prescribing the proper relationship between religion and government. The decision to "incorporate" the religion clauses represented, in effect, the reversal of that decision. By undertaking to review and regulate church-state relations at both the national and state levels, the federal judiciary necessarily committed itself to developing a substantive constitutional law for the subject. It would therefore be more accurate to say that this decision, far from "incorporating" the religion clauses, effectively repudiated– and hence repealed– those clauses.[20]

As will be noted in Question 10, the Supreme Court uses the Establishment Clause to forbid voluntary prayer and the posting of the Ten Commandments in public schools and otherwise to exclude from public activities any affirmation of God or of an objective moral law. The states are subjected to uniform, judge-made rules on matters that would be better left to the comparable protections of the state constitutions and to the common sense of the people.[21] The Supreme Court's intrusion into these matters is often itself a cause of the religious controversy that the Court claims to want to avoid. The prospect that every local incident can be transmuted into a federal case is an invitation to activist lawyers and judges to stir up trouble where there was none before. In the process, the federal judiciary is trivialized.

In applying the incorporation doctrine, the Court has interpreted the Bill of Rights to include new, unspecified rights which it has then applied against the states. In 1965, the Court struck down a Connecticut law prohibiting the use of contraceptives by married couples. To do this, the Court had to find a right of reproductive privacy in the Bill of Rights so as to hold that the due process clause of the Fourteenth Amendment forbids Connecticut to violate it. As Justice Black said in dissent, the framers did not have reproductive privacy in mind when they proposed the Bill of Rights. The Court majority, however, discovered such a right of privacy in the "penumbras formed by emanations

---

[20] Steven D. Smith, *Foreordained Failure* (1995), 49.

[21] See *Abington School District v. Schempp,* 374 U.S. 203 (1963); *Lynch v. Donnelly,* 465 U.S. 668 (1984).

from" the Bill of Rights.[22] This ruling was the precursor of *Roe v. Wade*,[23] where the Court held that the right of privacy prevents the states, in effect, from prohibiting any abortion.

The Supreme Court has used the incorporation doctrine to break down the division of powers between federal and state governments. Practically every form of state action is now subject to direct review by the federal courts, including nearly every aspect of criminal procedure, personal liberties, religion, obscenity, privacy, and other matters.

The incorporation doctrine is a judicial invention, unsupported by the history of the Fourteenth Amendment. In his definitive analysis, Charles Fairman analyzes the "mountain of evidence" in support of his conclusion that the framers and ratifiers of the Fourteenth Amendment did not intend to make the Bill of Rights applicable against the states.[24] He contrasts this "mountain of evidence" with "the few stones and pebbles that made up the theory that the Fourteenth Amendment incorporated Amendments I to VIII."[25] Nor can it be soundly argued that the Fourteenth Amendment made a "selective incorporation" of some of the provisions of the first eight amendments so as to apply only those provisions against the states.[26]

If the Fourteenth Amendment imposed the Bill of Rights upon the states, it would have required a change in state laws with respect to the necessity of indictments, the size of criminal juries, the right to jury trial in civil cases and other matters. Yet the states did not consider it to have that effect. When an Illinois state constitutional convention met in 1869-70, one of the hotly debated proposals was to abolish the grand jury. But the supporters of the grand jury "never so much as suggested that the Fourteenth Amendment incorporated the Bill of Rights and thus had fastened the grand jury upon the several states."[27] Five months after the adoption of the Fourteenth Amendment, the Supreme Judicial Court of New Hampshire ruled that "the whole power over the subject of religion is left exclusively to the state governments, to be acted upon according to their own sense of justice and the state constitutions."[28] And the Supreme Court agreed in several contemporaneous cases that

---

[22] *Griswold v. Conn.*, 381 U.S. 479, 484 (1965).

[23] 410 U.S. 113 (1973).

[24] Charles Fairman, "Does the Fourteenth Amendment Incorporate the Bill of Rights?" 2 *Stan. L. Rev.* 5, 134 (1949).

[25] *Ibid.*

[26] Louis Henkin, "'Selective Incorporation' in the Fourteenth Amendment," 73 *Yale L. J.* 74, 77 (1963); see also Raoul Berger, *Death Penalties: the Supreme Court's Obstacle Course* (1982), 15-16.

[27] Fairman, 2 *Stan. L. Rev.* at 99 (1949).

[28] *Hale v. Everett*, 53 N.H. 1, 124 (1868).

the Bill of Rights was not applied to the states.[29] Another indication is seen in the Blaine Amendment, which provided, "No State shall make any law respecting an establishment of religion, or prohibiting the free exercise thereof." The Congress which considered the Blaine Amendment in 1875 and 1876 included 23 members of the 39th Congress which had approved the Fourteenth Amendment, including Representative James G. Blaine himself. Yet not one member even hinted that the provisions of the Blaine Amendment were implicit in the amendment ratified just seven years earlier. Senator Frelinghuysen of New Jersey, for example, urged the adoption of the Blaine Amendment because it "prohibits the States for the first time, from the establishment of religion, from prohibiting its free exercise."[30]

A proper construction of the "privileges or immunities" clause would forbid the states to violate the right to life and other basic liberties.[31] The Court, however, having effectively nullified that clause,[32] has misused the due process clause to claim for itself the power of a continuing constitutional convention. "During the nineteenth century," said Robert Bork, "the Court often made up its own Constitution, most notoriously in the 1857 decision in *Dred Scott v. Sandford*. Chief Justice Roger Taney's opinion for the Court found a constitutional right, good against the federal government, to own slaves. But it wasn't until this century, when the Court invented the theory that the Bill of Rights limited states as well as the federal government, that the opportunities for judicial government exploded. The First Amendment speech clause has been made a guarantor of moral chaos, while its religion clauses have been reshaped to banish religious symbolism from public life. The Court invented a right of privacy and used it to create a wholly specious right to abortion. The list of such incursions into the legitimate sphere of democratic control goes on and on."[33]

THE MISUSE OF EQUAL PROTECTION

While the incorporation doctrine is the primary device the Court has used to gain dominance, we should note the Court's misinterpretation of the mandate of equal protection of the laws.[34] Every law, of

---

[29] See *Twitchell v. Pa.*, 74 U.S. (7 Wall.) 321 (1868); *Justices of the Supreme Court of New York v. U.S., ex rel. Murray,* 76 U.S. (9 Wall.) 274 (1870).

[30] See F. William O'Brien, S.J., *Justice Reed and the First Amendment* (1958), 116.

[31] See Raoul Berger, *Government by Judiciary* (2d ed., 1997), 57.

[32] *The Slaughter-House Cases,* 83 U.S. (16 Wall.) 36 (1873).

[33] Robert H. Bork, "Our Judicial Oligarchy," *First Things,* Nov. 1996, 21, 23.

[34] The Fourteenth Amendment provides, "Nor shall any State. . . deny to any person within its jurisdiction the equal protection of the laws." The Fifth Amendment's guarantee of "due process of law" has been held to include an implicit equal protection guarantee against the federal government. *Bolling v. Sharpe,* 347 U.S. 497 (1954).

course, involves a classification, treating some persons or subjects differently from others. The principle of equal protection would not prevent a state, for example, from setting educational qualifications for the practice of medicine. But some classifications, such as a racial restriction, could violate that principle.[35]

The Court, however, has interpreted the equal protection clause of the Fourteenth Amendment to diminish the power of the states with respect to various subjects, including public school desegregation,[36] the composition and apportionment of state legislatures,[37] and other matters. When the Court held that Virginia Military Institute's male-only policy denied equal protection to women, Justice Scalia, in dissent, said: "[I]t is one of the unhappy incidents of the federal system that a self-righteous Supreme Court, acting on its Members' personal view of what would make a 'more perfect union'. . . can impose its own favored social and economic dispositions nationwide. . . . The sphere of self-government reserved to the people of the Republic is progressively narrowed."[38]

In its interpretation of statutes as well as of the Fourteenth Amendment, the Court has distorted the concept of equal protection. "In *United Steelworkers of America v. Weber* (1979)," said former Attorney General Edwin Meese III, "the Supreme Court held for the first time that the Civil Rights Act of 1964 permits private employers to establish racial preferences and quotas in employment, despite the clear language of the statute. . . . Had the Court decided *Weber* differently, racial preferences would not exist in the private sector today. The *Weber* decision is a

---

[35] The "general rule" adopted by the Supreme Court is that a legislative classification "is presumed to be valid and will be sustained if [it] is rationally related to a legitimate state interest." *Cleburne v. Cleburne Living Center, Inc.,* 473 U.S. 432, 440 (1985). This "rational basis" test amounts to a presumption that the classification is constitutional. When the classification, however, is based on a "suspect" criterion, such as race, see *Miller v. Johnson,* 515 U.S. 900 (1995), or (with some exceptions) alienage, see *Graham v. Richardson,* 403 U.S. 365 (1971); *Ambach v. Norwick,* 441 U.S. 68 (1979), it "must serve a compelling govermental interest, and must be narrowly tailored to further that interest." *Adarand Constructors, Inc. v. Pena,* 515 U.S. 200, 235 (1995). This "compelling governmental interest" or "strict scrutiny" test amounts to a strong presumption of unconstitutionality. Classifications that burden a "fundamental right," such as the right to vote, *Kramer v. Union Free School District,* 395 U.S. 621 (1969) or the right to travel, *Shapiro v. Thompson,* 394 U.S. 618 (1969), are also subject to strict scrutiny. Classifications based on sex or illegitimacy receive an intermediate level of scrutiny, requiring that they "must serve important governmental objectives and must be substantially related to achievement of those objectives." *Craig v. Boren,* 429 U.S. 190, 197 (1976); *U.S. v. Virginia,* 518 U.S. 515 (1996).
[36] *Missouri v. Jenkins,* 515 U.S. 70 (1995).
[37] *Reynolds v. Sims,* 377 U.S. 533 (1964).
[38] *U.S. v. Virginia,* 518 U.S. 515, 601 (1996).

classic example of how unelected government regulators and federal judges have diverted our civil rights laws from a color-blind ideal to a complex and unfair system of racial and ethnic preferences and quotas that perpetuate bias and discrimination."[39]

The Court has interpretated "equal protection" to limit severely the power of the federal and state governments to make classifications that favor the traditional family founded on marriage. In *Romer v. Evans*,[40] the Court struck down an amendment to the Constitution of Colorado, adopted in a statewide referendum, which forbade any state or local law or policy "whereby homosexual, lesbian or bisexual orientation, conduct, practices or relationships shall constitute or otherwise be the basis of or entitle any person or class of persons to have or claim any minority status, quota preferences, protected status or claim of discrimination."[41] Justice Anthony M. Kennedy, writing for the Court, said, "Amendment 2 classifies homosexuals not to further a proper legislative end but to make them unequal to everyone else. . . . A State cannot so deem a class of persons a stranger to its laws. Amendment 2 violates the Equal Protection Clause."[42] Justice Scalia's dissent stated, "Despite all of its handwringing about the potential effect of Amendment 2 on general antidiscrimination laws, the. . . only denial of equal treatment [the Court's opinion] contends homosexuals have suffered is this: They may not obtain *preferential* treatment without amending the state constitution. That is to say, the principle underlying the Court's opinion is that one who is accorded equal treatment under the laws, but cannot as readily as others obtain *preferential* treatment under the laws, has been denied equal protection of the laws. If merely stating this alleged 'equal protection' violation does not suffice to refute it, our constitutional jurisprudence has achieved terminal silliness."[43]

---

[39] Edwin Meese III, "Putting the Federal Judiciary Back on the Constitutional Track," *Heritage Foundation Committee Brief,* June 30, 1997, 3.
[40] 517 U.S. 620 (1996).
[41] 517 U.S. at 624.
[42] 517 U.S. at 635.
[43] 517 U.S. 620 at 638-39.

9. DID CONGRESS SURRENDER TO THE SUPREME COURT?

Yes. The Supreme Court could not have achieved dominance if Congress had not acquiesced. The Incorporation Doctrine diminished the power of the states rather than of Congress, while Congress' powers are increased by the Court's misconstruction of the commerce clause and the general welfare clause. Why should Congress pick a fight with the Court, thus biting the hand that feeds it? Also, members of Congress find political benefit in being able to avoid tough questions on the ground that "our hands are tied" by the Court. "Recoiling from real power, our Congress is secretly delighted at being relieved of responsibility for resolving such blazing issues as busing, abortion, affirmative action, term limits, gun laws, doctor-assisted suicide, school prayer, English only and retention of all-male military schools."[1]

THE SUBMISSIVE CONGRESS

"Only in this century did it begin to become commonplace to regard the justices of the Supreme Court as the 'guardians' of the Constitution, as though only they. . . had this charge. . . . The Framers knew better. For them, the fate of republicanism. . . rested with 'the extent and proper structure of the Union,' and with institutions that 'divide and arrange the several offices in such a manner as that each may be a check on the other.'. . . Thus, they charged all public officials, indeed all citizens, with the duty to preserve the Constitution . . . . To forget that, to believe complacently that the highest task of our shared political existence is somebody else's business. . . is to let the cause of republican self-government slip through our fingers and to dishonor the. . . men from whom we inherited that cause."[2]

Congress has authority, under Article III, Section 2, of the Constitution, to remove a class of cases, such as those dealing with abortion or school prayer, from the appellate jurisdiction of the Supreme Court and from the trial and appellate jurisdiction of the lower federal courts. If Congress did so, for example, with respect to abortion, that would not overrule *Roe v. Wade*. But state courts would be free to decide the issue themselves without fear of review by the Supreme Court. Congress,

---

[1] Patrick Buchanan, Commentary, *Wash. Times,* July 2, 1997, p. A12.

[2] Matthew J. Franck, "Support and Defend: How Congress Can Save the Constitution from the Supreme Court," *The Heritage Lectures,* No. 604 (Heritage Foundation, 1997), 11-12; see *The Federalist,* nos. 10 and 51. See Edward A. Hartnett, "A Matter of Judgment, Not a Matter of Opinion," 74 *N.Y. Univ. L. Rev.*, 123 (1999).

however, appears to have no stomach for such an assertion of its prerogative.[3]

Section 5 of the Fourteenth Amendment [4] confers the power of enforcement on Congress, with no mention of an enforcement role for the
courts:

> It is not said that the judicial power of the general government shall
> extend to enforcing the prohibitions and protecting the rights and im-
> munities guaranteed. It is not said that branch of government shall be
> authorized to declare void any action of a State in violation of the pro-
> hibitions. It is the power of Congress which has been enlarged. Con-
> gress is authorized to enforce the prohibitions by appropriate legisla-
> tion. Some legislation is contemplated to make the amendment fully
> effective.[5]

The Supreme Court has abandoned that position. In 1997, in *City
of Boerne v. Flores*, the Court held that the application to the states of the
Religious Freedom Restoration Act (RFRA) is unconstitutional.[6] RFRA
prohibits "'[g]overnment' from 'substantially burden[ing]' a person's exercise of religion even if the burden results from a rule of general applica-
bility unless the government can demonstrate that the burden '(1) is in
furtherance of a compelling governmental interest; and (2) is the least restrictive means of furthering that interest.'"[7] RFRA was enacted in response to a Supreme Court decision,[8] which held that the requirement
that laws burdening the free exercise of religion must be justified by a
"compelling" governmental interest does not apply to "generally applicable prohibitions of socially harmful conduct."[9] The Court, in *City of
Boerne*, held that RFRA was not proper "enforcement legislation under §
5 of the Fourteenth Amendment"[10] because it crossed "the line between
measures that remedy or prevent unconstitutional actions and measures
that make a substantive change in the governing law."[11] The Court re-

---

[3] See Charles E. Rice, "Congress and the Supreme Court's Jurisdiction," 27 *Villanova
L. Rev.* 959 (1982); James McClellan, "Congressional Retraction of Federal Court Ju-
risdiction to Protect the Reserved Powers of the States: The Helms Prayer Bill and a
Return to First Principles," 27 *Villanova L. Rev.* 1019 (1982).

[4] "Section 5. The Congress shall have power to enforce, by appropriate legislation, the
provisions of this article."

[5] *Ex parte Virginia*, 100 U.S. 339, 345 (1879).

[6] *City of Boerne v. Flores*, 521 U.S. 507 (1997).

[7] 521 U.S. at 515-16.

[8] *Employment Division v. Smith*, 494 U.S. 872 (1990).

[9] 494 U.S. at 885.

[10] 521 U.S. at 529.

[11] 521 U.S. at 519.

gards its power to interpret the Fourteenth Amendment and the Free Exercise Clause as exclusive, barring any power of Congress to do so. "Legislation which alters the meaning of the Free Exercise Clause cannot be said to be enforcing the Clause. Congress does not enforce a constitutional right by changing what the right is. It has been given the power 'to enforce,' not the power to determine what constitutes a constitutional violation."[12]

In enacting RFRA, Congress accepted the premise of the Incorporation Doctrine, that the states are bound by the Free Exercise Clause and other provisions of the Bill of Rights.[13] But *City of Boerne* turned on the more basic question of the meaning of Congress' power to enforce the Fourteenth Amendment. In that context, RFRA ought to be regarded as an enforcement of the Free Exercise Clause rather than as a redefinition of it. In *City of Boerne*, not only did the Court reduce Congress' enforcement power to the performance of housekeeping chores implementing Supreme Court decisions, but also the Court confirmed its own seizure of power to redefine as well as enforce the Fourteenth Amendment. Consider the following passage from *City of Boerne*. If we substitute the *italicized* words for the bracketed words that were used by the Court, we can see that the Court is merely accusing Congress of doing what the Court itself does:

> If [Congress] *the Supreme Court* could define its own powers by altering the Fourteenth Amendment's meaning, no longer would the Constitution be "superior paramount law, unchangeable by ordinary means." It would be "on a level with ordinary [legislative acts] *judicial decisions,* and, like other [acts] *decisions,* . . . alterable when the [legislature] *Supreme Court* shall please to alter it.". . . . Under this approach, it is difficult to conceive of a principle that would limit [congressional] *Supreme Court* power. . . . Shifting [legislative] *Supreme Court* majorities could change the Constitution and effectively circumvent the difficult and detailed amendment process contained in Article V.[14]

The Supreme Court is not opposed to a single branch of government acting as a continuing constitutional convention to define the terms of the Constitution as it sees fit, so long as that branch is the Supreme Court. And Congress has thrown in the sponge without a fight.

---

[12] *Ibid.*

[13] See Matthew J. Franck, "Support and Defend: How Congress Can Save the Constitution from the Supreme Court," *The Heritage Lectures,* No. 604 (Heritage Foundation, 1997), 3-4.

[14] 521 U.S. at 529, quoting *Marbury v. Madison,* 5 U.S. (1 Cranch) 138, 177 (1803).

10. How did Secularism become the Official Religion of the Nation? And What Difference does it Make?

Can an event marked by about 90 percent of Americans become un-mentionable? Sure. School bus drivers in Fayette County, Ky., were warned not to say Merry Christmas to any of the children. Presumably, they would say, "Happy holidays," "Merry solstice," "Hail to winter" or something of the sort. In Pittsburgh, they could have said, "Happy Sparkle Season," the city's weird euphemism for Christmastime.

A high school dean in West Orange, N.J., reprimanded a student for singing "God Rest Ye Merry, Gentlemen" on school property. The student probably could have avoided criticism. . . by singing a song about overthrowing the government.

The nervous principal of Loudoun High School in Virginia told student editors to keep the newspaper as secular as possible and "to be careful that they don't associate the upcoming holiday with any particular religion." No, I guess not. You wouldn't want people to go around thinking that a Christian holy day is somehow associated with the Christian religion.

Why all these neurotic mental gymnastics? Christmas is the second most important feast on the Christian calendar (after Easter) and possibly now the second most important feast (after Thanksgiving) on the American civil, secular calendar. Though increasingly regarded as vaguely unmentionable, it is also a national public holiday like Independence Day and Memorial Day. Instead of acknowledging all this (along with the religious significance of Hanuka (sic) and Ramadan), our schools and other public institutions make their grim annual effort to pretend that Christmas isn't occurring. — *John Leo*[1]

The Original Intent

The First Amendment provides: "Congress shall make no law respecting an establishment of religion, or prohibiting the free exercise thereof." The Establishment Clause was intended to further the religious liberty which is the proper object of the Free Exercise Clause. Both clauses restricted only the federal government and left the subject of religion to be regulated by the states. The Free Exercise Clause was intended to protect, against federal infringement, the free exercise rights of all, evi-

---

[1] John Leo, "Bust Those Candy Cane Felons," *U.S. News & World Report*, Dec. 30, 1996/Jan. 6, 1997, 26.

dently including non-Christians, atheists and agnostics. The Establishment Clause required the federal government to maintain neutrality among religious sects.

> It is clear that neither the Constitution nor the First Amendment was designed to prohibit the recognition of God by the government of the United States or of any state. The Declaration of Independence acknowledged God in four places. Although the Constitution makes no reference to God, this was because the Constitution is a technical document, and not because of any secularizing purpose. The history of the colonies between 1775 and the Constitutional Convention in 1787 is replete with official acknowledgments of God and supplications for his aid. For example, the Treaty of Paris (with Great Britain at the close of the Revolution in 1783) begins: "In the name of the Most Holy and Undivided Trinity."[2] Pursuant to a resolution of both houses of Congress, an Anglican *Te Deum* service was conducted in St. Paul's Chapel as part of President Washington's first inauguration.[3] And on September 24, 1789, the very day it approved the First Amendment, the Congress called on President Washington to proclaim a national day of thanksgiving and prayer to acknowledge "the many signal favors of Almighty God."[4] President Washington proclaimed the day, and every president (except Thomas Jefferson and Andrew Jackson) has followed his example. If the First Amendment was intended to prevent governmental recognition of the existence of God, was it not strange for Congress to propose that amendment on the same day it called on the President to give thanks to that God whom he was not supposed to acknowledge?[5]

The Establishment Clause, as an allocation of federal-state jurisdiction, did not deny to the federal government the power to encourage belief in God and probably to encourage belief in the general principles of the Christian religion:

> Probably at the time of the adoption of the constitution, and of the first amendment to it. . ., the general, if not the universal sentiment in America was, that Christianity ought to receive encouragement from the state, so far as was not incompatible with the private rights of conscience, and the freedom of religious worship. An attempt to level all religions, and to make it a matter of state policy to hold all in utter indifference, would have created universal disapprobation if not universal indignation. . . .

---

[2] *Definitive Treaty of Peace between the United States of America and His Britannic Majesty,* Sept. 3, 1783, 8 Statutes 80.
[3] Douglas Southall Freeman, *George Washington* (1954), vol. VI, 196-97.
[4] *Annals of Congress,* I, 949.
[5] Charles E. Rice, *Beyond Abortion: The Theory and Practice of the Secular State* (1979), 61.

The real object of the amendment was not to countenance, much less to advance Mahometanism, or Judaism, or infidelity, by prostrating Christianity; but to exclude all rivalry among Christian sects, and to prevent any national ecclesiastical establishment which should give to a hierarchy the exclusive patronage of the national government.[6]

In *Holy Trinity Church v. United States*, in 1892, the Supreme Court unanimously held that a Congressional statute, prohibiting the immigration of persons under contract to perform labor, did not apply to an English minister who entered this country under a contract to preach at a New York church. The Court recited the legislative history of the act and then said:

> But beyond all these matters no purpose of action against religion can be imputed to any legislation, state or national, because this is a religious people. This is historically true. From the discovery of this continent to the present hour, there is a single voice making this affirmation. . . . If we pass beyond these matters to a view of American life as expressed by its laws, its business, its customs and its society, we find. . . a clear recognition of the same truth. . . . These, and many other matters which might be noticed, add a volume of unofficial declarations to the mass of organic utterances that this is a Christian nation.[7]

The result in *Holy Trinity* would probably have been the same if the Court had not relied on the religious factor. "All the other reasons permitting a nonliteral reading of the statute would still have been in place."[8] But the *Holy Trinity* opinion is significant to show that, a century ago, hospitality to theism and even to Christianity was regarded as consistent with the Establishment Clause.

THE ESTABLISHMENT OF SECULARISM

Until the Supreme Court incorporated the Bill of Rights into the Fourteenth Amendment, the handling of religious issues by the states was not a federal concern.[9] Rather, those issues were handled under the comparable bills of rights in state constitutions. In the 1940s, the Court applied the Establishment Clause,[10] and the Free Exercise Clause[11] to the

---

[6] Joseph Story, *Commentaries on the Constitution of the United States* (3rd ed., 1858), Secs. 1874, 1877.

[7] 143 U.S. 457, 470-71 (1892).

[8] Stuart Banner, "When Christianity Was Part of the Common Law," 16 *Law & History Review* 27, 42 (1998).

[9] See Question 8.

[10] *Everson v. Board of Education*, 330 U.S. 1 (1947).

[11] *Cantwell v. Conn.*, 310 U.S. 296 (1940).

states. By that time, the earlier Christian consensus had eroded. In the 1963 decision which outlawed prayer in public schools, Justice William Brennan aptly said:

> [O]ur religious composition makes us a vastly more diverse people than were our forefathers. They knew differences chiefly among Protestant sects. Today the Nation is far more heterogeneous religiously, including as it does substantial minorities not only of Catholics and Jews but as well of those who worship according to no version of the Bible and those who worship no God at all.[12]

As the American religious consensus eroded, the Court's conceptions reflected that erosion. The Court has interpreted the Establishment Clause to require not merely neutrality on the part of government among Christian and other theistic sects, but neutrality between theism and non-theism.[13]

> If we want an innocent target to blame for *Roe v. Wade*, we should not overlook Roy Torcaso. When he applied for appointment as a notary public in Maryland, he was refused because the Maryland constitution required that all public officers and employees declare their belief in God, which Torcaso refused to do. In deciding in his favor in 1961, the Supreme Court laid down the principles which made *Roe v. Wade* (or something of the sort) inevitable. In Torcaso's case, the Court struck down Maryland's oath requirement because it unconstitutionally invaded the applicant's "freedom of belief and religion" and because the "power and authority of the State of Maryland thus is put on the side of one particular sort of believers — those who are willing to say they believe in the existence of God."[14] Nontheistic creeds were defined by the court to be religions. The court held that "neither a State nor the Federal Government can constitutionally aid all religions as against non-believers, and neither can aid those religions based on a belief in the existence of God as against those religions founded on different beliefs."[15] In a footnote, Mr. Justice Black, speaking for the Court, said: "Among religions in this country which do not teach what would commonly be considered a belief in the existence of God are Buddhism, Taoism, Ethical Culture, Secular Humanism and others."[16]

---

[12] *Abington School District v. Schempp*, 374 U.S. 203, 239-40 (1963).
[13] See *Torcaso v. Watkins*, 367 U.S. 488 (1961); *Abington School District v. Schempp*, 374 U.S. 203 (1963).
[14] *Torcaso v. Watkins*, 367 U.S. at 490.
[15] 367 U.S. at 495.
[16] *Ibid.*, n. 11.

When the government of the United States, through the Supreme Court, thus declared its neutrality on the existence of God, the fate of millions of children was sealed. Not that the Supreme Court in the Torcaso case said anything about abortion; it did not have to. By 1961, our public philosophy had become thoroughly positivistic, but a lingering deference to God held matters in check. However, when the state declared its official indifference to God, the dam was breached. Thereafter, the Court would treat such issues as abortion only in secular and wholly amoral terms. Under those rules, the unborn child never had a chance.[17]

The Court-mandated neutrality between theism and non-theism influences the interpretations of both the Free Exercise and the Establishment clauses.[18] In practice, however, in the context of the American Founding, it is impossible for government to be neutral on the existence of God. Justice William Brennan argued, in his concurrence in the 1963 school prayer case, that the words "under God" could still be kept in the Pledge of Allegiance only because they "no longer have a religious purpose or meaning." Instead, according to Brennan, they "may merely recognize the historical fact that our Nation was believed to have been founded 'under God.'"[19] This supposed neutrality would logically prevent an assertion by any government official, whether President or school teacher, that the Declaration of Independence states the truth when it affirms the existence and providence of God. If a pupil asks his public school teacher whether God exists, as the Declaration affirms, and if the teacher says, "Yes," that is unconstitutional as a preference of theism; if the teacher says, "No," that is unconstitutional as a preference of atheism. The only thing the teacher can do, according to the theory of the Court, is to suspend judgment, to say, "I (the state) do not know." But this is an affirmation of the religion of agnosticism. In this way, the Court's requirement of suspension of judgment on the existence of God has resulted in the repudiation of the American Founding through the effective establishment of agnostic secularism as the national religion.

THE COURT FOLLOWS AND SHAPES THE CULTURE

Generations of public school children have passed through the system since the 1960s without ever seeing the state, in the person of their

---

[17] Charles E. Rice, *Beyond Abortion: The Theory and Practice of the Secular State* (1979), 59-60.

[18] See *Employment Division v. Smith*, 494 U.S. 872 (1990); *Rosenberger v. Rector of the Univ. of Virginia*, 515 U.S. 819 (1995); *Lemon v. Kurtzman*, 403 U.S. 602, 612-13 (1971); Dhananjai Shivakumar, "Neutrality and the Religion Clauses," 33 *Harvard Civil Rights–Civil Liberties L. Rev.* 505 (1998).

[19] *Abington School District v. Schempp*, 374 U.S. at 304.

teachers, acknowledge, in accord with the Declaration of Independence, that "the Laws of Nature and of Nature's God" limit the power of the state. Moreover, the Court's neutrality rule requires that public schools must treat issues such as homosexuality, promiscuity, abortion, etc., in a "non-judgmental" manner that cannot help but inculcate a relativistic attitude in the students. One result is a potential abridgment of the free exercise of religion of students who do not subscribe to the secular orthodoxy. Implicitly, the children are led to believe that there is no standard of right and wrong by which the decrees of the state can be judged other than the will of the state itself. "Nonjudgmental" sex education is part of the public school curriculum, but the Ten Commandments cannot be posted in the classroom.[20] In effect, a militant secularism is the established national religion. The Court both reflects and accelerates the cultural trend toward the privatization of religion as a sentiment irrelevant to law and public policy.

"The purpose of human law," said Aquinas, "is to lead men to virtue," although "not suddenly, but gradually."[21] Instead, through the Court's interpretations, the law has become a mere reflector of an increasingly secular consensus. The law in turn has advanced that consensus by its promotion of established secularism. The preference for secularism requires that the right to life of the unborn child and that of his retarded brother and his grandmother must be evaluated in secular, utilitarian terms, in which the odds are heavily against the "unwanted" one. Similarly, any legislative treatment of homosexual activity, pornography and divorce cannot be based on an objective moral law, let alone the Ten Commandments. When churches are intimidated into accepting these secular ground rules of public debate, they forego their most basic argument, that some things are out of bounds for any society because they violate the law of the Creator.

With respect to the family, its disintegration is accelerated by Supreme Court decisions which reflect an atomistic view of the family that is hostile to the Christian tradition.[22] There was a time when the Supreme Court defended the family as an institution essential to Christian civilization. In 1890, Justice Joseph P. Bradley, for the Court, described polygamy as a practice "contrary to the spirit of Christianity and of the civilization which Christianity has produced in the Western world." He

---

[20] *Stone v. Graham*, 449 U.S. 39 (1980); see *Wash. Times*, Aug. 12, 1998, p. A5; see Question 24.

[21] *ST,* I, II, Q.96, art. 2.

[22] See Carl A. Anderson, "The Supreme Court and the Economics of the Family," *The Family in America* (1987), 1; see generally, Allan C. Carlson, *Family Questions* (1990).

described it as "repugnant to our laws and to the principles of our civilization."[23] This approach has been abandoned by the Court.[24] The father, for example, whether he is married to the mother or not, does not even have a right to be informed that his unborn child is going to be killed.[25]

In his 1863 proclamation of a national day of fast and prayer, President Abraham Lincoln said, "it is the duty of nations as well as of men to own their dependence upon the overruling power of God. . . and to recognize the sublime truth, announced in the Holy Scriptures and proven by all history, that those nations only are blessed whose God is the Lord."[26] Unfortunately, in Lincoln's words, "we have grown in numbers, wealth and power as no other nation has ever grown. But we have forgotten God."[27] It is not the Supreme Court alone that has forgotten God. Rather, in its imposition of secularism as our national creed, the Court has reflected the erosion of our belief.

---

[23] *Church of Jesus Christ of Latter-Day Saints v. U.S.*, 136 U.S. 1, 49 (1890).

[24] See *Torcaso v. Watkins*, 367 U.S. 488 (1961); *Abington School District v. Schempp*, 374 U.S. 203 (1963).

[25] *Planned Parenthood v. Danforth*, 428 U.S. 52 (1976); *Planned Parenthood v. Casey*, 505 U.S. 833 (1992).

B.   Technology Has Made Murder a Private Matter

11.   HOW DID ABORTION BECOME A PRIVATE CHOICE BEYOND THE LAW?

> Exactly 50 years ago, Nazi tanks and Stukas were annihilating a Polish Army that had proclaimed itself ready for anything. A bulletin of the Polish Information Service dated July 1, 1939, just 60 days before the blitzkrieg fell, praised the late Marshal Pilsudski for his foresight in building "one of the first class military powers of Europe."
>
> Of special pride to the Poles was their horse cavalry, to which they had committed more than a quarter of their 132 standing regiments. A military observer of the day termed the cavalry "the outstanding feature of the Polish Army." He wrote "I should class this the best in Europe." And so it was. Regrettably, its skilled and courageous soldiers had prepared for the wrong war.— *Mitchell E. Daniels, Jr.*[1]

In his 1934 essay, *The Army of the Future*, Charles DeGaulle predicted what the next war would be like. He argued for mechanization of the French infantry, emphasizing the use of tanks. Unfortunately, the French military establishment continued to prepare for World War I-style combat. The French were ready for static warfare on the Maginot Line. But the Germans outflanked and defeated them.

Military establishments are often accused of preparing to fight the previous war rather than the next one. The pro-life establishment, unfortunately, is following the Maginot Line pattern. It still mobilizes the troops to fight for such marginal restrictions on surgical abortion as are permitted by the Supreme Court. This effort is counterproductive because it concedes that the intentional killing of some human beings can be validly legalized and therefore that some innocent human beings can be treated as nonpersons. More important, surgical abortions are rapidly going the way of the horse cavalry. In the new war, drugs and devices will dominate as early abortion techniques. The establishment pro-life movement, preoccupied with band-aid restrictions on surgical abortion and afraid to criticize contraception, is losing this new war by default. One reason for this failure is that the pro-death forces, in a pre-emptive strike more than three decades ago, succeeded in redefining early abortion as contraception.

---

[1] Mitchell E. Daniels, Jr., "The Decline of Central Government," *Hudson Opinion*, Nov. 1989, 1.

The Redefinition of Pregnancy

The Charles DeGaulle of the pro-life movement was Joseph R. Stanton, M.D., of the Value of Life Committee.[2] As DeGaulle warned of altered tactics of the Germans, so Dr. Stanton sounded the alarm in 1975 on the new anti-life tactic which has achieved a Blitzkrieg success, outflanking the pro-life establishment which has remained hunkered down in its Maginot Line, preparing defensive tactics to fight yesterday's war.

As Dr. Stanton noted, "Until 1964 there was no scientific disagreement whatsoever that human pregnancy began at fertilization. . . . Nor was there any dispute that conception occurred at the time of the fertilization of the human ovum by the human sperm. . . . Attempts to change the definition of the beginning of pregnancy from the time of fertilization to the more. . . imprecise time of implantation began seriously in 1964 at the Second International Conference on Intra-Uterine Contraception. . . . This was a. . . calculated effort to make induced abortion socially acceptable."[3]

The American College of Obstetricians and Gynecologists (ACOG) committee on terminology, in 1965, created new definitions of conception and the beginning of pregnancy, relating them both to implantation rather than fertilization of the ovum:

> Fertilization is the union of spermatozoon and ovum.
>
> Conception is the implantation of a fertilized ovum. . . .
>
> Pregnancy is the state from conception to expulsion of the products of that conception.[4]

Dorland's Medical Dictionary formerly defined "conception" as "the fecundation of the ovum."[5] However, the 26th and 27th editions of Dorland's, published in 1985 and 1988, defined conception as: "The onset of pregnancy, marked by implantation of the blastocyst; the formation of a viable zygote." As a *New England Journal of Medicine* editorial put it in 1997, "Pregnancy begins with implantation, not fertilization. Medical organizations and the federal government concur on this

---

[2] When Dr. Stanton died in 1997, the work of VOLCOM was taken over by the Sisters of Life, 1955 Needham Ave., Bronx, N.Y. 10466, (718) 881-7286.

[3] Joseph R. Stanton, M.D., and Marianne Rea-Luthin, *Why Human Life Should be Protected from Fertilization,* Onward (1975); see discussion in Germain Grisez, *Abortion: The Myths, the Realities and the Arguments* (1970), 106-16.

[4] *ACOG Terminology Bulletin* (Sept., 1965).

[5] *Dorland's Medical Dictionary* (25th edition, 1974).

point. Fertilization is a necessary but insufficient step toward pregnancy."[6] According to the federal Department of Health and Human Services, "'Pregnancy' encompasses the period of time from confirmation of implantation. . . until expulsion or extraction of the fetus."[7]

According to these re-definitions, even after fertilization, neither "conception" nor "the onset of pregnancy" takes place until implantation. Dr. W. N. Hubbard, M.D., Vice President of Upjohn Company, provided a frankly anti-life rationale for these changes in 1972:

> We are confronted with the problem of discrepancy between total productivity of the human race as it is now organized and its consumptive demands. This discrepancy has led to a threatening difference between the "have's" (sic) and "have-nots." If we are to have each human life fulfill its potential, then we will have to reduce this discrepancy between productivity and consumptive demand. With limited resources in an ecology that is subject to harmful alteration, there is some doubt about the strategy of only increasing production. Therefore, *for the first time, the medical profession is involved in the inhibition of life and here we look to the most effective and convenient means.* Considering the pathology of population concentration and the futility of trying to keep up with an explosive birth rate by increasing productivity alone, *the need for limitation of new human life becomes persuasive. It is our hope that by terminating or intercepting pregnancies at the embryonic disk or somate stage of development, we can avoid many of the problems, both aesthetic and physical, of abortions in later phases of conception. It is our hope that through the development of routes of optimum convenience, both oral and vaginal, it will be possible to obtain an effective inducer of menses at cycle end.*[8]

"In laymen's terms," said Dr. Stanton, "this means that it was anticipated that abortion would be more readily accepted by the American public if it could be done at very early stages of pregnancy. . . . Approval of 'drugs and devices intended to prevent implantation of the fertilized ovum' would effectuate the sanctioning in the public law of early induced abortion. Accepting the pragmatic redefinition of the beginnings of human pregnancy as the time of implantation sets the stage for acceptance of early self-administered abortion through the use of drugs, prostaglandins, etc."

[6] David A. Grimes, M.D., Editorial, "Emergency Contraception–Expanding Opportunities for Primary Prevention," 337 *N. England J. of Med.* 1078-79 (Oct. 9, 1997).
[7] 45 *C.F.R.* sec. 46.203(b).
[8] W. N. Hubbard, "Welcome Address," 9 *Journal of Reproductive Medicine,* 249 (Dec.1972). Emphasis added.

ABORTIFACIENTS AS "CONTRACEPTIVES"

While the attention of the pro-life movement was focused in 1996 on the effort to ban partial-birth abortions, the Food and Drug Administration gave conditional approval to the Population Council for the marketing of RU 486.[9] RU 486, or mifepristone, can be used as soon as a pregnancy test tells the woman she is pregnant.[10] It can be used at least until the seventh week of pregnancy. Another method using a combination of two drugs — methotrexate and misoprostil — that are now labeled for other purposes, is "highly effective" when used within the first nine weeks of pregnancy.[11] In September, 1998, the Food and Drug Administration approved marketing of "morning after" pills which, taken within 72 hours after intercourse, prevent implantation. "It's not a contraceptive. It is a very, very early abortive drug," said Dr. John C. Willke of the Life Issues Institute.[12] An alternate technique is "early surgical abortion," available as early as eight days after fertilization and through the fifth week of pregnancy, which uses vaginal ultrasound to detect the pregnancy when it is pea-size, or even microscopic, along with a hand-held syringe to extract the very early embryo.[13] Other kinds of pills, approved for use in this country, are inaccurately promoted as contraceptives although their effect is to prevent implantation of the embryo in the womb.[14] And the intrauterine device can operate as an abortifacient by preventing implantation.[15]

Early abortion drugs and devices could remove abortion from the political agenda since they are defined as contraceptive rather than as abortifacient. "There is a precedent for the abortion pill," notes Rutgers University Professor Leonard A. Cole: "A generation ago, much of the nation was divided over the legality of contraceptive devices. . . . By the mid-1960's, the then recently created birth control pill was becoming popular, and the contraception argument was settled as much by the new technology as by Government decision. . . . A few years from now,

---

[9] *N.Y. Times,* Sept. 19, 1996, p. A1.
[10] Margaret Talbot, "This Pill Will Change Everything About Abortion," *N.Y. Times Magazine,* July 11, 1999, 28.
[11] *N.Y. Times,* Sept. 12, 1996, p. A10; American Political Network, Lexis-Nexis, *Abortion Report,* Sept. 12, 1996.
[12] *Wash. Times,* Sept. 3, 1998, p. A1.
[13] *Boston Globe,* Mar. 25, 1998, p. B2.
[14] See *N.Y. Times,* Sept. 23, 1997, p. B15; *N.Y. Times,* Dec. 21, 1997, p. A1; See *Life Insight* (Nat'l. Conf. of Catholic Bishops, Oct. 1997), 1, 3, describing the abortifacient effect of so-called "emergency contraceptive pills."
[15] Updated lists of aborifacient drugs and devices are available from Pharmacists for Life, P.O. Box 130, Ingomar, PA 15127, (412) 487-8960.

the early pregnancy abortion pill is likely to be as much a nonissue as the birth control pill is today."[16]

Early abortifacients are beyond the effective reach of the law. It will usually be impossible to prove that a life was terminated in an early abortion; prosecution for abortion therefore would be practically impossible. The only way of controlling such abortifacients will be by licensing and by regulating the issuance of prescriptions. But some abortifacient drugs have legitimate, non-abortifacient uses. "Oral contraceptives can protect against cancer of the ovaries, even in women whose genetic makeup gives them an above-average risk for the tumor."[17] Since "contraceptive" drugs are licensed for legitimate uses, it is practically impossible to prevent their use for abortion. The legal obliteration of the distinction between contraception and abortion has put chemical abortions beyond the practical reach of the law.

In reality, conception, fertilization and the onset of pregnancy have always been synonymous. Margaret Sanger, the founder of Planned Parenthood, acknowledged this as long ago as 1920:

> If no children are desired, the meeting of the male sperm and the ovum must be prevented. When scientific means are employed to prevent this meeting, one is said to practice birth control. The means used is known as a contraceptive.
>
> If, however, a contraceptive is not used and the sperm meets the ovule and development begins, any attempt at removing it or stopping its further growth is called abortion.[18]

Supreme Court Justices Stevens and O'Connor, however, appear to regard abortifacients as contraceptives. The preamble to the Missouri statute in the 1989 *Webster* case stated that "the life of each human being begins at conception" and that "unborn children have protectable interests in life, health, and well-being."[19] Five Justices declined to decide the constitutionality of that preamble because it had no legal effect on abortions. Justice Stevens, however, argued that the preamble is unconstitutional. The statute defined conception as "the fertilization of the ovum of a female by a sperm of a male."[20] Justice Stevens stated that "standard

---

[16] Leonard A. Cole, "Abortions Will Be Moot Soon," *New York Times,* Oct. 9, 1989, p. 19.

[17] *Wash. Times,* Aug. 13, 1998, p. A6.

[18] Margaret Sanger, *Woman and the New Race* (1920), 124; see Germain Grisez, *Abortion: The Myths, the Realities and the Arguments* (1970), 114.

[19] *Webster v. Reproductive Health Services,* 492 U.S. 490, 504 (1989).

[20] 492 U.S. at 563.

medical texts equate 'conception' with implantation in the uterus, occurring about six days after fertilization. Missouri's declaration therefore implies regulation not only of previability abortions, but also of common
forms of contraception such as the IUD, and the morning-after pill."[21]
Justice Stevens noted that, "An intrauterine device, commonly called an
IUD, 'works primarily by preventing a fertilized egg from implanting.'. . . Other contraceptive methods that may prevent implantation include 'morning-after pills,' high dose estrogen pills taken after intercourse, particularly in cases of rape. . . and the French RU 486, a pill
that works 'during the indeterminate period between contraception and
abortion,'. . . Low-level estrogen 'combined' pills — a version of the ordinary, daily ingested birth control pill — also may prevent the fertilized
egg from reaching the uterine wall and implanting."[22] Justice O'Connor
appeared to agree with Justice Stevens when she described early
abortificients as "post fertilization contraceptive devices."[23]

These questions are not merely academic. If a majority of the Court
were to classify early abortifacients as contraceptives, any allowance by
the Court of restrictions on abortion (but not on contraceptives) would
be practically meaningless. It would allow no restraint on the chemical
and other early techniques which will be the usual abortions in the near
future. We have to recognize the impact of technology here. And we ultimately have to come to grips with the contraception issue if we are to do
anything effective on abortion.

[21] 492 U.S. at 563.
[22] 492 U.S. at 563, n. 7.
[23] 492 U.S. at 523.

12.   BUT ISN'T THE CLAIM THAT LIFE BEGINS AT CONCEPTION A "RELIGIOUS" POSITION?

No. Supreme Court Justice Stevens has led the charge here to dismiss scientific fact as mere theology. In the 1989 *Webster* case he said:

> Our jurisprudence. . . has consistently required a secular basis for valid legislation. . . . Because I am not aware of any secular basis for differentiating between contraceptive procedures that are effective immediately before and those that are effective immediately after fertilization,. . . I am persuaded that the absence of any secular purpose for the legislative declarations that life begins at conception and that conception occurs at fertilization makes. . . the preamble[1] invalid under the Establishment Clause of the First Amendment. . . . [T]he preamble, an unequivocal endorsement of a religious tenet of some but by no means all Christian faiths,. . . serves no identifiable secular purpose.[2]

Stevens regards the claim that life begins at fertilization as "theological."[3] "My concern," he writes, "can best be explained by reference to the position. . . accepted by. . . the Roman Catholic Church for many years. . . . 'It was widely held that the soul was not present until the formation of the fetus 40 or 80 days after conception, for males and females respectively. Thus, abortion of the 'unformed' or 'inanimate' fetus (from *anima,* soul) was something less than true homicide.'. . . This view received its definitive treatment in St. Thomas Aquinas."[4] The preamble to the Missouri statute declared that human life begins at fertilization. "If the views of St. Thomas were held as widely today as they were in the Middle Ages," wrote Stevens, "and if a state legislature were to enact a statute prefaced with a 'finding' that female life begins 80 days after conception and male life begins 40 days after conception, I have no doubt that this Court would promptly conclude that such an endorsement of a particular religious tenet is violative of the Establishment Clause. . . . [T]he difference between that hypothetical statute and Missouri's preamble reflects nothing more than a difference in theological doctrine. The preamble endorses the theological position that there is the same secular interest in preserving the life of a fetus during the first 40 or 80

---

[1] The preamble to the Missouri statute declared that "the life of each human being begins at conception" and the statute defined "conception" as "the fertilization of the ovum. . . by a sperm." 492 U.S. at 504, 563.

[2] *Webster v. Reproductive Health Services,* 492 U.S. 490, 566-67 (1989).

[3] 492 U.S. at 566.

[4] 492 U.S. at 567.

days of pregnancy as there is after viability — indeed, after the time when the fetus has become a 'person' with legal rights protected by the Constitution."[5]

Stevens' misuse of St. Thomas illustrates the technique of dismissing the fact that every abortion kills a human being as the expression of a merely theological belief. St. Thomas knew nothing of the ovum and fertilization. His lack of modern scientific knowledge led him to conclude that human life began and ensoulment took place, not at conception, but some time later, probably 40 days later for males and 80 for females. He concluded that abortion was not homicide until ensoulment, although he regarded abortion at every stage as a grave sin.[6] If St. Thomas were here today, he would surely accept the scientific reality that human life begins at fertilization.

"Some people," said Pope John Paul II, "try to justify abortion by claiming that the result of conception, at least up to a certain number of days, cannot yet be considered a personal human life. But in fact, 'from the time that the ovum is fertilized, a life is begun which is neither that of the father nor the mother; it is rather the life of a new human being with his own growth. It would never be made human if it were not human already. . . . [M]odern genetic science. . . has demonstrated that from the first instant there is established the programme of what this living being will be: a person, this individual person with his characteristic aspects already well determined. Right from fertilization the adventure of a human life begins, ... Even if the presence of a spiritual soul cannot be ascertained by empirical data, the results. . . of scientific research. . . provide 'a valuable indication for discerning by the use of reason a personal presence at the moment of the first appearance of a human life: how could a human individual not be a human person?'"[7]

TWINNING

Some have used questions raised by the process of identical twinning to rationalize early abortion as something other than the killing of a human being.[8] Fr. Norman Ford, S.B.D., argues that the embryo cannot

---

[5] *Ibid.*

[6] See Germain Grisez, *Abortion: The Myths, The Realities and The Arguments* (1970), 154-55; John T. Noonan, Jr., ed., *The Morality of Abortion: Legal and Historical Perspectives* (1970), 1, 22-26; Rudolph J. Gerber, "When is the Human Soul Infused?" 22 *Laval Theologique et Philosophique* 234, 236 (1966); Thomas Aquinas, *ST*, III, Q. 68, art. 2; Stephen J. Heaney, "Aquinas and The Humanity of the Conceptus," 15 *Human Life Rev.* 63 (1989).

[7] *EV*, no. 60.

[8] See Joseph F. Donceel, S.J., "Immediate Animation and Delayed Hominization," 31 *Theological Studies* 76 (1970).

be said to be a definitively individual human being until after the potential for identical twinning has passed, i.e., about 14 days after fertilization.[9] However, as Robert Joyce explained, the potential for twinning does not refute the reality of human life from fertilization:

> "The human *conceptus* is not necessarily an individual. But individuality is essential to personhood. Therefore, the *conceptus* cannot be reasonably regarded as a person." Proponents of this argument cite as evidence the fact of so-called "identical" twins and other multiple births resulting from. . . a single ovum and sperm. . . . But the evidence would seem to indicate *not* that there is *no* individual present at conception, but that there is at least one and possibly more. Jerome Lejeune of Paris. . . has indicated that individuality may be fully existent at the point of fertilization, but that thus far we do not have the technical capacity to discern how many individuals are present at that point.[10] Moreover. . . at this very early stage of human development there may occur at times a process of generation similar to that common in other species. In that case, we could say that one of the twins would be the parent of the other. The original zygote could be regarded as the parent of the second, even though we may never know which one was parthenogenically the parent.[11]

> There is also the disputed evidence that in the first days of life, twins or triples sometimes "recombine" into a single individual. . . . [T]his could. . . mean that one individual's body absorbs the body of the other, resulting in the latter's death at this particular, vulnerable stage in life.[12]

"I do not think Ford's objection," wrote Ronald K. Tacelli, S.J., "disproves the initial claim: that I am identical with the organism that began in my mother's body 48 years ago, the organism we call a zygote. . . . If you are an identical twin, then it *may* be that you cannot trace your own beginning back to the zygote your parents conceived; you may have

---

[9] Norman Ford, S.B.D., *When Did I Begin?: Conception of the Human Individual in History*, Philosophy and Science (1989); see Letters, in *The Tablet*, London, by John Finnis, Jan. 6, 1990 and Jan. 27, 1990 and Fr. Norman Ford, Jan. 27, 1990 and Feb. 3, 1990.

[10] Citing Jerome Lejeune, "The Beginning of a Human Being," paper presented to the Academie des Sciences Morales et Politiques (Paris, Oct. 1, 1973).

[11] Citing "The Position of Modern Science on the Beginning of Human Life," position paper of *Scientists For Life* (Fredericksburg, Virginia, 1975).

[12] Robert E. Joyce, "Personhood and the Conception Event," 52 *New Scholasticism* 97, 103-04 (1978). See Andre Hellegers, M.D., "Fetal Development," *Theological Studies*, March 1970, 4; Thomas Hilgers, M.D., "Human Reproduction: Three Issues for the Moral Theologian," *International Review of Natural Family Planning*, (1977), 115-116.

come to be at a later stage; and it may be that only your twin brother or sister can trace his or her history back to such an earlier beginning.[13] In any case, Ford's discussion does not prove that there are *not* real ontological individuals in the womb before the primitive streak stage — any more than the fact that I can be cloned proves that I am not a human individual."[14]

In short, we know that at least *one* human being is there at conception. There might be *more than one*, but that doesn't change the fact that at least *someone* is there. As Theodore Hall, O.P. put it, "We wonder if the biological process in twinning isn't simply another example of how nature reproduces from other individuals without destroying that person's or persons' individuality. Simply because modern embryology hasn't discovered the how of the reality doesn't mean that there isn't an answer. . . It is quite evident that man and woman accomplish the production of an individual without destroying their own individuality. . . . Thomistic philosophy demonstrates that it is the human soul which God immediately creates, and this soul informs the matter which was derived from pre-existing matter. Now, if unaided nature in the early embryonic stages so arranges the matter to provide another joined or disjoined individual to the previously existing individual (twinning), how does this negate the individuality of a previously existing human being? The one remains. The second begins to live, having had its material existence potentially in the former as in a parent cell. If God infuses a human soul into the first isolated matter, why not in the second and newly isolated matter?"[15]

A MATTER OF PRIVACY

As Dr. Stanton foretold, the pro-abortion strategy is to shield early abortions from restriction by defining them as contraceptives. The pro-life movement must insist on protection of life from the beginning, i.e., from fertilization. However, the reality is that early abortion techniques are beyond the practical reach of the law. With respect to surgical abor-

---

[13] "It may be, as Stephen Schwarz has argued (*The Moral Question of Abortion* 54-56), that twins can *already* exist, though in a materially unseparated way, *prior* to segmentation. Or perhaps the being your parents originally conceived died in giving rise to you and your brother or sister."

[14] Ronald K. Tacelli, S.J., "Were You a Zygote?" 4 *Josephinium J. of Theology*, 25, 33 (1997).

[15] Theodore Hall, O.P., S.T.D., "Human Life Begins: Integrated Senate Report," *Linacre Quarterly*, August, 1983, 253, 258-59; see also Joseph T. Culliton, "Rahner on the Origin of the Soul: Some Implications Regarding Abortion," 53 *Thought* 203 (June 1978); William H. Marshner, "Metaphysical Personhood and the IUD," *The Wanderer*, Oct. 10, 1974, 7.

tions, the Supreme Court will not uphold any effective prohibition of any of them at any stage of pregnancy. With respect to early abortions by pill or other devices, apart from the difficulty of proving that an abortion has actually occurred, the private nature of such techniques puts them beyond the effective reach of the law.

In *Roe v. Wade*, the Supreme Court based the newly invented right to an abortion on the right to privacy which it claimed in 1965 to have discovered lurking in the "penumbras formed by emanations from" the Bill of Rights.[16] In *Planned Parenthood v. Casey*,[17] the Court shifted the basis for the abortion right from privacy to a broader "liberty interest," just as technology was making abortion truly a matter of privacy.

---

[16] *Roe v. Wade*, 410 U.S. 113 (1973); *Griswold v. Conn.*, 381 U.S. 479, 484 (1965).
[17] 505 U.S. 833 (1992); see Question 4 for discussion of the significance of the "liberty interest" terminology.

13.   EUTHANASIA: HOW DID WE MOVE TOWARD A PRIVATIZED DUTY TO DIE?

"You've got a duty to die and get out of the way. Let the other society, our kids, build a reasonable life." — *Colorado Governor Richard Lamm, speaking to the elderly.* [1]

How does a "duty to die" develop in the law? Through the legal toleration of intentional killing and through the extension of that killing to the incompetent. Even if a state forbids assisted suicide, so that a physician may not legally prescribe for a consenting patient a drug that induces death, such a law will not prevent intentional killing by withholding medical treatment including nutrition and hydration, or by prescribing pain killers with the intent to hasten death, or by "terminal sedation" of the patient. In *Vacco v. Quill,* the Supreme Court noted that "respondents" (supporters of assisted suicide) argued that New York was irrational in forbidding assisted suicide but allowing "'terminal sedation,' a process respondents characterize as 'induc[ing] barbiturate coma and then starv[ing] the person to death.'" Petitioners (opponents of assisted suicide) argued that "'[a]lthough proponents of physician-assisted suicide and euthanasia contend that terminal sedation is covert physician-assisted suicide or euthanasia, the concept of sedating pharmacotherapy is based on informed consent and the principle of double effect.'" The Court agreed with petitioners and said: "Just as a State may prohibit assisting suicide while permitting patients to refuse unwanted lifesaving treatment, it may permit palliative care related to that refusal, which may have the foreseen but unintended 'double effect' of hastening the patient's death. . . . ('It is widely recognized that the provision of pain medication is ethically and professionally acceptable even when the treatment may hasten the patient's death, if the medication is intended to alleviate pain and severe discomfort, not to cause death')."[2]

The Court here refers to the double effect principle. Fr. John A. Hardon, S.J., described the legitimate operation of this principle with respect to the removal of a cancerous womb of a pregnant woman:

"To be licitly applied, the principle must observe four limiting norms:

1.   The action (removal of the diseased womb) is good; it consists in excising an infected part of the human body.

---

[1]   *So. Bend Tribune,* Mar. 28, 1984, p. 3; *N.Y. Times,* editorial, Mar. 31, 1984, p. 18.
[2]   521 U.S. at 807-08, n. 11.

2.   The good effect (saving the mother's life) is not obtained by means of the evil effect (death of the fetus). It would be just the opposite, e.g., if the fetus were killed in order to save the reputation of an unwed mother.

3.   There is sufficient reason for permitting the unsought evil effect that unavoidably follows. Here the Church's guidance is essential in judging that there is sufficient reason.

4.   The evil effect is not intended in itself, but is merely allowed as a necessary consequence of the good effect.

"Summarily, then, the womb belongs to the mother just as completely after a pregnancy as before. If she were not pregnant, she would clearly be justified to save her life by removing a diseased organ that was threatening her life. The presence of the fetus does not deprive her of this fundamental right."[3]

A Practice Beyond Legal Control

Dr. Timothy Quill, the physician who brought the *Vacco* case to the Supreme Court, stated in 1997 that "Physician-assisted suicide is a bad option. . . the practice of sedating a dying patient to the point they either stop breathing or die of dehydration. . . is a better option."[4] In *Vacco,* the Court noted that, unlike the physician who assists in suicide, the physician who sedates may or may not intend to hasten the death of his patient:

> [A] physician who withdraws, or honors a patient's refusal to begin, life-sustaining medical treatment purposefully intends, or may so intend, only to respect his patient's wishes and "to cease doing useless and futile or degrading things to the patient when [the patient] no longer stands to benefit from them."[5] The same is true when a doctor provides aggressive palliative care; in some cases, painkilling drugs may hasten a patient's death, but the physician's purpose and intent is, or may be, only to ease his patient's pain. A doctor who assists a suicide, however, "must, necessarily and indubitably, intend primarily that the patient be made dead."[6]

---

[3] John A. Hardon, S.J., *The Catholic Catechism* (1975), 337.

[4] American Political Network, *Abortion Report,* Apr. 21, 1997, p. 7.

[5] Quoting *Assisted Suicide in the United States,* Hearing, Subcommittee on the Constitution of the House Committee on the Judiciary, 104th Cong., 2d Sess., 368 (1996) (testimony of Dr. Leon R. Kass).

[6] 521 U.S. at 801-02.

In the absence of exceptionally clear proof of intent, the law cannot effectively distinguish among cases of sedation or removal of treatment so as to determine whether the physician acted with the intent to relieve pain or the intent to cause death. "What might be called managed deaths, as distinct from suicides, are now the norm in the United States. . . . The American Hospital Association says that about 70 percent of the deaths in hospitals happen after a decision has been made to withhold treatment. Other patients die when the medication they are taking to ease their pain depresses, then stops, their breathing. . . . 'It's called passive euthanasia,' said Dr. Norman Fost, director of the Program in Medical Ethics at the University of Wisconsin. 'You can ask who's involved and is it really consensual, but there is no question that these are planned deaths.'"[7]

It seems clear that the intent is to kill when food and water are withdrawn from a patient who is not dying, who is not in significant distress and who has been kept alive by the feeding tube. Yet, in *Cruzan*, the Supreme Court declined to treat such a case as involving the intent to kill. When death results from pain-killers or sedation, rather than withdrawal of treatment, it can be more difficult to determine whether the intent was to kill. In the 1997 right-to-die cases, the Supreme Court invited the states to turn a blind eye to euthanasia committed by withdrawal of food and water or by administration of palliatives and sedation. "The assisted-suicide debate has called the question on the health-care profession," said Dr. Steven Miles of the University of Minnesota. "The public is demanding assisted suicide, in part because they are justifiably afraid of the quality of end-of-life care. There is a demand for a new paradigm, and the paradigm is palliative care."[8] "Eventually. . . terminally ill patients will feel subtle yet clear pressure from family members or others to end their lives in order to save money. . . . The much-praised hospice movement may now be asked to help patients decide not how to die but when to die. That could turn them from spiritual and emotional refuges to places of semi-mechanized death."[9] In *Washington v. Glucksberg*, the Supreme Court commented on the evolution to involuntary euthanasia in the Netherlands, where the practice is not to prosecute for active assisted suicide:

> This concern is further supported by evidence about the practice of euthanasia in the Netherlands. . . . [I]n 1990, there were 2,300 cases of voluntary euthanasia (defined as "the deliberate termination of

---

[7] *N.Y. Times*, June 28, 1997, p. 1.

[8] *N.Y. Times*, June 30, 1997, p. A1.

[9] *The Economist*, Nov. 8, 1997, p. 30, describing a statement by Dr. Arthur Caplan, director of the Center for Bioethics at the University of Pennsylvania.

another's life at his request"), 400 cases of assisted suicide, and more than 1,000 cases of euthanasia without an explicit request. In addition to these latter 1,000 cases, the study found an additional 4,941 cases where physicians administered lethal morphine overdoses without the patients' explicit consent. . . . This study suggests that. . . euthanasia in the Netherlands has not been limited to competent, terminally ill adults who are enduring physical suffering, and that regulation of the practice may not have prevented abuses in cases involving vulnerable persons, including severely disabled neonates and elderly persons suffering from dementia.[10]

The Court noted the Netherlands' experience as a justification for Washington's judgment that allowing assisted suicide could lead to involuntary euthanasia. It appears, however, that the allowance of "passive" measures for ending life has the same potential to slide into involuntary termination, especially in light of the aging of the population. "In 1790, half the American people were under 16. It took two centuries, until 1990, for the median age to rise to 33. But by the middle of the next century, it will be over 40 and could approach 50."[11]

The Supreme Court should have drawn the line in *Cruzan*[12] to deny constitutional permission for the removal of food and water from non-dying patients who are kept alive by that feeding and who are not in substantial distress from the administration of the feeding. Removal of feeding in such cases would clearly appear to be done with the intent to cause death. If the Court had drawn the line there, it would have maintained the principle that the state may not constitutionally allow the intentional killing of the innocent. But not even such a result in *Cruzan* would prevent the practical privatization of euthanasia.

THE TRANSITION TO ACTIVE KILLING

The law recognizes the legal right of a competent adult to refuse any and all forms of medical treatment, including food and water, at least where they are provided by "artificial" means.[13] With respect to incompetent patients, the courts generally allow withdrawal of artificially provided food and water based on the patient's previously expressed intent, or on the decision of the family or authorized health care agent that the patient would have wanted such withdrawal or that the withdrawal would be in his best interest.[14] It is likely that the courts will agree with

---

[10] 521 U.S. at 734.
[11] *N.Y. Times*, Sept. 22, 1996, Sec. 4, p. 1.
[12] See Question 5.
[13] See *Bouvia v. Superior Ct.*, 179 Cal. App. 3d 1127 (1986).
[14] See *Matter of Conroy*, 486 A.2d 1209 (N.J., 1985); *In re Jobes*, 529 A.2d 434 (N.J., 1987).

the New Jersey Supreme Court that "the line between active and passive conduct in the context of medical decisions is far too nebulous to constitute a principled basis for decision making."[15]

Once the law permits euthanasia by withholding food and water, the allowance of active, intentional killing is inevitable. In *Brophy v. New England Sinai Hospital,* where the court approved removal of a feeding tube from a patient in a persistent vegetative state, Justice Neil L. Lynch remarked in dissent: "The withdrawal of the provision of food and water is a particularly difficult, painful and gruesome death; the cause of death would not be some underlying physical disability like kidney failure or the withdrawal of some highly invasive medical treatment, but the unnatural cessation of feeding and hydration which, like breathing, is part of the responsibilities we assume toward our bodies routinely. Such a process would not be very far from euthanasia, and the natural question is: Why not use more humane methods of euthanasia if that is what we indorse?"[16]

In a note to his opinion, Justice Lynch recounted the hardship which the evidence in the case showed to be normally associated with starvation and dehydration:

> Removal of the G. tube would likely create various effects from the lack of hydration and nutrition, leading ultimately to death. Brophy's mouth would dry out and become caked or coated with thick material. His lips would become parched and cracked. His tongue would swell, and might crack. His eyes would recede back into their orbits and his cheeks would become hollow. The lining of his nose might crack and cause his nose to bleed. His skin would hang loose on his body and become dry and scaly. His urine would become highly concentrated, leading to burning of the bladder. The lining of his stomach would dry out and he would experience dry heaves and vomiting. His body temperature would become very high. His brain cells would dry out, causing convulsions. His respiratory tract would dry out, and the thick secretions that would result could plug his lungs and cause death. At some point within five days to three weeks his major organs, including his lungs, heart, and brain, would give out and he would die.[17]

Paul Brophy died eight days after his feeding was terminated. "His death was extremely peaceful," said Mrs. Brophy's lawyer.[18] According to

---

[15] *Matter of Conroy,* 486 A.2d 1209, 1234 (1985).

[16] 497 N.E.2d 626, 641 (Mass., 1986).

[17] 497 N.E.2d at 642, n. 2.

[18] *N.Y. Times,* Oct. 24, 1986, p. B9

the attending physician, Mr. Brophy received practically no nutrition during the final eight days and only as much water as necessary to administer anti-convulsant medication.[19]

"'Let nobody think that this is an argument about putting to death people with terminal cancer. That will last about five minutes. Then it will move to, 'I don't want to be alive with Alzheimer's disease. I'm not terminally ill, but by the time I am I will not be able to ask for help in dying.' Or, [Dr. Caplan] said, there would be people saying, 'My mother always said she didn't want to be kept alive if she had Alzheimer's disease.'"[20] If you were a terminal AIDS or other patient, would you not prefer, as a "rational" choice, a painless exit by injection rather than a prolonged and painful death resulting from the withdrawal of food and water? And if such a patient, or an infirm octogenarian, declines to choose death when such is the "rational" choice, would not that irrationality indicate his incompetence so as to allow others to make that "rational" choice for him? The quick, painless injection is easier on the "care givers." And it is cost effective.

"Suicide. . . is always as morally objectionable as murder. . . . To. . . help in carrying it out through so-called 'assisted suicide' means to cooperate in, and at times to be the. . . perpetrator of, an injustice which can never be excused, even if it is requested."[21] But euthanasia, whether by assisted suicide or otherwise, is not itself the problem. *Evangelium Vitae* described euthanasia as "one of the more alarming symptoms of the 'culture of death,' which is. . . marked by an. . . excessive preoccupation with efficiency and which sees the growing number of elderly and disabled people as intolerable."[22]

Opponents of abortion have argued that the depersonalization and legalized execution of the unborn child would lead to similar treatment of his grandmother and his defective elder brother or sister. But the roots of euthanasia are deeper than abortion. With the advent of the contraceptive pill in the 1960s, man assumed the role of arbiter as to whether and when life should begin. In abortion and euthanasia, he acts as arbiter of when life shall end. Moreover, the contraceptive ethic is premised on the idea that there is such a thing as a life not worth living and that man has the right to enforce his own judgment in that regard. If he enforces that judgment as to prospective life through contraception, he will predictably enforce it as to existing life through abortion and euthanasia.

---

[19] *Ibid.*
[20] *N.Y. Times,* Oct. 20, 1996, Sec. 1, p. 14, quoting Dr. Arthur Caplan, Director of the Center for Bioethics at the University of Pennsylvania.
[21] *EV*, no. 65.
[22] *Ibid.*, no. 64.

Contraception and abortion have reduced the number of taxpayers available to support the elderly and disabled. By 2050, one American in 20 will be age 85 or over and one in five will be over 65. The fertility rate in this country has been below the replacement level of 2.1 children per woman continuously for two decades.[23]

> The population is rapidly growing older and will continue to do so in the next half-century. Between 1995 and 2010, the population of people 65 and older will grow slowly by about 6 million, from 33.5 million to 39.4 million, as people born in the 1930's and early 1940's (when fertility was low) age. By contrast, between 2010 and 2030, with the baby boomers aging, the number will soar by about 30 million, from 39.4 million to 69.3 million. Meanwhile, the population in the prime working ages of 20 to 59 will remain stationary at 160 million. In 1900, there were 10 times as many children below 18 as there were adults over 65. By 2030, there will be slightly more people over 65 than under 18.

> In fact, the population is aging because both fertility and mortality rates are below their long-term historic averages. Unless fertility rates increase, the population will not become younger even after the boomers have left the scene.[24]

We should not be surprised when the secular, contraceptive society turns to euthanasia as a remedy for the financial and other problems caused by the increasing proportion of old people which itself is a result of contraception and abortion. Nor is it a long step to the unspoken enforcement of a "duty to die," as shown in Governor Lamm's statement at the beginning of this question. "A duty to die is more likely when continuing to live will impose significant burdens — emotional burdens, extensive caregiving, destruction of life plans, and, yes, financial hardship — on your family and loved ones. This is the fundamental insight underlying a duty to die. It is one of the tragedies of our lives that someone who wants very much to live can nevertheless have a 'duty to die.'" [25]

In political and cultural terms, the pro-life movement has already lost the euthanasia fight. It will take a while for the mop-up operation to be completed, but the legalization and social acceptance of active as well as passive euthanasia on request, or at the direction of others for incom-

---

[23] See Samuel H. Preston, "Children Will Pay," *N.Y. Times Magazine*, Sept. 29, 1996, 96.

[24] *Ibid.*, 97.

[25] John Hardwig, "Is There a Duty to Die?" 27 *Hastings Center Report* 34 (Mar. 13, 1997).

petent patients, is a foregone conclusion. Through its compromises on legalized abortion, even the pro-life movement has conceded that the intentional killing of innocent human beings may validly be allowed by law. Legalized, active, involuntary euthanasia will be the price for our treatment of the life of the unborn child as a matter for political negotiation and compromise. If the pro-life movement itself treats the child in the womb as a nonperson whose life is negotiable, should we be surprised when the pro-death people do the same thing to his elder retarded brother and his grandmother?

C.   The Problem is Spiritual and Cultural

14.   WHAT ENLIGHTENMENT IDEAS CORRUPTED OUR CULTURE?

> Over half a century ago, while I was still a child, I recall hearing a
> number of older people offer the following explanation for the great
> disasters that had befallen Russia: "Men have forgotten God; that's
> why all this has happened.". . .
>
> And if I were called upon to identify the principal trait of the entire
> twentieth century,. . . I would repeat once again: *Men have forgotten
> God.* — *Aleksandr Solzhenitsyn.* [1]

Francis Canavan, S.J., aptly described the present stage of Western
culture as "the fag end of the Enlightenment."[2] The Enlightenment rejected not only the Church but also revealed religion in general, the objective moral law and the capacity of the intellect to know truth. It
sought to organize society as if God did not exist.

The Enlightenment view of the person and of the state differed radically from what had gone before in the Christian tradition and the common law. Hobbes, Locke and Rousseau postulated a mythical state of
nature in which autonomous, isolated individuals were milling around
and, for various reasons, agreed to form the state. Hobbes thought
people were hostile and needed the state, or Leviathan, to keep them
from killing each other. The individual surrendered total power to the
state, reserving only his right to life and his right not to incriminate himself. Locke's state of nature was more pleasant, but men needed a common judge to settle disputes. And so they formed the state to protect
their rights, but in that state the majority would rule. Rousseau, on the
other hand, thought men formed the state to carry out the general will
which is the unlimited will, not of the majority, but of the man in
charge, the sovereign.[3]

In the traditional Christian view, the state derives its authority from
God (although the people may from time to time decide who exercises
that authority) and the state is subject to the law of God including the
natural law. In the Enlightenment view, the state derives its authority
horizontally, from the people. It is the people, rather than the law of

[1] Aleksandr Solzhenitsyn, *Address,* Templeton Univ., May 10, 1983; see *Immaculata,*
    Sept. 1983, p. 6.
[2] Francis Canavan, S.J., Commentary, *Catholic Eye,* Dec. 10, 1987, 2.
[3] See generally, Heinrich Rommen, *The Natural Law* (1948), 75-109.

God, which defines in what way, if any, the power of the state will be limited. And, if the people give rights, the people can take them away. Nineteenth century utilitarianism added to this mix the idea, as seen in Jeremy Bentham, John Stuart Mill and others, that the purpose of law and society is to achieve the greatest good of the greatest number.[4] The good is the maximization of pleasure and the minimization of pain. There is no knowable objective morality and no common good beyond the sum of individual goods. The family is an aggregation of individuals rather than a society in itself. The person comes to be regarded as merely "economic man." The Enlightenment philosophy has dominated the twentieth century in different forms. It devalues the role of mediating institutions, such as the family and social groups, between the individual and the state. It tends to deteriorate into either an individualist capitalism or a totalitarian collectivism. Enlightenment law is wholly an exercise of will, while Aquinas affirmed that the essence of law is reason. Enlightenment jurisprudence will be utilitarian and postivist, with no inherent limits on what the state can do.[5]

The Enlightenment project, which dominates American culture, has three decisive characteristics:

1. *Secularism.* The Enlightenment rejected any revealed religion as irrelevant. "Only in the past two generations, in my lifetime," wrote Professor Harold Berman, "has the public philosophy of America shifted radically from a religious to a secular theory of law, from a moral to a political or instrumental theory, and from a historical to a pragmatic theory."[6] Man made himself the autonomous arbiter of right and wrong. The scientific method was the only way to search for truth, which was necessarily tentative. Man, rather than God, became the ultimate judge. "[A]s the autonomous individual of liberal theory lost his faith in divine revelation and in the ability of reason to perceive a natural moral order, he became an independent self, a subject of rights rather than of obligations, and a sovereign will bound by no law to which he himself had not consented. In the end, he became a bundle of appetites, because his will, lacking any anchorage in a divinely-created moral order, was submerged in and identified with his desires. That, too, is a kind of individualism, but a different kind from the freedom of the sons of God."[7]

---

[4] See Peter Bristow, "Utilitarianism at Work," *Position Paper* 136 (Dublin, Ireland), Aug. 1985, 125.

[5] See Question 15.

[6] Harold Berman, "The Crisis of Legal Education in America," 26 *Boston Coll. L. Rev.* 347, 348 (1985).

[7] Francis Canavan, S.J., "Commentary," *Catholic Eye,* Mar. 17, 1988, 2.

This autonomous man practices the religion of secular humanism, which "sees man as a product of this world — of evolution and human history — and acknowledges no supernatural purposes."[8] "The fool," said John Paul II, "thinks that he knows many things, but really he is incapable of fixing his gaze on the things that truly matter. . . . And so when he claims that 'God does not exist'. . . he shows. . . how deficient his knowledge is and just how far he is from the full truth of things, their origin and their destiny."[9] If there is no God and therefore no ultimate Lawgiver higher than the state, then there is no basis for affirming the transcendent dignity of the human person over and against the state. And there are no limits to what the state — and science under its patronage — can do to manipulate human beings.

2. *Relativism.* The Enlightenment denied the capacity of reason to know objective moral truth. The prevailing American culture agrees, as typified by the professors who are absolutely sure that they cannot be sure of anything. Only a few decades ago, public debate was premised on an assumed objective morality. Today, as Allan Bloom noted, "Relativism is. . . the only virtue. . . which all primary education for more than fifty years has dedicated itself to inculcating. Openness. . . is the great insight of our times. The true believer is the real danger. The study of history and of culture teaches that all the world was mad in the past; men always thought they were right, and that led to wars, persecutions, slavery, xenophobia, racism, and chauvinism. The point is not to correct the mistakes and really be right; rather it is not to think you are right at all. The students, of course, cannot defend their opinion. It is something with which they have been indoctrinated. The best they can do is point out all the opinions and cultures there are and have been. What right, they ask, do I or anyone else have to say one is better than the others?"[10]

In *Fides et Ratio*, John Paul II said that "different forms of agnosticism and relativism" have led to a "widespread scepticism. . . . A legitimate plurality of opinions has yielded to an undifferentiated pluralism, based upon the assumption that all positions are equally valid, which is one of today's most widespread symptoms of the lack of confidence in truth. . . . [E]verything is reduced to opinion; and there is a sense of being adrift."[11] "[I]n the last century. . .various forms of atheistic humanism. . . expressed in philosophical terms. . . regarded faith as alienating and damaging to the development of a full rationality. They did not

8   *The Humanist* (Statement of Purpose), May-June 1973, 3.
9   *FR*, no. 18.
10   Allan Bloom, *The Closing of the American Mind* (1987), 25-26.
11   *FR*, no. 5.

hesitate to present themselves as new religions serving as a basis for projects which, on the political and social plane, gave rise to totalitarian systems which have been disastrous for humanity.

"In the field of scientific research, a positivistic mentality abandoned the Christian vision of the world [and] rejected every appeal to a meta-physical or moral vision. . . . [C]ertain scientists, lacking any ethical point of reference, are in danger of putting at the centre of their concerns something other than the human person and the entirety of the person's life. . . .[S]ome of these. . . succumb not only to a market-based logic, but also to the temptation of a quasi-divine power over nature and even over the human being. As a result of the crisis of rationalism, what has appeared finally is nihilism. As a philosophy of nothingness, it has a certain attraction for people of our time. Its adherents claim that the search is an end in itself, without any hope or possibility of ever attaining the goal of truth. In the nihilist interpretation, life is no more than an occasion for sensations and experiences, in which the ephemeral has pride of place. Nihilism is at the root of the widespread mentality which claims that a definitive commitment should no longer be made, because everything is fleeting and provisional."[12]

Relativism denies the existence of an objective moral law derived from the unchanging nature of man, which we can know through reason and Revelation. The relativist says that the morality of abortion depends on the circumstances. He declares that all propositions are relative except, of course, his proposition that all things are relative. The absurdity of skepticism lies in the skeptic's certainty that he cannot be certain of anything. If he is not even certain about that, at least he is certain that he is not certain. A science professor not long ago at a professedly Catholic university began his first class of the year by declaring, "The first thing you have to understand is that there are no absolutes." A student of my acquaintance asked from the back row, "Are you absolutely sure of that?" The professor changed the subject. Several generations of Americans have been raised on relativistic theories of progressive education, life adjustment, situation ethics and values clarification, which encourage the students to form their own morality without obedience to the law of God. These theories are evident in Catholic as well as in public schools.[13]

This denial of objective morality permeates our culture. "Post-modernists now place quotation marks around words like 'reality,' insisting that the old notion of objective knowledge has become obsolete.

---

[12] *FR*, no. 46.

[13] See Robert Spencer, "Desert Blossoms," *Sursum Corda,* Special edition, 1998, 21; Kimberly J. Gustin, "Letter from a Jesuit Prep School," *Crisis,* Sept. 1989, 45.

Multiculturalists argue for new curriculums not on the basis of factual accuracy, but on the basis of 'self-esteem.' And politicians and their spin doctors use pseudo-events and photo-ops to market virtual-reality versions of themselves to the public. Throughout our culture, the old notions of 'truth' and 'knowledge' are in danger of being replaced by the new ones of 'opinion,' 'perception' and 'credibility.'" [14]

"Our age," said John Paul II, "has been termed by some thinkers the age of 'postmodernity.'. . . [According to] currents of thought which claim to be postmodern. . . the time of certainties is irrevocably past, and the human being must now learn to live in a horizon of total absence of meaning, where everything is provisional and ephemeral. . . . [A] positivist cast of mind continues to nurture the illusion that, thanks to scientific and technical progress, man and woman may live as a demiurge, single-handedly and completely taking charge of their destiny."[15]

3. *Individualism.* The Enlightenment looks on the human person, not as *social* by nature, but as an isolated individual who is merely *sociable* in that he can be made social by his consent. The isolated, autonomous individual has relation to others only if he so chooses. That is the origin of "pro-choice" rhetoric on abortion and other issues. The mother has relation to the child she is carrying only if she so chooses. A husband and wife have a continuing relation to each other only if they continue to consent. The autonomous individual is the creator of his own morality, i.e., he is his own god. *Fides et Ratio* noted the "'tendency to grant to the individual conscience the prerogative of independently determining the criteria of good and evil and then acting accordingly. Such an outlook is quite congenial to an individualist ethic, wherein each individual is faced with his own truth different from the truth of others.'"[16]

As John Paul II put it, "the roots of the contradiction between the solemn affirmation of human rights and their tragic denial in practice lies in a *notion of freedom* which exalts the isolated individual in an absolute way, and gives no place to solidarity, to openness to others and service of them. While it is true that the taking of life not yet born or in its final stages is sometimes marked by a mistaken sense of altruism and human compassion, it cannot be denied that such a culture of death. . . betrays a completely individualistic concept of freedom, which ends up by becoming the freedom of 'the strong' against the weak who have no choice but to submit. . . . If the promotion of the self is understood in

---

[14] *N.Y. Times,* Jan. 28, 1994, p. B1.
[15] *FR,* no. 91.
[16] *FR,* no. 98, quoting *VS,* no. 32.

terms of absolute autonomy, people inevitably reach the point of rejecting one another. Everyone else is considered an enemy from whom one
has to defend oneself. Thus society becomes a mass of individuals placed
side by side, but without any mutual bonds. Each one wishes to assert
himself independently of the other and in fact intends to make his own
interests prevail. Still,. . . some kind of compromise must be found if
one wants a society in which the maximum possible freedom is guaranteed to each individual. In this way, any reference to common values and
to a truth absolutely binding on everyone is lost and social life ventures
onto the shifting sands of complete relativism. At that point, *everything
is negotiable, everything is open to bargaining*: even the first of the fundamental rights, the right to life."[17]

IMPACT ON CONSTITUTIONAL LAW

These distorted notions of freedom have permeated the law as well
as the culture. They have had a special impact on the constitutional freedoms of speech and religion. The Enlightenment philosophy would protect speech from government restraint on the theory that speech is
merely a scientific datum because no one can know what is true. Influenced by that philosophy, the Constitution is now interpreted to permit
only limited restraint on such types of speech as incitement to imminent
unlawful violence, some defamation and hard-core pornography. Enlightenment philosophy also requires the exclusion of religion from influence on public affairs on the ground that any statements about religion are nonrational:

> Eric Voegelin has written that the principles of the Enlightenment. . . "seek to
> enthrone the Newtonian methods of science as the only valid method of arriv-
> ing at truth.". . . [This] had enormous implications for a theory of freedom of
> speech. The criteria by which words should be judged shifted from their moral
> and spiritual content to their utility as objects of science. In effect words corre-
> sponded to scientific data. . . . [A]s in science the freedom to consider all data
> was the precondition to progress.

> When this philosophy of science was applied to constitutional juris-
> prudence there could be almost no constitutional justification for the
> regulation of speech and expression. . . . [T]here did not yet exist all
> the scientific tools by which we could make a definite choice between
> good and bad data; better to allow almost all speech than to risk elimi-
> nating what would be later found as an advancement. . . . [T]hese sen-
> timents. . . became the. . . justification for an almost unlimited expan-
> sion of the right to freedom of expression and an almost complete
> purging of religion from prominent areas of public life.

---

[17] *EV*, nos. 19-20.

Religion had to be purged from public life because, with the enshrine-
ment of "reason" as the guide of man, the experiences which inspired
religious symbolisms were deemed unscientific [and] "irrational" because they cannot be understood in scientific categories. Religion was
valuable. . . only as a visible device of social utility which compelled
men to act in an orderly fashion. . . . . [A]ny affirmations of the spirit
such as prayer had to be eliminated as a precondition to progress in
public life. Any such affirmations were bound to lead backwards to a
"darker period" in history when men were at war over phantasms. The
thoroughness with which religious symbolisms have been eliminated
from American public life demonstrates the degree to which the legal
community has accepted the progressivist philosophy of history and
affirmed its major tenet — that expressions of religious experience
have a disordering and reactionary effect on public life.[18]

So the next time you wonder why pornography abounds on the
Internet, why prime time TV reaches a new moral low every year, and
why your local high school football team can't pray before a game, remember to reserve part of the blame for the Enlightenment folks of long
ago and of today.

THE LOSS OF GOD

The moral collapse of Western culture, under the influence of secularism, relativism and individualism, has accelerated over the past four
decades.[19] Ideas have consequences:[20] "Could not the whole nature of
the current civilization," asked Czech President Vaclav Havel, "with its
shortsightedness, with its proud emphasis on the human individual as
the crown of all creation — and its master — and with its boundless
trust in humanity's ability to embrace the Universe by rational cogni-
tion, could it not all be only the natural manifestation of a phenomenon
which, in simple terms, amounts to the loss of God? Or more specifically: the loss of respect for the order of existence of which we are not the
creators but mere components. . . . [T]he crisis. . . is. . . due to the fact
that we have lost the certainty that the Universe, nature, existence and
our lives are the work of creation guided by a definite intention, that it
has a definite meaning and follows a definite purpose."[21]

---

[18] William Smith, "The First Amendment and Progress," *Humanitas,* Summer 1987, 1,
5-6.
[19] See M. Stanton Evans, *The Theme is Freedom: Religion, Politics, and the American Tradition* (1994).
[20] Richard Weaver, *Ideas Have Consequences* (1948).
[21] Vaclav Havel, "Faith in the World," *Civilization,* Apr./May 1998, 51, 52-53; See
Wash. Times, May 22, 1998, p. A2.

Every society has to have a god, an ultimate moral authority. If the real God is displaced, another will take his place. Today, the replacement god is the autonomous individual who makes himself the defining authority. Inevitably, such authority will be assumed by the state. "Nowadays," said Pope John Paul in 1991, "there is a tendency to claim that agnosticism and skeptical relativism are the philosophy and the basic attitude which correspond to democratic forms of political life. . . . [But] if there is no ultimate truth to guide and direct political activity, then ideas and convictions can easily be manipulated for reasons of power. As history demonstrates, a democracy without values easily turns into open or thinly disguised totalitarianism."[22] John Paul could have cited the United States for that analysis.

The United States Constitution justified Lord Bryce's description of it as "the greatest single contribution ever made to Government as an applied science."[23] Unfortunately, no paper constitution can survive the erosion of its moral and cultural base.

---

[22] Pope John Paul II, *Centesimus Annus* (1991), no. 46, quoted in *VS*, no. 101.
[23]Viscount Bryce, O.M., *The Study of American History* (1921), 53.

15. HOW DOES LEGAL POSITIVISM SEPARATE LAW AND MORALITY?

Hamilton College Professor Robert L. Simon provides a glimpse of the thinking that is common among students today:

'Of course I dislike the Nazis,' one of my students commented, 'but who is to say they are morally wrong?' Other students in my classes on moral and political philosophy have made similar remarks about apartheid, slavery, and ethnic cleansing. They make the assertion as though it were self-evident; no one, they say, has the right even to criticize the moral views of another group or culture. . . . In an increasingly multicultural society, it is not surprising that many students believe that criticizing the codes of conduct of other groups and cultures is either unwise or prohibited. They equate such criticism with intolerance and the coercive imposition of a powerful culture's norms on the less powerful.[1]

As far as these students are concerned, there is no standard of justice that anyone can know. They have made themselves incapable of measuring the laws of their own country by any higher standard. They are setting themselves up to behave as "good Germans" with respect to the laws of the United States. The jurisprudence of their relativism is legal positivism, under which law becomes wholly a question of power, without moral limits. Positivism, in various forms, dominates modern American jurisprudence.

DEPERSONALIZATION

The subjection of innocent human beings to depersonalization at the will of the legislature is legal positivism in action. A clear example was the decision of the highest court of New York, in *Byrn v. New York City Health and Hospitals Corp.*,[2] upholding the permissive 1970 New York abortion law. The court first found as a fact that the unborn child is a human being "upon conception."[3] But it said that it is up to the legislature to decide which human beings are persons and are therefore entitled to the right to live: "What is a legal person is for the law, including, of course, the Constitution, to say, which simply means that upon according legal personality to a thing the law affords it the rights and privileges of a legal person (e.g., Kelsen, *General Theory of Law and State*,

---

[1] Robert L. Simon, "The Paralysis of Absolutophobia," *The Chronicle of Higher Education*, June 27, 1997, p. B5, B6.

[2] 31 N.Y.2d 194, 335 N.Y.S.2d 390, 393 (1972), appeal dismissed, 410 U.S. 949 (1973).

[3] 31 N.Y.2d at 199.

pp. 93-109. . . .) . . . . The point is that it is a policy determination whether legal personality should attach and not a question of biological or 'natural' correspondence."[4] The Supreme Court took this same route in *Roe v. Wade*.

It was fitting for the *Byrn* court to cite Hans Kelsen, who has been well described as "the jurist of our century."[5] Kelsen was influential in Germany between the two World Wars. He denied the possibility of natural law and insisted on the separation of law and morality. He rejected what he called "philosophical absolutism," the "metaphysical view that there is an absolute reality, i.e., a reality that exists independently of human knowledge."[6] He thought that the claim that one can actually know reality and what is right and wrong leads to "political absolutism," or tyranny, because the rulers will impose on the people what the rulers "know" to be for the people's good.[7] Instead, he adopted what he called "philosophical relativism," the "empirical doctrine that reality exists only within human knowledge, and that, as the object of knowledge, reality is relative to the knowing subject. The absolute, the thing in itself, is beyond human experience; it is inaccessible to human knowledge and therefore unknowable."[8] This "philosophical relativism," in Kelsen's view, leads to democracy and the tolerance of divergent views, because "what is right today may be wrong tomorrow," and the minority "must have full opportunity of becoming the majority. Only if it is not possible to decide in an absolute way what is right and what is wrong is it advisable to discuss the issue and, after discussion, to submit to a compromise."[9]

Law, according to Kelsen, is a system of coercive rules called "legal norms." These rules are prescribed by the legislator in accord with the "basic norm" or constitution of the community. That basic norm may or may not be in a written constitution. It is entirely up to the legislator to decide what the basic norm is and whether any particular enactment is in accord with it. Nor is there any restriction on the content of legal rules. "Any content whatsoever can be legal; there is no human behavior which could not function as the content of a legal norm." The only requirement for a law to be valid and binding is that "it has been constituted in a particular fashion, born of a definite procedure and a definite

---

[4] 31 N.Y.2d at 201.
[5] Hans Kelsen, *Essays in Legal and Moral Philosophy* (Ota Weinberger, ed., 1973), ix.
[6] Hans Kelsen, "Absolutism and Relativism in Philosophy and Politics," 42 *Am. Pl. Sci. Review* 906 (1948).
[7] *Ibid.*, at 908, 913.
[8] *Ibid.*, at 906.
[9] *Ibid.*, at 913.

rule."[10] The legislator decides what law will be useful and in accord with the basic norm as he has defined it. Once a law is enacted, it is obligatory. There is no higher law of nature or of God, and the positive law cannot be criticized as unjust. According to Kelsen, justice "is not ascertainable by rational knowledge at all. Rather, from the standpoint of rational knowledge there are only interests and conflicts of interests. . . . Justice is an irrational ideal."[11]

So what happens if the majority, or those in control of the political process, decide to oppress or even to exterminate a minority? The positivist can raise no moral objections. His only objections to Auschwitz will be those of utility or esthetics: "It is not *useful* to kill millions of Jews and if we set that precedent, someday they may come looking for us." Or he may object because the mass slaughter of the Jews is offensive to his sensibilities. He cannot say it is *unjust* because he does not believe he can know what is just or unjust.

Kelsen's "pure theory of law" is the most clear-cut form of positivism. All positivist systems, however, are characterized in some degree by the denial of the capacity of human reason to know what is right and wrong. They are concerned only with what the law is, not with what it ought to be. For Oliver Wendell Holmes, the leading figure of American Legal Realism, "law" is not an ordinance of reason, but merely "a statement of the circumstances in which the public force will be brought to bear upon men through the courts."[12] For Holmes, "the sacredness of human life is a purely municipal ideal of no validity outside the jurisdiction. I believe that force, mitigated so far as may be by good manners, is the *ultima ratio,* and between two groups that want to make inconsistent kinds of world I see no remedy except force."[13] Holmes defined truth as "the majority vote of the nation that could lick all others."[14] "I see no reason for attributing to man," he wrote, "a significance different in kind from that which belongs to a baboon or a grain of sand."[15]

In 1942, Francis E. Lucey, S.J., described the contrast between the natural law and the postivist Legal Realism espoused by Holmes and his successors under various labels:

---

[10] Hans Kelsen, "The Pure Theory of Law, Part II," 51 *Law Quart. Rev.* 517, 518-19 (1935).

[11] Hans Kelsen, "The Pure Theory of Law, Part I," 50 *Law Quart. Rev.* 474, 482 (1934).

[12] 2 *Holmes-Pollock Letters* (1941), 212.

[13] 2 *Holmes-Pollock Letters* (1942), 36; See Oliver Wendell Holmes, "The Natural Law," 32 *Harv. L. Rev.* 40 (1918).

[14] Oliver Wendell Holmes, *The Natural Law: Collected Legal Papers* (1920), 310.

[15] 2 *Holmes-Pollock Letters* (1942), 252; see discussion in William Kenealy, S.J., "The Majesty of the Law," 5 *Loyola Law Rev.* 101, 107-08 (1950); Charles E. Rice, *Beyond Abortion: The Theory and Practice of the Secular State* (1979), chs. 2 and 6.

Non-natural law systems of Jurisprudence rest on a view of man's nature that makes man independent of his creator and hence the helpless prey of his fellow men. For Holmes and the Realist he is a sort of superior animal. For Scholastic Natural Law, man is a being with a mind and a soul, and hence, superior to animals. He derives his dignity not from other men, but from God his creator. This question of God and morals in law is the real basic difference between Natural Law and other philosophies of law. If there is no God, man is only an animal. He has no innate dignity and no *de jure* independence. He is bound by no norm. Morals have no place in law. Man is subject to the law for animals, physical force. This much must be said for Realism. If man is only an animal, Realism is correct, Holmes was correct, Hitler is correct.[16]

THE NAZI EXPERIENCE

The fruits of a positivist jurisprudence can be seen in Nazi Germany. Prior to World War I, positivism was dominant in Germany. "According to this new positivistic jurisprudence, the legislator, and he alone, *creates* the law. Everything prior to legislative enactment is at best 'custom,' but never true law. Thus, law and right became wholly identified, and bare 'legality' takes the place of substantive justice as an ideal."[17]

The Weimar Constitution, under which Germany was governed from 1918 to 1933, did not recognize any law higher than itself. Certain principles of the natural law, it is true, were embodied in Weimar constitutional guarantees, but the constitution could be readily changed and it was often disregarded through the enactment of unconstitutional laws. The constitution also empowered the president to abrogate basic rights in some situations. "But the greatest obstacle to the recognition of natural law was the doctrine of positivism which equated right and might to begin with and, hence, assigned to the legislator full discretion as to the detailed content or provisions of the law, to the point of injustice, indeed to the point of complete, highhanded arbitrariness. A decision of the Supreme Court of the Reich of November 4, 1927, makes this fully clear: 'The legislator is absolutely autocratic, and bound by no limits save those he has set for himself either in the constitution or in some other laws.'"[18]

---

[16] Francis E. Lucey, S.J., "Natural Law and American Legal Realism: Their Respective Contributions to a Theory of Law in a Democratic Society," 30 *Georgetown L. J.* 493, 531 (1942). See also Charles E. Rice, *Beyond Abortion: The Theory and Practice of the Secular State* (1979), 7-15.

[17] Ernst von Hippel, "The Role of Natural Law in the Legal Decisions of the Federal German Republic," 4 *Natural Law Forum* 106, 107 (1959).

[18] *Ibid.*, 109.

This sort of positivism was dominant during the Hitler years, from 1933 to 1945. "A decision of the Fuhrer in the express form of a law or decree may not be scrutinized by a judge," said a 1936 decree of the Reich Commissar of Justice. "In addition, the judge is bound by any other decisions of the Fuhrer, provided that they are clearly intended to declare law."[19] The most striking example of Nazi positivism was the extermination program.[20]

The legal positivist has to concede that an extermination law is valid. "Philosophical relativism" and its jurisprudential offspring, legal positivism, can prescribe no moral limit to what the law can do. After World War II, Hans Kelsen acknowledged that the laws of the Nazi, Soviet and Italian fascist regimes were valid, regardless of their content, simply because they were duly enacted and enforced: "The legal order of totalitarian states authorizes their governments to confine in concentration camps persons whose opinions, religion, or race they do not like; to force them to perform any kind of labor, even to kill them. Such measures may be morally or violently condemned; but they cannot be considered as taking place outside the legal order of those states." Thus, "from the point of view of the science of law, the law under the Nazi-government was law. We may regret it but we cannot deny that it was law."[21]

Gustav Radbruch, a German legal philosopher, who renounced positivism during the Nazi regime, said that positivism "disarmed the German jurists against law of an arbitrary and criminal content."[22] He described the subversion of the German legal profession by the positivistic idea that might makes right:

> For the soldier an order is an order; for the jurist, the law is the law. But the soldier's duty to obey an order is at an end if he knows that the order will result in a crime. But the jurist, since the last natural law men in his profession died off a hundred years or so ago, has known no such exception and no such excuse for the citizen's not submitting to the law. The law is valid simply because it is the law; and it is law if it has the power to assert itself under ordinary conditions. Such an attitude towards the law and its validity [i.e., positivism] rendered both lawyers and people impotent in the face of even the most capricious, criminal, or cruel of laws. Ultimately, this view that only where there

---

[19] *Ibid.*,110.

[20] Charles E. Rice, *Beyond Abortion: The Theory and Practice of the Secular State* (1979), 10-11.

[21] Hans Kelsen, *Das Naturrecht in der politischen Theorie* (F.M. Schmoelz, ed., 1963), 148, quoted in translation in F.A. Hayek, *Law, Legislation and Liberty* (1976), vol. 2, 56.

is power is there law is nothing but an affirmation that might makes right. [Actually] law is the quest for justice. . . if certain laws deliberately deny this quest for justice (for example, by arbitrarily granting or denying men their human rights) they are null and void; the people are not to obey them, and jurists must find the courage to brand them unlawful.[23]

Note that Radbruch said jurists must brand unjust laws as "unlawful." West German courts did that after World War II, in holding certain Nazi laws void. Rejecting the claim by certain physicians that their "experimental killings" of prisoners and patients were sanctioned by the laws of the Third Reich, an appellate court at Frankfurt declared:

Law must be defined as an ordinance or precept devised in the service of justice [citing Radbruch]. *Whenever the conflict between an enacted law and true justice reaches unendurable proportions,* the enacted law must yield to justice, and be considered a "lawless law.". . . An accused may not justify his conduct by appealing to an existing law if this law offended against certain self-evident precepts of the natural law.[24]

THE UNITED STATES CONSTITUTION

The constitutions of the United States and of all the states incorporate natural law principles, such as due process and equal protection, so that laws contrary to those principles would ordinarily violate the constitution without any need for recourse to a supraconstitutional higher law. There is no need to resort to natural law to strike down a law allowing abortion, for example, because such a law violates the constitutional guarantee of equal protection of the laws. Nevertheless, "although it is the highest enacted law of the nation, the Constitution is itself a form of human law and is therefore subject to the higher standard of the natural law."[25] If the Constitution were amended to explicitly allow abortion, that amendment should be held void, as contrary to the natural law, just as should be a constitutional amendment repealing the Thirteenth Amendment and reinstituting slavery.

The prevailing approach in the United States, unfortunately, is positivistic, as seen in the Supreme Court abortion rulings which deperson-

---

22 See Heinrich Rommen, "Natural Law in Decisions of the Federal Supreme Court and of the Constitutional Courts in Germany," 4 *Natural Law Forum* 1, 1 (1959).

23 Quoted in Ernst von Hippel, "The Role of Natural Law in the Legal Decisions of the German Federal Republic," 4 *Natural Law Forum* 106, 110 (1959).

24 *Ibid.,* at 111 (emphasis added); See Charles E. Rice, "Some Reasons for a Restoration of Natural Law Jurisprudence," 24 *Wake Forest L. Rev.* 539 (1989).

25 Charles E. Rice, *50 Questions on the Natural Law* (2nd ed., 1999), Question 17.

alized the unborn.[26] Despite the lessons of experience, absolute faith in the "democratic" political process dies hard, even among leading proponents of constitutional integrity. At Gregorian University in Rome, in 1996, Supreme Court Justice Antonin Scalia acknowledged that "[a] Christian should not support a government that suppresses the faith or that sanctions the taking of innocent human life."[27] However, he said, "we should select our economic and political systems on the basis of what seems to produce the greatest material good for the greatest number, and leave theology out of it."[28] He continued:

> It just seems to me incompatible with democratic theory that it's good and right for the state to do something that the majority of the people do not want done. Once you adopt democratic theory. . . you accept that proposition. If the people, for example, want abortion, the state should permit abortion in a democracy. If the people do not want it, the state should be able to prohibit it as well. . . . I do not know how you can argue on the basis of democratic theory that the government has a moral obligation to do something that is opposed by the people. . . . The whole theory of democracy. . . is that the majority rules. . . . You protect minorities only because the majority determines that there are certain minorities or certain minority positions that deserve protection. Thus, in the U.S. Constitution we have listed those things that the majority cannot do such as taking someone's life without due process of law,. . . impeding freedom of religion and so forth. But my only authority as a judge to prevent the state from doing what may be bad things is the authority that the majority has given to the courts. But ultimately the formation of the state is by the majority, and what the majority decides shall be the rights of minorities is what their rights are, under that legal system.

> To say, "Ah, but it is contrary to the natural law" is simply to say that you set yourself above the democratic state and presume to decide what is good and bad in place of the majority of the people. I do not accept that as a proper function. If you want to set yourself above the state, do it the good, old-fashioned, honest way: Lead a revolution!. . . I do not feel empowered to revoke those laws that I do not consider good laws. If they are stupid laws, I apply them anyway, unless they go so contrary to my conscience that I must resign.

> But the alternative is not to do what is good or apply the law. The alternatives are apply the law or resign because the law is what the people have decided. And if it is bad, the whole theory of a democratic

---

[26] See Questions 3 and 4.
[27] 26 *Origins* 82, 83 (1996).
[28] 26 *Origins* at 86.

system is you must persuade the people that it is bad. . . . [W]ith respect to the Nuremberg laws, I would have resigned. But I would certainly not have the power to invalidate them because they are contrary to the natural law. I have been appointed to apply the Constitution and positive law. God applies the natural law.[29]

The problem with this approach is that, if a human law "deflects from the law of nature," as Aquinas said, it is unjust and "is no longer law but a perversion of law."[30] Unjust laws "are acts of violence rather than laws; because as Augustine says,. . .'a law that is not just, seems to be no law at all.'"[31] As a West German court said, "the positive legislative act is intrinsically limited. It loses all obligatory power if it violates the generally recognized principles of international law or the natural law. . .or if the contradiction between positive law and justice reaches such an intolerable degree that the law. . . must give way to justice."[32] In the face of an unjust law, it is not a sound response for a judge merely to excuse himself from the case or resign his position. The proper response of a judge to an unjust law is to declare it void and refuse to enforce it.[33]

Democracy, as a process, can offer no assurance that the laws generated by that process will be just. In *Veritatis Splendor*, John Paul insisted that "obedience to universal and unchanging moral norms" is essential for "genuine democracy."[34] "[T]here can be no freedom apart from or in opposition to the truth. . . . [O]nly by obedience to universal moral norms does man find full confirmation of his personal uniqueness and the possibility of authentic moral growth. For this very reason. . . [t]hese norms. . . represent the foundation of genuine democracy, which can. . . develop only on the basis of the equality of all its members, who possess common rights and duties. *When it is a matter of the moral norms prohibiting intrinsic evil, there are no privileges or exceptions for anyone.* It makes no difference whether one is the master of the world or the 'poorest of the poor' on the face of the earth. Before the demands of morality, we are all absolutely equal."[35]

TOWARD TOTALITARIANISM

If we do not affirm objective norms that always prohibit certain conduct, how can we define any moral limits to what the state can do?

---

[29] 26 *Origins* at 87-89.
[30] *ST*, I, II Q. 95, art. 2.
[31] *ST*, I, II, Q. 96, art. 4.
[32] Heinrich Rommen, "Natural Law in Decisions of the Federal Supreme Court and of the Constitutional Courts in Germany," 4 *Natural Law Forum* 1, 11 (1959).
[33] See the opinion of Justice Samuel Chase in *Calder v. Bull*, discussed in Question 47.
[34] *VS*, no. 85; see also no. 99.
[35] *VS*, no. 96.

"[A] democracy without values easily turns into open or thinly disguised totalitarianism."[36] In two respects, legal positivism has had a decisive impact on the right to life in American law:

1. The treatment of law as will rather than as reason. If no one can *know* what is just, reason loses its capacity to serve as an essential element and measure of law. Aquinas, as did Aristotle, Cicero and the common law tradition, affirmed that law, to be valid, must be in accord with reason and the natural law.[37] In legal positivism, however, the will of the lawmaker controls. A clear example is in the abortion rulings of the Supreme Court. Exactly as the New York court did in *Byrn*, the Supreme Court decrees the nonpersonhood of the unborn child regardless of what the *Byrn* court called "biological or 'natural' correspondence."[38]

2. The adoption of a functional definition of the person. If no one can *know* the essence of human nature, there is no basis to conclude that there is a natural and necessary entitlement of all human beings to be treated as persons in any legal system in which personhood is the condition for possession of rights. As discussed in Questions 5, 11 and 13, ability to function is becoming for some the determinant as to whether they will be subjected to death through abortion or through withholding medical treatment that would be given to a patient with a prospect for return to useful functioning.

The roots of these two approaches are in the epistemology of the Enlightenment. "Philosophical relativism" leads to "nonjudgmentalism." The result can be a cultural as well as a legal tyranny, as described by John Leo:

> Overdosing on nonjudgmentalism is a growing problem in the schools. . . . In the new multicultural canon, human sacrifice is hard to condemn, because the Aztecs practiced it. In fact, however, this nonjudgmental stance is not consistently held. Japanese whaling and the genital cutting of girls in Africa are criticized all the time by white multiculturalists. Christina Hoff Sommers,. . . professor of philosophy at Clark University. . . says that students who can't bring themselves to condemn the Holocaust will often say flatly that treating humans as superior to dogs and rodents is immoral. Moral shrugging may be on the rise, but old-fashioned and rigorous moral criticism is alive and

---

[36] *VS*, no. 101.
[37] *ST*, I, II, Q. 90, art. 4; see Charles E. Rice, *50 Questions on the Natural Law* (2d ed. 1999), Questions 4, 6.
[38] 31 N.Y.2d at 201.

well on certain selected issues — smoking, environmentalism, women's rights, animal rights.[39]

As Fr. Lucey described the choice between natural law and positivist legal realism: "These two philosophies are worlds apart. Yet it must be one or the other. The one alone can be the basis for Democracy or for popular sovereignty. The other. . . can be the basis for nothing but the absolute state."[40]

---

[39] John Leo, "Moral Perspective as a College Elective," *Wash. Times,* July 16, 1997, p. A13.

[40] Francis E. Lucey, S.J., "Natural Law and American Legal Realism: Their Respective Contributions to a Theory of Law in a Democratic Society," 30 *Georgetown L. J.* 493, 532 (1942).

16. WHY IS CONTRACEPTION THE DECISIVE ISSUE?

It is impossible to reconcile the doctrine of the divine institution of marriage with any modernistic plan for the mechanical regulation or suppression of human birth. The church must either reject the plain teachings of the Bible or reject schemes for the "scientific" production of human souls. Carried to its logical conclusion, the committee's report [approving the use of contraceptives] if carried into effect would sound the death-knell of marriage as a holy institution, by establishing degrading practices which would encourage indiscriminate immorality. The suggestion that the use of legalized contraceptives would be "careful and restrained" is preposterous. —*Washington Post*, editorial, March 22, 1931.

Times have changed. Can you imagine a *Washington Post* editorial like that today? It was written in response to the Federal Council of Churches which had followed the Anglican Lambeth Conference by endorsing "careful and restrained" use of contraceptives.

Is contraception a "Catholic issue"? Not really.[1] The 19th century laws restricting distribution of contraceptives were enacted by legislatures dominated by Protestants. It was not until 1930, with the Anglican Lambeth Conference, that any Christian denomination ever said that contraception could ever be objectively right. The Lambeth Conference was cautious in its approval of contraception, stating its "strong condemnation of the use of any methods of birth control from selfishness, luxury or mere convenience. The conference further records its abhorrence of the sinful practice of abortion."[2]

"My concern," said G. K. Chesterton about Lambeth, "is. . . with all to whom I might once have looked to defend the country of the Christian altars. They ought surely to know that the foe now on the frontiers offers no terms of compromise; but threatens a complete destruction. And they have sold the pass."[3] The Lambeth statement also met with strong Protestant criticism. "Lambeth," said editor James Douglas, of the *London Sunday Express*, "has delivered a fatal blow to marriage, to motherhood, to fatherhood, to the family and to morality."[4] Dr. Samuel A. Craig, the Presbyterian editor of *Christianity Today*, said the conference's approval of contraception "seems somewhat equivalent to

---

[1] See Dr. Les Hemingway, *Contraception and Common Sense* (1997).
[2] *N.Y. Times*, Aug. 15, 1930, p. 1, col. 6.
[3] Quoted in Cahal B. Daly, *Morals, Law and Life* (1966), 115.
[4] *N.Y. Times,* Aug. 17, 1930, p. 5, col. 1.

saying that there are circumstances under which we may lie or steal, provided we do so in the light of Christian principles."[5]

Seven decades after Lambeth,"some Protestants are re-discovering a view of marriage and children lost to their families for two or three generations."[6] "Ten years ago," says Pastor Matt Trewhella, of Milwaukee, founder of Missionaries to the Preborn, "it was virtually unheard of to meet or hear of a Protestant opposed to birth control. Now it is rather commonplace."[7] "For too long," according to the Missionaries, "birth control has been looked on as a Catholic issue. It is fast becoming a Protestant issue, however. . . . We must understand that the Church, whether Catholic, Protestant or Orthodox, spoke consistently for 1900 years against birth control."[8]

WHY IS CONTRACEPTION WRONG?

As spelled out in papal statements, contraception is wrong for three reasons:

1. *Contraception deliberately separates the unitive and procreative aspects of sex.*

In his 1968 encyclical, *Humanae Vitae,* Pope Paul VI said that the law of God prohibits "every action which, either in anticipation of the conjugal act, or in its accomplishment, or in the development of its natural consequences, aims, whether as an end or as a means, at making procreation impossible."[9] This teaching "is founded upon the inseparable connection — which is willed by God and which man cannot lawfully break on his own initiative — between the two meanings of the conjugal act: the unitive and the procreative meanings."[10] In his *Letter to Families,* John Paul II said:

> In particular, responsible fatherhood and motherhood directly concern the moment in which a man and a woman, uniting themselves in one flesh, can become parents. This is a moment of special value both for their interpersonal relationship and for their service to life: They can become parents — father and mother — by communicating life

[5] *N.Y. Times,* Sept. 20, 1930, p. 20, col. 6.
[6] Elizabeth Altham, "Converging Paths," *Sursum Corda,* Summer 1998, 60, 61. See also Margaret White, M.D., "Protestant View on Contraception," *Heartbeat,* Spring 1983, 18; Charles D. Provan, *The Bible and Birth Control* (Zimmer Printing, 410 W. Main St., Monongahela, PA 15063, 1989).
[7] Altham, *ibid.,* at 61.
[8] *Ibid.*
[9] *Humanae Vitae,* no. 14.
[10] *Ibid.,* no. 12.

to a new human being. The two dimensions of conjugal union, the unitive and the procreative, cannot be artifically separated without damaging the deepest truth of the conjugal act itself.[11]

2. *The acceptance of contraception asserts that man, rather than God, is the arbiter of when life shall begin.*

"At the origin of every human person there is a creative act of God. . . . [I]t follows that the procreative capacity, inscribed in human sexuality, is — in its deepest truth — a cooperation with God's creative power. It also follows that men and women are not the arbiters, are not the masters of this same capacity, called as they are, in it and through it, to be participants in God's creative decision. When, therefore, through contraception, married couples remove from the exercise of their conjugal sexuality its potential procreative capacity, they claim a power which belongs solely to God: the power to decide, in *a final analysis,* the coming into existence of a human person. They assume the qualification not of being cooperators in God's creative power, but the ultimate depositaries of the source of human life. . . . [C]ontraception is. . . so profoundly unlawful as never to be, for any reason, justified. To think or to say the contrary is equal to maintaining that in human life situations may arise in which it is lawful not to recognize God as God."[12]

3. *Contraception destroys the total mutual self-donation which ought to characterize the conjugal act.*

Contraception is degrading to the persons who practice it and to the integrity of the spousal relationship.[13] Pope John Paul made this point in *Familiaris Consortio* in 1981:

> When couples, by means of recourse to contraception, separate these two meanings that God the Creator has inscribed in the being of man and woman and in the dynamism of their sexual communion, they act as "arbiters" of the divine plan and they "manipulate" and degrade human sexuality and with it themselves and their married partner by altering its value of "total" self-giving. Thus the innate language that expresses the total reciprocal self-giving of husband and wife is overlaid through contraception, by an objectively contradictory language, namely, that of not giving oneself totally to the other. This leads not only to a positive refusal to be open to life but also to a falsification of

---

[11] *LF,* no. 12.

[12] Pope John Paul II, *Discourse,* Sept. 17, 1983; 28 *The Pope Speaks* 356, 356-57 (1983).

[13] See John F. Crosby, "The Mystery of 'Fair Love,'" *Catholic World Report,* Apr. 1999, 52, 57.

the inner truth of conjugal love, which is called upon to give itself in personal totality.[14]

Contraception transforms the sexual act from an act of total self-do-nation to a mutual pursuit of self-centered gratification.[15] It becomes, in effect, assisted masturbation.

WHAT ABOUT NATURAL FAMILY PLANNING?

At the 1994 National Prayer Breakfast, Mother Teresa of Calcutta said:

> We are fighting abortion by. . . care of the mother and adoption for her baby. . . . *[B]ut I never give a child to a couple who have done something not to have a child.* . . . The way to plan the family is natural family planning, not contraception. In destroying the power of giving life through contraception a husband or wife is doing something to self. This turns the attention to self and so destroys the gift of love in him or her. In loving, the husband and wife must turn the attention to each other, as happens in natural family planning, and not to self, as happens in contraception. Once that living love is destroyed by contraception, abortion follows very easily.
>
> I also know that there are great problems in the world — that many spouses do not love each other enough to practice natural family planning. We cannot solve all the problems in the world, but let us never bring in the worst problem of all, and that is to destroy love. And this is what happens when we tell people to practice contraception and abortion.[16]

Despite Mother Teresa's endorsement, is natural family planning (NFP) merely another form of contraception?[17] In the words of Pope John Paul, NFP and contraception involve "two irreconcilable concepts of the human person and of human sexuality. The choice of the natural rhythms involves accepting the cycle of the person, that is, the woman, and thereby accepting dialogue, reciprocal respect, shared responsibility,

---

[14] Pope John Paul II, *Familiaris Consortio* (1981), no. 32. See also Question 20.
[15] See Scott Hahn, "Sex, Lies and Sacraments," *CCC Family Foundations* (Couple to Couple League), May-June 1999, 4.
[16] *Family Resources Center News,* May 1994, p. 13 (emphasis added).
[17] For information on natural family planning, contact American Life League, Box 1350, Stafford, VA 22554, (540) 659-4171; Couple to Couple League, Box 111184, Cincinnati, OH 45211, (513) 661-7612; Pope Paul VI Institute, 6901 Mercy Road, Omaha, NE 68106, (402) 390-6600; Family of the Americas Foundation, Box 219, Mandeville, LA 70448; see discussion in Charles E. Rice, *Fifty Questions on the Natural Law* (2d ed., 1999), Question 43.

and self-control. To accept the cycle and to enter into dialogue means to recognize both the spiritual and corporal character of conjugal communion and to live personal love with its requirement of fidelity."[18] With NFP, "[t]he wife preserves herself from intrusive chemicals or devices and remains true to her natural cycle. The husband shares in the planning and responsibility for NFP. Both learn a greater degree of self-mastery and a deeper respect for each other."[19] They are open to life and do nothing to impede the life-giving potential of that conjugal act.

Natural family planning, however, is *"not an end in itself."*[20] "Marriage and married love are by nature ordered to the procreation and education of children."[21] As Paul VI stated, it is only "for grave motives," "serious motives" and "just motives," that married couples may rightly choose to avoid pregnancies even by partial abstinence.[22] Doubts about the sufficiency of such reasons may be resolved in consultation with a confessor. If natural family planning is used without serious reason it becomes, in purpose rather than in technique, an alternative form of contraception. "The Encyclical *Humanae Vitae,*" said John Paul II, "presents 'responsible parenthood' as an expression of a high ethical value. *In no way is it exclusively directed* to limiting, much less excluding, children; it means also the willingness to accept a larger family. Above all,. . . 're-sponsible parenthood' implies 'a deeper relationship with the objective moral order instituted by God — the order of which a right conscience is the true interpreter.'"[23]

Education about contraception should emphasize openness to life and the advantages of large families. At the Capitol Mall in Washington, DC in 1979, John Paul II reminded us of this point:

> Decisions about the number of children and the sacrifices to be made for them must not be taken only with a view to adding to comfort and preserving a peaceful existence. Reflecting upon this matter before God, with the graces drawn from the sacrament, and guided by the teaching of the Church, parents will remind themselves that it is certainly less serious to deny their children certain comforts or material advantages than to deprive them of the presence of brothers and sis-

---

[18] *Familiaris Consortio,* no. 32.

[19] Archbishop Charles Chaput, Pastoral, *Of Human Life* (1998); *Catholic World Report,* Oct. 1998, 56, 60.

[20] Pope John Paul II, *Address,* June 8, 1984; 29 *The Pope Speaks* 246 (1984).

[21] Vatican II, *Gaudium et Spes, Pastoral Constitution On The Church In The Modern World,* no. 50; see also no. 48.

[22] *Humanae Vitae,* nos. 10, 16.

[23] Pope John Paul II, *Audience,* Sept. 5, 1984; *L'Osservatore Romano* (English edition), Sept. 10, 1984, p. 10.

ters, who could help them to grow in humanity and to realize the beauty of life at all its ages and in all its variety.[24]

Why Does Contraception Determine So Many Other Issues?

Events have verified the analysis of an Irish cardinal, Cahal Daly, more than three decades ago. "Birth control mores," he wrote, "create a mentality of 'unwanting' babies. Furthermore, it is not a practice only but a new philosophy of man and sex, a new 'way of life.' It means the abandonment of self-control over sexual urges; it implicitly authorizes sexual promiscuity. The real problem of our time is that society tolerates a continuous and ubiquitous display, by every medium of mass communication, of artificial libidinous solicitation, which makes it unnaturally difficult for people, particularly young people, to be continent; and then offers a remedy, contraceptives, which merely increases the incontinence. Promiscuity is the logic of birth control; but to have promiscuity with impunity there must also be abortion and infanticide, sterilization and euthanasia. The logical contraceptionist must insist that if these cannot be generalized by persuasion, they must be imposed by law. It has long been recognized that there is a connection between eroticism and totalitarianism."[25]

Through secularism we deny the subjection of human conduct to the law of God; through relativism we deny objective morality and our ability to know right from wrong; through individualism, each of us makes himself his own god, so that whatever he wills to do is "right" for him. All three are symptoms of a loss of faith in the reality, love and providence of God. The contraceptive mentality is the leading manifestation of that loss. Any "pro-life" effort that temporizes on contraception will be futile because the trajectory is a straight line from the approval of contraception to the acceptance of the following evils:

Abortion. If man (of both sexes) makes himself, through contraception, the arbiter of when life begins, he will predictably make himself the arbiter of when it shall end. Contraception prevents life while abortion kills existing life. But both involve the deliberate separation of the unitive and procreative aspects of sex. A contraceptive society requires abortion as a backup for contraception. The availability of abortion is also a factor in the decision of some to engage in sexual relations without using contraception. And many so-called contraceptives are abortifacient in that they cause the destruction of the developing human being. "[T]he

[24] *The Pope in America* (The Wanderer Press, 1979), 79, 80.
[25] Cahal Daly, *Morals, Law and Life* (1966), 94-95.

historical evidence indicates that conspicuous consumption, contraception, and abortion are alike symptoms of a master principle: the urge to control life and life's environment. . . . The tendency for Christians' reasons for contraception and abortion to match is a function of this underlying desire for material security."[26]

Pope John Paul has noted that "the pro-abortion culture is especially strong precisely where the Church's teaching on contraception is rejected. Certainly, from the moral point of view, contraception and abortion are *specifically* different evils: the former contradicts the full truth of the sexual act as the proper expression of conjugal love, while the latter destroys the life of a human being. . . . But despite their differences of nature and moral gravity, contraception and abortion are often closely connected, as fruits of the same tree. It is true that in many cases contraception and even abortion are practiced under the pressure of real-life difficulties, which nonetheless can never exonerate from striving to observe God's law fully. Still, in very many other instances such practices are rooted in a hedonistic mentality unwilling to accept responsibility in matters of sexuality, and they imply a self-centered concept of freedom, which regards procreation as an obstacle to personal fulfillment. The life which could result from a sexual encounter thus becomes an enemy to be avoided at all costs, and abortion becomes the only possible decisive response to contraception. The close connection between. . . contraception and. . . abortion. . . is being demonstrated in an alarming way by the development of chemical products, intrauterine devices and vaccines which, distributed with the same ease as contraceptives, really act as abortifacients in the very early stages of the development of the life of the new human being."[27]

Euthanasia. More than three decades of contraception and abortion have left the United States with a diminished pool of workers to support the elderly, sick and disabled. Contraception and abortion accustomed people to the idea that some lives are not worth bringing into existence or continuing in existence. This clears the way for euthanasia of those whose lives are considered "useless."

If, through contraception, man makes himself the arbiter of when life begins, he will predictably make himself the arbiter, through suicide and euthanasia, as well as abortion, of when it ends. All are based on a utilitarian approach. Euthanasia, said John Paul II, is "one of the more

---

[26] Jeremy C. Jackson, "The Shadow of Death: Abortion in Historical and Contemporary Perspective," in Richard L. Granz (ed.), *Thou Shalt Not Kill: The Christian Case Against Abortion* (1978), 93-94.

[27] *EV,* nos. 13, 15.

alarming symptoms of the 'culture of death,'. . . in prosperous societies, marked by [a] preoccupation with efficiency. . . which sees. . . elderly and disabled people as intolerable and too burdensome. These people are. . . isolated by their families and by society, which are organized. . . on. . . criteria of productive efficiency, according to which a hopelessly impaired life no longer has any value."[28] The prevailing culture "presents recourse to contraception, sterilization, abortion and even euthanasia as a mark of progress and a victory of freedom, while depicting as enemies of freedom and progress those positions which are unreservedly pro-life."[29]

Pornography. Pornography reduces sex to an exercise in self-gratification, as contraception reduces it to an exercise in mutual masturbation. Both involve the separation of sex from life. Pope Paul, in *Humanae Vitae,* warned that contraception would cause women to be viewed as sex objects, that "man, growing used to the employment of anti-conceptive practices, may finally lose respect for the woman and, no longer caring for her physical and psychological equilibrium, may come to the point of considering her as a mere instrument of selfish enjoyment, and no longer as his respected and beloved companion." The theologians of The Church of Where It's At laughed at Pope Paul. But now that the objectification of woman is obvious, nobody is laughing any more.

Promiscuity. In the nature of things, one reason why sex is reserved for marriage is that sex is inherently connected with procreation and the natural way to raise children is in a marriage. But if it is entirely up to us to decide whether sex will have anything to do with procreation, why should it be reserved for marriage?

Divorce. One reason, in the nature of things, why marriage should be permanent is that sex is inherently related to procreation and it is good for children to be raised in a home with parents permanently married to each other. But if sex is not intrinsically related to procreation, marriage loses its reason for permanence.[30] It tends to become a temporary alliance for individual gratification — what Paul VI called "the juxtaposition of two solitudes."[31]

Homosexual Activity. In any sane society, if George and Harry apply for a license to "marry" each other, the response would be some variant

---

[28] *EV,* no. 64.
[29] *EV,* no. 17.
[30] See Bob & Gerri Laird, "Birth Control: It Almost Cost Us Our Marriage," in *Family Foundations,* Couple to Couple League Newsletter, July-Aug. 1998, 1.
[31] "Conversations with Pope Paul VI," *McCall's,* Oct. 1967, 93, 138.

of "Get lost." But if it is entirely up to man (of both sexes) to decide whether sex will have any relation to procreation, why should marriage be limited to male-female combinations? The contraceptive society cannot deny legitimacy to the homosexual lifestyle without denying its own basic premise. Its only objections to homosexual activity and homosexual "marriage" will be pragmatic or aesthetic. "Homosexual activity, like contraception, also frustrates the interpersonal communion that is intrinsic to the conjugal act. And where that act should be open to life, homosexual activity is a dead end. It rejects life and focuses instead on excrement, which is dead."[32]

In vitro fertilization (IVF). This is the flip side of contraception. IVF engineers procreation without sexual union, while contraception seeks to take the unitive without the procreative. As a by-product of IVF, spare embryos are frozen and used for later implantation in the mother or in other women. And they are used for experimentation, as objects of utility.[33] Or they are flushed down the drain.

Cloning. Dolly the sheep, the first verifiably cloned animal, was introduced to the world by Dr. Ian Wilmut in Edinburgh in February, 1997. Dr. Wilmut took from an adult "donor" sheep a cell which he then treated so that all its genes could be activated so as to develop into a lamb. He electrically fused that cell with the unfertilized egg of a ewe, from which egg the nucleus containing the DNA of the ewe had been removed. The fused cell and egg interacted and developed into a lamb embryo. Since the ewe's DNA had been removed, the only DNA in the embryo was that of the "donor." The embryo was then implanted in a "surrogate mother" sheep and carried to term. The result is Dolly, a sheep that is a genetic copy of the "donor" sheep. Dr. Wilmut predicted that we can "produce, in the next two or three years, [cloned] animals" whose milk would contain "proteins to treat human illnesses, such as hemophilia." Cloned sheep "will offer. . . models to study cystic fibrosis. . . . [T]here could be no limits on the possible diseases to be treated." But he said it would be "inhumane" to clone human beings.[34] Nine months later, however, the *New York Times* reported that "There has been an enormous change in attitudes in just a few months; scientists

---

[32] Charles E. Rice, *50 Questions on the Natural Law* (2d ed.,1999), Question 42. See also Questions 28 and 29 in this book.

[33] See Richard Doerflinger, "Destructive Stem-Cell Research on Human Embryos," 28 *Origins* 770 (1999); for information on stem-cell research, contact American Bioethics Advisory Commission, c/o American Life League, P.O. Box 1350, Stafford, VA 22554, (540) 659-4171.

[34] *Wash. Times,* Mar. 13, 1997, p. A1.

have become sanguine about the notion of cloning and, in particular, cloning a human being."[35]

"Scientists. . . envision. . . circumstances in which it might be acceptable to clone humans. Grieving parents may want to reproduce a terminally ill child. Or a woman may want a child but be infertile. Is it worse somehow for her to clone herself than to obtain an embryo made-to-order with donated egg and sperm, the kind that many fertility clinics are already offering the infertile? In fact, said Dr. Joseph Schulman, director of the Genetics and IVF Institute in Fairfax, Va., if a woman has no eggs and her husband makes no sperm, they might consider cloning both husband and wife. Then they could have one of each, Dr. Schulman said. . . . The fact is that, in America, cloning may be bad but telling people how they should reproduce is worse, Dr. [Steen] Willadsen said. In the end, Dr. Willadsen said, 'America is not ruled by ethics. It is ruled by law.'"[36]

The Catholic Church condemns human cloning, which shares the basic premises of contraception. The 1987 *Instruction on Bioethics* said that "attempts. . . for obtaining a human being without any connection with sexuality through. . . cloning. . . are. . . contrary to the moral law, since they are in opposition to the dignity both of human procreation and of the conjugal union."[37] Cloning shares with contraception the treatment of woman as an object of utility. Human cloning would confirm the status of woman as an object, an impersonal egg bank. It is futile, however, to try to put the brakes on human cloning, as on abortion or euthanasia, without restoring the conviction that God, and not man, is the arbiter of when and how life begins and ends. This requires a reassessment and rejection of contraception.

A DEFINING VICE

The acceptance of contraception has led to the diversion of medical resources from therapeutic ends to the alteration of healthy organisms for behavioral purposes. "Nature is manipulated every day as. . . the natural progress of disease is checked by surgery or drugs. So people ask: 'What is the difference between removing a diseased appendix and tying fallopian tubes, or between taking an antibiotic and taking the contraceptive pill?' One difference is easily explained. Appendices are only removed when they become diseased. Antibiotics are taken to kill danger-

---

[35] *N.Y. Times*, Dec. 2, 1997, p. A1.

[36] *Ibid.*

[37] Congregation for the Doctrine of the Faith, *Instruction on Bioethics* (1987), I, 6; 32 *The Pope Speaks* 137, 146 (1987).

ous micro-organisms. Such therapeutic procedures restore patients to health — by destroying pathological bacteria or removing malfunctioning bodily parts. Contraceptives function in a totally different way. Instead of removing a malfunction they actually *produce* one. Contraceptives turn normal fertility into an abnormal, sterile state. They impair the function of healthy reproductive organs. Contraceptives *damage* the bodies of those who use them and they are taken for that express purpose."[38]

"[B]y giving women the means to prevent pregnancy," said Francis Fukuyama, "the pill freed men from the social responsibility of dealing with the consequences of sex."[39] As evolutionary anthropologist Lionel Tiger said in 1996:

> Two mysteries haunt the relationship of men and women. First, there has been an inexorable change in their productive and reproductive roles. In both areas, men's place is declining; their share of income and wealth falls as women's rises, and an increasing number of men are less involved with their mates and offspring. This is accompanied by men's belligerence. The second mystery is why the numbers of single mothers and abortions have risen at the same time there are more and better contraceptives than ever in history. I think these two phenomena are linked and that that helps explain the tension between the sexes. I think the introduction of widespread contraception use in the 1960s caused this revolutionary break between men and women. . . . As happens frequently, technology (contraception, in this case) has generated an unexpected result: more abortions, more single-parent families, more men abandoning their role of being good providers and a higher divorce rate.[40]

The National Right to Life Committee and other "pro-life" organizations concentrate on restricting abortion and euthanasia, but they refuse to take a position against contraception.[41] It is no surprise that organizations which temporize on contraception are ineffective. Contraception is the defining vice of this era. As long as the cultural dominance of the contraceptive ethic continues, there is no practical chance to prevent the legal implementation of that ethic in abortion, euthanasia and its other manifestations:

---

[38] Dr. Les Hemingway, *Contraception and Common Sense* (1997), 1.

[39] Francis Fukuyama, "At Last, Japan Gets the Pill. Is This Good News?" *Wash. Times*, June 9, 1999, p. A31.

[40] *U.S. News & World Report*, July 1, 1996, 57.

[41] See *National Right to Life News*, May 24, 1994, 10, 11; The major exceptions, to their credit, are American Life League, P.O. Box 1350, Stafford, VA 22554, (540) 659-4171; and Human Life International, Front Royal, VA 22630, (540) 635-7884.

For three decades or so, the American culture has embraced a belief that contraception brings freedom — freedom from unwanted pregnancy, overpopulation, child abuse, frustration in sexual relationships, AIDS and most importantly, freedom from having (or being able) to say "no" at any time for any reason. Our nation practices contraception more than ever in its history. How interesting that we also experience more sexual disease, more abortion, more smashed marriages, more alienation from one another and from God, more self-indulgence at earlier and earlier ages — and less peace and discipline and joy than the world has ever known. Contraceptives set us free, all right — from spiritual growth. . . .

Pope Paul VI predicted that contraceptive technology would lead to general moral decline, the use of women as mere objects and the demeaning of their dignity as persons; he also prophesied promiscuity and marital infidelity on a heretofore unimaginable scale and added that coercive government intervention in family planning would not be far behind. Those who laughed him to scorn predicted more stable marriages, a virtual (if not virtuous) end to unwanted pregnancies and greater personal happiness and freedom for all. Who told the truth?[42]

---

[42] Anne Collopy, "Contraception Creates More Ills than It Solves," *Minneapolis Star Tribune,* Aug. 16, 1993, p. A9.

17. HOW DOES CONTRACEPTION PUT A DANGEROUS WEAPON IN THE HANDS OF GOVERNMENT?

[A] dangerous weapon would thus be placed in the hands of those public authorities who take no heed of moral demands. Who could blame a government for applying to the solution of the problems of the community those means acknowledged to be licit for married couples in the solution of a family problem? Who will stop rulers from even imposing upon their peoples. . . the method of contraception which they judge to be most efficacious? In such a way men. . . would reach the point of placing at the mercy of. . . public authorities the most personal and most reserved sector of conjugal intimacy. — *Pope Paul VI, Humanae Vitae* [1]

During the 1960s the federal government subsidized family planning research and services on a limited basis. In 1970 the Family Planning Services and Population Research Act was passed to make "comprehensive voluntary family planning services readily available to all persons desiring such services" in the United States. That Act added a new Title X to the Public Health Service Act.[2] Title X authorized grants and contracts to states and nonprofit private entities for "voluntary family planning projects."[3] In signing the Act, on Christmas Eve, President Nixon stated his goal as "providing adequate family planning services. . . to all those who want them but cannot afford them."[4] Title X prohibited use of its funds "in programs where abortion is a method of family planning."[5] But that restriction has been ineffective: "Title X provides funding for chemical abortions as well as funding for organizations that promote abortion."[6] Since the mid-1970s, curtailment of population growth also in "developing countries" has become an "important component"[7] of United States foreign policy and of United Nations programs supported by the United States.[8] "Without foreign aid programs from wealthier nations in the past three decades, the world would probably have 500 million more people, and be 'more crowded, more pol-

---

[1] No. 17. See William B. Smith, "Population Control - Voluntary?" *Homiletic & Pastoral Review*, June 1999, 67.

[2] 42 U.S. Code, Ch. 6A.

[3] Sec. 1001(a).

[4] *Public Papers of the Presidents of the United States* (1970), 1157.

[5] Sec. 1008.

[6] Judie Brown et al., *The Facts About Title X: The Six Billion Dollar Scam* (American Life League, 1997), 4-5.

[7] Statement of Secretary of State Madeleine Albright, *APN Abortion Report*, Feb. 12, 1997.

[8] See Antonio Gaspari, "The War Against Babies," *Catholic World Report*, Apr., 1993, 23.

luted and poorer,' according to the Federal Agency for International Development."[9]

The domestic and international family planning programs of the federal government initially funded only contraception. But that funding quickly expanded to include abortion, especially early abortions.[10] Those programs tend to be at least implicitly coercive. And they are persistently weighted against non-white populations.

GENOCIDE BY PILL

Reproductive methods and technology have historically been used in this country as a mechanism for social control. 'At various times in American history fear of blacks, immigrants, Native Americans, working people, Hispanics, and welfare recipients has been expressed in explicit, although, unofficial, attempts to control their growth rates.' Similarly, compulsory or coercive contraception statutes which would mandate or coerce women on welfare, including numerous minority women, to submit to mandatory birth control 'has [sic] vast class and racial implications.'. . . Both the Eugenicists and today's politicians who have proposed compulsory contraceptive welfare reform have decided certain groups are unfit to procreate. By making such a judgment, both Eugenic policy and so called welfare 'reform' policy impose the morality of its lawmakers (generally middle and upper class, white males) on the rest of society. 'The idea behind all of these projects is the same: only those women. . . who conform to majoritarian middle-class values deserve government subsistence benefits.'[11]

As Rev. Johnny Hunter, director of the Life, Education & Resource Network (LEARN), put it, abortion has "killed more blacks than the Ku Klux Klan ever lynched."[12] Although blacks make up 12 percent of the nation's population they account for 31 percent of its abortions. "When you're a minority," says Rev. Hunter, "you can't take that kind of hit and survive as a race." He echoed Rev. Edward V. Hill, of Mount Zion Missionary Baptist Church in Los Angeles, who said in 1982:

It is clear that present government policies of abortion on demand have a disproportionate effect on racial minorities: more black babies

---

[9] *Atlanta Journal/Constitution*, June 29, 1998, p. A3.
[10] See the discussion of Title X in Question 35.
[11] Meredith Blake, "Welfare and Coerced Contraception: Morality Implications of State Sponsored Reproduction Control," 34 *U. of Louisville J. of Family Law* 311, 342-43 (1995-96); see also, *Note*, "Involuntary Contraceptive Measures: Controlling Women at the Expense of Human Rights," 10 *Boston U. Int'l. Law J.* 351 (1992).
[12] *Wash. Times*, Jan. 10, 1997, p. A2.

are being killed by abortion and more black women, men and children suffer the psychological consequences than members of any other group. This is occurring despite the fact that polls show black people to be more strongly against abortion than other groups. Subtle coercion in a new welfare plantation system is continuing where slavery left off to destroy black family structures. This new war on the black family benefits a new breed of college-educated overseers.[13]

In *Centesimus Annus*, Pope John Paul II denounced "systematic anti-childbearing campaigns which, on the basis of a distorted view of the demographic problem and in a climate of 'absolute lack of respect for the freedom of choice of the parties involved,' often subject them 'to intolerable pressures. . . to force them to submit to this new form of oppression.' These policies are extending their field of action by the use of new techniques, to the point of poisoning the lives of millions of defenseless human beings, as if in a form of 'chemical warfare.'"[14]

In Brazil, said Cardinal Lopez Trujillo, about 40 percent of women have been sterilized through 'contraceptive imperialism.'"[15] With reason, the Brazilian Catholic Bishops' Conference concluded that "The desired result of [population control] is always the same: to reduce the growth of the countries of the Third World so that the industrialized nations can continue to exploit them and dominate them as they always have."[16] And coercion is implicit in the linkage of population control to economic aid. As University of Maryland demographer Prof. Julian Simon summarized: "Sugarcoat the matter as U.N. functionaries do, attaining [their population control] goal means government policies that will propagandize, bribe and coerce couples to have fewer children than they would otherwise choose to have."[17]

CONTRACEPTIVE IMPERIALISM

The concentration of people in megacities and the maldistribution of resources do create major problems. But it is simplistic to ascribe them to an overall excess of people. If you took the six billion people now on the earth and gave each one six square feet to stand on, you

---

[13] 128 *Cong. Rec.,* S 12913-8 (Sept. 30, 1982).
[14] Pope John Paul II, *Centesimus Annus* (1991), no. 40.
[15] *The Sooner Catholic* (Oklahoma City), June 16, 1996, 13.
[16] See Georgie Anne Geyer, "Listening for the Voices of Reason at Cairo Conference," *Chicago Tribune*, Sept. 4, 1994, p. C3. See also "Tribal Leaders See Sterilization as a Form of Genocide," *Wash. Times*, May 4, 1999, p. A15.
[17] *N.Y. Times*, Aug. 21, 1994, Sec. 4, p. 15; see also G. Joseph Rees, "The American Connection," *Catholic World Report*, Mar. 1998, 45; Steven W. Mosher, "Sterilizing Peru?" *Inside the Vatican*, Mar. 1998, 27.

could fit them all into Nassau and Suffolk counties on Long Island in New York, with 281 square miles left over. Nobody would propose that expedient, least of all the people of Long Island. But the heated rhetoric can cause us to assume that there are more people on earth than there actually are.

The total fertility rate at which a population replaces itself is 2.1. In 1991, the rate for the world was 3.35, with 3.20 for Asia, 4.75 for the Near East/No. Africa, 6.43 for sub-Saharan Africa and 3.24 for Latin America. The figure for North America/Europe was 1.91. By 2020, the rate will decline in every region, but only in North America/Europe will it be below the 2.1 replacement level, at 1.86.[18] "Contraceptive imperialism" is a utilitarian attack on rising Third World populations by Western peoples who have lost the will even to reproduce themselves. "Today the estimated populations of Europe and Africa are almost exactly equal. But by the middle of the next century,. . . Africans will outnumber Europeans by over three to one. A list of the world's 12 largest countries will include not only China, India and Pakistan, but Nigeria, Indonesia, Brazil, Bangladesh, Ethiopia, Congo, Iran and Mexico. Not a single European country will be able to match the population of even the Philippines, and the only Western survivor among the top 12 will be the U.S."[19] A survey released by the Population Reference Bureau in 1999 put "[f]ertility rates for the world's more developed countries at 1.5 children per woman [the replacement rate is 2.1] compared to 3.8 children for the non-developed world (excluding China) and 5.8 children for sub-Saharan Africa."[20]

"What do these demographic numbers tell us?" asked Pat Buchanan. "That the Western hour in world history is ending, that by its hedonistic embrace of the sexual revolution — of birth control and of abortion — Western civilization, that great vibrant part of the world once called Christendom, is marching merrily along toward civilizational suicide. God is not mocked."[21]

Facing demographic suicide, the developed nations choose to suppress populations in developing countries rather than turn from the contraceptive ethic. Nor can this choice be justified in the name of promoting development. As Prof. Julian Simon, noted: "In the 1980's, there was a U-turn in the consensus of population economists about the effects of population growth. In 1986, the National Research Council of the Na-

---

[18] *Atlanta Journal/Constitution,* Aug. 28, 1994, p. D4.
[19] Richard Grenier, "Overpopulation Myths," *Wash. Times,* Sept. 12, 1997, p. A19.
[20] *Wash. Times,* May 27, 1999, p. A15.
[21] *Wash. Times,* Nov. 17, 1997, p. A16.

tional Academy of Sciences. . . reversed the worried view it expressed in 1971. Its report noted that there was no statistical evidence of a negative connection between population increase and economic growth. . . . This shift has gone unacknowledged by the media, by environmental organizations and by the agencies that foster population control abroad."[22] Malcolm S. Forbes, Jr., points out that "The real issue is the assumption that curbing population growth is critical for economic development. The premise is preposterous. A growing population is not a drag on economic development. When combined with freedom, it is a stimulant."[23]

Pope John Paul II in his opening address at the five-day UN World Food Summit on Nov. 14, 1996, "chided" those who link hunger and overpopulation: "We must renounce the sophist view which holds that 'to be many is to condemn ourselves to be poor.'" "It would be illusory," said the Pope, "to believe that an arbitrary stabilization of the world population, or even its reduction, could solve the problem of hunger directly." The Pope urged leaders instead to close the "intolerable" gap between "those who lack the bare necessities and those who squander freely."[24] Before the 1994 Cairo Conference, Vatican spokesman Joaquin Navarro-Valls described the anti-life premises of the population control movement:

> World population is to be set at some such figure as 7-1/2 billion. Since that figure is said to represent the "carrying capacity" of the earth — something itself purely arbitrary — this end justifies the means to achieve it. . . . We thus need to impose a widespread system of control of the reproductive act's consequences. All activity that results in children will be subject to political scrutiny and, if need be, to force.

> All essentially sterile acts, on the other hand, are said to be relatively insignificant. Homosexual or lesbian activity, contraception or sterilization, all are viewed in a positive light because they have no visible consequences. Sex becomes literally insignificant. The social and political freedom of homosexual activity is thus rooted precisely in its lack of any real existential purpose or consequence. Only sexual activity that has potential consequences in the conception of a child has any political importance. And this activity must be limited and controlled as much as possible by the eugenic state. This theoretical position has its own prior logic. Its premise is that there is no nature or

---

[22] *N.Y. Times,* Aug. 21, 1994, p. E15.
[23] *Forbes,* Sept. 12, 1994, p. 25.
[24] *N.Y. Times,* Nov. 4, 1996, p. A15.

principle of morality that is not subject to the state. The state cannot be itself limited by anything except necessity.[25]

THE CONDOM GOES TO WAR

The record of federal birth-control programs vindicates Paul VI's warning that the acceptance of contraception would place "a dangerous weapon" in the hands of government. The government's claim to competence in this area, however, reaches back beyond the 1960s. A firm precedent was set in World War II, with the general distribution of condoms to military personnel. The armed forces in World War II justified that program as a disease-prevention measure, just as condom distribution to school children is justified today as prevention of AIDS. Very few Catholic or other voices were raised in public opposition to the military condom program. *America* magazine was the most outspoken critic.

America objected to "the apparent belief of the authorities that to prevent disease they are at liberty to use means and methods which are themselves immoral, and which. . . suggest that immoral practices may be indulged in provided that precautions against disease are taken."[26] Editor Paul L. Blakely, S.J., protested "any military regulation which can lead the young soldier to conclude that sexual immorality does not matter much, provided that mechanical and chemical means are taken to avoid the diseases which commonly follow promiscuity."[27] The *America* writers objected to the provision of condoms, but not to medical treatment of diseases resulting from sexual activity. The arguments for provision of condoms were the same used today to justify condom distribution to school children:

> The answer of the Catholic Chaplains is unanimous: "The majority of men in the Army are decent, clean-living men. It is only a minority who are offenders in this matter. They must and can be cured of consequent disease *after* the offense in the prophylactic stations already provided. The offering for use of these devices *beforehand* is an incentive to sin and a condoning of immorality. . . . This is not a question of a purely Catholic point of view — it is a question of fundamental morality and social decency. It is using a bad means for a good end. In effect, the Army is saying: 'We assume that you are going to commit this sin and we are going to assist you so that, at least, you will not suffer any bad consequences.'". . .What particularly worries Chaplains in

---

[25] *Wall St. Journal*, Sept. 1, 1994, p. A12.
[26] *America*, editorial, Aug. 2, 1941, 463-64.
[27] Paul L. Blakely, S.J., "Morals Versus Health of the Men in the Camp," *America*, Aug. 9, 1941, 481.

this whole bad business is the effect it will have on good, but easily led boys whose characters are not thoroughly formed. They may easily argue that if the Government recognizes promiscuous sexual indulgence as normal and to be expected, that perhaps it is not so bad after all. Possibly the ideals they were trained in at home were a trifle narrow.[28]

America's objections are worth recalling, if only to remind us that the principles and arguments have not changed. The American Catholic Church and all of us would do well to imitate the wisdom and courage of those Jesuits in their opposition to the utilitarian liberation of government from moral limits.

In 1959, President Dwight D. Eisenhower rejected proposals that the United States help other nations to control population growth by providing them with birth control information:

> I cannot imagine anything more emphatically a subject that is not a proper political or governmental activity or function or responsibility. . . . That's not our business.[29]

Would that the government had adhered to that policy. "It should be obvious," said the November 14, 1966 statement of the National Conference of Catholic Bishops, "that a full understanding of human worth, personal and social, will not permit the nation to put the public power behind the pressures for a contraceptive way of life. . . . History has shown that as a people lose respect for any life and a positive and generous attitude toward new life, they move fatally to inhuman infanticide, abortion, sterilization, and euthanasia; we fear that history is, in fact, repeating itself on this point within our own land at the moment."[30]

---

[28] J. Gerard Mears, S.J., "Chaplains Labor to Uphold Army Morals and Morale," *America,* Aug. 23, 1941, 539.

[29] *N.Y. Times,* Dec. 6, 1959, p. E5.

[30] *Pastoral Letters of the United States Catholic Bishops* (vol. III, 1962-74), 69, 71-72.

PART III:

THE SOLUTION

A. The Culture of Life

18. WAIT A MINUTE. FIRST, WHAT IS THE ANSWER TO THE IDEAS OF THE ENLIGHTENMENT?

Veritatis Splendor (The Splendor of Truth) was "the first time. . . that the Magisterium. . . set forth in detail the fundamental elements of [Christian moral] teaching and presented the principles for. . . discernment. . . in practical and cultural situations."[1] *Veritatis* is not a sectarian directive. "I have been a Protestant minister for nearly half a century," wrote Rev. Harvey N. Chinn, "but I consider *The Splendor of Truth* to be a. . . compelling analysis of the world's current moral dilemma. . . . *Splendor of Truth* is biblical. . . . It. . . is about. . . immutable, eternal standards of right and wrong that are built into the very structure of the universe. It is a witness that above and beyond our pretenses and. . . sophistication there shines a moral north star that never changes. . . . I am a better Protestant for having studied this magnificent Catholic document."[2] "That encyclical," said University of California Prof. James Q. Wilson, "is not a list of specific moral rules. It is about the universal law of nature that is discoverable by human reason; it exists in all people regardless of culture, and leads us inevitably to judge actions as right or wrong — whatever their intentions and whether or not they help or harm others."[3]

THE UNITY OF FAITH AND REASON

"Moral truth is objective," said John Paul II at World Youth Day in Denver, "and a properly formed conscience can perceive it."[4] Though reason can attain to moral truth, our intellects are weakened by original sin and sincere advocates can be found on both sides of most issues, including abortion. They cannot both be right. As St. Thomas tells us, "If. . . we consider one action in the moral order, it is impossible for it to be morally both good and evil."[5] But how are we to know what the natural law requires? Although the natural law can be known by reason without the aid of explicit supernatural revelation, St. Thomas states that "Besides the natural and the human law it was necessary for the directing

---

[1] *VS*, no. 115.

[2] Harvey N. Chinn, "Protestant Cheers Pope's Message," *Sacramento Bee,* Jan.15, 1994, p. SC 10.

[3] James Q. Wilson, "Calvin and Hobbes and John Paul," *N.Y. Times,* Nov. 26, 1993, p. A19.

[4] *N.Y. Times,* Aug. 15, 1993, sec. 1, p. 12.

[5] *ST.* I, II, Q. 20, art. 6.

of human conduct to have a Divine law. . . . [O]n account of the uncertainty of human judgment,. . . different people form different judgments on human acts. . . . In order. . . that man may know without any doubt what he ought to do and what he ought to avoid, it was necessary for man to be directed. . . by a law given by God, for it is certain that such a law cannot err."[6]

In *Fides et Ratio,* John Paul discussed this weakness of reason in the context of Christ. "[I]t was part of the original plan of the creation that reason should without difficulty reach beyond the sensory data to the origin of all things: the Creator. But because of the disobedience by which man and woman chose to set themselves in. . . autonomy in relation to the One who had created them, this ready access to God the Creator diminished. . . . The coming of Christ was the saving event which redeemed reason from its weakness, setting it free from the shackles in which it had imprisoned itself."[7] It is Christ who integrates faith and reason for us:

> This truth, which God reveals to us in Jesus Christ, is not opposed to the truths which philosophy perceives. . . . [T]he two modes of knowledge lead to truth in all its fullness. The unity of truth is a fundamental premise of human reasoning, as the principle of non-contradiction makes clear.[8] . . . It is the one and the same God who establishes. . . the intelligibility and reasonableness of the natural order of things upon which scientists. . . depend, and who reveals himself as the Father of our Lord Jesus Christ. This unity of truth, natural and revealed, is embodied in a living and personal way in Christ, as the Apostle reminds us: "Truth is in Jesus." [9]

FAITH AS A WAY OF KNOWING

John Paul affirms the "profound and indissoluble unity between the knowledge of reason and the knowledge of faith."[10] Like reason, faith itself is a way of knowing. Indeed, "the world and the events of history cannot be understood in depth without professing faith in the God who is at work in them. . . . [W]ith the light of reason human beings can

---

[6] *Ibid.,* I, II, Q. 91, art. 4.

[7] *FR,* no. 22.

[8] "The first principle of the speculative reason is the principle of contradiction (or non-contradiction), that a thing cannot be and not be at the same time under the same aspect, or 'that the same thing cannot be affirmed and denied at the same time.'" Charles E. Rice, *50 Questions on the Natural Law* (2d ed., 1999), Question 19, quoting *ST,* I, II, Q. 94, art. 2.

[9] *FR,* no. 34.

[10] *Ibid.,* no. 16.

know which path to take, but they can follow that path to its end, quickly and unhindered, only if. . . they search for it within the horizon of faith."[11] The "knowledge which is peculiar to faith" is more excellent, "surpassing the knowledge proper to human reason."[12]

So what is faith? It is "an obedient response to God. . . . [T]he act of entrusting oneself to God [is] a moment of fundamental decision . . . . Men and women can accomplish no more important act in their lives than the act of faith; it is here that freedom reaches the certainty of truth and chooses to live in that truth."[13]

Every act of belief involves trust in another person. When you rely on the turn signal given by the other driver, you place your trust, and perhaps your life, in his hands. Belief in others is one of the ways we reach the truth. "[B]elief. . . involves an interpersonal relationship. . . . [T]he truths sought in this interpersonal relationship are not primarily empirical or philosophical. Rather, what is sought is the truth of the person — what the person is and what the person reveals from deep within. Human perfection, then, consists not simply in acquiring an abstract knowledge of the truth, but in a dynamic relationship of faithful self-giving with others. It is in this faithful self-giving that a person finds a fullness of certainty and security. At the same time. . . knowledge through belief, grounded as it is on trust between persons, is linked to truth: in the act of believing, men and women entrust themselves to the truth which the other declares to them."[14]

So it is with faith in Christ. "It is the nature of the human being to seek the truth. . . . [I]t is. . . a search which can reach its end only in reaching the absolute. . . . Such a truth. . . is attained not only by way of reason but also through trusting acquiescence to other persons who can guarantee the authenticity and certainty of the truth itself . . . . [M]en and women are on. . . a search for the truth and a search for a person to whom they might entrust themselves. Christian faith comes to meet them, offering the concrete possibility of reaching the goal which they seek. Moving beyond the stage of simple believing, Christian faith immerses human beings in the order of grace, which enables them to share in the mystery of. . . Jesus Christ, who is the Truth."[15]

Faith, therefore, is "a communion of love and of life between the believer and Jesus Christ . . . . which enables us to live as he lived. . . in

---

[11] *Ibid.*, no. 16.
[12] *Ibid.*, no. 8.
[13] *Ibid.*, no. 13.
[14] *Ibid.*, no. 32.
[15] *Ibid.*, no. 33.

profound love of God and of our brothers and sisters. . . in the gift of self, *even to the total gift* of self, like that of Jesus."[16] John Paul, therefore, is not expounding a set of abstract principles: "[T]he Christian faith. . . is not simply a set of propositions to be accepted with intellectual assent. Rather, faith is a lived knowledge of Christ. . . and a *truth to be lived out*. . . . Through the moral life, faith becomes 'confession' not only before God but also before men; it becomes witness."[17] In *Veritatis Splendor*, John Paul said, "Following Christ is. . . the essential and primordial foundation of Christian morality. . . . To imitate the Son, 'the image of the invisible God'. . . means to imitate the Father."[18]

ON SECULARISM

"[T]he challenge of secularism," the Pope said, "has become apparent especially in the West, which is highly developed from the standpoint of technology but is interiorly impoverished by its tendency to forget God or to keep him at a distance."[19] Against secularism, John Paul insists that freedom must be grounded in Truth and that morality must not be separated from faith: "The attempt to set freedom in opposition to truth, and indeed to separate them radically, is the. . . consummation of another more serious and destructive dichotomy, that which separates faith from morality."[20] As he said in *Evangelium Vitae*, "*[W]hen the sense of God is lost, there is also a tendency to lose the sense of man*, of his dignity and his life."[21]

For three centuries the Enlightenment project has tried to construct a morality without faith and a society without God. If natural law was mentioned, it was assumed that, unlike every other law, it had no Lawgiver. If a god was mentioned it was only as a deistic watchmaker. "[W]e are living in an atmosphere of deism," said Joseph Cardinal Ratzinger. "Our notion of natural law does not facilitate us in believing in any action of God in our world. It seems that there is no room for God himself to act in human history and in my life. And so we have the idea of God who can no longer enter into this cosmos, made and closed against him. What is left? Our action. And we are the ones who must transform the world. We are the ones who must generate redemption. We are the ones who must create the better world, a new world. And if that is how one

---

[16] *VS*, no. 88-89.
[17] *Ibid.*, nos. 88 and 89.
[18] *Ibid.*, no. 19.
[19] *Tertio Millennio Adveniente*, no. 52.
[20] *VS*, no. 88.
[21] *EV*, no. 21.

thinks, then Christianity is dead and the language of religion becomes a purely symbolic, empty language."[22]

John Paul reminds us that the Enlightenment project is futile. "[W]hen God is forgotten the creation itself grows unintelligible. . . . Life itself becomes a mere 'thing,' which man claims as his exclusive property, completely subject to his control and manipulation."[23] On the contrary, "[t]he truth of Christian Revelation, found in Jesus. . . summons human beings to be open to the transcendent, whilst respecting both their autonomy as creatures and their freedom. At this point the relationship between freedom and truth is complete, and we understand the full meaning of the Lord's words: 'You will know the truth, and the truth will make you free.'"[24]

ON RELATIVISM

John Paul insists on the reality of an objective moral norm. That norm, however, is not an abstraction but a Person, Jesus Christ. "Jesus' way of acting and his words, his deeds and his precepts constitute the moral rule of Christian life. Indeed, his actions, and in particular his Passion and Death on the Cross, are the living revelation of his love for the Father and for others. This is exactly the love that Jesus wishes to be imitated by all who follow him."[25] "The truth," said John Paul in *Fides et Ratio,* "is that only in the mystery of the Incarnate Word does the mystery of man take on light. . . . Christ. . . fully reveals man to himself and brings to light his most high calling."[26]

The twentieth century has produced more declarations of human rights than ever before. Yet it has also produced the greatest violations of those rights ever seen. *Veritatis Splendor* explains why the denial of objective truth ultimately reduces law to an exercise of raw, totalitarian power:

> Totalitarianism arises out of a denial of truth in the objective sense. If there is no transcendent truth. . . there is no sure principle for guaranteeing just relations between people. Their self-interest as a class, group or nation would inevitably set them in opposition to one another. If one does not acknowledge transcendent truth, then the force of power takes over, and each person tends to. . . impose his own interests or his own opinion, with no regard for the rights of others. . . . [T]he root of modern totalitarianism is. . . the denial of the transcen-

---

[22] "The Power and Grace," *30 days,* no. 10, 1998, 26, 32.
[23] *EV,* no. 22.
[24] *FR,* no. 15.
[25] *VS,* no. 20.
[26] *FR,* no. 60; quoting *Gaudium et Spes,* no. 22; see also *Redemptor Hominis,* no. 8.

dent dignity of the human person who, as the visible image of the invisible God, is therefore by his very nature the subject of rights which no one may violate. . . . Not even the majority of a social body may violate these rights, by going against the minority, by isolating, oppressing, or exploiting it, or by attempting to annihilate it.[27]

This makes sense. If we do not affirm objective norms that always prohibit certain conduct, how can we define any moral limits to what the state can do? Abstract moral affirmations, however, will be of little use if they are not lived in practice. In *Veritatis Splendor*, John Paul mentioned "the need for a radical personal and social renewal capable of ensuring justice, solidarity, honesty and openness."[28] This is a matter, not of official proclamations, but of life on the street, in "personal and social" life. The Pope raises this point with respect to the nations of the former Soviet Union. He sees a "grave" danger in those nations of *"an alliance between democracy and ethical relativism,* which would remove any sure moral reference point from political and social life, and on a deeper level make the acknowledgment of truth impossible. Indeed, 'if there is no ultimate truth to guide and direct political activity, then ideas and convictions can easily be manipulated for reasons of power. As history demonstrates, a democracy without values easily turns into open or thinly disguised totalitarianism.'"[29]

In *Fides et Ratio*, John Paul mentioned "the fundamental questions which pervade human life: *Who am I? Where have I come from and where am I going? Why is there evil? What is there after this life?"*[30] Regrettably, American universities have an abundant supply of professors who are absolutely sure that they cannot be sure of the answers to these questions or of anything else. Such an attitude has precedent. "Pilate's question: 'What is truth?'," said John Paul, "reflects the distressing perplexity of a man who often no longer knows *who he is, whence* he comes and *where* he is going. Hence we not infrequently witness the fearful plunging of the human person into situations of gradual self-destruction."[31]

ON INDIVIDUALISM

John Paul reminds us that freedom without truth degenerates into a self-centered individualism. The answer to this separation of freedom and truth is the person of Christ. "Christ reveals, first and foremost, that

---

[27] *VS*, no. 99. See Question 14.
[28] *Ibid.*, no. 98.
[29] *Ibid.*, no. 101.
[30] *FR*, no. 1.
[31] *VS*, no. 84.

the frank and open acceptance of truth is the condition for authentic freedom."[32] Moreover, "*in the Crucified Christ. . . the Church finds the answer* to the question troubling so many people today: how can obedience to universal and unchanging moral norms respect the uniqueness and individuality of the person, and not represent a threat to his freedom and dignity?. . . *The Crucified Christ reveals the authentic meaning of freedom; he lives it fully in the total gift of himself* and calls his disciples to share in his freedom."[33]

John Paul noted "a tendency to grant to the individual conscience the prerogative of independently determining the criteria of good and evil and then acting accordingly. Such an outlook is quite congenial to an individualist ethic, wherein each individual is faced with his own truth different from the truth of others."[34] The erroneous "*notion of freedom*" today "exalts the isolated individual in an absolute way, and gives no place to solidarity, to openness to others and service of them."[35] On the contrary, "every man is his 'brother's keeper,' because God entrusts us to one another. And it is also in view of this entrusting that God gives everyone freedom, a freedom which possesses an *inherently relational dimension*."[36] Thus, "the full meaning of freedom [is] the gift of self in *service to God and one's brethren*."[37] Our model is the "*Crucified Christ* [who] *reveals the authentic meaning of freedom*."[38] As John Paul described it, "the deepest and most authentic meaning of life [is] that of being *a gift which is fully realized in the giving of self*." [39]

An essential point in the recent teaching of the Magisterium is the idea that relation to others is of the essence of every person. The "identity" of the human person is that he is "a spiritual and bodily being in relationship with God, with his neighbor and with the material world."[40] He can fulfill himself only through the gift of himself:

> The Persons in God are. . . not three isolated individuals. Rather, "relation" to the other divine Persons "is the divine essence itself."[41] This concept of a divine person as essentially involving relation to others goes beyond the classic definition of a person in general as "an indi-

---

[32] *Ibid.*, no. 87.
[33] *Ibid.*, no. 85.
[34] *FR*, no. 98.
[35] *EV*, no. 19.
[36] *Ibid.*
[37] *VS*, no. 87.
[38] *Ibid.*, no. 85.
[39] *EV*, no. 49.
[40] *VS*, no. 13.
[41] *ST*, I, Q. 29, art 4.

vidual substance of a rational nature." Saint Thomas did not apply this idea of person-as-relation to human as well as to divine persons. However, the Second Vatican Council began that application: "[T]he Lord Jesus, when praying to the Father 'that they may all be one. . . even as we are one.'. . . has opened up new horizons closed to human reason by implying that there is a certain parallel between the union existing among the divine persons and the union of the sons of God in truth and love. It follows, then, that if man is the only creature on earth that God has wanted for its own sake, man can fully discover his true self only in a sincere giving of himself."[42] More recently, John Paul II and others have further developed this idea that relation to others is of the essence of the human person just as it is of the essence of the divine Persons of the Trinity.[43]

Relation to others is not something we do. It is something we are; it is of our essence. Father Robert Connor explained the importance of this new, relational understanding of the human person:

> With the introduction of the notion of person in the *Pastoral Constitution on the Church*. . . as "achieving self by the gift of self," the notion of person as "gift," and hence as relation, has universally and constantly been offered as the core concept in all the papal pronouncements and magisterial offerings. . . since Vatican II and particularly. . . in the pontificate of John Paul II. That this notion has impacted heavily in the East as a rallying point for Solidarity and in the collapse of Marxism, as well as in the West where it collides with the individualism of what we could call the "autonomous man," gives testimony to the enormous import of the notion.[44]

Through Vatican II and John Paul II, the Church has shown the way to an understanding of the human person as gift. This understanding is the definitive answer to the sterile individualism and alienation of the Enlightenment.

ON THE COMMANDMENTS

The Ten Commandments are specifications of the obligations of the natural law.[45] "Both the Old and the New Testaments explicitly affirm that *without love of neighbor*, made concrete in keeping the commandments, *genuine love for God is not possible*."[46] "God, who alone is good,

---

[42] Vatican II, *Gaudium et Spes*, no. 24.
[43] Charles E. Rice, *50 Questions on the Natural Law* (2d ed., 1999), Question 36.
[44] Robert A. Connor, "The Person as Resonating Existential," 66 *Am. Catholic Phil. Q.* 39, 42 (1992).
[45] See *VS*, no. 79.
[46] *Ibid.*, no. 14.

knows perfectly what is good for man, and by virtue of his very love proposes this good to man in the commandments."[47] The positive precepts of the natural law, such as to honor one's parents, may not apply in a specific situation "in view of other duties which may be more important or urgent."[48] If his parents ordered a child to steal, he would be obliged to disobey them. "The *negative precepts* of the natural law," however, such as the prohibition of adultery, "oblige each and every individual, always and in every circumstance. . . . [T]he choice of this kind of behavior is in no case compatible with the goodness of the will of the acting person, with his vocation to life with God and to communion with his neighbor. . . . The Church has always taught that one may never choose kinds of behavior prohibited by the moral commandments expressed in negative form in the Old and New Testaments. . . . Jesus himself reaffirms that these prohibitions allow no exceptions."[49]

Such prohibitions, of course, include murder in all its forms. In *Evangelium Vitae*, John Paul explicitly declared the immorality of all intentional killing of the innocent, including abortion and euthanasia:

> Therefore, by the authority which Christ conferred upon Peter and his Successors, and in communion with the Bishops of the Catholic Church, *I confirm that the direct and voluntary killing of an innocent human being is always gravely immoral.*[50]

Evangelium Vitae defined "procured abortion" as "*the deliberate and direct killing, by whatever means it is carried out, of a human being in the initial phase of his or her existence, extending from conception to birth.* The moral gravity of procured abortion is apparent in all its truth if we recognize that we are dealing with murder."[51] "Therefore, by the authority which Christ conferred upon Peter and his Successors, in communion with the Bishops — who on various occasions have condemned abortion and who. . . albeit dispersed throughout the world, have shown unanimous agreement concerning this doctrine — *I declare that direct abortion, that is, abortion willed as an end or as a means, always constitutes a grave moral disorder,* since it is the deliberate killing of an innocent human being."[52] As John Paul said, "a law which violates an innocent person's natural right to life is unjust and, as such, is not valid as a law."[53]

---

[47] *Ibid.*, no. 35.
[48] *Ibid.*, no. 67; see also no. 52.
[49] *Ibid.*, no. 52.
[50] *EV,* no. 57.
[51] *Ibid.*, no. 58.
[52] *Ibid.*, no. 62.
[53] *Ibid.*, no. 90.

Evangelium Vitae defined "*Euthanasia in the strict sense* [as] an action or omission which of itself and by intention causes death, with the purpose of eliminating all suffering. 'Euthanasia's terms of reference, therefore, are to be found in the intention of the will and in the methods used.' . . . Taking into account these distinctions, in harmony with the Magisterium of my Predecessors and in communion with the Bishops of the Catholic Church, *I confirm that euthanasia is a grave violation of the law of God*, since it is the deliberate and morally unacceptable killing of a human person."[54]

The Apostolic Letter, Motu Proprio, *Ad Tuendam Fidem*, issued June 30, 1998, inserted into Canon Law an explicit requirement, subject to "just penalty," that "everything set forth definitively by the Magisterium. . . on faith and morals must be firmly accepted and held."[55] As Cardinals Ratzinger and Bertone noted in their official explanation of *Ad Tuendam Fidem*, this obligation includes "the doctrine on the grave immorality of direct and voluntary killing of an innocent human being."[56]

THE NEW SPRINGTIME

"Dechristianization which weighs heavily upon entire peoples. . . once rich in faith and Christian life," said John Paul, "involves not only the loss of faith or in any event its becoming irrelevant for everyday life, but also, and of necessity, *a decline or obscuring of the moral sense*."[57] This dechristianization presents "a formidable challenge to undertake a 'new evangelization'" which "*also involves the proclamation and presentation of morality*. . . . [T]he new evangelization will. . . unleash all its missionary force when it is carried out through the gift not only of the word proclaimed but also of the word lived."[58] In this way we can hope for "that new springtime of Christian life which will be revealed by the Great Jubilee, if Christians are docile to the action of the Holy Spirit."[59]

So what is the answer to the Enlightenment? "This crisis of civilization must be countered by the civilization of love, founded on the universal values of peace, solidarity, justice and liberty, which find their full attainment in Christ."[60]

---

[54] *Ibid.*, nos. 64-66.
[55] *Code of Canon Law (1983)*, Canons 750, 1371; see the statement by Joseph Cardinal Ratzinger and Archbishop Tarcisio Bertone, *Inside the Vatican*, Aug.-Sept. 1998, 26. See also Canons 598, 1436.
[56] *Inside the Vatican, Ibid.*, at 27.
[57] *VS*, no. 106.
[58] *Ibid.*, nos. 106, 107.
[59] *Tertio Millennio Adveniente*, no. 18.
[60] *Ibid.*, no. 52.

19. So what is the culture of life?

The theme of this book is that the answer to the culture of death in the United States will not be found in politics, lawsuits or press releases. Each person and family will find that answer by living out the social and moral teachings of the Catholic Church. In *Evangelium Vitae*, Pope John Paul II gave prescriptions "For a New Culture of Human Life." The best thing we can do here is to let him say it for himself:

JESUS CHRIST AS THE NORM

"Faced with the. . . threats to life. . . in the modern world," John Paul writes, "one could feel overwhelmed by sheer powerlessness: good can never be powerful enough to triumph over evil! At such times the People of God. . . is called to profess. . . its faith in Jesus Christ, 'the Word of life'. . . . Through the words, the actions and the very person of Jesus, man is given the possibility of 'knowing' the *complete truth* concerning the value of human life. . . . In Christ, the *Gospel of Life* is definitively proclaimed and fully given. This is the Gospel which. . . has echoed in every conscience 'from the beginning,'. . . in such a way that, despite the. . . consequences of sin, *it can also be known in its essential traits by human reason.*"[1]

[T]he deepest element of God's commandment to protect human life is the *requirement to show reverence and love* for every person and the life of every person.[2]

[T]his message. . . is the presentation of human life as a life of relationship, a gift of God, the fruit and sign of his love. It is the proclamation that Jesus has a unique relationship with every person, which enables us to see in every human face the face of Christ. It is the call for a "sincere gift of self" as the fullest way to realize our personal freedom. . . . Not only must human life not be taken, but it must be protected with loving concern. The meaning of life is found in giving and receiving love, and in this light human sexuality and procreation reach their true and full significance. Love also gives meaning to suffering and death. . . . Respect for life requires that science and technology should always be at the service of man and his integral development. Society. . . must. . . promote the dignity of every human person, at every moment and in every condition of that person's life.[3]

---

[1] *EV*, no. 29.
[2] *Ibid.*, no. 41.
[3] *Ibid.*, nos. 80-82.

INITIATIVES FOR LIFE

"We need. . . to *'show care' for all life and for the life of everyone* . . . .
[P]rogrammes of *support for new life* must be implemented, with special
closeness to mothers who, even without the help of the father, are not
afraid to bring their child into the world and to raise it. Similar care
must be shown for the life of the marginalized or suffering, especially in
its final phases. All of this involves. . . *education* aimed at encouraging
one and all to bear each other's burdens. . . It requires a. . . promotion of
vocations to service, particularly among the young. It involves. . . long-
term practical *projects and initiatives* inspired by the Gospel."[4] John Paul
then enumerated some of those "projects and initiatives":

> At the first stage of life, *centres for natural methods of regulating fertility*
> should be promoted. . . in which all individuals, and in the first place
> the child, are. . . respected in their own right, and where every deci-
> sion is guided by the ideal of the sincere gift of self. *Marriage and fam-*
> *ily counseling agencies.* . . help in rediscovering the meaning of life, and
> in supporting. . . every family in its mission as the "sanctuary of life."
> Newborn life is also served by *centres of assistance and homes or centres*
> *where new life receives a welcome.* Thanks to. . . such centres, many un-
> married mothers and couples in difficulty discover new hope and find
> assistance and support. . . .
>
> [O]ther programmes — such as *communities for treating drug addic-*
> *tion, residential communities for minors or the mentally ill, care and relief*
> *centres for AIDS patients, associations for solidarity especially toward the*
> *disabled.* . . give everyone new reasons for hope and practical possibili-
> ties for life.
>
> And when earthly existence draws to a close,. . . charity. . . finds
> the. . . means for enabling the *elderly.* . . and the *terminally ill* to en-
> joy. . . humane assistance and to receive an adequate response to their
> needs, in particular their anxiety and their loneliness. In these cases the
> role of families is indispensable, yet families can receive much help
> from social welfare agencies and, if necessary, from recourse to *pallia-*
> *tive care,* taking advantage of suitable medical and social services avail-
> able in public institutions or in the home."[5]

The Pope emphasized the role of hospitals and health care personnel
and went on to discuss the need for *"social activity and commitment in the*
political field . . . . *Individuals, families.* . . *and associations.* . . have a re-

---

[4] *Ibid.,* nos. 87-88.
[5] *Ibid.,* no. 88.

sponsibility for. . . the building of a society in which the dignity of each person is recognized and protected and the lives of all are defended and enhanced. . . . *[C]ivil leaders*. . . have a duty to make courageous choices in support of life, especially through *legislative measures*. . . . [N]o one can ever renounce this responsibility, especially when he or she has a legislative or decision-making mandate, which calls that person to answer to God, to his or her own conscience and to the whole of society for choices which may be contrary to the common good. Although laws are not the only means of protecting human life, nevertheless they do play. . . a sometimes decisive role in influencing patterns of thought and behaviour. I repeat once more that a law which violates an innocent person's natural right to life is unjust and, as such, is not valid as a law."[6]

SOCIAL AND FAMILY POLICY

"[I]t is difficult to mount an effective legal defence of life in pluralistic democracies . . . . [T]he Church encourages political leaders, starting with those who are Christians, not to give in, but to make those choices which, taking into account what is realistically attainable, will lead to the re-establishment of a just order in the defence and promotion of the value of life. . . [I]t is not enough to remove unjust laws. The underlying causes of attacks on life have to be eliminated, especially by ensuring proper support for families and motherhood.[7]

"Within the 'people of life and the people for life,' *the family has a decisive responsibility* . . . . It is above all in *raising children* that the family fulfills its mission to proclaim the *Gospel of life*. . . through *daily prayer,* both individual prayer and family prayer. . . . [T]he celebration which gives meaning to every other form of prayer and worship is found in *the family's actual daily life together,* if it is a life of love and self-giving. . . . through *solidarity*. . . . A. . . significant expression of solidarity between families is a willingness to *adopt or take in* children abandoned by their parents or in. . . serious hardship. . . . [S]olidarity also needs to be practiced through *participation in social and political life*. . . to ensure that the laws and institutions of the State in no way violate the right to life, from conception to natural death, but rather protect and promote it.[8]

BUILDING A CULTURE OF LIFE

What is urgently called for is a *general mobilization of consciences* and a *united ethical effort* to activate a *great campaign in support of life*. All to-

---

6 *Ibid.,* no. 90.
7 *Ibid.*
8 *Ibid.,* nos. 92-93.

gether we must build a new culture of life. . . . We need to begin with *the renewal of a culture of life within Christian communities themselves* . . . . [W]e need to question how widespread is the culture of life today among individual Christians, families, groups and communities in our Dioceses. . . . [W]e need to promote a serious. . . exchange about basic issues of human life with everyone, including non-believers. . . .

The first. . . step towards this cultural transformation consists in *forming consciences* with regard to the incomparable and inviolable worth of every human life. It is of the greatest importance *to re-establish the essential connection between life and freedom.* . . . There is no true freedom where life is not welcomed and loved; and there is no fullness of life except in freedom. . . . Love, as a sincere gift of self, is what gives the life and freedom of the person their truest meaning.

No less critical in the formation of conscience is *the recovery of the necessary link between freedom and truth.* . . . [W]hen freedom is detached from objective truth it becomes impossible to establish personal rights on a firm rational basis; and the ground is laid for society to be at the mercy of the unrestrained will of individuals or the oppressive totalitarianism of public authority.[9]

"In a word," said John Paul, "the cultural change which we are calling for demands from everyone the courage to *adopt a new life-style,* consisting in making practical choices — at the personal, family, social and international level — on the basis of a correct scale of values: *the primacy of being over having, of the person over things.* This renewed life-style involves a passing *from indifference to concern for others, from rejection to acceptance of them.*"[10] He offered "a special word to *women who have had an abortion.* The church is aware of the many factors which may have influenced your decision, and she does not doubt that in many cases it was a painful and even shattering decision. The wound in your heart may not yet have healed. Certainly what happened was and remains terribly wrong. But do not give in to discouragement and do not lose hope. Try rather to understand what happened and face it honestly. If you have not already done so, give yourselves over with humility and trust to repentance. The Father of mercies is ready to give you his forgiveness and his peace in the Sacrament of Reconciliation. You will come to understand that nothing is definitively lost and you will also be able to ask forgiveness from your child, who is now living in the Lord. With the. . . help of other people, and as a result of your own painful experience, you can be among the most eloquent defenders of everyone's right to life. Through

---

[9] *Ibid.,* nos. 95-96.
[10] *Ibid.,* no. 98.

your commitment to life, whether by accepting the birth of other children or by welcoming and caring for those most in need of someone to be close to them, you will become promoters of a new way of looking at human life."[11]

The Pope emphasized that "Jesus himself has shown us by His own example that prayer and fasting are the first and most effective weapons against the forces of evil. . . . As he taught his disciples, some demons cannot be driven out except in this way. . . . Let us therefore discover anew the humility and the courage to *pray and fast* so that power from on high will break down the walls of lies and deceit: the walls which conceal from the sight of so many of our brothers and sisters the evil of practices and laws which are hostile to life."[12]

"*The Gospel of Life*," moreover, "is not for believers alone: *it is for everyone*. . . . The value at stake is one which every human being can grasp by the light of reason; thus it necessarily concerns everyone. . . .When the Church declares that unconditional respect for the right to life of every innocent person — from conception to natural death — is one of the pillars on which every civil society stands, she 'wants simply *to promote a human State.*'. . . There can be no *true democracy* without a recognition of every person's dignity and without respect for his or her rights.[13]

The Pope concluded *Evangelium Vitae* with emphasis on the role of Mary: "The one who accepted 'Life' in the name of all and for the sake of all was Mary, the Virgin Mother; she is thus most closely and personally associated with the *Gospel of Life*. . . . Mary thus helps the Church to *realize that life is always at the center of a great struggle* between good and evil, between light and darkness. . . . [A]s we. . . the people of life, make our way in confidence 'towards a new heaven and a new earth'. . . we look to her who is for us 'a sign of sure hope and solace.'"[14]

---

[11] *Ibid.,* no. 99.
[12] *Ibid.,* no. 100.
[13] *Ibid.,* no. 101.
[14] *Ibid.,* nos. 102, 104, 105.

B. Some Family Questions

20. WHAT IS THE FAMILY AND HOW DOES IT WORK?

For openers, every married couple — and every person contemplating marriage — ought to read Pope John Paul's *Letter to Families*. Written in 1994 for the UN's International Year of the Family, the *Letter* was addressed "not to families in the abstract but to every particular family in every part of the world."[1] Unfortunately, some people do not read their mail and probably very few have read this *Letter*.

WHAT *IS* THE FAMILY?

"[T]he family," wrote Fr. Paul Scalia, "is the fundamental source and support of a civilization of love because the family preserves the proper understanding of the human person."[2]

The human person is made in the image and likeness of the persons of the Trinity so that relation to others is of his essence. So, too, "the. . . model of the family is. . . in God himself, in the Trinitarian mystery of his life. The divine *we* is the eternal pattern of the human *we*, especially of that *we* formed by the man and the woman created in the divine image and likeness."[3]

The family, "the basic cell of society,"[4] is a relation characterized by covenant, communion and community. The family, "the first human society,. . . arises whenever there comes into being the conjugal covenant of marriage, which opens the spouses to a lasting communion of love and of life, and it is brought to completion. . . with the procreation of children. The communion of the spouses gives rise to the community of the family. The community of the family is. . . pervaded by. . . communion."[5]

> Love causes man to find fulfillment through the sincere gift of self. . . .
> By its very nature the gift of the person must be lasting and irrevocable. The indissolubility of marriage flows in the first place from the very essence of that. . . gift of one person to another person. . . .

---

[1] *LF,* no. 4.
[2] Paul Scalia, "The Role of the Family in John Paul II's Program for Building the Civilization of Love," 23 *Faith & Reason*, 255, 256 (1997-98).
[3] *Ibid.,* no. 6.
[4] *Ibid.,* no. 4.
[5] *Ibid.,* no. 7; on solidarity as experienced within and around the family, see *EV,* no. 93.

In the newborn child is realized the common good of the family. . . . A child comes to take up room when it seems that there is less and less room in the world. But is it really true that a child brings nothing to the family and society?. . . The child becomes a gift to its. . . entire family. . . .

The family is. . . the place where an individual can exist for himself through the sincere gift of self. This is why it. . . neither can nor should be replaced: It is the "sanctuary of life."[6]

"The family is. . . a community of generations. In prayer every one should be present; the living and those who have died, and also those yet to come into the world. [T]he times in which we are living tend to restrict family units to two generations. Often this is the case because. . . housing is too limited. . . . But it is not infrequently due to the belief that having several generations living together interferes with privacy and makes life too difficult. But is this not where the problem really lies? Families today have too little 'human' life. There is a shortage of people with whom to create and share the common good; and yet that good, by its nature, demands to be created and shared with others."[7]

RESPONSIBLE PARENTHOOD

What is "responsible fatherhood and motherhood"? John Paul puts this often misused term in a new perspective. In "the moment of conjugal union. . . a man and woman. . . become a mutual gift to each other. All married life is a gift; but this becomes most evident when the spouses. . . bring about that encounter which makes them one flesh. . . . Both are responsible for their potential and later actual fatherhood and motherhood. The husband cannot fail to acknowledge and accept the result of a decision which has also been his own. He cannot hide behind expressions such as, 'I don't know,' 'I didn't want it' or 'you're the one who wanted it.' In every case conjugal union involves. . . a potential responsibility which becomes actual when the circumstances dictate. . . . The man and the woman must assume together. . . the responsibility for the new life which they have brought into existence. . . . [T]he total gift of self to the other involves a potential openness to procreation: In this way the marriage is called to even greater fulfillment as a family. Certainly the mutual gift of husband and wife does not have the begetting of children as its only end, but is in itself a mutual communion of love and of life."[8]

---

[6] *LF,* no. 11.
[7] *Ibid.,* no. 10.
[8] *Ibid.,* no. 12.

COMMUNION

"The two dimensions of conjugal union," the *Letter* said, "cannot be artificially separated without damaging the deepest truth of the conjugal act itself."[9] In other words, the contracepting couple, who seek the unitive while deliberately frustrating the procreative, will end up with neither. John Paul spells out the contrast between this "truth about freedom and the communion of persons" and the utilitarian "civilization in which persons are used in the same way as things are used."

> [C]ontemporary civilization is linked to a scientific and technological progress which is often. . . one-sided. . . and. . . positivistic. Positivism. . . results in agnosticism in theory and utilitarianism in practice and in ethics. In our own day history is in a way repeating itself. Utilitarianism is a civilization of production and of use,. . . of things and not of persons,. . . in which persons are used in the same way as things are used. In. . . a civilization of use, woman can become an object for man, children a hindrance to parents, the family an institution obstructing the freedom of its members. To be convinced that this is the case, one need only look at certain sexual education programs introduced into the schools, often notwithstanding. . . the protests of many parents; or pro-abortion tendencies which vainly try to hide behind the so-called right to choose. . . .
>
> So-called safe sex. . . is radically not safe. . . . It endangers both the person and the family. . . . It is the loss of the truth about one's own self and about the family, together with the risk of a loss of freedom and consequently of a loss of love itself. . . .
>
> A love which is. . . reduced only to the satisfaction of concupiscence. . . or to a man's and a woman's mutual "use" of each other, makes persons slaves to their weaknesses. Do not certain modern "cultural agendas" lead to this enslavement?. . .
>
> The civilization of love evokes joy: joy, among other things, for the fact that. . . spouses have become parents. . . . But a civilization inspired by a consumerist, anti-birth mentality. . . cannot ever be a civilization of love.[10]

INDIVIDUALISM VS. PERSONALISM

The contrast between individualism and personalism is a major component of John Paul's analysis of what he calls the "civilization of

---

[9] *Ibid.*, no. 12.
[10] *Ibid.*, no. 13.

love." "In this concept what is important is not so much individual actions (whether selfish or altruistic), so much as the radical acceptance of the understanding of man as a person who 'finds himself' by making a sincere gift of self. A gift, is obviously, 'for others.' This is the most important dimension of the civilization of love."[11]

"We thus come," continues John Paul, "to the very heart of the Gospel truth about freedom. The person realizes himself by the exercise of freedom in truth. Freedom cannot be. . . a license to do absolutely anything; it means a gift of self. . . . The idea of gift contains not only the free initiative of the subject, but also the aspect of duty. All this is made real in the 'communion of persons.' We find ourselves again at the very heart of each family.

"Continuing this line of thought, we also come upon the antithesis between individualism and personalism. Love, the civilization of love, is bound up with personalism. Why with personalism? And why does individualism threaten the civilization of love? We find a key to answering this in the council's expression, a 'sincere gift.' Individualism presupposes a use of freedom in which the subject does what he wants, in which he himself is the one to 'establish the truth' of whatever he finds pleasing or useful. He does not tolerate the fact that someone else 'wants' or demands some thing from him in the name of an objective truth. He does not want to 'give' to another on the basis of truth, he does not want to become a 'sincere gift.' Individualism thus remains egocentric and selfish. The real antithesis between individualism and personalism emerges not only on the level of theory, but even more on that of ethos. The ethos of personalism is altruistic. It moves the person to become a gift for others and to discover joy in giving himself. . . .

"Opposed to the civilization of love is certainly. . . so-called free love; this is. . . usually suggested as a way of following one's 'real' feelings, but it is. . . destructive of love. . . . Free love exploits human weaknesses. It gives them a certain veneer of respectability with the help of seduction and the blessing of public opinion. In this way there is an attempt to soothe consciences by creating a 'moral alibi.' But not all of the consequences are taken into consideration, especially when *the ones who end up paying are, apart from the other spouse, the children, deprived of a father or mother and condemned to be in fact orphans of living parents* . . . .

"[A]t the foundation of ethical utilitarianism. . . is the continual quest for 'maximum' happiness. But this is a utilitarian happiness, seen

---

[11] *Ibid.*, no. 14. See also Mark Zwick and Louise Zwick, "Personalism vs. Individualism," *Houston Catholic Worker*, Mar.-Apr. 1998, p. 1.

only as pleasure, as immediate gratification for the exclusive benefit of the individual. . . . The program of utilitarianism based on an individualistic understanding of freedom — freedom without responsibilities — is the opposite of love . . . . When this concept of freedom is embraced by society and quickly allies itself with varied forms of human weakness, it soon proves a systematic and permanent threat to the family."[12]

PERMISSIVENESS

John Paul defined the family so as to exclude homosexual unions from that definition and to affirm the family as a society in its own right vis-a-vis the State:

> Marriage,. . . is constituted by the covenant whereby "a man and a woman establish. . . a partnership of their whole life," which. . ."is ordered to the well-being of the spouses and to the procreation and upbringing of children." Only such a union can be recognized. . . as a "marriage" in society. Other interpersonal unions. . . cannot be recognized, despite. . . trends which represent a. . . threat to the future of the family and of society itself.

> No human society can run the risk of permissiveness. . . regarding the nature of marriage and the family. Such moral permissiveness cannot fail to damage. . . peace and communion among people. . . . As a community of love and life, the family is . . . . in a way entirely its own, a sovereign society, albeit conditioned in certain ways. . . .

> But the rights of the family are not simply the sum total of the rights of the person, since the family is much more than the sum of its individual members. It is a community of parents and children, and at times a community of several generations. . . . The Charter of the Rights of the Family. . .consolidates the existence of the institution of the family in the social and juridical order of the "greater" society — those of the nation, of the state and of international communities. . . . Only in those situations where the family is not really self-sufficient does the state have the authority and a duty to intervene.[13]

THE HUMAN BODY

In his Wednesday general audiences between September 1979 and November 1984, John Paul spoke on the theology of the body. He returned to that theme in *Letter to Families,* noting a "tendency to consider the human body, not in accordance with. . . its. . . likeness to God,

---

[12] *LF.,* no. 14 (emphasis added).
[13] *Ibid.,* nos. 16-17.

but. . . on the basis of its similarity to all the other bodies. . . in the world of nature, bodies which man uses as raw material in his efforts to produce goods for consumption. But everyone can. . . realize what. . . dangers lurk behind the application of such criteria to man. When the human body, considered apart from spirit and thought, comes to be used as raw material in the same way that bodies of animals are used. . . for example in experimentation on embryos and fetuses — we will inevitably arrive at a dreadful ethical defeat. . . .

"[T]he human family is facing. . . a new Manichaeism, in which body and spirit are put in radical opposition, the body does not receive life from the spirit, and the spirit does not give life to the body. Man thus ceases to live as a person and a subject. . . . [H]e becomes merely an object. This neo-Manichaean culture has led. . . to human sexuality being regarded more as an area for manipulation and exploitation. . . . If an individual is exclusively concerned with use, he can reach the point of killing love by killing the fruit of love. For the culture of use, the 'blessed fruit of your womb' (Lk. 1:42) becomes in a certain sense an 'accursed fruit.'"[14]

WITNESS

John Paul concludes his *Letter to Families*: "Written testimonies alone. . . will not suffice. Much more important are living testimonies. As Pope Paul VI observed, 'Contemporary man listens more willingly to witnesses than to teachers, and if he listens to teachers, it is because they are witnesses.'. . . The history of mankind, the history of salvation, passes by way of the family. . . . May Mary, mother of fairest love, and Joseph, guardian of the Redeemer, accompany us all with their constant protection."[15]

---

[14] *Ibid.*, nos.19, 21; see Christopher West, "John Paul's Distinctive Contribution," *Inside the Vatican*, Nov. 1998, 42.

[15] *LF,* no. 23.

21. How can the civil law help the family?

In *Evangelium Vitae,* John Paul said: "*a family policy must be the basis and the driving force of all social policies.* . . . It is also necessary to rethink labour, urban, residential and social service policies so as to harmonize working schedules with time available for the family, so that it becomes effectively possible to take care of children and the elderly."[1] And in his *Letter to Families,* John Paul said: "[T]he Holy See published in 1983 the *Charter of the Rights of the Family;* even today this document has lost none of its relevance. . . . The *Charter.* . . consolidates the. . . family in the social and juridical order of. . . the nation, of the state and of international communities."[2]

In its preamble the *Charter* states: "[T]he family, a natural society, exists prior to the state or any other community, and possesses inherent rights which are inalienable. . . . Society. . . must protect the family. . . so that it can exercise its specific function."[3]

The *Charter of the Rights of the Family* is more than a cookbook listing of legislative proposals. Rather it is a road map to the principles and objectives that ought to guide legislators and citizens as to the duty of the state toward the family. It has to be read in full to be appreciated:

Article 1
All persons have the right to the free choice of their state of life and, thus, to marry and establish a family or to remain single.

a) Every man and every woman, having reached the age of marriage and having the necessary capacity, has the right to marry and establish a family without any discrimination whatsoever; legal restrictions to the exercise of this right, whether. . . permanent or temporary. . . can be introduced only when they are required by grave and objective demands of the institution of marriage itself and its social and public significance; they must respect in all cases the dignity and the fundamental rights of the person.

b) Those who wish to marry and establish a family have the right to expect from society the moral, educational, social and economic conditions which will enable them to exercise their right to marry in all maturity and responsibility.

---

[1] *EV,* no. 90.
[2] *LF,* no. 17.
[3] 29 *The Pope Speaks* 78, 80 (1984).

c) The institutional value of marriage should be upheld by the public authorities; the situation of non-married couples must not be placed on the same level as marriage duly contracted.

Article 2

Marriage cannot be contracted except by the free and full consent of the spouses duly expressed.

a) With due respect for the traditional role of the families in certain cultures in guiding the decision of their children, all pressure which would impede the choice of a specific person as spouse is to be avoided.

b) The future spouses have the right to their religious liberty. Therefore, to impose as a prior condition for marriage a denial of faith or a profession of faith which is contrary to conscience, constitutes a violation of this right.

c) The spouses, in the natural complementarity which exists between man and woman, enjoy the same dignity and equal rights regarding the marriage.

Article 3

The spouses have the inalienable right to found a family and to decide on the spacing of births and the number of children to be born, taking into full consideration their duties toward themselves, their children already born, the family and society, in a just hierarchy of values and in accordance with the objective moral order which excludes recourse to contraception, sterilization and abortion.

a) The activities of public authorities and private organizations which attempt in any way to limit the freedom of couples in deciding about their children constitute a grave offense against human dignity and justice.

b) In international relations, economic aid for the advancement of peoples must not be conditioned on acceptance of programs of contraception, sterilization or abortion.

c) The family has a right to assistance by society in the bearing and rearing of children. Those married couples who have a large family have a right to adequate aid and should not be subjected to discrimination.

Article 4

Human life must be respected and protected absolutely from the moment of conception.

a) Abortion is a direct violation of the fundamental right to life of the human being.

b) Respect of the dignity of the human being excludes all experimental manipulation or exploitation of the human embryo.

c) All interventions on the genetic heritage of the human person that are not aimed at correcting anomalies constitute a violation of the right to bodily integrity and contradict the good of the family.

d) Children, both before and after birth, have the right to special protection and assistance, as do their mothers during pregnancy and for a reasonable period of time after child-birth.

e) All children, whether born in or out of wedlock, enjoy the same right to social protection, with a view to their integral personal development.

f) Orphans or children who are deprived of the assistance of their parents or guardians must receive particular protection on the part of society. The state, with regard to foster-care or adoption, must provide legislation which assists suitable families to welcome into their home children who are in need of permanent or temporary care. This legislation must, at the same time, respect the natural rights of the parents.

g) Children who are handicapped have the right to find in the home and the school an environment suitable to their human development.

Article 5

Since they have conferred life on their children, parents have the original, primary and inalienable right to educate them; hence they must be acknowledged as the first and foremost educators of their children.

a) Parents have the right to educate their children in conformity with their moral and religious convictions, taking into account the cultural traditions of the family which favor the good and the dignity of the child; they should also receive from society the necessary aid and assistance to perform their educational role properly.

b) Parents have the right to choose freely schools or other means necessary to educate their children in keeping with their convictions.

Public authorities must ensure that public subsidies are so allocated that parents are truly free to exercise this right without incurring unjust burdens. Parents should not have to sustain, directly or indirectly, extra charges which would deny or unjustly limit the exercise of this freedom.[4]

c) Parents have the right to ensure that their children are not compelled to attend classes which are not in agreement with their own moral and religious convictions. In particular, sex education is a basic right of the parents and must always be carried out under their close supervision, whether at home or in educational centers chosen and controlled by them.

d) The rights of parents are violated when a compulsory system of education is imposed by the state from which all religious formation is excluded.

e) The primary right of parents to educate their children must be upheld in all forms of collaboration between parents, teachers and school authorities, and particularly in forms of participation designed to give citizens a voice in the functioning of schools and in the formulation and implementation of educational policies.

f) The family has the right to expect that the means of social communication will be positive instruments for the building up of society, and will reinforce the fundamental values of the family. At the same time the family has the right to be adequately protected, especially with regard to its youngest members, from the negative effects and misuse of the mass media.

Article 6
The family has the right to exist and to progress as a family.

a) Public authorities must respect and foster the dignity, lawful independence, privacy, integrity and stability of every family.

b) Divorce attacks the very institution of marriage and of the family.

c) The extended family system, where it exists, should be held in esteem and helped to carry out better its traditional role of solidarity and mutual assistance, while at the same time respecting the rights of the nuclear family and the personal dignity of each member.

---

[4] See Question 23, recommending an increase in the personal income tax exemption as an alternative to school vouchers.

Article 7

Every family has the right to live freely its own domestic religious life under the guidance of the parents, as well as the right to profess publicly and to propagate the faith, to take part in public worship and in freely chosen programs of religious instruction, without suffering discrimination.

Article 8

The family has the right to exercise its social and political function in the construction of society.

a) Families have the right to form associations with other families and institutions, in order to fulfill the family's role suitably and effectively, as well as to protect the rights, foster the good and represent the interests of the family.

b) On the economic, social, juridical and cultural levels, the rightful role of families and family associations must be recognized in the planning and development of programs which touch on family life.

Article 9

Families have the right to be able to rely on an adequate family policy on the part of public authorities in the juridical, economic, social and fiscal domains, without any discrimination whatsoever.

a) Families have the right to economic conditions which assure them a standard of living appropriate to their dignity and full development. They should not be impeded from acquiring and maintaining private possessions which would favor stable family life; the laws concerning inheritance or transmission of property must respect the needs and rights of family members.

b) Families have the right to measures in the social domain which take into account their needs, especially in the event of the premature death of one or both parents, of the abandonment of one of the spouses, of accident, or sickness or invalidity, in the case of unemployment, or whenever the family has to bear extra burdens on behalf of its members for reasons of old age, physical or mental handicaps or the education of children.

c) The elderly have the right to find within their own family or, when this is not possible, in suitable institutions, an environment which will enable them to live their later years of life in serenity while pursuing those activities which are compatible with their age and which enable them to participate in social life.

d) The rights and necessities of the family, and especially the value of family unity, must be taken into consideration in penal legislation and policy, in such a way that a detainee remains in contact with his or her family and that the family is adequately sustained during the period of detention.

Article 10
Families have a right to a social and economic order in which the organi-zation of work permits the members to live together, and does not hinder the unity, well-being, health and the stability of the family, while offering also the possibility of wholesome recreation.

a) Remuneration for work must be sufficient for establishing and maintaining a family with dignity, either through a suitable salary, called a "family wage," through other social measures such as family allowances or the remuneration of the work in the home of one of the parents; it should be such that mothers will not be obliged to work outside the home to the detriment of family life and especially of the education of the children.

b) The work of the mother in the home must be recognized and re-spected because of its value for the family and for society.

Article 11
The family has the right to decent housing, fitting for family life and com-mensurate to the number of the members; in a physical environment that provides the basic services for the life of the family and the community.

Article 12
The families of migrants have the right to the same protection as that ac-corded other families.

a) The families of immigrants have the right to respect for their own culture and to receive support and assistance toward their integration into the community to which they contribute.

b) Emigrant workers have the right to see their family united as soon as possible.

c) Refugees have the right to the assistance of public authorities and international organizations in facilitating the reunion of their fami-lies.[5]

---

[5] 29 *The Pope Speaks* 78, 81-85 (1984) (emphasis added).

THE SOVEREIGN FAMILY

The family has a claim on society and the state for recognition and support, as specified in the *Charter*. However, the family is not a mere adjunct of the state and the culture. "Every effort should be made," said John Paul, "so that the family will be recognized as the primordial and in a certain sense sovereign society! The sovereignty of the family is essential for the good of society. A truly sovereign and spiritually vigorous nation is always made up of strong families who are aware of their vocation and mission in history."[6]

---

[6] *LF*, no. 17.

22. IF WE ARE GOING TO LIVE THE CULTURE OF LIFE, HOW SHOULD WE EDUCATE OUR KIDS? SHOULD WE GIVE UP ON THE PUBLIC SCHOOLS?

I think that the most important factor moving us toward a secular society has been the educational factor. Our schools may not teach Johnny to read properly, but the fact that Johnny is in school until he is sixteen tends to lead toward the elimination of religious superstition. The average American child now acquires a high-school education, and this militates against Adam and Eve and all other myths of alleged history. . . . When I was one of the editors of *The Nation* in the twenties, I wrote an editorial explaining that golf and intelligence were the two primary reasons that men did not attend church. Perhaps I would now say golf and a high-school diploma. — *Paul Blanshard* [1]

About 64% of American students are enrolled in public schools. 51,484,000 students were enrolled in public elementary and secondary schools in 1996-97.[2] In 1995-96, 6,357,000 students were in private non-sectarian schools, 8,248,000 were in Catholic schools and 13,081,600 in other religious schools,[3] for a total private school enrollment of 27,686,000. In 1996-97 an estimated 1,230,000 students, at elementary and secondary level, were educated in home schools in the United States. Home schooling is permitted in every state, subject to regulations.[4] Various organizations provide advice and assistance to supporters of private schools and home schools with respect to government efforts to restrict and obstruct those schools.[5]

While "parents. . . must. . . be recognized as being primarily and principally responsible for the education of their children,"[6] the common good may require that the state itself conduct schools at appropriate levels: "[W]hen the efforts of the parents and of other organizations are inadequate, [civil society] should itself undertake the duty of educa-

---

[1] Paul Blanshard, "Three Cheers for Our Secular State," *Humanist*, Mar.-Apr. 1976, 17.
[2] U.S. Dept. of Education, Nat'l. Center for Education Statistics, *Digest of Education Statistics*, 1996, table 3.
[3] U.S. Dept. of Education, Nat'l. Center for Education Statistics, *Private School Survey*, 1995-96.
[4] See *National Survey of State Laws* (Richard A. Leiter, ed., 1997), ch. 13. For statistical information on home schooling, contact National Home Education Research Institute, P.O. Box 13939, Salem, OR 97309, (503) 364-1490.
[5] Contact Home School Legal Defense Assn., P.O. Box 3000, Purcellville, VA 20134, (540) 338-5600; see Kimberly Hahn and Mary Hasson, *Catholic Education: Homeward Bound* (1996); see Dr. Mary K. Clark, "Home Schoolers: Educators Because They Are Parents," *Forum Focus* (Wanderer Forum Foundation, Fall 1998), 23.
[6] Vatican II, *Declaration on Christian Education*, no. 3.

tion with due consideration. . . for the wishes of the parents [and] insofar as the common good requires it, it should establish its own schools
and institutes."[7] We ought to recognize, however, three widely misun-
derstood realities about the role of the state — that is, the federal, state
or local government — in education in the United States:

> *First*, the state did not become the major provider of education,
> through its own schools, until the middle of the nineteenth century.
> Until then, education was the responsibility of families and churches.

> *Second*, the state, at least in recent decades, has not demonstrated its
> competence in education; and

> *Third*, the state schools have become instruments for the inculcation
> of a secular religion.

1. The state is a latecomer to the education business.

Elementary and secondary education in the United States was private and religious in its origin and it had a generally Christian stamp for
much of its history, even after the state assumed the role of educator. In
the colonial period, schooling was essentially a function of the church.
Where a colony had an official religion, as in New England, the schools
of that religion received state support. They were "sectarian public
schools, where the public supported a single established religion and
where dissenters' schools were not allowed to function."[8] The religious
character of the schools, including those with public support, generally
continued into the post-Revolutionary period. It was "an age of sectarian
public education."[9]

Interest in public schools began to grow in the 1830s and 1840s,
with the emergence of Horace Mann as a crusader for nonsectarian public schools in which the great "common truths" of Christianity would be
taught. One reason for the success of his movement was a reluctance to
subsidize Catholic schools and the fear that, if the publicly supported
schools remained sectarian, the increasing proportion of Catholics
would cause those schools to become effectively Catholic:

> The period from 1830 through the 1840's saw not only an increase in
> the number of Protestant sects, but an enormous influx of Roman

---

[7] *Ibid.*

[8] Donald E. Boles, *The Bible, Religion, and the Public Schools* (1965), 4.

[9] Charles E. Rice, "Conscientious Objection to Public Education: The Grievance and
the Remedies," *Brigham Young L. Rev.* (1978), 847, 850.

Catholic immigrants. The fear that early Catholic opposition to Bible reading and other Protestant practices in the public schools would lead to Catholic domination led to open and at times violent hostility toward Roman Catholics. Debates over the efficacy of Bible reading became increasingly common during this time, and the extreme Protestant opposition to the Catholic viewpoint finally crystallized in the Know-Nothing political movement which was organized officially as a party in 1853. During this period of strife, Horace Mann, the father of the public school system in America, emerged as the great crusader against sectarianism in the public schools.[10]

The public or common schools under Mann's concept were nonsectarian, but not in the way we use that term today. They incorporated into their teaching a common denominator Protestantism anchored on Scripture. But the point to remember here is that the state-conducted school cannot trace its dominance to the founding of the nation. It did not become the major player on the American educational scene until at least the mid-nineteenth century.

2. The state, at least in recent decades, has not shown its competence in education.

Res ipsa loquitur. The thing speaks for itself. The massacre in April, 1999 at Columbine High School in Littleton, Colorado, and similar incidents reinforce the perception of public schools as potentially dangerous places under siege.[11] While the metal detector has become a symbol of the modern public school, those schools are also failing in their primary educational mission. In fairness, however, we have to recognize that elementary and secondary education in general, whether public or private, is not as effective as it used to be, especially in literacy and math. If you doubt this, take a look at *The Federalist,* the essays written by Hamilton, Madison and Jay to persuade the people of New York to support the Constitution. Those essays were published in newspapers read by upstate New York farmers who had three or four years of church school education. Try them out today on a high school or college student. I can tell you that law students today find them intricate and challenging. Some years ago I assigned to a law school class in constitutional law a passage from Blackstone to the right of property. Several of those college graduates remarked that it was more demanding than the usual material. It was difficult for them, whether they were products of public, Catholic or other private schools. I then told them I had copied it from

---

[10] *Boles,* at 23.
[11] See *N.Y. Times,* Apr. 22, 1999, p. A1; *N.Y. Times,* May 21, 1999, p. A1.

McGuffey's sixth reader, which was a staple in the education of pre-teens in the nineteenth century. Students in 1911 in Indiana rural public schools who wanted to attend public high school had to pass an exam– covering Geography, Grammar, Arithmetic, Physiology, Reading and History– that would perhaps daunt a Ph.D. candidate today.[12]

It is fair to say, however, that the public, or state, schools have generally sunk to a performance level far below that of Catholic and other private schools.[13] That state schools have "dumbed down" their students is beyond dispute, as any non-comatose parent can attest. "The best thing we can do for American education is to abolish university education departments and the U.S. Department of Education, and fire education 'experts.'. . . Over the last 30 years, achievement-test scores have been in free fall. . . . On a recent test, one-third of high school seniors couldn't identify Abraham Lincoln or the countries we fought during W.W. II. Only 6 percent could solve the following math problem: 'Christine borrows $850 for one year at 12 percent. What will be the total amount of money she repays?' A major insurance company reports that 44 percent of its applicants couldn't read at the ninth-grade level. Eighty percent of a major manufacturer's applicants flunked its fifth-grade math and seventh-grade English competency tests. Few Americans need more proof that our education system is in shambles — but why it's in shambles is important for the cure. . . . [T]he widely used book, 'Secondary Math: An Integrated Approach,' features color photos and essays on the Dogon tribe of Africa, and pictures of Maya Angelou and Bill Clinton. It also asks questions such as 'What role should zoos play in today's society?'. . . Much of the explanation for educational rot is connected to the fact that 1960s hippies have taken over colleges of education and dominate the education establishment. Their vision is that high academic standards are elitist. To discriminate among students, based on academic excellence, risks injuring their self-esteem; failure must be defined out of existence."[14]

"The public schools," said Thomas Sowell, "do not merely fail to develop a sense of systematic reasoning, they actively promote an emphasis on 'feeling,' lofty rhetoric and psycho-babble."[15] "There were four birds in a nest and one flew away. How do you think the bird felt that flew

---

[12] See *Letter* from William H. Bell, *Wall St. Journal*, July 25, 1983, p. 9.

[13] See John Chodes, "Public Education — Dump It," *N.Y. Times*, Dec. 19, 1988, p. 23. Star Parker, "The Money Trail to Better Education," *Wash. Times*, Aug. 4, 1998, p. A17; John Leo, "Dumbed Down," *Dallas Morning News*, Sept. 12, 1996, p. A31.

[14] Walter Williams, "Misguided by the Experts," *Wash. Times*, May 10, 1997, p. D1.

[15] Thomas Sowell, "The Larger Suicide That Confronts Us," *Wash. Times*, Apr. 6, 1997, p. B1.

away from the nest? This was a 'math' question that a baffled parent in Pennsylvania discovered was asked of her child in a public school."[16] Examples could be multiplied, but we can lay on the public schools the reality that standard, literate English is now a foreign language for many younger Americans.

Apart from the poor quality of the education they provide, the public schools ought to be rejected for another reason by parents who seek to raise their children in the culture of life. That reason is the character of public education as an aggressive promoter of a secular religious approach hostile to Christian belief.

3. The state schools indoctrinate their students in a religion of secularism.

"In reaction to the pre-Civil War Catholic efforts to remove 'common denominator' Protestant influence from the public schools, Protestant support for those schools increased. The resolution of the controversy. . . was that public funds would not be used for parochial schools of any denomination, but the public schools would retain their common denominator Christianity with Bible reading at least encouraged and, if possible, required. This condition continued through the late nineteenth and the early twentieth centuries. The decades of the 1930s and 1940s, however, saw a rise in opposition on the part of secularists and others to such theistic manifestations in public schools. In the 1960s, this opposition prevailed with the elimination of prayer, Bible reading, and other theistic practices from public schools."[17]

"The essence of education is that it be religious," wrote Alfred North Whitehead.[18] The legitimacy of religious influence in education, whether public or private, was acknowledged throughout our history, until recently. Today, the public school purports to be nonreligious. Justice Robert Jackson, in his 1947 *Everson* dissent, accurately observed that the public school "is organized on the premise that secular education can be isolated from all religious teaching. . . . The assumption is that after the individual has been instructed in worldly wisdom he will be better fitted to choose his religion."[19] But that stance of the public school is itself a religious position, affirming the separability of religion from secu-

---

[16] Richard Grenier, "Dumb Times Ahead with Fuzzy Math," *Wash. Times,* Oct. 24, 1997, p. A23.

[17] Charles E. Rice, "Conscientious Objection to Public Education: The Grievance and the Remedies," *Brigham Young Univ. L. Rev.* (1978) 847, 849-53.

[18] Alfred North Whitehead, *The Aims of Education* (1929), 25.

[19] *Everson v. Board of Education,* 330 U.S. 1, 23-24 (1947) (Jackson, J., dissenting).

lar life. If elementary and secondary education has an inherent religious character, how could the state's assumption of the role of educator be consistent with the neutrality mandate of the Establishment Clause as presently interpreted?[20] The nonjudgmental treatment of moral issues without any affirmation of the supernatural is itself an implicitly religious assertion that contradictory moral positions are equally tenable, that there is therefore no objective and binding moral order, and that the supernatural is not a necessary factor in the making of moral decisions. As Patrick Cardinal O'Boyle commented:

> Of course, it may be argued that the public schools need not favor any particular religion or religion at all, for they can proceed on strictly humanistic, pragmatic and secular conceptions. But this is precisely the point. To proceed in this way is itself to establish a religion– secular humanism — and to favor this religion over all others. . . .

> Historically, John Dewey, who has so much to do with progressive education, which deeply affected the philosophical foundations of our present public schools, spoke of his own beliefs, which were a form of secular humanism, in religious terms. In a statement first published in 1897, entitled *My Pedagogic Creed,* Dewey said that in shaping children as members of secular society the teacher is "always the prophet of the true God and the usherer in of the kingdom of God."

> For Dewey, the true God is not the Holy Trinity, but is the human community; the true kingdom of God is not heaven, but is the secular city perfected by applied science. Dewey claimed that public schools, in contributing to the realization of this ideal, would be doing a genuinely religious work, more so indeed than could be done with all of the paraphernalia of traditional religion.[21]

"The public school is a religious institution whose creed is secularism. This condition would not be cured by working a prayer into the school day or even by allowing instruction by religious groups on public school premises. At best, an amorphous theism would come to be the religion of the public school. In fact, the public schools are not worth saving. Through their 'objective' presentation of all points of view they tend to indoctrinate their pupils with agnostic secularism and pragmatism. Through sex education and similar activities, they undermine the family and corrupt the youth by the inculcation of contraceptive and other anti-life attitudes. Whatever parental influence existed in those schools a

---

[20] See Question 10.
[21] *Catholic Currents,* Nov. 15, 1971, p. 3.

decade ago has been minimized by the schools' intrusion into the subjects of family life and sex and by the breakup of neighborhood schools under the edicts of federal judges."[22]

A properly ordered state can be justified in conducting schools when parents and churches cannot do it. But that justification cannot apply where the state is embarked on the establishment of secular humanism as its national creed.[23] Such a state has no moral right to educate the young. In this country, moreover, parents and churches, and especially the Catholic Church, have the potential to be fully capable of educating the youth. The major difficulty is financial, and it is created by the appetite of the state for taxes to support a public school system which is unnecessary and detrimental.

We ought not to underestimate the impact of the secular religion of the public schools. A steady classroom diet of suspended judgment and laissez faire on moral issues can influence the students away from an acknowledgment of an objective law of God. There is logic in this comment by a writer in *The American Atheist*:

> And how does a god die? Quite simply because all his religionists have been converted to another religion, and there is no one left to make children believe they need him.

> Finally, it is irresistible — we must ask how we can kill the god of Christianity. We need only insure that our schools teach only secular knowledge; that they teach children to constantly examine and question all theories and truths put before them in any form; and that they teach that nothing is proven by the number of persons who believe a thing to be true. If we could achieve this, god would indeed be shortly due for a funeral service.[24]

Public schools have never been religiously neutral. Today, the religion of secular humanism has merely displaced the old common denominator Protestantism. The many abuses in the areas of sex education, "values clarification" and such are not aberrations in the system. They are rather inevitable developments of the religion of secular humanism. There is no point in trying to sanitize the public schools. We should not disparage the numerous teachers and administrators who do their best within a failed system. Nor can we deny that some public

---

[22] Charles E. Rice, *Beyond Abortion: The Theory and Practice of the Secular State* (1979), 67-68.

[23] See Question 10.

[24] G. Richard Bozarth, "On Keeping God Alive," *American Atheist*, Nov. 1977, 7, 8.

schools are academically excellent and that, in some circumstances, a student can become stronger in his faith through attending a public school.[25] However, in general, public elementary and secondary education in this country is an idea whose time has gone. It is time to reduce and eventually eliminate the compulsion of taxpayers to support the failed enterprise of public education.

In Question 23 we will discuss tax and other policies which could enable parents to regain control of the education of their children. The movement to separate school and state has gained ground in recent years.[26] That movement is not merely an attack on public schools. Rather it seeks to assert the rights of parents and to enhance the ability of private and home schools to do their job. The leaders of the future will come from those schools. Among other reasons, because they can read and write.

---

[25] See Germain Grisez, "How Can Catholics in Public Schools Avoid Being of Their World?" *Lay Witness,* Sept. 1996, p. 8.

[26] For information, contact Separation of School and State Alliance, 4578 N. First, Fresno, CA 93726, (209) 292-1776.

23. BUT SHOULDN'T THE STATE PROVIDE VOUCHERS OR TAX CREDITS FOR STUDENTS IN PRIVATE SCHOOLS?

This is a tough question. Parents who support vouchers or other forms of "school choice" seek only justice. Many of them pay taxes to support a failed system of state schools which they find objectionable for their own children on grounds of educational quality, morality or safety. Their tax burden can be the decisive factor in preventing those parents from paying tuition at the nonpublic schools they would prefer. In fairness, should not the government pay a mere fraction of the per pupil cost of public education to parents who would prefer to use the private schools? Private education serves a public purpose, and the cost of having a student use a voucher to attend a private school is less than what it would cost to educate that child in a public school. And when that child is from a family in poverty, the voucher can appear as his only ticket out of a dead-end public school. The "school choice" movement affirms parental rights, it promotes fairness and it challenges the arbitrary interpretations of the First Amendment that prevent even indirect public aid to religious schools.

These and other arguments for vouchers or educational tax credits are powerful. There is, however, another perspective from which government aid can be seen as a trap. Vouchers or tax credits can be used only at schools approved by the state and they expose those schools to detrimental control by the state.

How would history evaluate the judgment of a passenger on the Titanic who had escaped but then climbed back on board so he could ride the ship to the bottom? His deficiency of judgment would be comparable to that of Catholic and other parents who support vouchers (or tax credits) to pay tuition at private schools. The Titanic here is the system of state schools, which is sinking of its own weight. Instead of moving clear so as to keep the Catholic and other private schools afloat, voucher proponents are climbing aboard the public school wreck as it slides beneath the waves.

THE MILWAUKEE PROGRAM

In 1998, the Supreme Court of Wisconsin upheld school vouchers under the Milwaukee Parental Choice Program (MPCP).[1] The Supreme Court of the United States declined to review the case.[2] The Supreme Court's decision not to review was not an endorsement of the MPCP.

---

[1] *Jackson v. Benson*, 578 N.W.2d 602 (Wis., 1998).
[2] *Jackson v. Benson*, 119 S.Ct. 466 (1998).

But it leaves the Wisconsin court's ruling in place as the highest judicial ruling upholding the constitutionality of vouchers.[3]

Under the MPCP, the parent or guardian receives a voucher, a check, which he can endorse to a participating school to pay for his child's education in grades K-12 at that school. "Pupils are eligible under the amended MPCP," said the Wisconsin court, "if they reside in Milwaukee, attend public schools (or private schools in grades K-3) and meet certain income requirements." Of the 122 private schools eligible to participate in the MPCP, 89 are sectarian.

The MPCP "is the most mature example of vouchers at work."[4] It was hailed as a model by voucher proponents. "Today's decision [by the Wisconsin Supreme Court] will help school choice spread like wildfire across the nation," said Chip Mellor of the Institute for Justice, which represented parents in the Wisconsin case.[5] "School choice is working in Milwaukee," said Cal Thomas when the Supreme Court declined to review the case. "It can work everywhere."[6]

The Wisconsin court upheld the MPCP under the Establishment Clause of the First Amendment because the MPCP has a "secular purpose, does not have the primary effect of advancing religion, and does not create an excessive entanglement of government with religion."[7] "The program," said the court, "does not involve the State in any way with the schools' governance, curriculum, or day-to-day affairs."[8] Although the MPCP does not of itself increase the role of government in overseeing the quality of education in the participating schools, there is no constitutional bar to such an increase of supervision. Once the private school chooses to participate in the program it will be subject, as a condition of further funding, to whatever requirements might be thereafter imposed by the state to foster educational quality in those schools. To some extent the state will be precluded from interfering with the religious character of those schools or from otherwise fostering an "excessive entanglement" of government with religion. This assurance, however, is far from an absolute protection. Indeed, the MPCP already incorporates restrictions which give reason for concern about their impact on the integrity of the participating schools:

---

[3] *N.Y. Times*, Nov. 10, 1998, p. A1. Several state courts have held vouchers unconstitutional. *Wash. Times*, June 12, 1995, p. A3.

[4] *National Catholic Register*, Mar. 7-13, 1999, p. 1.

[5] *N.Y. Times*, June 11, 1998, p. A1.

[6] *Wash. Times*, Nov. 15, 1998, p. B1. See *N.Y. Times*, Apr. 28, 1999, p. A1, describing the Florida voucher program to enable students at low-rated public schools to attend private schools including religious schools; see also *Wash. Times*, May 1, 1999, p. A2.

[7] 578 N.W.2d at 620.

[8] *Ibid.*

First, students are not eligible to enter MPCP if they are already enrolled in the participating private school unless they are in grades K-3.

Second, the private school has no control over selection of the participating students who will attend that school. The school must select the students "on a random basis," except that it may give preference to siblings of students already accepted in that school.[9]

Third, the original MPCP was amended in 1995 to add an "opt-out" provision prohibiting a private school from requiring "a student attending the private school under this section to participate in any religious activity if the pupil's parent or guardian submits to the teacher or the private school's principal a written request that the pupil be exempt from such activities."[10]

NO FREE LUNCH

These restrictions in the MPCP reflect the reality that government subsidies create the potential for government control.

The Second Vatican Council said that "public authority. . . is bound according to. . . distributive justice to ensure that public subsidies to schools are so allocated that parents are truly free to select schools for their children in accordance with their conscience."[11] Jerry Topczenski, communications director for the Archdiocese of Milwaukee, said, "We do not expect that the [MPCP] regulations will be overly burdensome. From a Catholic perspective," he said, "we already operate with a quasi opt-out clause. None of our non-Catholic students is forced to participate in any ceremony they may disagree with. We have no intention of using Catholic schools to proselytize. We do not do it with our Catholic hunger or poverty programs. Why would we do it with our education programs?"[12] Perhaps the answer is that educational programs are different. Religious belief cannot be coerced. "It is, however, the special function of the Catholic school to develop in the school community an atmosphere animated by a spirit of liberty and charity based on the Gospel. . . . It. . . so orients the whole of human culture to the message of salvation that the knowledge which the pupils acquire of the world, of life and of men is illumined by faith."[13] In carrying out this mission the Catholic school will properly take reasonable steps to avoid giving of-

---

[9] 578 N.W.2d. at 617.
[10] 578 N.W.2d at 609.
[11] Vatican II, *Declaration on Christian Education,* no. 6.
[12] *National Catholic Register,* June 28-July 4, 1998, p. 1.
[13] Vatican II, *Declaration on Christian Education,* no. 8.

fense to its non-Catholic students. But an "opt-out" provision in a voucher program gives a large measure of control to the objecting student and his parents; this control is reinforced by the threat of the school's exclusion from the voucher program.

The later addition of the "opt-out" restriction to the MPCP confirms that once a school enters a voucher program of any sort it has made itself a hostage for whatever restrictions might be imposed down the line. The recognition of a state-enforced right of objecting students to excuse themselves from "any religious activity" could be reasonably expected to lead to the elimination of such activities on the ground that they are divisive and potentially productive of litigation. And what does the "opt-out" provision mean by "any religious activity"? Presumably that could include prayer in class, putting a crucifix or a copy of the Ten Commandments on a wall, holding a religiously oriented school assembly and even making an affirmation of Catholic doctrine in a classroom presentation. And would classroom discussions on abortion have to be balanced and nonjudgmental to avoid imposing on students the "religious" view that human life begins at conception and that abortion is murder?[14] Even where a local government is hospitable to religious education, a restriction such as the "opt-out" clause has the potential to dilute the religious character of the school.

Apart from an explicit restriction such as the "opt-out" provision, the acceptance of public subsidies tends to lead to the absorption of the subsidized schools into the public education universe. "According to the stipulated facts" in the MPCP case, "the State's system of per-pupil school financing, in which public funds follow each child, now encompasses a wide range of school choices — mainly public, but some private or religious. Numerous programs have amended the number and type of educational options available to public school students. Qualifying public school students may choose from among the Milwaukee public district schools, magnet schools, charter schools, suburban public schools, trade schools, schools developed for students with exceptional needs, and now sectarian or nonsectarian private schools participating in the amended MPCP. In each case, the programs let state funds follow students to the districts and schools their parents have chosen."[15] The MPCP voucher, apart from private school students in grades K-3, is usable only by public school students who choose to use the public money to attend the private school. It is fair to say that the Catholic and other

---

[14] See the discussion in Question 12 of Justice Stevens' position on the "theological" nature of the claim that life begins at conception.
[15] 578 N.W.2d. at 618, n. 16.

private schools participating in MPCP have made themselves, in effect, auxiliaries of the state educational establishment. It is unrealistic to think that achievement of that status will not be accompanied ultimately by an erosion of the religious character that ought to permeate those schools. A similar problem arises in some jurisdictions which make public school textbooks available to parochial school students.[16] It is doubtful at best that Catholic schools can rely on such public school books without compromising the performance of their duty to permeate the study of every subject by the light of faith.

The reality of government control over participating schools is inherent in any program of government aid to private schools, whether direct subsidies, vouchers or tuition tax credits. "Heretofore, the universe of American education has consisted of two major institutions, the public school and the private school. If voucher programs such as the Milwaukee Parental Choice Program take hold in the country, that educational universe will change. There will still be public schools and private schools. Somewhere between the two, however, in an amorphous and as-yet-indistinct middle ground, there will be a third educational entity—the publicly-regulated private school."[17] Under a voucher program, less authentic but subsidized schools would drive from the market more authentic, unsubsidized schools:

> Proponents of vouchers are quick to note that no school would ever be *forced* to accept the voucher. That is true enough, but look at the Sophie's Choice that vouchers put before parents and private schools. A Christian school deeply committed to its mission may bite the bullet and refuse to accept the voucher, but a less committed Christian school down the street decides it can live with the regulations and oversight and accepts the voucher. Some parents from the first school decide they can get roughly the same result from the voucher-redeeming school down the street and beat a fast path to free Christian schooling. The first school may now be faced with the prospects of dropping its music program, not renovating a gym in bad repair, or even closing its doors. The mere existence of the voucher pits mission-compromising schools against uncompromising schools, with the upper hand given to the compromisers. . . .

> Once a private school begins accepting vouchers, it is unlikely to go back. Voucher-receiving schools will increase wages and debt for ex-

---

[16] See *Bd. of Education v. Allen*, 392 U.S. 236 (1968); for a list of state laws, see U.S. Dept. of Education Home Page, http://www.ed.gov/pubs/RegPrivSchl/chart3.hmtl.

[17] Frank R. Kemerer, Joe B. Hairston and Keith Lauerman, "Vouchers & Private School Autonomy," 21 *J. of Law & Education* 601, 623-24 (1992).

pansion and otherwise assume financial obligations that will make opting out very difficult when more restrictions are imposed.[18]

A BETTER WAY

The campaign for school vouchers is part of a broader and commendable effort to ameliorate the hostility to theistic religion which the Supreme Court has built into its Establishment Clause jurisprudence over the past five decades.[19] Unfortunately, there really is no free lunch. The proper response to the terminal crisis of public education is not to attach Catholic and other private schools to that failed system. A more constructive approach would be to increase the personal exemption from income for federal income tax purposes. It began in 1948 at $600 and for 1998 it was $2700. For that exemption to represent the same percentage of per capita income as it did in 1948, it would now have to be at least $10,000[20] for each parent and each dependent child. Such an increase would improve the ability of parents to pay tuition, and the ability of Catholic schools, to which that tuition would be paid, to open their doors to the poor so as to offer them a genuinely Catholic education. Also, privately-funded scholarships currently assist 14,500 children in private schools. In 1998, a group of businessmen, including John Walton, of Wal-Mart, and Theodore Forstmann of Gulfstream Aerospace, pledged a total of $200 million each for this purpose. This program alone would fund 50,000 scholarships, all free from government control.[21]

These remarks are not meant to disparage those who work for vouchers, tuition tax credits, textbook loans, etc. The point is, rather, that such programs are imprudent in the United States. The leaders of the future in this country will come from private schools, especially religious schools. And they will come from home schools which would be either excluded or subverted by a voucher program. Public elementary and secondary education is a terminal case. As that failed system slides beneath the waves, the objective of Catholic and other private schools ought to be to help the students in need, not to climb aboard the sinking hulk.

---

[18] Douglas Dewey, "Vouchers and Educational Freedom: A Debate," *Policy Analysis* (Cato Institute, Mar. 12, 1997), 3, 40-41.

[19] See Question 10.

[20] Michael J. McIntyre and C. Eugene Steurle, *Federal Tax Reform: A Family Perspective* (The Urban Institute, 1998), 3; *Minneapolis Star Tribune*, July 15, 1998, p. 38.

[21] See *The New American*, Aug. 17, 1998, 35. See *Kotterman v. Killian*, 972 P.2d 606 (Ariz., 1999), where the Arizona Supreme Court upheld state income tax credits for contributions to a private, nonprofit "school tuition organization" which uses the money for scholarships for students at any private, elementary or secondary school that operates lawfully under state law; see *Liberty & Law* (Institute for Justice, Feb., 1999), 1.

24. WHAT ABOUT "SEX EDUCATION"?

Alan Guttmacher, former president of Planned Parenthood, was asked, "What makes abortion so secure in America?" He answered in two words: "Sex education." Atheist Madalyn Murray O'Hair wrote: "The issue of abortion is a red herring. . . . The fight is over sex education, including information on birth control." — *Rev. Vernon J. Schaefer*[1]

"Sex education in the schools is not new," writes Barbara Dafoe Whitehead, "but never before has it attempted to expose children to so much so soon. Comprehensive sex education. . . begins in kindergarten and continues into high school. It sweeps across disciplines, taking up the biology of reproduction, the psychology of relationships, the sociology of the family, and the sexology of masturbation and massage. It seeks not simply to reduce health risks to teenagers but also to build self-esteem, prevent sexual abuse, promote respect for all kinds of families, and make little boys more nurturant and little girls more assertive."[2] Classroom sex education typically includes information about sexual methods, including birth control, precautions against sexually transmitted disease, and related matters including homosexual relationships. It can be taught in mixed groups of boys and girls and it can be a separate course or integrated into other courses.

In response to the AIDS problem, sex education has become largely an exercise in understanding the homosexual and his lifestyle, with an emphasis on the need for fairness and compassion in dealing with him (or her). In the process, a relativistic, non-judgmental attitude tends to be fostered. This can be so in Catholic as well as public schools.[3] Programs in public schools promote "safe sex" as a means of preventing AIDS and other sexually transmitted diseases. The urgency of the AIDS problem tends to sweep away inhibitions that otherwise might have exerted a moderating influence.

BASIC PRINCIPLES

Nothing has happened to lessen the cogency of Pope Pius XI's warning, seven decades ago, in his encyclical, *On the Christian Education of Youth*:

---

[1] Vernon J. Schaefer, "Classroom Sex Education," *Homiletic & Pastoral Review*, Mar., 1995, 53.

[2] Barbara Dafoe Whitehead, "The Failure of Sex Education," *Atlantic Monthly*, Oct. 1994, 55.

[3] For analyses of sex education in Catholic schools, contact Human Life International, Front Royal, VA 22630, (540) 635-7884; see *HLI Special Report No. 164* (Aug. 1998); see "The 'Catholic' AIDS Ed. Battle," *The Orator* (St. Brigid's Assn., P.O. Box 71022, Ottawa Ontario, K2P 219, Canada), Apr. 1998, 1.

Another very grave danger is that naturalism which nowadays invades the field of education in that most delicate matter of purity of morals. Far too common is the error of those who with dangerous assurance and under an ugly term propagate a so-called sex-education, falsely imagining they can forearm youths against the dangers of sensuality by means purely natural, such as a foolhardy initiation and precautionary instruction for all indiscriminately, even in public; and, worse still, by exposing them at an early age to the occasions, in order to accustom them, so it is argued, and as it were to harden them against such dangers.

Such persons grievously err in refusing to recognize the inborn weakness of human nature, and the law of which the Apostle speaks, fighting against the law of mind; and also in ignoring the experience of facts, from which it is clear that, particularly in young people, evil practices are the effect not so much of ignorance of intellect as of weakness of a will exposed to dangerous occasions, and unsupported by the means of grace.

In this extremely delicate matter, if, all things considered, some private instruction is found necessary and opportune, from those who hold from God the commission to teach and who have the grace of state, every precaution must be taken.[4]

"As they grow older" said the Second Vatican Council, "[children] should receive a positive and prudent education in matters relating to sex."[5] In 1995 the Pontifical Council for the Family issued *The Truth and Meaning of Human Sexuality* (*TMHS*).[6] As Alfonso Cardinal Lopez Trujillo, President of the Council, said, *TMHS* "does not pretend to be a didactic manual."[7] It "aims. . . to offer an anthropological framework as the basis of sexual education, and to provide methodological guidelines that involve the family. . . . [A] kind of expropriation has taken place by the schools, or rather by personnel who are not in syntony with the parents, who act using methods not in accord with the parents, and who are often only concerned with promoting their own pragmatic or ideological conceptions or the interests of agencies outside the real interest of persons and families. . . . Moreover,. . . . organizations promoting *family planning* and guided by the precepts of anti-natalism have found ways of inserting themselves into the 'education' of adolescents and of taking the place of families. [*TMHS*] does not exclude the school or other educa-

---

[4] Pope Pius XI, *Divini Illius Magistri, On the Christian Education of Youth* (1929), nos. 65-66.
[5] *Declaration on Christian Education*, no. 1.
[6] 25 Origins 529 (1996).

tional associations, but it does. . . reclaim the irreplaceable role of parents and the family. . . as the constant reference points for schools, religious communities, and associations."[8]

PARENTS AS THE PRINCIPAL EDUCATORS

"Other educators. . . can only take the place of parents for serious reasons of physical or moral incapacity. . . .[P]arents are the first and most important educators of their children, and they also possess a fundamental competency in this area: They are educators because they are parents."[9] *TMHS* sets out "four principles regarding information about sexuality":

1. *Each child is a unique and unrepeatable person and must receive individualized formation.* Since parents know, understand and love each of their children in their uniqueness, they are in the best position to decide what the appropriate time is for providing. . . information. . . . No one can take this capacity for discernment away from conscientious parents.[10]

2. *The moral dimension must always be part of their explanations.*[11]

3. *Formation in chastity and timely information regarding sexuality must be provided in the broadest context of education for love.*[12]

4. *Parents should provide this information with great delicacy, but clearly and at the appropriate time.*[13]

TMHS said that the imparting of information by parents should be gradual and appropriate to the age of the child. "[A] child is in. . . 'the years of innocence' from about 5 years of age until puberty. . . . This period. . . must never be disturbed by unnecessary information about sex. . . . In some societies today there are planned and determined attempts to impose premature sex information on children. . . . [I]n "puberty. . . . parents are. . . bound to give more detailed explanations about sexuality (in an ongoing relationship of trust and friendship) each time girls confide in their mothers and boys in their fathers. . . . But it is still not necessary to give detailed explanations about sexual union unless this is explicitly requested."[14]

---

[7] *The Truth and Meaning of Human Sexuality* (Wanderer Press, 1996), 27.
[8] *Ibid.,* 24-27.
[9] *Ibid.,* no. 23.
[10] *Ibid.,* no. 65.
[11] *Ibid.,* no. 68.
[12] *Ibid.,* no. 70.
[13] *Ibid.,* no. 75.
[14] *Ibid.,* nos. 78-90.

School Programs

TMHS does not exclude the school from a possible, though limited, role in assisting the parents, provided that the primary role of the parents is maintained. "'Sex education. . . must always be carried out under [the parents'] attentive guidance, whether at home or in educational centers chosen and controlled by them.'"[15]

"No one can bind children or young people to secrecy about. . . instruction provided outside the family. We are aware of the difficulty and often the impossibility for parents *to participate fully in all supplementary instruction provided outside the home.* Nevertheless, they have the right to be informed about the structure and content of the program. In all cases, their right to be present during classes cannot be denied. It is recommended that parents attentively follow every form of sex education that is given to their children outside the home, *removing their children whenever this education does not correspond to their own principles.* However, such a decision of the parents must not become grounds for discrimination against their children. On the other hand, parents who remove their children from such instruction have the duty to give them an adequate formation appropriate to each child or young person's stage of development."[16]

"Since each child or young person must be able to live his or her own sexuality in conformity with Christian principles and hence be able to exercise the virtue of chastity, *no educator— not even parents— can interfere with this right to chastity. . . .*It is recommended that respect be given to the *right of the child or young person to withdraw from any form of sexual instruction imparted outside the home.*"[17]

Working Principles and Norms

TMHS sets out "four working principles and their norms":

1. *Human sexuality is a sacred mystery and must be presented according to the doctrinal and moral teaching of the Church, always bearing in mind the effects of original sin. . . .*

2. *Only information proportionate to each phase of their individual development should be presented to children and young people. . . .*

(a)   In later adolescence young people can first be introduced to the knowledge of the signs of fertility and then to the natural regulation of

---

[15]   *Ibid.*, no. 43, quoting John Paul II, *Familiaris Consortio,* no. 37.
[16]   *TMHS,* nos. 115-117.
[17]   *Ibid.*, nos. 118, 120.

fertility, but only in the context of education for love, fidelity in marriage, God's plan for procreation and respect for human life.

(b) Homosexuality should not be discussed before adolescence unless a specific serious problem has arisen in a particular situation. This subject must be presented only in terms of chastity, health and "the truth about human sexuality in its relationship to the family as taught by the Church."

(c) Sexual perversions that are relatively rare should not be dealt with except through individual counseling as the parents' response to genuine problems.

3. *No material of an erotic nature should be presented to children or young people of any age, individually or in a group. . . .*

4. *No one should ever be invited, let alone obliged, to act in any way that could objectively offend against modesty or which could subjectively offend against his or her own delicacy or sense of privacy.*

This principle of respect for the child excludes all improper forms of involving children and young people. . . . [T]his can include the following methods that abuse sex education: (a) every "dramatized" representation, mime or "role playing" which depict genital or erotic matters; (b) making drawings, charts or models etc. of this nature; (c) seeking personal information about sexual questions, or asking that family information be divulged; (d) oral or written exams about genital or erotic questions.[18]

METHODS AND IDEOLOGIES

After describing the governing "principles and norms," *TMHS* sets out its own "Recommended Methods" and "Methods and Ideologies to Avoid." They emphasize the parental role, the need for moral formation of the young, and the dangers that can occur in school programs:

"The. . . method. . . proposed. . . is *personal dialogue between parents and their children,. . . individual formation within the family circle. . . .* In certain situations parents can *entrust part of education for love to another trustworthy person,* if there are matters which require a specific competence or pastoral care in particular cases. . . ." [P]arents must reject *secularized and anti-natalist sex education,* which puts God at the margin of life and regards the birth of a child as a threat. This. . . is spread by large organizations and international associations that promote abortion, sterilization and contraception. These organizations want to impose a false lifestyle against the truth of human sexuality. . . .[19]

---

18 *Ibid.,* nos. 121-27.
19 *Ibid.,* nos. 129, 132, 136.

One widely used but possibly harmful, approach goes by the name of 'values clarification.' Young people are encouraged to reflect upon,. . . moral issues with. . . 'autonomy,' ignoring. . . the moral law. . . and disregarding the formation of consciences on. . . Christian moral precepts as affirmed by the Magisterium. . . . Young people are given the idea that a moral code is something which they create themselves, as if man were the source and norm of morality.[20]

Parents should also be attentive to ways in which sexual instruction can be inserted in the context of other subjects. . .(for example, health and hygiene, personal development, family life, children's literature, social and cultural studies etc.). In these situations it is more difficult to control the content of sexual instruction. This *method of inclusion* is used. . . by those who promote sex instruction within the perspective of birth control or in countries where the government does not respect the rights of parents in this field. But catechesis would also be distorted if the inseparable links between religion and morality were to be used as a pretext for introducing into religious instruction the biological and affective sexual information which the parents should give according to their prudent decision in their own home.[21]

Another abuse occurs whenever *sex education* is given to children by teaching them all the intimate details of genital relationships, even in a graphic way. Today this is often motivated by wanting to provide education for "safe sex," above all in relation in the spread of AIDS. In this situation parents must also reject the promotion of so-called "safe sex" or "safer sex," a dangerous and immoral policy based on the deluded theory that the condom can provide adequate protection against AIDS. Parents must insist on continence outside marriage and fidelity in marriage as the only true and secure education for the prevention of this contagious disease.[22]

"Therefore," concluded *TMHS*, "explicit and premature sex education can never be justified in the name of a prevailing secularized culture. On the contrary, parents must educate their own children to understand and face up to the focus of this culture so that they may always follow the way of Christ."[23]

"CATHOLIC" SEX EDUCATION

"The fact of the matter," said former U.S. Assistant Secretary of Education Kenneth D. Whitehead, is that *TMHS* "almost completely

---

[20] *Ibid.*, no. 140.
[21] *Ibid.*, no. 141. See H. Vernon Sattler, C.S.S.R., *Challenging Children to Chastity—A Parental Guide* (1992).
[22] *TMHS*, no. 139.
[23] *Ibid.*, no. 143.

vindicates what the critics of classroom sex education in Catholic schools have been saying for the past quarter of a century":

> Nearly a generation ago, Catholic school educators. . . began buying into secular sex-ed programs as if they were. . . antidotes to the sexual immorality of our day, rather than. . . reflections of it. Considering the public schools'. . . record of failure, why Catholic educators would have looked to them for anything is a mystery. But in. . . classroom sex-education. . . Catholic educators. . . adopted. . . models developed by organizations like Planned Parenthood that were designed to promote. . . the sexual revolution. Oftentimes these educational models were uncritically adapted for Catholic schools with only minimal modifications to give them the semblance of accord with Catholic doctrine and morality.
>
> It was. . . startling to see in these programs the subordination of Catholic teaching to. . . psychologism, an accent on autonomous decision making, an obsession with self-esteem, and a denigration of "puritanism." In fact, these classroom sex-education programs are not based on any traditional Christian view of man. Rather, they are based on the fashionable view that neither sin, nor temptation, nor the Church's remedies for sin are to be taken very seriously.[24]

Mr. Whitehead noted that the letter issued in response to *TMHS* by the president of the National Conference of Catholic Bishops "credits [*TMHS*] with providing 'welcome warnings in regards to the dual problems of sexually permissive cultures and of poorly done, values-neutral, overly explicit sex-education programs.' Yet it is really doubtful if a single one of the current 'Catholic' sex-education programs published by typical Catholic textbook publishers could escape the same characterization. The Catholic educators. . . have been. . . uncritical of them. The bishops,. . . have relied on. . . experts, in this as in so many other respects. . . . [B]oth educators and bishops regularly have rejected and set aside any criticism of classroom sex education. . . . There never has been a Catholic tradition of imparting sexual information in a classroom setting. . . . Neither does the fact that sex is now discussed so openly in our society. . . invalidate the principle of keeping sexual instruction private. On the contrary–when the. . . school is employed to promote. . . an equal frankness concerning sexual matters, the lower standards of society are implicitly validated. . . . [T]he school has taken over the role of the parents. These programs. . . . co-opt those parents who become actively

---

[24] Kenneth D. Whitehead, "Secular Drift in Catholic Sex Education," *Crisis,* Jan. 1997, 37, 37-38.

involved, while the school retains total control over the programs themselves. Have you ever tried to tell a school principal or teacher what to teach in the classroom?. . . [T]hese programs usurp the rights and responsibilities of those parents who do not get actively involved. Such parents either do not know what these programs contain, or somehow they go on believing that the Catholic schools are still functioning properly as they furnish indoctrination in modern sexual attitudes to captive student audiences in mixed classrooms."[25]

Kenneth Whitehead wondered "why more parents have not protested these programs' inclusion in the Catholic schools."[26] But perhaps the reason for their silence is that Catholic parents are as heavily immersed in the practice of the contraceptive ethic as anyone else. Such parents have no real disagreement with what is taught in the Catholic and even public school courses. They are happy to have somebody take their parental responsibility off their hands.

Classroom sex education is virtually an intrinsically imprudent idea. Nor should we be surprised that such "education" results in an increase of sexual activity among its alleged beneficiaries. As Robert M. Patrick put it, "you don't teach Driver's Training to clear the highways."[27]

The secular public school ought to be entirely excluded from the subject of sex education. Those schools cannot perform their basic duty of teaching their students to read, write, add and subtract. By what warrant can they claim the right to teach a subject such as sexuality? They are precluded by the Supreme Court from treating the subject in the context of objective morality and the dignity of the person as made in the image and likeness of God. It would be far better to leave this subject untaught than to teach it the way the public schools have to teach it. Even in Catholic schools, however, common sense and experience mandate a virtually irrebutable presumption against including sex education as a separate course in the curriculum.[28]

WHY IT WON'T WORK

One problem with any classroom sex education is that the teacher cannot possibly know the background and personal history of every child in the classroom. When children in a group are given detailed lectures on sexual topics, whether or not the sexes are mixed in the group,

---

[25] *Ibid.*
[26] *Ibid.*
[27] *Catholic Eye,* Oct. 26, 1994, 2.
[28] Rev. Vernon J. Schaefer, "Classroom Sex Education," *Homiletic & Pastoral Review* Mar. 1995, 53.

the potential for emotional damage is real. The problem is compounded when the children are encouraged to discuss in the group or among themselves their own feelings on the subject. The feelings of young people are mercurial from day to day. But when a pupil is induced to voice those feelings in a group, he establishes a "public record" which can create unpredictable consequences. He may say what he thinks is the consensus of the group, in which case he is implicitly accepting the peer group as his norm of thought and behavior. Or he may blurt out what is really on his mind, with a resulting loss of the personal reserve which is an important aspect of his privacy. In either case, the teacher has no reliable idea of what is going on in the minds and emotions of the pupils.

The potential for unpredictable consequences is present even when there is no group discussion and the pupils merely listen to the teacher, watch a film or fill out self-evaluation sheets. The teacher does not know what he is doing to each child. He is not merely imparting ideas as he would in an ordinary academic subject. Rather, he is meddling with the emotions of young people who are relative strangers to him. The process can fairly be described as a verbal form of child molesting. It destroys modesty which, in the era of sex education and pagan culture, has become a "lost virtue."[29] Nothing has happened to rebut psychoanalyst Bruno Bettelheim's observation that "sex education is impossible in a classroom."[30]

Such group instruction devalues the parental role, overlooks the individuality of the children, invades their privacy and tends towards relativism and experimentation. The adverse consequences of classroom sex education are especially significant with children in the latency period. As Dr. Sean O'Reilly, professor of medicine at George Washington University wrote, "Explicit sex instruction during latency, even in private, but *a fortiori* in the classroom, is a grave and potentially dangerous invasion of the child's right to privacy." Dr. O'Reilly quoted Dr. Myre Sim, professor of psychiatry at the University of Ottawa. "Sex education cannot be equated with other forms of learning. . . . Sex is basically a private matter and does not lend itself at serious and responsible levels to public display, and this is what modern sex educators are doing. . . . I agree entirely. . . that disturbances of the latency period interfere with the most productive learning phase in child development. In this respect it is anti-educational."[31]

---

[29] Wendy Shalit, *A Return to Modesty: Discovering the Lost Virtue* (1999).
[30] Bruno Bettelheim, "Our Children Are Treated Like Idiots," 2 *Psychology Today* 28, 38. (July 1981).
[31] Sean O'Reilly, M.D., *Sex Education in the Schools* (1978), 5.

As the Second Vatican Council affirmed, parents are the primary educators of their children. It is a matter for parental decision, not only how, when and by whom children should be given explicit sexual instruction, but also whether it should be given at all. With some children, explicit instruction may be appropriate. With others it may not be. The decision is for the parents. The certainty that some or even most parents will not give their children explicit sexual instruction, whether as a result of parental choice, timidity or neglect, involves a lesser evil than does the herding of all children into groups for such detailed instruction.

In teaching the moral law in religion, ethics or other courses, Catholic schools must teach about sex and they must do so in the classroom. But such teaching is not equivalent to "sex education," especially in the AIDS era. A separate course in sex education should be avoided, whether it is called "chastity education" or something else. Numerous books and other teaching materials are suitable for the teaching of Catholic sexual morality without involving explicit and other objectionable features of classroom sex education. The difference may be hard to define but any prudent parent who is doing his or her job can tell that difference.

Perhaps we can best summarize by quoting the conclusion of *TMHS*:

> There are various ways of helping and supporting parents in fulfilling their fundamental right and duty to educate their children for love. Such assistance never means taking from parents or diminishing their formative right and duty, because they remain 'original and primary,' 'irreplaceable and inalienable.' Therefore, the role which others can carry out in helping parents is always (a) *subsidiary*, because the formative role of the family is always preferable and (b) *subordinate*, that is, subject to the parents' attentive guidance and control.[32] . . . [T]hose who are called to help parents in educating their children for love must be disposed and prepared to teach in conformity with the authentic moral doctrine of the Catholic Church.[33]

---

[32] *TMHS*, no. 145.
[33] *Ibid.*, no. 146.

25. WHAT HAPPENED TO THE CATHOLIC UNIVERSITIES? ARE ANY OF THEM STILL CATHOLIC?

If they were in the business of selling cookies instead of education, the leaders of some "Catholic" universities might need a good defense lawyer.[1] It can be a federal crime to label products in a misleading way. For example, the "labeling of products as — 'Butter Cookies,'. . . is. . . false and misleading unless all of the shortening ingredient is butter. The use of the term 'butter flavored' is appropriate for products that contain both butter and shortening but which have sufficient butter to give the product a butter flavor. If the product contains any artificial butter flavor it would have to be so labeled."[2] The law also provides civil remedies for consumer fraud. If a mechanic sold you a "new" transmission when he knew it was a rebuilt one, you could get your money back and punitive damages as well. The reluctance of the law to involve itself in religious and educational disputes has left the consumer of "Catholic" higher education with less protection than the buyers of "butter" cookies.

Students at Catholic universities (including colleges) are entitled to an opportunity to study sound philosophy and theology, as well as the teachings of the Church, so as to be able to make an informed judgment on those matters. For nearly four decades I have taught at Catholic law schools. Most of the students have come from Catholic colleges and probably most from Catholic grade and high schools as well. With exceptions and through no fault of their own, they tend to be ignorant or misinformed as to the teachings of the Church and the reasoned foundations of those teachings. Worse yet, they frequently think they know all they need to know because they went to a "Catholic" college where, too often, all they heard about those things was filtered through the lens of a hostile professor. Every term I teach a Jurisprudence course at Notre Dame Law School. There is nothing original about the course. It examines the teaching of Thomas Aquinas on the natural law and its relation to the civil law, as that teaching is incorporated into the teaching of Christ by the Magisterium. And it examines in detail the positivist and utilitarian jurisprudence of the Enlightenment. We get into foundational questions: Can you know anything? Is it unreasonable not to believe in God? Is there an objective moral order? Who is Christ? What is the role of the teaching Church? And so on. It has never failed: Every

---

[1] This Question is an adaptation of Charles E. Rice, "Esau's Bargain: A Potted Message," *Catholic Dossier,* July-Aug. 1997, 17.

[2] *Food Drug Cosmetic Law Reporter,* Vol. 4, § 50, 124.211 quoting *FDA Compliance Policy Guide § 505.200* (CPG 7102.05), Mar. 8, 1988.

term, either before or shortly after the end of the course, at least one student has come into my office and said, "I have gone through eight (twelve) (fifteen) (or whatever) years of Catholic schooling and I never heard any of this." Those students have been shortchanged, through no fault of their own, by the Catholic educational system on which they relied. They and their parents contracted for a "Catholic" education. What they got was "Catholic flavored" at best. And frequently the seller adds insult to injury by exhorting them to make voluntary contributions to that seller so that he can more effectively perpetrate that deception on others.

This shortchanging reflects the impact on Catholic universities of the Enlightenment culture which attempts to organize society as if God does not exist. The dominance of that Enlightenment culture, especially in the prestigious universities, raises two issues here: Must the Catholic university, as an institution, affirm objective moral truth? Must that university recognize the Church, and specifically the Pope, as the authoritative interpreter of that truth?

These issues were not directly covered in the *Code of Canon Law* of 1917, but they simmered until the expansion of higher education after World War II. In response to the lament of some that there was no "Catholic Harvard" and that the Catholic universities were not producing "Catholic Einsteins," some of those universities pursued the academic "excellence" exemplified by the Ivy League schools which had gained influence after terminating their ties to the religious groups by which they were founded. Those striving Catholic universities obtained money from foundations for studies which told them how to pursue that excellence. Acceptance of the authority of the Church was regarded as a hindrance to that pursuit. Later, "the spirit of Vatican II" advanced the "magisterium of the theologians" so as to reduce the pope to merely one voice among many, with the faithful enjoying a cafeteria choice among doctrines. The decisive factor, however, that made those ideas in concrete the new orthodoxy in Catholic universities was the lure of government money. Or at least it was a decisive pretext.

In the 1966 case of *Horace Mann League v. Board of Public Works,*[3] the highest court of Maryland held unconstitutional grants by the state to three colleges because the schools were too religious. In response, the major Catholic universities shifted to secular control. Rev. Leo McLaughlin, S.J., then President of Fordham University, said, "one reason that the changes are being made in the structure of the boards of

---

[3] 220 A.2d 51 (Md., 1966).

trustees is money. . . . [M]any Catholic. . . colleges simply cannot continue to exist without state aid. . . . [T]he choice offered to Catholic institutions is going to be quite clear: changes will have to be made within the structure of the Catholic institutions which will made them eligible for federal and state aid or many of them will have to close their doors."[4] Incidentally, there is no sound legal basis for the claim that the secularization of Catholic universities was necessary to make those institutions eligible for government aid.[5]

In 1967, a statement on "The Nature of the Contemporary Catholic University" was issued at Land O'Lakes, Wisconsin, by officials of the leading Catholic universities in the United States. The statement provided the rationale for the severance of the juridical link between the universities and the Church. It declared:

> To perform its teaching and research functions effectively the Catholic university must have a true autonomy and academic freedom in the face of authority of whatever kind, lay or clerical, external to the academic community itself. . . . There must be no theological or philosophical imperialism, all scientific and disciplinary methods, and methodologies, must be given due honor and respect.[6]

The importance of the severance of the juridical connection between a university and its founding church was described by Fr. James T. Burtchaell, C.S.C., who detailed the secularization of the major Protestant universities, using Vanderbilt as an example, after they severed their connection to the founding churches. He suggested also, without naming any particular Catholic university, that "secularization is rapidly bleaching the Catholic character out of that church's universities and colleges, with all the elements we saw typified in the Vanderbilt story." Fr. Burtchaell noted that, after their formal secularization, "the Catholic institutions enjoyed an immediate honeymoon period wherein autonomy actually enhanced the institution as both a faith community and a house of liberal learning. But then the slow and inexorable gravity pull of the secularism dominant in the force-field of the academy begins to retard and then counteract the inertial momentum that has hitherto set the course of the Catholic college or university, until, after a period when the forms and symbols of Christian identity are gradually evacu-

---

[4] *Address to Fordham Alumni Federation,* Jan. 24, 1967.
[5] See Kenneth D. Whitehead, *Catholic Colleges and Federal Funding* (1988); Kenneth D. Whitehead, "Religiously Affiliated Colleges and American Freedom," *America,* Feb. 7, 1987, 96.
[6] "The Catholic University of Today," *America,* Aug. 12, 1967, 54.

ated of their conviction, the institution finally emerges as a wraith of the Christian community it once was."[7]

Ex Corde Ecclesiae, the 1990 Apostolic Constitution on Catholic Universities, does not mandate a formal legal connection between the Catholic university and the Church. But it does require an essential relationship between the two.[8] Cardinal Newman thought along similar lines: "If the Catholic Faith is true, a University cannot exist externally to the Catholic pale, for it cannot teach Universal Knowledge if it does not teach Catholic theology. . . .[But] still, though it had ever so many theological Chairs, that would not suffice to make it a Catholic University; for theology would be included in its teaching only as a branch of knowledge. . . . Hence a direct and active jurisdiction of the Church over it and in it is necessary, lest it should become the rival of the Church with the community at large in those theological matters which to the Church are exclusively committed, — acting as the representative of the intellect, as the Church is the representative of the religious principle."[9]

The prevailing view in American Catholic universities today was expressed by Fr. Richard McBrien, former chairman of the Notre Dame Theology Department and now [in 1997] president of the Notre Dame Faculty Senate: "Just the idea of even suggesting any kind of oversight by non-academic people in the academic operations of a university — Catholic or not — is odious to anybody in an academic institution," he said. "I'm not saying we're above criticism. But I want the criticism to come from people with the credentials to criticize." He added: "Bishops should be welcome on a Catholic university campus. Give them tickets to ball games. Let them say mass. Bring them to graduation. Let them sit on the stage. But there should be nothing beyond that. They should have nothing to say about the internal academic affairs of the university or any faculty member thereof."[10] A comparison of the Newman and McBrien statements should give pause to any who still maintain the theory of the upward intellectual evolution of the academy.

The American Catholic universities have resisted *Ex Corde Ecclesiae.* The matter is under discussion among the universities, the American Catholic bishops and the Vatican. The areas of disagreement include:

---

[7] James T. Burtchaell, C.S.C., "The Decline and Fall of the Christian College," *First Things,* Apr. 1991, 16, and May 1991, 30, 37. See also James T. Burtchaell, C.S.C., *The Dying of the Light: The Disengagement of Colleges and Universities from Their Christian Churches* (1998).
[8] See *Ex Corde Ecclesiae,* Nos. 27, 28, 29 and *General Norms,* Articles 4 and 5.
[9] John Henry Newman, *The Idea of a University* (1982), 163.
[10] *Chronicle of Higher Education,* Nov. 22, 1996, A8.

1. *The mandate for theologians.* Canon Law requires that "It is necessary that those who teach theological disciplines in any institute of higher studies have a mandate from the competent ecclesiastical authority."[11]

2. *Adherence to the Magisterium.* Ex Corde Ecclesiae requires that: "Catholic theologians, aware that they fulfill a mandate received from the church, are to be faithful to the magisterium of the church as the authentic interpreter of sacred Scripture and sacred tradition."[12] *Ex Corde* also states that: "One consequence of its essential relationship to the church is that the institutional fidelity of the university to the Christian message includes a recognition of and adherence to the teaching authority of the church in matters of faith and morals."[13]

3. *The requirement that a majority of the faculty be Catholic.* Ex Corde provides: "In order not to endanger the Catholic identity of the university or institute of higher studies, the number of non-Catholic teachers should not be allowed to constitute a majority within the institution, which is and must remain Catholic."[14]

When the Catholic universities terminated their juridical link to the Church, they substituted for the relatively benign authority of the Church the more peremptory authority of the secular academic establishment. The mission of those universities came to be defined, not as an apostolic endeavor, but as the pursuit of a reputation for excellence as determined by the criteria of that secular establishment. Yet, for fundraising and recruitment purposes, those universities still claim to be "Catholic." The result is a consumer fraud.

The Catholic universities vary in the degree of their secularization. We have to be careful about making automatic judgments about any particular institution. The University of Notre Dame, for example, is unusual because of its notoriety and large resources. Developments at Notre Dame offer some insight into the deterioration which may be perceived, to varying degrees, in other Catholic universities. Nevertheless, I would recommend Notre Dame to a prospective student with a strong faith who was willing to be careful in course selection, especially in theology, to be prudent in his personal life, and, most important, to pray. A student can readily come through Notre Dame with a sound education

---

[11] Canon 812.

[12] *Ex Corde Ecclesiae, General Norms,* art. 3.

[13] *Ex Corde Ecclesiae,* no. 27.

[14] *Ibid., General Norms,* art. 4. Estimates of the Catholics on the faculty at Boston College vary from 20 to 35%. James T. Burtchaell, *The Dying of the Light* (1998), 617. At the University of Notre Dame, 56% of the tenured and tenure-track faculty list themselves as Catholic; the percentage is headed south. *Notre Dame Fact Book,* 1998-99.

and moral formation. This is particularly true, incidentally, of Notre Dame Law School which maintains a Catholic character. Notre Dame provides abundant sacramental and other spiritual resources for those students who want to use them, in part through the example provided by numerous priests including an encouraging number of younger ones. And the figure of Mary does stand in a place of honor atop the Golden Dome. Nevertheless, the reality is that at practically all the major Catholic universities, including Notre Dame, the students are shortchanged as a result of the false autonomy claimed by those institutions and their mislabeling of themselves as Catholic when they fail to fulfill the criteria for a Catholic university spelled out in *Ex Corde Ecclesiae.*

In several major respects, the Catholic universities' pursuit of secular "excellence" has operated to the detriment of their students:

1. *They fail to offer the students an opportunity to study systematically the rich heritage of the Catholic faith, its underlying philosophy and the teachings of the Church.* In many cases, students are offered instead actively heterodox teaching. Most regrettable is the missed opportunity to provide the students with the intellectual background that would enable them to make intelligent choices in matters of faith and morals for the governance of their lives. Notre Dame proclaims its Catholic identity, in the final report of its Colloquy for the Year 2000, in a mission statement that does not even mention the Catholic Church. Notre Dame insists on its identity as Catholic. However, it defines that term, as a Protestant would, according to its own lights rather than according to the mind of the Church as specified in *Ex Corde Ecclesiae.* If a university professes to be Catholic, it ought at least to give all of its students an opportunity to study the Catholic Faith as it is understood by the teaching Church. Otherwise, the students will hardly have a fighting chance to make an informed judgment on whether to accept or reject the faith.

2. *They refuse to affirm, as an institution, the truth of Catholic moral and social teaching.* This has led to the spectacle of some "Catholic" universities distributing condoms, conferring honors on notoriously pro-abortion figures, affording recognition to student homosexual activist groups and otherwise conveying the message that the teaching of the Church is not to be taken seriously. The word for this is scandal. Even at Notre Dame, which has refused to recognize GLND/SMC, the student gay and lesbian activist group, the University places that rejection only on the ground that homosexual acts are forbidden by "the official teaching of the Church." The University refuses to affirm that the inclination to homosexual acts is itself disordered. Its denial of recognition therefore appears to be based on an arbitrary Church edict rather than on the real-

ity of nature. This failure to affirm the fullness of Church teaching has resulted in an ambivalence that disserves the students, especially those with homosexual inclinations.[15]

3. *They focus on research to the detriment of undergraduate education.* Two decades ago, Notre Dame, for example, began to define itself as a National Catholic Research University. "The reputations of universities," said Fr. Edward A. Malloy, C.S.C., the Notre Dame President, "are driven by the research and graduate programs, not by the undergraduate schools."[16] One consequence is the devaluation of undergrad education. Notre Dame is far from the worst offender in this respect. But there is cause for concern, for example, at the fact that: "Within any given semester, approximately 15 percent of arts and letters courses, including Freshman Composition and Freshman Seminar, are taught by graduate students."[17] Our family has had undergraduate students enrolled at Notre Dame continuously, except for two years, since 1977. Empirically, we can guarantee that the quality of undergrad education at Notre Dame is inferior, in course offerings and the quality of the undergrad experience, to what it was 20 years ago. The leaders of the University have meant well in altering the character of Notre Dame. But the results have been harmful to the students.

Nor is it merely incidental that the formerly pastoral Notre Dame has been transformed into a very crowded urban-style campus like those at the big Research Universities. As one senior professor in another college of the University said to me, "A few years ago, professors normally taught three courses or sections. Now they teach one. So they have to hire more professors, or reduce the number of courses or overcrowd the sections, or use grad students to teach. And the professor, to do his research, needs research assistants and they need office space. That's why we have some of the new buildings." And there seems to be no end to the building frenzy in sight.

Research is only marginally related to education. And, in the pursuit of Research Greatness, the Catholic character of the University tends to become a secondary concern. As Timothy O'Meara, then Notre Dame Provost, stated in 1993, "I personally am confident that Notre Dame will be a university first of all, and secondly a Catholic university, for a long time to come."[18] Interestingly, the overemphasis on research is itself

[15] See Charles E. Rice, "Right or Wrong?" *The Observer* (Univ. of Notre Dame), Oct. 4, 1996, p. 10, and Apr. 18, 1997, p.13.
[16] *The Observer,* Feb. 12, 1992, p. 7.
[17] Report of Graduate Studies Committee to Academic Council, *Notre Dame Report,* Sept. 16, 1994, 29.
[18] Interview, WNDU-TV, Oct. 5, 1993.

a cause of the dilution of a university's Catholic character. "[E]mphasizing research causes Catholicism [as well as teaching] to be de-emphasized. This is true, not because there is any problem with doing excellent Catholic research, but because it is more difficult to publish such research in prestigious journals and with elite university presses than to publish the kind of scholarship respected by secular universities."[19]

4. *They have unjustifiably priced themselves out of reach of the middle class families who formed their basic constituency.* In 1978-79 Notre Dame's undergrad tuition, room and board totaled $5,180. In 1994 dollars, on the Consumer Price Index, that amounts to $11,758. In 1999-2000, the Notre Dame total is $27,660. Given the estimated 3.5 inflation rate since 1994, that is about double, in real money, what it was before Notre Dame began its drive for Research Prestige. The 1999-2000 figure rose over the previous year by $1,435, or 5.47%. It is doubtful that many students realize that they are paying twice as much, in real money, as in the pre-Research University days. And there are lower-cost alternatives. The College Board stated in 1996 that "a majority of all students at four-year colleges and universities pay less than $4,000 for tuition and fees [not including room and board] and that nearly three-quarters of them pay less than $6,000."[20] "80 percent of students attend four-year public universities where tuition, even after years of hikes, averages $3,200."[21]

"In most industries, competition cuts costs. In higher education, it sparks an arms race of amenities that raise them. Schools vie for the best students and faculty to win better rankings, which raise prestige, which draws better students, which boosts alumni giving, which finances new labs, which draws new top faculty and so on. . . . The Federal Government has unintentionally fueled this arms race by vastly expanding access to student loans. . . . What we're left with is a higher-education establishment that consumes $200 billion each year. . . in part relying on an explosion in student indebtedness to bankroll facilities and research having little to do with undergraduate learning."[22]

Student borrowing for college has increased more than 50% since 1992. A 1978 law removed income restrictions on federal loans. But, as *Fortune* magazine warned, "anything that makes it easier to pay tuition bills will also make it easier to raise tuition charges."[23] The major univer-

---

[19] Letter from Dr. David W. Lutz, *The Observer*, Feb. 16, 1993, p. 9.
[20] College Board, *Release*, Sept. 25, 1996.
[21] Matthew Miller, "$140,000 – And a Bargain," *N.Y. Times Magazine*, June 13, 1999, 48.
[22] *Ibid.*, 49.
[23] See discussion in *N.Y. Times*, Dec. 29, 1994, p. A21.

sities have lobbied Congress to increase the loan limits. As the loan limits have gone up, so has the tuition, with the universities financing their research and expansion projects on the backs of the borrowing students. In 1996-97, reports the College Board, federal loan programs provided 60% of all financial aid. "For most of those loans, the. . . government pays the interest while borrowers are. . . in school. However, a growing share of. . . loans are now unsubsidized, adding in-school interest charges to the borrower's total cost. . . . In contrast to loan aid,. . . federal grant support per student has steadily declined."[24]

Notre Dame and other schools commendably help students bridge the gap between the student's resources, including loans, and the costs. The student loan, however, remains the basic form of "financial aid." Among indebted Notre Dame law students, for instance, total indebtedness of $120,000 is not uncommon, with more than a few well over that total. The figures for undergrads are proportionately comparable.

While students mortgage their futures, university endowments continue to grow. The 1998-99 Notre Dame Fact Sheet stated that the market value of the Endowment is "more than $1.2 billion," an increase in one year of $400 million or $38,929 for each of the approximately 10,275 students at Notre Dame. In Fiscal Year 1995, cash contributions to the University totalled a record $70.2 million, or $6,685 per student. One can fairly ask: Why does tuition keep going up when money in such amounts is cascading into the University's coffers and when the Endowment is more than ten times the $113 million Endowment of 1978? As the 1998-99 Fact Sheet said, "student tuition and fees. . . generally account for about 42 percent of [University] income." As former Provost O'Meara put it, Notre Dame's budget is "tuition driven."[25] In terms of availability and quality of courses and quality of teaching, it can hardly be claimed that undergrads are receiving anything remotely close to twice the value in their education than they did two decades ago.

The main impact of the escalating tuition and loan burden at Notre Dame, as elsewhere, is the practical foreclosing of a Notre Dame education to middle class students, apart from ROTC students, scholarship athletes, faculty and staff children and special scholarships students. The old Notre Dame, owned by the Congregation of Holy Cross, defined its primary mission as part of the educational effort of the Church. That mission was to make available to students, even those of modest means, a sound undergraduate education in the Catholic tradition. Research

---

[24] College Board, *Release*, Sept. 29, 1997.
[25] See Charles E. Rice, "Fact Sheet Should Display Real Cost of N.D. Degree," *The Observer* (Notre Dame), Oct. 18, 1996, p. 13.

and graduate studies played a balanced role in the enterprise, but undergrad education was valued on its own merits as a Catholic intellectual work and resources were used primarily to keep it accessible to students. As *Notre Dame Magazine* stated in 1950, "Still, as always, Notre Dame refuses to turn down any more worthy applicants than necessary, even those in need of financial assistance. This is one reason why Notre Dame, unlike many other universities, never has known wealth — or even appreciable financial reserve."[26] Notre Dame's endowment in 1949 was $4,077,587, "the lowest among all major colleges and universities."[27] Interestingly, Notre Dame took its small endowment (they spelled it with a small "e") as a point of pride because it was using its income to lessen the burden on students. And the quality and breadth of the undergrad program counted for more than did the achievement of recognition by the secular "academic community." The striving "Catholic" universities now focus on research and graduate programs, where the money is. This has led to the depersonalization of the undergrad experience and the exploitation of undergrad students and their families to finance the pursuit of research prestige. It is deeply immoral for a supposedly Catholic university to exact inflated tuition from those to whom it falsely promises a Catholic education, so as to exploit those students and their parents for the support of research programs which have only a marginal relation, at best, to the education of those students. In effect, in so breaching their duty of truth in labeling, those universities offer their product to students only at the price of financial burdens which will make it more difficult for those students to make career choices freely and to be open to children in their married lives.

SECULARIZATION AS A MARKET RESPONSE

The secularization of Catholic universities over the past three decades is an exercise in market economics. Fifty years ago everyone knew what a Catholic university was supposed to be. But as the Catholics who had been educated in those universities became affluent, their concern with Catholicity lessened. The 1967 change of Catholic universities to lay control came five years after the contraceptive pill was approved by the Food & Drug Administration and two years after the close of Vatican II. The change to lay control promised easy access to government money. There was little or no resistance among alumni and parents who reflected a "bottom line" consumer mentality. For the time being the claim was made to students, parents and donors that the university was unequivocally Catholic despite the change to lay control. Today,

---

[26] *Notre Dame Magazine*, vol. 3, no. 1, p. 5 (1950).

[27] *Ibid.*, 10.

however, those universities can safely resist the bishops and even the Pope because that is what their constituents do. Many of the affluent "cultural Catholics" who send their children to Georgetown, Fordham, Notre Dame, etc., reject in their own lives the authority of the Church. Catholics practice contraception to the same extent as others, and their attitudes toward moral and social issues, including abortion, are nearly indistinguishable from those of the community at large. The Catholic universities, in declaring their autonomy from Church authority, reflect their market, although they also shape that market by producing graduates who are clueless as to what the Church actually teaches. Moreover, even though their market may prefer "Catholic flavored" education, it is a fraud for the universities to pass it off as authentically "Catholic."

WHAT IS TO BE DONE?

The reclamation of the Catholic universities cannot be accomplished merely by changes in governance, the hiring of Catholic faculty, etc., as essential as those changes surely are. The reclamation has to include a reaffirmation of the principles of truth in labeling, and an effective restoration of the link between those universities and the Church as defined in *Ex Corde Ecclesiae*.

If the Vatican effectively implements *Ex Corde*, the consumers of Catholic higher education will at least have the benefit of some measure of truth in labeling. If *Ex Corde* were enforced against the American Catholic universities, however, it is likely that some would refuse to submit and would forego the right to call themselves "Catholic." In any event, some of those universities have evidently gone past the point of no return, especially in cases where the faculty is predominantly non-Catholic and hostile to restoration of the Catholic character of the institution. Until now, the American Catholic bishops have preferred to deal with the Catholic universities through dialogue, trusting those universities to implement *Ex Corde* themselves. "The strengthening of Catholic identity," said Bishop John M. D'Arcy of Fort Wayne-South Bend, "must be done within the university and by the university, according to the university's statutes, and we accept that."[28] The bishops mean well, but their confidence in the willingness of the universities to strengthen their own Catholic identity is unrealistic. And we — and the bishops — ought to recall Fr. McBrien's view that the bishops should only be given "tickets to ball games" and be allowed to "say mass" and "sit on the stage" at graduation.

---

[28] *So. Bend Tribune,* June 28, 1996, p. D1.

RESTORATION OF CATHOLIC GOVERNANCE?

As Fr. James T. Burtchaell, C.S.C. concludes, the severance by the Protestant universities of their juridical and authoritative links with the founding churches made secularization inevitable.[29] However, in at least some Catholic universities it may be possible to restore that juridical link. Notre Dame, for example was governed until 1967 by six Fellows, all of whom were required to be Holy Cross priests. In 1967, the Fellows were increased to twelve: six lay-people and six Holy Cross priests. A lay-dominated board of trustees was also created then. However, the Holy Cross priests have not relinquished actual control of the University. The governance of the University is ultimately in the twelve Fellows, six of whom must be Holy Cross priests. The Fellows "have and exercise all power and authority granted by" the State of Indiana to Notre Dame. The Fellows, "a self-perpetuating body," elect the Trustees, amend the bylaws, approve any substantial transfer of University property and are responsible for maintaining the "essential character of the University as a Catholic institution."

Through the six Holy Cross priests who are Fellows, the Congregation may fairly be said to have the de facto power to run Notre Dame or at least to prevent any action of which those Fellows disapprove. But this power is divorced from any corporate responsibility on the part of the Congregation. The separation of power from responsibility for its exercise violates basic principles of leadership and management. When Notre Dame's President, Fr. Edward A. Malloy, C.S.C., exercised his clear authority to appoint an abundantly qualified Holy Cross priest as a visitor to the theology department, he was resisted by that department and the Faculty Senate.[30] We ought not to be surprised that Holy Cross priests are treated at Notre Dame with something less than the deference they received when they had the will, as a Congregation, to run the place they had founded. They owned the place and imprudently gave it away. The University statutes provide for preferential treatment of members of the Congregation in faculty appointments, but they have surrendered their right, as a Congregation, to ensure it. In the spirit of Land O'Lakes they have put themselves on the road to a marginalization which invites disdain. They have made themselves the most pathetic characters in the picture. Nevertheless, they could take the place back if they could summon the will to do so. If they did, Notre Dame would have a chance to

---

[29] See, for example, his discussion of Lafayette College and Davidson College in James T. Burtchaell, C.S.C., *The Dying of the Light* (1998), 127-239.

[30] See Charles E. Rice, "Right or Wrong?" *The Observer,* Jan. 17, 1997, p.10; *National Catholic Reporter,* Jan. 31, 1997.

resume its rightful role as the leading authentically Catholic university in the nation.

SOME POSSIBLE CORRECTIVES

"Newman clubs," or orthodox alternatives, should be established near, or if possible on, "Catholic" university campuses. If those universities will not provide their students a predictable opportunity for formation in the Faith, somebody else will have to do it from the outside. Newman club-type efforts should be emphasized as well at state and private universities. The escalation of private college tuition requires a high school grad to consider the lower-cost state colleges if he is contemplating post-graduate education. Incidentally, the increasing availability of distance education may open new prospects for low-cost education that may drive the high-priced "Catholic-flavored" universities into irrelevance.[31] If a student can gain credits from an accredited university for courses taken at home through interactive technology, why should he mortgage his future to attend an overpriced and misrepresented "Catholic" university?

Some Catholic institutions, such as Ave Maria Institute and Ave Maria School of Law in Ann Arbor, Michigan, Franciscan University of Steubenville, Christendom College, Thomas Aquinas College, Thomas More College, the St. Ignatius Institute of the University of San Francisco, Magdalen College and others, offer an opportunity for sound intellectual and moral formation. They should be supported and considered by students and parents as increasingly attractive alternatives to the "Catholic flavored" institutions which misrepresent themselves as "Catholic."

The leaders of the secularized Catholic universities have squandered a heritage that was not theirs to diminish. In some cases, at least, they have done so, not under the pressure of events, but apparently out of a desire to conform and to be accepted by the secular society and its government. Perhaps we should heed Father Robert I. Gannon, S.J., who was president of Fordham University when the Jesuits were doing the job for which they were founded. Fr. Gannon criticized the administrators and faculties of Catholic colleges who "would rather be modern than right [and] would go to any lengths to avoid the stigma of conservatism. In the eyes of such educators a university must be a place where obvious error has a right to equal time. That is why they would maintain that a Catholic university is a contradiction in terms. It is our handicap to know from revelation that some things are false. . . . If the sad day

---

[31] See, for example, the program of the International Catholic University, P.O. Box 495, Notre Dame, IN 46556.

ever comes when the tendency to secularize our campuses not only appears but starts to move toward realization, then indeed the time will have come to auction them for industrial parks and send the money to the foreign missions."[32]

A POSTSCRIPT

It is unlikely that the leaders of the major American Catholic universities will ever voluntarily accept any effective implementation of the norms of *Ex Corde*. In 1997 the Vatican had asked the bishops to include "juridical elements for an effective functioning institutionally of Catholic universities as Catholic in all aspects of their organization, life and activity."[33] At this writing, in 1999, the bishops and the university leaders continue to discuss proposed norms to enforce *Ex Corde Ecclesiae*. The university presidents resist enforcement of Canon Law and other requirements of *Ex Corde* against the universities.[34]

It may be useful to reconsider a proposal made in 1987 by William Bentley Ball, the great constitutional lawyer who died in January 1999.

"My suggestion," Ball wrote, "would. . . enable any institution which desired to meet Church criteria. . . to be accredited as a Catholic institution. The [universities tell] us that accreditation processes, by secular and government agencies, are. . . acceptable — even though they involve a great deal of monitoring,. . . inspection [and] record-keeping,. . . even [as to] 'whether the institution is meeting its stated objectives.' A. . . far less cumbersome, accrediting process. . . could. . . be adopted by the Church [so] the Church [could] provide Catholics and the public. . . a list, in each diocese, of Church-accredited colleges and universities. We would then all know who is who. If a student, or parents, desired higher education at a college of the faith, they would run no risk of being deceived. If a college desired to be all-out orthodox, it would not be subject to unfair competition by those who tell the government that they are nonsectarian and the Catholic market that they are Catholic. But what of the [secularizing universities]? Their problem with the Church would be over. They could label themselves anything they wished. . . . They could,. . . do their own thing. But now everyone would know that that thing is not the real thing."[35]

---

[32] *The Jesuit*, Autumn 1969.
[33] 27 *Origins*, 53, 54 (1997).
[34] See J. Donald Monan, S.J., and Edward A. Malloy, C.S.C., "'Ex Corde Ecclesiae' Creates an Impasse," *America*, Jan. 30, 1999, 6.
[35] William Bentley Ball, "Faith and Freedom," *Crisis*, Mar. 1987, 8.

It could be useful to consider an adaptation of Mr. Ball's proposal in the context of *Ex Corde*. The general norms of *Ex Corde* "are valid for all Catholic universities and other Catholic institutions of higher studies throughout the world."[36] Those norms are to be applied "concretely at the local and regional levels by episcopal conferences and other assemblies of Catholic hierarchy. . . . After review by the Holy See, these local or regional 'ordinances' will be valid for all Catholic universities and other Catholic institutes of higher studies in the region, except for ecclesiastical universities and faculties [such as the Catholic University of America, which] are governed by the norms of the apostolic constitution *Sapientia Christiana*."[37]

Instead of forcing institutions to comply with standards they resist, the objective under the Ball approach would be to afford any institutions that do accept *Ex Corde*, Canon Law and their implementations the opportunity to affirm that acceptance and to pledge to put it into effect.

The burden would be on the college or university. If it accepts those requirements, it could say so. The bishops, including the bishop of the diocese in which the school is located, could publish a list of institutions that have made that commitment. If the institution reneges on its commitment, the bishops could remove it from the list. Any oversight by bishops on the universities would be limited. And juridical enforcement of the norms and ordinances would be minimized if not eliminated.

If the presidents of Catholic universities were selling meat instead of education and if they labeled generic hamburger as ground round, they could find themselves in legal difficulty. The government properly sets binding standards for labeling food. The Catholic Church, speaking through the Vicar of Christ, properly sets binding standards for labeling institutions as Catholic. Canon Law provides that "Even if it really be Catholic, no university may bear the title or name *Catholic university* without the consent of the competent ecclesiastical authority."[38] In *Veritatis Splendor*, John Paul II, citing Canon 808, said: "It falls to [bishops], in communion with the Holy See, both to grant the title 'Catholic' to Church-related schools, universities, health care facilities and counseling services and, in cases of a serious failure to live up to that title, to take it away."[39]

---

[36] *Ex Corde Ecclesiae, General Norms*, 1(1).
[37] *Ibid.*, 1(2).
[38] Canon 808.
[39] *VS*, no. 116.

The criteria that make a university "Catholic" are defined by the Pope who is the only person in the world with ultimate authority to make that definition. If a university will not live by those criteria, it is a species of consumer fraud for it to claim to be "Catholic." The controversy over Catholic universities need not be an occasion to start World War III. But it involves a non-negotiable principle, of truth in labeling. The way to vindicate that principle may simply be to consider an adaptation of Mr. Ball's proposal.

26. WHEN IS IT RIGHT TO "PULL THE PLUG" ON A FAMILY MEMBER?

It may seem abrupt to move the discussion from higher education to terminal care. But both are persistent family questions today. Every reader of this book is likely to confront the problem of "pulling the plug" on a family member. Our pagan culture permits the termination of medical treatment, including artificially provided food and water, whenever the patient's life is seen as no longer worth living, which includes the judgment that the patient's life is burdensome not only to himself but to those who make the decision as to whether he should die.

THE BASIC PRINCIPLE

"*[T]he direct and voluntary killing of an innocent human being is always gravely immoral.*"[1] This includes euthanasia which "*in the strict sense* is understood to be an action or omission which of itself and by intention causes death, with the purpose of eliminating all suffering.*"[2] "*[E]uthanasia is a grave violation of the law of God,* since it is the deliberate and morally unacceptable killing of a human person.*"[3]

So when family members are sitting around wondering what to do about Grandma, who is in a persistent vegetative state and could go on like that for years, they must remember that they cannot morally do or omit anything with the intent of ending her life. If Grandma herself were conscious and competent she would be bound by the same command and could not morally do or omit anything with the intention of ending her own life. "Suicide is always as morally objectionable as murder."[4] She would not, however, be morally required to use all possible means to preserve life:

> Everyone has the duty to care for his or her own life and health and to seek necessary medical care from others, but this does not mean that all possible remedies must be used in all circumstances. One is not obliged to use either "extraordinary" means or "disproportionate" means of preserving life — that is, means which are understood as offering no reasonable hope of benefit or as involving excessive burdens. Decisions regarding such means are complex, and should ordinarily be made by the patient in consultation with his or her family, chaplain or pastor and physician when that is possible.[5]

---

[1] *EV,* no. 57.
[2] *Ibid.,* no. 65.
[3] *Ibid.*
[4] *Ibid.,* no. 66.
[5] U.S. Bishops' Pro-Life Committee, "Nutrition and Hydration: Moral and Pastoral Reflections," 21 *Origins* 705, 706 (1992).

"In the final stage of dying one is not obliged to prolong the life of a patient by every possible means. . . '[w]hen inevitable death is imminent in spite of the means used.'"[6] We are not morally required to turn the dying process into a technological circus in which extraordinary and disproportionate means are used to stave off the inevitable. *Evangelium Vitae* explained:

> Euthanasia must be distinguished from the decision to forego so-called "aggressive medical treatment,". . . medical procedures which. . . are. . . disproportionate to any expected results or [which] impose an excessive burden on the patient and his family. In such situations, when death is clearly imminent and inevitable, one can in conscience "refuse forms of treatment that would only secure a precarious and burdensome prolongation of life, so long as the normal care due to the sick person in similar cases is not interrupted.". . . To forego extraordinary or disproportionate means is not the equivalent of suicide or euthanasia; it rather expresses acceptance of the human condition in the face of death. . . . [I]ncreased attention is being given to what are called "methods of palliative care". . . . Pius XII affirmed that it is licit to relieve pain by narcotics, even when the result is decreased consciousness and a shortening of life, "if no other means exist". . . . In such a case, death is not willed or sought,. . . there is simply a desire to ease pain. . . . All the same, "it is not right to deprive the dying person of consciousness without a serious reason": as they approach death people ought to be able to satisfy their moral and family duties, and above all they ought to be able to prepare in a fully conscious way for their definitive meeting with God.[7]

Note that John Paul's limited endorsement of palliative care, if "death is not willed or sought," is light years removed from the use of such care, or of "terminal sedation," as a cloak for the intentional killing of the patient.[8]

NUTRITION AND HYDRATION

Artificially provided nutrition and hydration are intended to sustain life, not to cure the underlying illness. As long as they are useful in sustaining life, they should be continued unless they themselves are disproportionately painful or burdensome to the patient. Moreover, "[e]ven in the case of the imminently dying patient. . . any action or omission

---

[6] *Ibid.*, quoting Congregation for the Doctrine of the Faith, *Declaration on Euthanasia* (1980), Part IV.

[7] *EV,* no. 65.

[8] See discussion in Question 13.

that of itself or by intention causes death is to be absolutely rejected."[9] Regrettably, as the U.S. Bishops' Pro-Life Committee explained:

> The harsh reality is that. . . nutrition and hydration (whether orally administered or medically assisted) are sometimes withdrawn not because a patient is dying, but precisely because a patient is not dying (or not dying quickly) and someone believes it would be better if he or she did, generally because the patient is perceived as having an unacceptably low "quality of life" or as imposing burdens on others.[10]

In his 1991 pastoral letter, *Instruction for Healthcare Administrators*, Bishop John J. Myers, of Peoria, noted "a subtle distinction which is precisely the heart of the matter. *It is euthanasia to intend to bring an end (through action or omission) to human life which is burdensome or miserable. It is not euthanasia to bring an end to a burdensome means of prolonging life.*"[11] The principles on nutrition and hydration, as applied to different kinds of patients, were spelled out by Bishop James McHugh, of Rockville Centre, New York. His analysis is worth quoting at length:

> [N]utrition and hydration should be provided as part of a patient's normal care, even if [it] requires medical technology, unless or until the benefits of nutrition and hydration are clearly outweighed by a definite danger or burden, or they are clearly useless in sustaining life.

> Artificially assisted nutrition and hydration are not customarily burdensome. . . . They do not usually increase the suffering of the patient. They are not useless, in that they sustain the life of a person who is alive but impaired in terms of function. They provide the basic nourishment necessary for life and maintain a bond of solidarity between caretakers and the helpless person who is dependent upon them.

> There is also the matter of intent. If the withholding or withdrawal of nutrition is *intended* to cause or hasten death, the intention then is euthanasia, and the withholding or withdrawing is morally impermissible. In fact, it seems that in many cases those favoring withholding or withdrawal do *intend* to bring the patient's life to an end because of the lack of any likelihood that consciousness will be regained or restored.

> Claiming that the patient is deprived of autonomy and human dignity because of the dependence on the medical technology, some argue that

---

[9] U.S. Bishops' Pro-Life Committee, "Nutrition and Hydration: Moral and Pastoral Reflections," 21 *Origins* 705, 706 (1992).

[10] 21 *Origins* at 707.

[11] See *The Wanderer*, Oct. 31, 1991, p. 6.

there is no point in sustaining life in such circumstances, and they justify withholding or withdrawing technologically provided food and water to bring on or hasten death. They further argue that this allows the patient to die with dignity and it saves family members the cost and emotional burden of long-term care. However, in such cases discontinuing nutrition and hydration does not simply allow the patient to die from some existing pathology, but introduces a new cause of death, that is, starvation and dehydration. This does not seem morally justifiable in light of the church's teaching on euthanasia.

In light of the above analysis and commentary, the principles should be applied to specific cases in the following manner:

1. *Unconscious, Imminently Dying Patient*: In the unconscious, imminently dying patient (i.e., progressive and rapid deterioration), the dying process has begun and cannot be reversed. Nutrition and hydration are now useless and, all things considered, no longer a reasonable burden.

2. *Conscious, Imminently Dying Patient*: In the conscious, imminently dying patient, nutrition and hydration are useless, possibly burdensome and need not be artificially provided but may be if desired by the patient.

3. *Conscious, Irreversibly Ill, Not Imminently Dying Patient*: In the conscious, irreversibly ill, not imminently dying patient, the person is conscious, beyond cure or reversal of the disease but able to function to some degree. Nutrition and hydration sustain life, so they are not useless; and usually they are not unreasonably burdensome. Nutrition and hydration should be provided unless or until there is clear evidence that [it] constitutes an unreasonable burden for the patient.

4. *Unconscious, Non-Dying Patient*: In the unconscious, non-dying patient, nutrition and hydration should be supplied. Feeding is not useless, because it sustains human life. There is no indication that the person is suffering nor is there any clear evidence that the provision of nutrition and hydration is an unreasonable danger or burden. In such a case, the withdrawal of nutrition/hydration brings about death by starvation/dehydration. Absent any other indication of a definite burden for the patient, withdrawal of nutrition/hydration is not morally justifiable.[12]

---

[12] Bishop James McHugh, "Principles in Regard to Withholding or Withdrawing Artificially Assisted Nutrition/Hydration," 19 *Origins* 314, 315-16 (1989).

This analysis by Bishop McHugh is sound, but a caution is necessary. The determination of whether a patient is "imminently dying" is subject to abuse. The crucial point is whether the withdrawal of nutrition and hydration will introduce "a new cause of death, that is, starvation and dehydration." If the patient is "imminently dying" in the sense that continuation of nutrition and hydration will not prolong his life, it may be justified to remove the nutrition and hydration. The determination that the patient is "imminently dying," however, cannot justify the withdrawal of nutrition and hydration which is effective to keep the patient alive. The fact that you think the patient is "imminently dying" from a pathology cannot justify you in substituting starvation and dehydration as the cause of his death. The potential for abuse here underlines the inability of the law to forbid intentional killing in such situations.[13]

The bottom line: No one ever has the right, on whatever pretext, intentionally to kill Grandma. Or any other innocent human being.

---

[13] See Question 13.

27. SHOULD I HAVE A LIVING WILL?

"If I become a 'human vegetable,' I don't want to be kept alive. I want them to 'pull the plug' and let me go." A common reaction. If a patient is competent he can legally refuse all treatment, including food and water, despite the moral obligation to use ordinary and proportionate means to sustain life.[1] If a patient is incompetent, the living will or the durable power of attorney, which he executed when he was competent, can provide restrictions on the care to be given to him:

> When a patient is not competent to make his or her own decisions, a proxy decision-maker. . . such as a family member or guardian, may be designated to represent the patient's interests and interpret his or her wishes. Here, too, moral limits remain relevant — that is, morally the proxy may not deliberately cause a patient's death or refuse what is clearly ordinary means, even if he or she believes the patient would have made such a decision.[2]

ADVANCE DIRECTIVES

The basic advance directives for health care are the living will and the durable power of attorney.[3] A living will is a written statement of your intentions as to the health care you will receive if you become incompetent. It must be interpreted and implemented by others, including the physician and your family members. A durable power of attorney for health care is an appointment by you of an agent to make health care decisions for you if you become incompetent. It is called "durable" because it allows your agent to act on your behalf even if you become incompetent. An ordinary power of attorney, by which you appoint someone to handle personal or business matters on your behalf, cannot be exercised if you become incompetent. An advance directive, however, is not a magic solution:

> Advance directives do not always resolve what to do in an emergency. . . both because patients and families often waver when confronted with imminent death and because it is often hard to predict whether an emergency intervention will improve the patient's quality of life or consign him to a long painful process of high-tech dying. . . .

---

[1] See *Bouvia v. Superior Ct.*, 179 Cal.App.3d 1127 (1986).

[2] U.S. Bishops' Pro-Life Committee, "Nutrition and Hydration: Moral and Pastoral Reflections," 21 *Origins* 705, 710 (1992).

[3] See Richard A. Leiter, ed., *Right to Die*, 441-96, in *National Survey of State Laws* (1997).

Over the last two decades, every state has provided mechanisms for people to declare, in advance, what measures they want taken if they are incapacitated, or to name a proxy who will make such decisions, or both. Since 1990, the Federal Patient Self-Determination Act has required hospitals and nursing homes to tell patients, on admission, of their right to file an advance directive, and to refuse treatment. . . .

[A]dvance directives have done little to change end-of-life medical care, according to a study financed by the Robert Wood Johnson Foundation. . . . The study. . . found that fewer than half the doctors knew when patients wanted to avoid resuscitation. . . . What stunned the medical community even more was another finding, that intensive efforts to improve matters, using nurses to talk to families and doctors and encourage planning, had no influence on how much the patients' wishes were followed or how much aggressive treatment they received before dying.[4]

Advance directives must be executed in the form prescribed by state law. You should consult an attorney before executing an advance directive. The directive can include additional restrictions as you choose. It is difficult to list in a living will all the contingencies that might arise at the time of your hospitalization. The durable power of attorney is therefore preferable. As the Maryland Catholic Bishops said in their pastoral, *Care of the Sick and Dying*:

. . . [T]he written appointment of a health care agent is preferable to a living will or to an oral directive. . . The chief advantage of appointing a health care agent is that it leaves decision making in the hands of a person of your own choosing . . . . [Y]ou may want to consider the following points:

A.   You should appoint someone who has the strength of character to make good judgments in painful circumstances.

B.   You should appoint someone. . . you can trust to make decisions on the basis of the Church's teaching. The prudent person will select an agent who will act as he or she would have acted. . . .

C.   No one should agree to act as an agent for another person if that person would expect. . . the agent to make decisions which disregard the teaching of the Church. It is not morally acceptable to carry out immoral decisions on behalf of someone else. . . .

---

[4] *N.Y. Times,* June 2, 1996, p. A1.

D. You should appoint someone who is likely to be available to care for you in the distant future. The law implies that only one agent need be designated; it may be advisable, however, to name alternate agents, in the event that your first choice proves unable or unwilling to act for you. . . .

E. Discuss the specifics of your directive with the person whom you wish to choose as your agent. You also are well advised to discuss these specifics with your physician. You also should discuss them with an attorney to ensure that they meet the requirements of the law.[5]

These cautions of the Maryland bishops are important. You could also stipulate that the power of attorney is subject to binding restrictions on the authority of the agent you appoint to act for you, perhaps along the following or similar lines:

1. If I am ill or injured and I am incompetent, all ordinary means must be used to sustain my life and any treatment or procedure may be withheld or withdrawn from me only if such treatment or procedure is extraordinary or disproportionate and therefore optional under the teaching of the Catholic Church; provided that no treatment or procedure may be withheld or withdrawn from me with the intent of causing, or contributing to, my death; and provided further that

2. If I am ill or injured and I am incompetent, nutrition and hydration, whether orally or artificially provided, may be withheld or withdrawn from me only where, in the judgment of my Agent and two attending physicians, such nutrition and hydration are ineffective in sustaining my biological life. I do not authorize, and I forbid, my Agent or any other person to withhold from me nutrition or hydration, whether orally or artificially provided, with the intent or effect of causing, or contributing to, my death.[6]

So, in response to the question, when can you pull the plug? the answer is: you never have a moral right intentionally to kill the innocent, including even yourself. And, whether you are young or old, you ought to take prudent measures to make sure that no one kills you when you are vulnerable.

---

[5] Catholic Bishops of Maryland, *Care of the Sick and Dying* (Oct. 14, 1993), http://www.ewtn.com/library/BISHOPS/SICK.TXT.

[6] For various formulations of advance directives, contact American Life League, P.O. Box 1350, Stafford, VA 22555; Human Life International, Front Royal, VA 22630; CURE, Ltd., 812 Stephen St., Berkeley Springs, WV 25411; Robert C. Cetrulo, P.S.C., 620 Washington St., Covington, KY 41011; Right to Life of Michigan Resource Center, P.O. Box 901, Grand Rapids, MI 49509; Human Life Alliance of Minnesota, 3570 Lexington Ave. N., Suite 205, St. Paul, MN 55126.

28. IS HOMOSEXUALITY A SIN?

No, but the homosexual inclination is a disorder. A person's inclination toward excessive drinking, shoplifting or any other morally disordered act would be a disordered inclination. But the inclination itself would not be sinful so long as it is not acted upon. So it is with the homosexual inclination.

"In 1973– under intense pressure from gay activists– the American Psychiatric Association voted to remove homosexuality from its Diagnostic Manual, and effectively silenced professional discussion of homosexuality as a disorder. Although modern psychology had considered the condition pathological for over 100 years, and all cultures have considered it deviant throughout recorded history, the official view of homosexuality changed overnight."[1] A politicized change in terminology, however, cannot change the reality of nature.

As the *Letter on the Pastoral Care of Homosexual Persons*, issued with the approval of John Paul II in 1986, stated: "Although the particular inclination of the homosexual person is not a sin, it is a more or less strong tendency ordered toward an intrinsic moral evil, and thus the inclination itself must be seen as an objective disorder. Therefore special concern and pastoral attention should be directed toward those who have this condition, lest they be led to believe that the living out of this orientation in homosexual activity is a morally acceptable option. It is not."[2]

Homosexual acts are intrinsically wrong. "It is only in the marital relationship that the use of the sexual faculty can be morally good. A person engaging in homosexual behavior therefore acts immorally. To choose someone of the same sex for one's sexual activity is to annul the rich symbolism and meaning, not to mention the goals, of the Creator's sexual design. . . . This does not mean that homosexual persons are not often generous and giving of themselves; but when they engage in homosexual activity they confirm within themselves a disordered sexual inclination which is essentially self-indulgent. As in every moral disorder, homosexual activity prevents one's own fulfillment and happiness by acting contrary to the creative wisdom of God."[3] The teaching of the Church emphasizes respect for the dignity of the person with a homosexual inclination, but also recognition that the inclination itself is disordered as are the homosexual acts. As the *Catechism* sums it up:

---

[1] *Taking a Stand* (National Assn. for Research and Therapy of Homosexuality (NARTH), undated), 2.

[2] No. 3; 16 *Origins* 378, 379 (1986).

[3] 1986 *Letter*, no. 7.

2358.   The number of men and women who have deep-seated homosexual tendencies is not negligible. This inclination, which is objectively disordered, constitutes for most of them a trial. They must be
accepted with respect, compassion, and sensitivity. Every sign of unjust discrimination in their regard should be avoided. These persons
are called to fulfill God's will in their lives and, if they are Christians,
to unite to the sacrifice of the Lord's Cross the difficulties they may
encounter from their condition.[4]

The reality that the homosexual condition is itself a disorder is dis-
positive. It makes no sense to insist that homosexual acts are intrinsically
evil while denying that the inclination toward those acts is disordered. If
the acts are disordered, how could the inclination toward those acts be
anything but disordered? And if the inclination is not disordered, why
may it not be acted upon? If the homosexual inclination is not recognized as disordered, the prohibition of homosexual acts will be seen as an
arbitrary edict of an insensitive Church. Homosexual acts, and the inclination to them, are "intrinsically disordered," not because of "official
Church teaching," but because they are contrary to nature and the law
of God.

"[D]eparture from the Church's teaching or silence about it, in an
effort to provide pastoral care, is neither caring nor pastoral. Only what
is true can ultimately be pastoral. The neglect of the Church's position
prevents homosexual men and women from receiving the care they need
and deserve. . . . The human person, made in the image and likeness of
God, can hardly be adequately described by a reductionist reference to
his or her sexual orientation. Everyone living on the face of the earth has
personal problems and difficulties, but challenges to growth, strengths,
talents and gifts as well. Today the Church provides a badly needed context for the care of the human person when she refuses to consider the
person as a 'homosexual' and insists that every person has a fundamental
identity: the creature of God and, by grace, his child and heir to eternal
life."[5]

---

[4] See also *CCC*, nos. 2357, 2359.
[5] 1986 *Letter*, nos. 15-16.

29. What should our attitude be on "gay rights"?

[T]he Centers for Disease Control says that if a lifelong smoker dies from any smoking-related disease he or she loses an average of 12 years of life, the same as for lung cancer. . . . Homosexual sex is the largest single cause of AIDS among American men. . . . Deaths from AIDS are less than 28 percent of the deaths from lung cancer, but because AIDS victims die so young, the years of potential life lost from AIDS [average] over 35 years per death, according to figures provided by the National Center for Health Statistics. . . . Like smoking, AIDS is almost entirely the result of a lifestyle choice. Many young lives that will be snuffed out 35 years prematurely could be saved if there were a campaign to make that lifestyle unacceptable to vulnerable youngsters. . . . [H]omosexual conduct is an even greater threat to long life than Joe Camel ever was.[1] — *Reed Irvine and Joe Goulden*

While Joe Camel was being driven off the billboards, the Provincetown, Mass., school board voted "to begin teaching preschoolers about homosexual lifestyles and backed hiring preferences for 'sexual minorities,' cementing the town's position as the nation's leader on homosexual issues."[2] The rest of the country, or at least its elite, is not far behind Provincetown. "Sexual orientation" is increasingly protected by anti-discrimination legislation. Through "domestic partnership" legislation and coverage for employment benefits, same-sex couples are accorded some benefits of marriage in many states and corporations.[3] Public schools inculcate the idea that the homosexual lifestyle is a normal alternative.[4] The media support that idea and cover up the excesses of the homosexual movement:

> Since I've been to enough Gay Pride parades to last me half a dozen lifetimes, I decided to give this year's exercise in public deviance a miss. As a Catholic, you can take only to many spectacles like the Sisters of Perpetual Indulgence, the grotesque mockery of the pope, cardinal and church, the celebration of perversion, and displays of unimaginable vulgarity before you call enough.

> Television's lying, dishonest, double-standard coverage is even worse. Every year, the city's TV stations send their cameras, producers and re-

---

[1] Reed Irvine and Joe Goulden, "Deadlier Habit Than Smoking," *Wash. Times,* Aug. 27, 1997, p. A13.

[2] *Wash. Times,* Aug. 21, 1997, p. A1.

[3] See Jay Alan Sekulow and John Tuskey, "Sex and Sodomy and Apples and Oranges– Does the Constitution Require States to Grant a Right to Do the Impossible?" 12 *B.Y.U.J. of Public Law* 309 (1998).

[4] See Question 24.

porters out and they all come back with glowing accounts. With almost conspiratorial censorship, all six stations automatically delete the lewdness, nudity, profanity and blasphemy that are the intrinsic ingredients of the parade. . . . Instead, they present the parade as a fun festival, rich in color, pageantry and pride. The distortion is a criminal abuse of truth. . . .

The WABC/Channel 7 anchors could hardly contain their enthusiasm. "It was a wild and fun afternoon. . . a fun affair." None of them told of the reported half-dozen men who were stark naked except for their green condoms. None told of the bare-breasted women prancing down the avenue. None showed the lurid excesses of the drag queens and cross-dressers. None find it offensive that this essentially obscene promenade starts at 52nd Street so it will pass the front doors of St . Patrick's Cathedral and dishonor the religion it represents.

The anti-Catholic thrust of the gay parade is recognized by the mayors (Ed Koch and Rudy Giuliani) who invariably join the march at 48th Street, past the cathedral. They wouldn't dare join this parade at any point if it insisted on passing and desecrating a sacred black church or synagogue. Indeed, if the media thought the Gay Pride Parade was racist or anti-Semitic in tone, they would pour the fires of hell on it. Let it be anti-Catholic, and it's suddenly fun and festive, a tribute to the First Amendment.

Public acceptance of the double-standard is part of the virulent Christian-bashing binge that seems to be sweeping the country. It's in the movies, on television, on the stage, in art, in politics. . . everywhere. I'm tired of it. So is William Donohue, president of the Catholic League for Religious and Civil Rights. "Could you imagine, say, a pro-life demonstration with some lunatics going naked in the streets?" he asked. "It would be front page everywhere. Puerto Ricans, Irish, Italians, Jews, Poles, West Indians all have parades, but none feels compelled to disrobe. The Gay Pride Parade itself demonstrates it is genitally derived."

"I believe it all comes down to sex," Donohue said. "The church teaches restraint, its opponents want to abandon restraint, so the church is an impediment to their libertine understanding of sexuality."[5]

IT'S A WAR

The homosexual movement is at war with the Catholic Church and the family. "The cause of this cultural war. . . is the relentless drive by

---

[5] Ray Kerrison, "Media Coverage of Gay Parade Reeks of Christian-Bashing," *New York Post,* June 30, 1998, p. 16.

homosexuals and their allies to use schools and media to validate and propagate their moral beliefs, to convert America to those beliefs, and to codify them in federal law."[6]

When the European Parliament approved homosexual marriage and the adoption of children by homosexual couples, John Paul II said that the Parliament "does not merely defend people with homosexual *tendencies* by rejecting unjust discrimination in their regard. The Church agrees with that — indeed, she supports and approves it . . . . What is not morally acceptable is the legal approval of homosexual *activity*. Being understanding towards the sinner who is unable to free himself from this tendency is not the same as lessening the requirement of the moral norm . . . . Without a basic awareness of the moral law, human life and human dignity are subject to decadence and ruin. Forgetting Christ's words, 'the truth will set you free' (Jn 8:32), the attempt has been made to tell the inhabitants of this continent that moral evil, deviation, a kind of slavery, is the way to liberation, thus distorting the true meaning of the family. The relationship of two men or two women cannot constitute a true family; still less can one grant such a union the right to adopt children who lack a family. These children suffer great danger, grave harm, because in these 'substitute families' they do not have a father and mother, but two fathers or two mothers. This is dangerous."[7]

THE DIGNITY OF THE PERSON

"The Roman Catholic Church is now the counterculture," says Father John F. Harvey, O.S.F.S., director of Courage, a support group for Catholic men and women — and their families — who try to live chaste lives in accord with Catholic teaching on homosexuality.[8] The homosexual movement insists that the homosexual inclination is a permanent, unchangeable condition, contrary to the abundant evidence, provided by Courage, Exodus (an ex-gay ministry), Focus on the Family, and other sources, that some homosexuals can overcome their homosexual inclination and lead normal heterosexual lives.[9] Joseph Nicolosi, Ph.D., executive director of NARTH, the National Association for the Research and Therapy of Homosexuality, states: "[O]ver 300 professionally published studies. . . have shown reparative therapy to bring about change. You can go back in the literature and find such studies back in the 1920s. Besides that, NARTH has just completed its own two-year re-

---

[6] Patrick Buchanan, "Commentary," *Wash. Times*, Sept. 14, 1994, p. A16.
[7] 39 *The Pope Speaks* 249, 250 (1994).
[8] Contact Courage at St. John the Baptist Church, 210 West 31st St., New York, NY 10001, (212) 268-1010.
[9] See *Wash. Times*, Aug. 4, 1998, p. A2; *Today's Catholic*, Sept. 27, 1998, p. 10.

search project. We have more than 860 individuals who say that they have experienced varying degrees of sexual reorientation change and over 200 licensed psychotherapists who say they have participated in the successful treatment of homosexuality. There's lots of information, but it's being politically covered up."[10]

The 1986 Letter from the Congregation for the Doctrine of the Faith emphasized the duty of "the entire Christian community" to "recognize its own call to assist its brothers and sisters, without deluding them or isolating them."[11] "It is deplorable that homosexual persons have been and are the object of violent malice in speech or in action. Such treatment deserves condemnation. . . . The intrinsic dignity of each person must always be respected in word, in actions and law. But the proper reaction to crimes committed against homosexual persons should not be to claim that the homosexual condition is not disordered. When such a claim is made and when homosexual activity is consequently condoned, or when civil legislation is introduced to protect behavior to which no one has any conceivable right, neither the Church nor society at large should be surprised when other distorted notions and practices gain ground, and irrational and violent reactions increase."[12]

On July 23, 1992, the Congregation for the Doctrine of the Faith released to the public a "background resource" analysis on legislative proposals to forbid discrimination on the ground of sexual orientation. Although not "an official and public instruction on the matter," it offers pertinent insights on the homosexual issue:

> "Sexual orientation" does not constitute a quality comparable to race, ethnic background, etc., in respect to non-discrimination. Unlike these, homosexual orientation is an objective disorder. . . . There are areas in which it is not unjust discrimination to take sexual orientation into account, for example, in the placement of children for adoption or foster care, in employment of teachers or athletic coaches, and in military recruitment. Homosexual persons, as human persons, have the same rights as all persons, including the right of not being treated in a manner which offends their personal dignity. . . . Among other rights, all persons have the right to work, to housing, etc. Nevertheless, these rights are not absolute . . . . The "sexual orientation" of a

---

[10] *National Catholic Register,* Dec. 7-13, 1997, p. 20. Contact NARTH, 16633 Ventura Blvd., Suite 1340, Encino, CA 91436-1801, (818) 789-4440.

[11] Congregation for the Doctrine of the Faith, "The Pastoral Care of Homosexual Persons," 160 *Origins* 378 (1986).

[12] *Ibid.*, no. 11.

person is not comparable to race, sex, age, etc. also for another reason. . . . An individual's sexual orientation is generally not known to others unless he publicly identifies himself as having this orientation or unless some overt behavior manifests it. . . . Homosexual persons who assert their homosexuality tend to be precisely those who judge homosexual behavior or lifestyle to be "completely harmless, if not an entirely good thing" and hence worthy of public approval.[13]

The 1986 *Letter* noted that "increasing numbers of people today, even within the church, are bringing enormous pressure to bear on the church to accept the homosexual condition as though it were not disordered and to condone homosexual activity. . . . The movement within the church, which takes the form of pressure groups of various names and sizes, attempts to give the impression that it represents all homosexual persons who are Catholics. As a matter of fact, its membership is by and large restricted to those who either ignore the teaching of the church or seek somehow to undermine it. It brings together under the aegis of Catholicism homosexual persons who have no intention of abandoning their homosexual behavior. One tactic used is to protest that any and all criticism of or reservations about homosexual people, their activity and lifestyle are simply diverse forms of unjust discrimination."[14]

The misnamed "gay rights" movement is not about "rights" in any legitimate sense of that term. Rather, its objective is to impose upon society a view of the person and of the family that is at war with nature and the divine law. The proper response to that movement is to refuse compromise on its objectives and to speak the truth. The teaching of the Church on the homosexual issue is hopeful, constructive and balanced. It adheres to the truth and it respects the dignity of the person. Our attitude should reflect that teaching.

---

[13] Nos. 10-14, quoting from 1986 *Letter*.
[14] 1986 *Letter*, nos. 8, 9.

30.   SHOULD WE MAKE SUNDAY A SPECIAL KIND OF DAY?

> Why must Little League and soccer league games be scheduled on
> Sunday mornings? Why create this conflict for kids or for their par-
> ents?. . . Church has been traditional on Sunday mornings. . . since
> the earliest days of our republic and before . . . . Is it more important
> for a youngster to go to church than to play baseball or soccer? Don't
> we normally give prime time to what we believe is most important?. . .
> There are Saturday evening Masses and Sunday evening Masses,
> and. . . many Protestant bodies have divine services at varying
> times. . . But why is it religion that must always accommodate? This is
> the constant erosion, the constant secularization of our culture, that
> I. . . believe to be a serious mistake. — *John Cardinal O'Connor*[1]

Unfortunately, nobody paid much attention to the Cardinal. "Years
ago," commented the president of Southern Baptist Theological Seminary, "a statement like this — from the man known simply as His Emi-
nence to most New Yorkers — would have brought Little League to a
Sunday standstill. No more. Americans now treat Sundays like any other
day, though for many work takes a back seat to leisure activities. . . . The
erosion of Sunday observance is the. . . result of a decline of Christian
conviction. A loss of faith preceded the encroachment of Little League.
If enough parents refused to let their children play on Sundays, the
league would have to adjust. Committed Christians know Sunday is the
Lord's Day — the day set aside for the worship of God. . . . A secular society has no use for a day of Christian worship."[2]

THE CHANGING SIGNIFICANCE OF SUNDAY

Sunday closing laws in America, from the beginning, combined religious and other purposes. Their main initial purpose was to promote the
Sabbath duty to God. "But even during the seventeenth and eighteenth
centuries those laws served secular purposes, providing workers with a
common day of rest and protecting small shopkeepers from larger com-
petitors able to operate on Sunday with hired workers."[3]

In 1961, the Supreme Court held that the "present purpose and effect" of Maryland's Sunday closing laws were not religious and therefore
did not violate the Establishment Clause.[4] While "the original laws

---

[1] John Cardinal O'Connor, *New York Online,* July 16, 1998, 1.
[2] *Raleigh News and Observer,* July 10, 1998, p. F4.
[3] Alan Raucher, "Sunday Business and the Decline of Sunday Closing Laws: A Historical Overview," 36 *J. of Church and State* 29 (1994).
[4] *McGowan v. Maryland,* 366 U.S. 420, 445 (1961).

which dealt with Sunday labor were motivated by religious forces," those laws are now secular in that "secular justifications have been advanced for making Sunday a day of rest, a day when people may recover from the labor of the week just passed and may. . . prepare for the week's work to come. [It] would seem unrealistic. . . to require a state to choose a common day of rest other than that which most persons would select of their own accord."[5]

> When the discount chain, Two Guys from Harrison-Allentown, Inc., challenged Pennsylvania's Sunday closing law in 1957, Herbert Hubschman, president of Two Guys, condemned the law as out of touch with the changing times: "Shopping is a recreation," he reportedly quipped, "Look at the way your wife enjoys it.". . . As "habits of the heart" changed, America abandoned. . . the myth of community order based on a common day of rest. . . . [B]y the mid-twentieth century Sunday had become. . . secular, even for a great many Christians. By then consumer-oriented mass marketing. . . had made Sunday closing laws anachronistic. . . .[P]ragmatism was already "working in favor of the customer, who demands certain products and services for his family on Sunday.". . . Many busy people. . . could not easily find time to shop other than on Sundays. Just as the once austere American Sunday had earlier yielded to rational recreation and other exceptions, so too did business interests and changing public attitudes bring down the last significant legal barriers to retailing on Sundays. And when the laws changed, Sunday business usually flourished.[6]

"THE WEEKLY EASTER"

"'The erosion of Sunday as a day of rest is a profound loss,' said Harvard economist Juliet Schor, author of 'The Overworked American.' 'America is a more frenzied and harried society than it was 20 or 25 years ago.'"[7] However, the "main point" of the Sabbath commandment, said Pope John Paul in his 1998 encyclical, *Dies Domini*, is "not just any kind of *interruption* of work, but the *celebration* of the marvels which God has wrought."[8] John Paul described Sunday as "the weekly Easter. . . *the day of the Risen Lord*, celebrating God's work of creation and 'new creation.'"[9]

---

[5] 366 U.S. at 431, 434, 452.
[6] Raucher, at 29, 32-33.
[7] William Bole, "Sunday Blue Laws Fading into History," *Cleveland Plain Dealer,* Jan. 1, 1995, p. 3-I.
[8] *Dies Domini,* no. 17.
[9] *Ibid.*, nos. 55, 57.

"Unfortunately," the Pope said, "when Sunday loses its fundamental meaning and becomes merely part of a 'weekend,' it can happen that people stay locked within a horizon so limited that they can no longer see 'the heavens'. . . . The disciples of Christ, however, are asked to avoid any confusion between the celebration of Sunday, which should truly be a way of keeping the Lord's Day holy, and the 'weekend,' understood as a time of simple rest and relaxation."[10]

"Since the Eucharist is the very heart of Sunday, it is clear why, from the earliest centuries, the Pastors of the Church have not ceased to remind the faithful of *the need to take part in the liturgical assembly*. . . . When. . . their assemblies were banned with the greatest severity, many were courageous enough to defy the imperial decree and accepted death rather than miss the Sunday Eucharist. This was the case of the martyrs of Abitina. . .who replied to their accusers: 'Without fear of any kind we have celebrated the Lord's Supper, because it cannot be missed; that is our law'; 'We cannot live without the Lord's Supper.' As she confessed her faith, one of the martyrs said: 'Yes, I went to the assembly and I celebrated the Lord's Supper with my brothers and sisters, because I am a Christian.'"

Today, "[t]he Code of Canon Law [states] that 'on Sundays and other holy days of obligation the faithful are bound to attend Mass.' This legislation has normally been understood as entailing a grave obligation; this is the teaching of the Catechism of the Catholic Church and it is easy to understand why if we keep in mind how vital Sunday is for the Christian life."[11]

THE DAY OF REST

The character of Sunday as a day of rest is related to the spiritual character of the day. "The alternation between work and rest, built into human nature, is willed by God himself, as appears in the creation story in the Book of Genesis . . . . [R]est is. . .'sacred' because it is man's way of withdrawing from. . . earthly tasks. . . to renew his awareness that everything is the work of God."[12]

"Ever since Apostolic times," John Paul said, "the Sunday gathering has been for Christians a moment of fraternal sharing with the very poor. . . . If Sunday is a day of joy, Christian should declare by their. . . behavior that we cannot be happy 'on our own.' They look around to find people who may need their help. . . . It is true that commitment to

---

[10] *Ibid.*, no. 4.
[11] *Ibid.*, no. 47; see *Code of Canon Law*, Canon 1247; *CCC*, nos. 2180-86.
[12] *Dies Domini,* no. 65.

these people cannot be restricted to occasional Sunday gestures. But. . . why not make the Lord's Day a more intense time of sharing. . .? Inviting to a meal people who are alone, visiting the sick, providing food for needy families, spending a few hours in voluntary work and acts of solidarity: these would certainly be ways of bringing into people's lives the love of Christ received at the Eucharistic table. Lived in this way, not only the Sunday Eucharist but the whole of Sunday becomes a great school of charity, justice and peace."[13]

The law should recognize Sunday as a day of rest. "[T]he link between the Lord's Day and the day of rest in civil society has a meaning and importance which go beyond the distinctly Christian point of view. . . . Pope Leo XIII, in his encyclical *Rerum Novarum,* spoke of Sunday rest as a worker's right which the State must guarantee. . . . Therefore, also in the particular circumstances of our own time, Christians will naturally strive to ensure that civil legislation respects their duty to keep Sunday holy. In any case, they are obliged in conscience to arrange their Sunday rest in a way which allows them to take part in the Eucharist, refraining from work and activities which are incompatible with the sanctification of the Lord's Day."[14]

Sunday is related to the culture of life issues discussed in this book. The Sunday observance is an affirmation of the dignity of the person over utility. The observance of other holy days by adherents of other religions can serve the same purpose. Man needs time to reflect on himself and on his God. As Jonathan Wilson, professor of religious studies at Westmont College, said, "I think we are getting a little worn down as a people and as a culture and we're saying, 'Wouldn't it be nice if we all were off on this day?' Part of it is nostalgia, but maybe we're also saying, 'There may be something emotionally and psychologically right about this idea of the Sabbath. Maybe God knew what he was doing.'"[15]

---

[13] *Ibid.,* nos. 70-73.
[14] *Ibid.,* nos. 67; see *CCC* 2187-88.
[15] *Dallas Morning News,* July 5, 1998, p. 1A.

C.   The Right to Life: No Exception

31.   WHY IS ABORTION NEVER MORALLY OR LEGALLY JUSTIFIED IN ANY CASE?

In 1995, at least 1,210,883 American babies were legally executed by abortion, not including the uncounted but larger number killed by chemical and other early abortifacients.[1] In all the wars this nation has fought, from the Revolution through Desert Storm in Iraq, including both sides of the Civil War, American battle deaths total 650,604.[2] The body count of unborn babies reaches that figure about every six months. Every year abortion wipes out the combined populations of Atlanta, Boston, and Louisville.[3]

Is even a single one of these killings of unborn babies morally or legally justified? Three decades ago the California Medical Association editorially observed that a new ethic of killing is taking over this nation: "Since the old ethic has not yet been fully displaced it has been necessary to separate the idea of abortion from the idea of killing, which continues to be socially abhorrent. The result has been a curious avoidance of the scientific fact, which everyone really knows, that human life begins at conception and is continuous whether intra– or extra– uterine until death."[4]

LIFE OF THE MOTHER

Many abortion opponents concede that abortion is killing, but claim that it ought to be allowed in "hard cases," to preserve the life or health of the mother, when pregnancy results from rape or incest or where the unborn child is defective. However, there appear to be no situations where abortion is medically or psychiatrically necessary to save the life of the mother.[5]   Bernard Nathanson, M.D., who himself had been

---

[1]   Centers for Disease Control, *Morbidity and Mortality Weekly Report*, July 3, 1998, p. 31. The Alan Guttmacher Institute, the research affiliate of Planned Parenthood, consistently reports higher numbers of abortions than the CDC. AGI gets its data directly from abortion providers, while CDC relies on government health agencies. For 1994, the CDC put the total abortions at 1,267,416 and the AGI put it at 1,435,000. See *Abortion in the United States: Statistics and Trends* (National Right to Life Committee, June 4, 1997).

[2]   *World Almanac and Book of Facts* (1998), 161.

[3]   *Ibid.*, 385.

[4]   113 *California Medicine* 67 (Sept. 1970).

[5]   David C. Wilson, "The Abortion Problem in the General Hospital," in Harold Rosen, *Abortion in America* (1967); see discussion in Kenneth D. Whitehead, *Respectable Killing: The New Abortion Imperative* (1972), 93; Frederick L. Good, *Marriage, Morals & Medical Ethics* (1951), 148-49; and see the discussion of testimony at a Rhode Island legislative hearing, *The Wanderer*, Apr. 23, 1981, p. 3, col. 1.

responsible for 30,000 abortions, said, "In our first book [after he stopped doing abortions], we proposed a lengthy list of illnesses (including but not limited to heart or kidney disease) which would justify abortion. We regard that list now with. . . . disbelief: if women with heart and liver transplants can be carried successfully through pregnancy, we can no longer conceive of any medical condition which would legitimize abortion. In short, we have slowly evolved to an unshakable posture of no exceptions . . . . [W]orkable, morally acceptable legislation proscribing abortion can have no exceptions written into it– not even medical ones."[6] As Dr. Hymie Gordon, the Mayo Clinic geneticist, put it, "A doctor who kills a preborn baby to save the mother should surrender his license."[7]

We must distinguish, however, cases such as the cancerous uterus and extra-uterine pregnancies. If a pregnant woman has a cancerous uterus which imminently threatens her life and the operation cannot be postponed until the baby it contains is able to survive outside the womb, then the uterus may be removed even though the removal results in the death of the unborn child. Similarly, when the fertilized ovum lodges in the fallopian tube and grows there, the damaged portion of the tube, containing the human being, may be removed where it is clearly and imminently necessary to save the mother's life. Such operations are moral even under Catholic teaching.[8] Morally, they are considered indirect abortions and are justified by the principle of the double effect, since the death of the child is an unintended effect of an operation independently justified by the necessity of saving the mother's life.[9] They do not involve the intentional killing of the unborn child for the purpose of achieving another good, for example, the preservation of the mother's life. Legally, such operations are not considered abortions at all. No prosecution has ever been attempted in this country based on the removal of any of those conditions, even where the mother's life was not immediately threatened. There is no need, therefore, to provide a specific exception for such cases in a statute or constitutional amendment prohibiting abortion.

Apart from cases such as the ectopic pregnancy and the cancerous uterus, there appears to be no medical or psychiatric justification for ter-

---

[6] *Bernadell Technical Bulletin,* April 1991; see generally Bernard N. Nathanson, M.D., *The Abortion Papers: Inside the Abortion Mentality* (1983); Bernard Nathanson, M.D., *The Hand of God* (1996), 128-31.

[7] Human Life International, *Special Report,* Apr. 1991.

[8] *Ethical and Religious Directives for Catholic Health Facilities* (National Conference of Catholic Bishops, 1994), nos. 47, 48; 24 *Origins* 450, 458 (1994).

[9] See John A. Hardon, S.J., *The Catholic Catechism* (1975), 337. Fr. Hardon's explanation of the principle of the double effect is quoted in Question 13.

minating a pregnancy. Even if there were, abortion should not be allowed. If two people are on a one-man raft in the middle of the ocean, the law does not permit one to throw the other overboard even to save his own life.[10] Otherwise, might would make right. In maternity cases, the duty of the doctor is to use his best efforts to save both his patients, the mother and her child. He should not be given a license to kill intentionally either of them.

"Never and in no case," said Pope Pius XII in 1951, "has the Church taught that the life of the child must be preferred to that of the mother. It is erroneous to put the question with this alternative: either the life of the child or that of the mother. No, neither the life of the mother nor that of the child can be subjected to direct suppression. In the one case as in the other, there can be but one obligation: to make every effort to save the lives of both, of the mother and the child."[11]

NO OTHER EXCEPTION

If an exception should not be made where the life of the mother is concerned, it follows that it should not be made for any lesser reason. To allow abortion to prevent injury to the mother's mental or physical health (where her life is not in danger) is to allow killing for what amounts to convenience. And to kill the unborn child because he may be defective is to do what the Nazis did to the Jews whose lives they regarded as not worth living.

Politically, the most appealing reasons to allow abortion are for rape and incest. Of the two, rape is the broader category. Every act of intercourse by a minor, i.e., a girl below the age of legal consent, is rape, whether forcible or statutory or both. The fact that the intercourse is incestuous does not change its character as a rape. An act of intercourse, incestuous or otherwise, by an adult woman against her will or where she is incapable of consent, is also rape. Pro-abortion literature misleadingly refers to "rape *or* incest" as if they were totally separate categories. But the only case of pregnancy resulting from incestuous intercourse which would not fall within the broader category of rape would be that resulting from a voluntary act of intercourse by an adult woman capable of consent. A victim of rape has the right to resist her attacker. But the unborn child is an innocent non-aggressor who should not be killed because of the crime of his father. Since the woman has the right to resist the rapist, she has the right to resist his sperm. Non-abortive measures

---

[10] See *Regina v. Dudley and Stephens*, 14 Q.B.D. 624 (1884); *U.S. v. Holmes*, 26 Fed. Cas. 360 (no. 15,383) (C.C.E.D. Pa., 1842).

[11] 53 *AAS* (1951), 855.

can be taken, consistent with the law and Catholic teaching, promptly after the rape, which are not intended to abort and which may prevent conception.[12] However, once the innocent third party, the child, is conceived, he should not be killed. The state and society have the duty to solve the problems constructively with personal and financial support through delivery and beyond. It is not enough merely to forbid the abortion without providing all necessary help.[13] But a license to kill is never a constructive solution to a troubled pregnancy.

"Human life is sacred," according to *Evangelium Vitae,* "because from its beginning it involves 'the creative action of God,' and it remains forever in a special relationship with the Creator, who is its sole end. God alone is the Lord of life from its beginning until its end: no one can, in any circumstance, claim for himself the right to destroy directly an innocent human being."[14]

There are no exceptions to the moral prohibition of abortion nor to the duty of the state to protect innocent life. "The Catholic Church," said John Paul II in his 1998 address to the Pontifical Academy of Life, "insists that the recognition of the dignity of the human being as a person from the moment of conception also be guaranteed by law."[15] As John Paul said, "a law which violates an innocent person's natural right to life is unjust and, as such, is not valid as a law."[16]

---

[12] "A female who has been raped should be able to defend herself against a potential conception from the sexual assault. If, after appropriate testing, there is no evidence that conception has occurred already, she may be treated with medications that would prevent ovulation, sperm capacitation or fertilization. It is not permissible, however, to initiate or to recommend treatments that have as their purpose or direct effect the removal, destruction or interference with the implantation of a fertilized ovum." *Ethical and Religious Directives for Catholic Health Care Facilities,* no. 36; 24 *Origins* 450-456 (1994).

[13] Contact Life After Assault League, 1336 W. Lindbergh St., Appleton, WI 54914, (414) 739-4489.

[14] *EV,* no. 53, quoting *Instruction on Bioethics* (1987).

[15] 43 *The Pope Speaks* 235, 236 (1998).

[16] *EV,* no. 90.

32. CAN IT EVER BE MORAL TO PURSUE AN INCREMENTAL STRATEGY, PROPOSING OR SUPPORTING LAWS THAT WOULD LIMIT ABORTION BUT ALLOW IT IN SOME CASES?

It can be moral to pursue such an incremental strategy, in the limited circumstances spelled out in *Evangelium Vitae.*

THE LAW *MUST* PROTECT INNOCENT LIFE

The civil law is under a moral duty to protect innocent life. At the Capitol Mall in Washington, in 1979, Pope John Paul II declared, "If a person's right to life is violated at the moment in which he is first conceived in his mother's womb, an indirect blow is struck also at the whole of the moral order, which serves to ensure the inviolable goods of man. Among those goods, life occupies the first place. . . . And so, we will stand up every time that human life is threatened. When the sacredness of life before birth is attacked, we will stand up and proclaim that no one ever has the authority to destroy unborn life."

The duty of the civil law to protect the right to life was emphasized in the *Instruction on Bioethics*, issued in 1987, with papal approval, by the Congregation for the Doctrine of the Faith. While the *Instruction*, with respect to the civil law, focused on "techniques of artificial transmission of life and. . . "experimentation," it enunciated principles that apply as well to abortion. The *Instruction* declared that "The human being is to be respected and treated as a person from the moment of conception; and therefore from that same moment his rights as a person must be recognized, among which in the first place is the inviolable right of every innocent human being to life."[1]

The *Instruction* recognized that the "civil law. . . must sometimes tolerate. . . things which it cannot forbid without a greater evil resulting. However," the *Instruction* continued, "the inalienable rights of the person must be recognized and respected by civil society and the political authority."[2] Among the "fundamental rights" that must be "recognized and respected" by the civil law, the *Instruction* enumerated first "every human being's right to life and physical integrity from the moment of conception until death."[3] Therefore, *"the law must provide appropriate penal sanctions for every deliberate violation of the child's rights."*[4] *Evangelium Vitae* similarly emphasized the duty of the civil law to protect the right to life:

[1]   *Part I* (1).
[2]   *Part III.*
[3]   *Ibid.*
[4]   *Ibid.* (emphasis added).

[C]ivil law must ensure that all members of society enjoy respect for certain fundamental rights which. . . every positive law must recognize and guarantee. First and fundamental. . . is the inviolable right to life of every innocent human being. While public authority can sometimes choose not to put a stop to something which — were it prohibited — would cause more serious harm, it can never presume to legitimize as a right of individuals. . . an offence against other persons caused by the disregard of so fundamental a right as the right to life. The legal toleration of abortion or of euthanasia can in no way claim to be based on respect for the consciences of others, precisely because society has the right and the duty to protect itself against the abuses which can occur in the name of conscience and under the pretext of freedom.[5]

The civil law can never validly tolerate the intentional killing of the innocent by abortion, euthanasia or in any other way. "[A] civil law authorizing abortion or euthanasia ceases by that very fact to be a true, morally binding civil law. . . . In the case of an intrinsically unjust law, such as a law permitting abortion or euthanasia, it is therefore never licit to obey it, or to 'take part in a propaganda campaign in favour of such a law, or vote for it.'"[6]

The Legislator's Dilemma

The Pope went on to examine the responsibility of legislators "where a legislative vote would be decisive for the passage of a more restrictive law, aimed at limiting the number of authorized abortions, in place of a more permissive law already passed or ready to be voted on. . . . [W]hen it is not possible to overturn or completely abrogate a pro-abortion law, an elected official, whose absolute personal opposition to procured abortion was well known, could licitly support proposals aimed at *limiting the harm* done by such a law and at lessening its negative consequences at the level of general opinion and public morality. This [is] not in fact an illicit cooperation with an unjust law, but rather a legitimate and proper attempt to limit its evil aspects."[7]

When a legislator votes for a "more restrictive law" that would still permit abortion, that vote can be "a legitimate and proper attempt to limit [the] evil aspects" of the more permissive law. This can be a worthy tactic to save lives. Legislators who so act, in accord with the criteria of *Evangelium Vitae*, merit respect for their efforts to save the lives of the

---

[5]   *EV,* no. 71.
[6]   *EV,* nos. 72-73, quoting from Congregation for the Doctrine of the Faith, *Declaration on Procured Abortion* (1974), no. 22.
[7]   *EV,* no. 73.

innocent. However, it does not follow that pursuit of such a tactic is practical and prudent.

The Pope says that a legislator "could" licitly support such a proposal. He does not say that he "should." This leaves open the prudential question of whether pro-life support for such compromise measures might increase the "negative consequences" of legalized abortion "at the level of general opinion and public morality," especially when such compromises are promoted by "pro-life" advocates themselves. This is not to say that a legislator is acting immorally if he reluctantly votes as a last resort for a bill that would allow some abortions, e.g., with parental consent or for rape, incest, or the life of the mother. But it is relevant to ask whether the requirements of *EV*, no. 73 are met in a particular case, especially with respect to the requirement that a legislator must make "well known" his "absolute personal opposition to procured abortion." Many legislators who seek cover under no. 73 do not appear to fulfill its terms. In such cases, their actions would not be morally justified. However, it is not fruitful to question whether they are subjectively acting morally. Instead, a prudent response would be simply to state the terms of no. 73, emphasizing that even in its stated circumstances, it says "could," not "should," and then address the question of whether the incremental approach is practical in prudential terms.

Evangelium Vitae does not explicitly address the morality of support for exceptions by others than legislators. John Paul asserts that "we all [have] the inescapable responsibility of *choosing to be unconditionally pro-life*."[8] However, since a legislator "could licitly support" exceptions in the circumstances defined in no. 73, pro-life individuals and groups could morally assist him in drafting and explaining such legislation. At some point, such individuals and groups could exceed the bounds of permissible material cooperation in their work on exception provisions. *Evangelium Vitae* does not address the limits of such assistance. Nor does it address the moral obligations of voters with respect to candidates for public office who favor exception. The moral issues here with respect to legislators, those who assist them, voters and others are governed in general by the criteria relating to permissible cooperation with evil.

While a pro-life legislator or other pro-life person may be morally justified in supporting imperfect legislation, the further question is whether such support is prudent, as will be discussed in Question 34.

---

[8] *EV*, no. 28.

33.   WHAT PRINCIPLES GOVERN THE MORALITY OF COOPERATION WITH ABORTION OR OTHER EVILS?

Evangelium Vitae addressed the cooperation issue:

Christians, like all people of good will, are called upon. . . not to cooperate formally in practices which, even if permitted by civil legislation, are contrary to God's law. Indeed. . . it is never licit to cooperate formally in evil. Such cooperation occurs when an action, either by its very nature or by the form it takes in a concrete situation, can be defined as a direct participation in an act against innocent human life or a sharing in the immoral intention of the person committing it. This cooperation can never be justified either by invoking respect for the freedom of others or by appealing to the fact that civil law permits it or requires it. — *Evangelium Vitae*[1]

Formal cooperation in evil, which is never morally justified, therefore consists of "direct participation" in the evil act "or a sharing in the immoral intention of the person committing it."[2] *Evangelium Vitae* did not explicitly state the principles of material, as opposed to formal, cooperation. "Material cooperation is that in which the cooperator performs an act which in itself is not wrong, though it is used by the principal agent to help him commit sin. This type of cooperation, as opposed to formal cooperation in evil, is not always wrong. Its morality depends on the proximity to the immoral act itself and whether there is a proportionate reason. Thus, material cooperation may be either proximate or remote."[3]

In his 1990 pastoral statement, *The Obligations of Catholics and the Rights of Unborn Children,* Bishop John J. Myers, of Peoria, explained the principles of formal and material cooperation with reference to abortion. It is worth extensive quotation:

VOTERS

As voters, Catholics are under an obligation to avoid implicating themselves in abortion. There can be no assurance that voters will. . . have a qualified pro-life candidate to choose. . . . [A]bstention is a permissible political response. There are. . . circumstances (as in an election between two pro-abortion candidates, one of whom is more extreme than the other) in which it is possible for a Catholic legitimately

---

[1] *EV,* no. 74.
[2] *Ibid.*
[3] Rev. Edward J. Hayes, Msgr. Paul J. Hayes, Dorothy Ellen Kelly, R.N., James J. Drummey, *Catholicism and Ethics: A Medical/Moral Handbook* (1997), 72.

to vote for a pro-abortion candidate. However, a Catholic may never count an office seeker's advocacy of legal abortion or public funding of abortion as a reason to favor that person's candidacy. Indeed, it is wrong not to count such advocacy as a very weighty reason against the candidacy. A Catholic may support the candidacy of someone who would permit unjust killing only when the real alternatives are candidates who would permit even more unjust killing. . . .

LEGISLATORS

Formal complicity in any legislation or public policy promoting abortion is gravely wrong. Under certain limited circumstances, a Catholic legislator may. . . vote for a measure that would protect some unborn children, but not all of them,. . . only if the legislator decides there is at that time no reasonable hope of enacting legislation which would protect equally all unborn children; a legislator in this position should make it clear that the legislation. . . is not adequate and should work to make possible the eventual enactment of more just legislation. . . .

One is formally complicit in the injustice of abortion when one votes for a candidate even partially on the basis of his or her pro-abortion positions. The same is true when a legislator votes for legislation even partially for the purpose of making abortion available.

One who supports legal abortion cannot avoid formal complicity by maintaining that he or she wills not abortion as such, but only the freedom of others to choose abortion. . . . From the ethical point of view, there is no distinction between being "pro-choice" and being "pro-abortion."

MATERIAL COOPERATION

One *materially* cooperates in another's wrongdoing when one's acts help to make that wrongdoing possible, although one does not *intend* that wrongdoing. Material cooperation in abortion takes place when *one does not will* that an abortion happen or that the unborn be left unprotected from abortion, *but where one's actions — although motivated by another purpose — nevertheless help to make an abortion possible.*

All formal cooperation in abortion is gravely immoral. So is most material cooperation in abortion. However, there may be limited circumstances under which certain forms of material cooperation are permissible. For example, a hospital worker responsible for cleaning and maintaining an operating room where abortions are sometimes performed may carry out his or her tasks without being implicated in the immoral act. The worker may oppose abortion and *intend* only to facilitate the morally upright, indeed laudable, surgical procedures performed there. He or she merely accepts as an unintended albeit foreseen consequence that the well-maintained facility will enable physicians to perform abortions. Another acceptable form of material cooperation is that of the citizen who votes for a pro-abortion candidate with the intention of helping to prevent the election of someone whose pro-abortion position is even more extreme. The same is true for the legislator who votes for legislation permitting some abortions in order to prevent the enactment of legislation permitting even more.[4]

"PERSONALLY OPPOSED BUT. . . ."

It is all too common for Catholic politicians to say they are "personally" opposed to abortion, but will nevertheless vote to permit it and even fund it out of respect for the consciences of those who hold different views. This "respect" for another's conscience should never require abandoning one's own.[5]

In their 1998 statement, *Living the Gospel of Life: A Challenge to American Catholics*, the Catholic Bishops of the United States acknowledged that when it is "impossible to overturn or prevent passage of a law" which allows abortion, "an elected official, whose position in favor of life is known, could seek legitimately to limit the harm done by the law. However, no appeal to policy, procedure, majority will or pluralism ever excuses a public official from defending life to the greatest extent possible." The bishops urged "those Catholic officials who choose to depart from Church teaching on the inviolability of human life in their public life to consider the consequences for their own spiritual well-being, as well as the scandal they risk by leading others into serious sin."[6]

So it *can* be morally permissible to pursue an incremental strategy on abortion, but only subject to the criteria governing permissible cooperation with evil. The further question is whether that strategy is counterproductive.

---

[4] 20 *Origins* 65 (1990).
[5] *Ibid.*
[6] Nat'l. Conf. of Catholic Bishops, *Living the Gospel of Life: A Challenge to American Catholics*, (Nov. 19, 1998), no. 32.

34. ALTHOUGH AN INCREMENTAL STRATEGY OF LIMITING ABORTION CAN BE MORALLY JUSTIFIED, DOES IT MAKE PRACTICAL SENSE?

No. Period, paragraph, next case.

THE FOUR CARDINALS

The years immediately following *Roe v. Wade* offered an opportunity to reverse its basic holding before the cultural acquiescence in legalized abortion put such a remedy beyond reach. Three weeks after *Roe*, the Administrative Committee of the National Conference of Catholic Bishops condemned it and urged "legal and constitutional conformity to the basic truth that the unborn child is a 'person' in every sense of the term from conception."[1] The bishops said, "we reject this decision of the Court because, as John XXIII says, 'if any government does not acknowledge the rights of man or violates them,. . . its orders completely lack juridical force.'"[2]

After *Roe*, constitutional amendments to forbid abortion were introduced in Congress. When Cardinals Krol, Manning, Cody and Medeiros testified before a Senate Subcommittee in March 1974, they insisted on full constitutional protection for the unborn child. "The constitutional amendment," said Cardinal Medeiros, "should clearly establish that, from conception onward, the unborn child is a human person in the terms of the Constitution." "The right to life," he noted, "is described in the Declaration of Independence as 'unalienable' and as a right with which all men are endowed by the Creator. The constitutional amendment should restore the basic protection for this human right to the unborn, just as it is provided to all other persons in the United States."[3]

The Cardinals declined to endorse the amendment proposed by Senator James L. Buckley (R.-NY) because it would have allowed abortion "in an emergency when a reasonable medical certainty exists that the continuation of the pregnancy will cause the death of the mother." Cardinal Cody said, "The Senator's proposal here, as it stands, I don't think would be justified on moral grounds."[4] Cardinal Medeiros, re-

---

[1] *Documentation on the Right to Life and Abortion* (Nat'l. Conf. of Catholic Bishops, 1974), 55, 58.

[2] *Ibid.* at 56, quoting *Pacem in Terris*, no. 61.

[3] *Record of Hearings*, Subcommittee on Constitutional Amendments (93rd Cong., 2d Sess.) on S.J. Res. 119 and S.J. Res. 130; *New York Times*, Mar. 8, 1974, p. 11; *The Wanderer*, Mar. 14, 1974, p. 1; *The Wanderer*, Mar. 21, 1974, p. 1.

[4] *Record of Hearings*, 171.

sponding to a question about the Buckley Amendment, said, "if direct taking of life and intentional taking of life to save the life of the mother, is what we have in mind, then it is not licit. . . . I could not endorse any wording that would allow for direct abortion."[5] In his prepared statement, Cardinal Medeiros said, "A 'States rights' amendment which would simply return jurisdiction over the abortion law to the States, does not seem to be a satisfactory solution to the existing situation. Protection of human life should not depend upon geographical boundaries. . . . The Constitution should express a commitment to the preservation of all human life. Therefore, the prohibition against the direct and intentional taking of innocent human life should be universal and without exceptions. . . . As for an amendment, which would generally prohibit abortion but permit it in certain exceptional circumstances, such as when a woman's life is considered to be threatened, the Catholic Conference does not endorse such an approach in principle and could not conscientiously support it." Neither the Buckley Amendment nor any other constitutional amendment on abortion gained sufficient support in Congress to be submitted to the states for ratification.

A Seamless Garment?

The years immediately following *Roe* provided a pro-life window of opportunity to restore personhood to the unborn child before the abortion mentality achieved cultural dominance. The Cardinals' no-compromise stand was sound in prudential as well as moral terms. It would have framed the debate accurately: "Why *shouldn't* all human beings be treated as persons entitled to the right to life?" Unfortunately the bishops' bureaucracy, the National Right to Life Committee and other elements of the right-to-life establishment chose to follow the route of compromise. Instead of regarding the right to life of the innocent as non-negotiable, they came to regard that right as no less subject to compromise than would be the size of a government subsidy.

The Cardinals' 1974 position was wholly repudiated when the Bishops endorsed the states' rights Hatch Amendment in 1981; abortion later became one pro-life issue among many in a "seamless garment" of Catholic "pro-life" positions on war, poverty, capital punishment and other matters.

There really is a "seamless garment" of pro-life issues, as John Paul II has made clear in his advocacy of a total culture of life.[6] The foundation of this authentic seamless garment is the dignity of the human person,

---

[5] *Ibid.*
[6] See *EV,* nos. 8, 27, 75-76.

including the absolute inviolability of innocent human life. But the "seamless garment," as advanced by some in response to *Roe*, had an effect of providing a cover for pro-abortion politicians to pose as pro-life because of their positions on welfare reform, the environment and other issues.[7]

THE INCREMENTAL APPROACH

Since at least 1981, major elements of the pro-life establishment, including the Catholic bishops' bureaucracy, have themselves promoted incremental legislation that would allow abortion for the life or health of the mother, in pregnancies caused by rape or incest and for minors with parental consent.[8] And they have urged the states' rights solution, which would permit the states to allow or forbid abortion.[9] Both the incremental and states' rights approaches affirm the nonpersonhood of the unborn child by subjecting him to execution at the discretion of another whenever the legislature so decrees.

The unborn child is as much a human being as is his elder brother. Suppose the Supreme Court had sanctioned, not the murder of the unborn, but the execution of any grade school child at the discretion of his mother. What sort of legislation should a pro-life movement propose to stop those killings? How about a law requiring that no grade school child may be executed without the consent of his grandmother? Or perhaps merely after notice to one of his grandparents? Or maybe a requirement that no grade-school child may be stood against a wall and shot unless his mother's physician said her health would be improved if the child were no longer around? Or that no such child may be executed unless he was fathered by a rapist or was physically or mentally disabled? The incremental approach makes no more sense on abortion than it would in the case of the murder of grade school children.

George Weigel and Harvard law professor Mary Ann Glendon accurately described the incremental approach, which they favor:

> The goal of conscientious Catholic politicians must be the maximum possible legal protection for unborn human life. There can be no compromise. They must support the principle of the protection of inno-

---

[7] See Human Life International, *Special Report,* Feb. 1993; Michael Pakaluk, "A Cardinal Error: Does the 'Seamless Garment' Make Sense?" *Crisis,* Nov. 1988, 10 .

[8] See *Morning Advocate* (Baton Rouge, LA), June 21, 1991, p.1; *Legisletter,* American Life League, Jan.-Feb. 1992, p. 2.

[9] See *Newsletter,* National Committee for a Human Life Amendment, Sept. 21, 1981; *National Catholic Register,* Jan. 10, 1982, p. 4; *National Right to Life News,* Nov. 23, 1981, p. 1.

cent human life, and the implementation of that principle in law. The goal of "maximum legal protection" will have to be pursued incrementally. . . . A conscientious Catholic legislator may "settle" for, say, prohibiting sex-selection abortions if that is all that is feasible in a given state. Indeed, that minimal protection establishes a legal beachhead for the principle that human life must be legally respected. . . . [T]he conscientious Catholic politician will seek the principled recognition of the state's interest in the protection of unborn human life and the maximum possible legal implementation of that principle, given local political and cultural realities. A. . . strategy of incremental gains does not involve an abandonment of principle. For, according to classic Catholic understandings and the common moral intuitions of the American people, an America in which fewer and fewer abortions are performed each year is morally preferable to the present America, in which there are 1.6 million abortions annually, and rising.[10]

This approach can be morally justified under the criteria discussed in Question 32. But, as a strategy it founders upon its own logic. A "legal beachhead" for the principle that "human life must be legally respected" cannot be established through supporting the proposal that unborn life can be taken for any reason except sex selection. Such a proposal denies that principle. To "settle" for it concedes that, at least until "political and cultural realities" permit, all other unborn lives need not be respected. To "settle" for such a law undermines the legislator's professed principle that all human life "must be legally respected." If, on the other hand, the principle is that only certain human life must be legally respected, it is not much of a principle. If every abortion really is the murder of an innocent human being, how can a movement be pro-life unless it insists that the killing be stopped, absolutely? Is it effectively pro-life to "settle" instead for a rule that the killings can be done only for certain reasons, under certain conditions and with prescribed formalities?

PRAGMATISM DOES NOT WORK

It would be unjust to reproach those who do their best to achieve total protection for the unborn and then reluctantly support or vote for legislation that includes exceptions to that protection. There is a difference, however, between the pro-life advocate who fights the good fight, is beaten down and then, under protest, takes what he can get, and the one who himself takes the initiative in promoting, as an "incremental" strategy, laws that allow abortion. Sometimes, pro-lifers and legislators

---

[10] Mary Ann Glendon and George Weigel, "Catholic Politicians Must Fight Abortion," *Newsday*, May 9, 1990, p. 61.

convince themselves that an authentically pro-life law cannot be enacted; consequently, they propose compromises that validate the anti-life position by implicitly defining the lives of some unborn children as negotiable. "If we can support exceptions at the bitter end," they ask, "why can't we propose them in the first place if we honestly believe they are inevitable?" One answer is that, in practical terms, that tactic is not only a predictable loser but also a contributor to the dominance of the anti-life ethic. Every time a pro-lifer proposes a law that would tolerate the execution of some unborn children, his pro-life rhetoric is drowned out by the loud and clear message of his action, that he concedes that the law can validly tolerate the intentional killing of innocent human beings. The incremental approach should be rejected not as necessarily immoral but as counterproductive.

Exceptions were urged on pragmatic grounds. Yet their concession has brought only a string of retreats and defeats. The Supreme Court has carved in stone the principle that unborn children are nonpersons and that the right to live, at both ends of life, is a political issue as negotiable as a highway appropriation. The public accepts the principle that innocent human beings can rightly be killed by euthanasia as well as by abortion. The political pro-life movement can hardly complain. That principle underlies some of its own activity. Through its proposal of exceptions it has corrupted the public discourse and undermined the pro-life cause. While this undermining effect can neither be quantified nor empirically demonstrated, it stands to reason that a movement created to defend a right as inalienable will lose credibility and render itself laughable by conceding exceptions to that "inalienable" right.

CORRUPTION OF THE PUBLIC DISCOURSE

The dominant abortions of the near future will be committed by pills, implants or other devices. The only way that the law can reach such early abortions will be by licensing or other regulations including limits on prescriptions. Such restraints will have limited effect, especially on items that have non-abortive as well as abortive uses. The only way to mobilize support for any restrictions on early abortifacients will be to restore the public conviction that all life is sacred and must be protected by the law. The incremental strategy, which seeks to regulate rather than prohibit abortion, undermines that conviction because it permeates the public discourse with the message that even the "pro-life" advocates agree that innocent life is negotiable.

Consider one local example. Station KELO-TV in Sioux Falls, SD, conducted polls on abortion in late 1990 and late 1991. In 1991 the major pro-life effort in South Dakota was an attempt to forbid abortions except for rape, incest, and the life or physical health of the mother. After that campaign, the second poll, identical to the first and covering the same audience, showed that more people favored some abortion, and fewer opposed all abortions, than had been the case with the first poll. "[T]he large body of the public who remain 'unsure' where they stand on abortion look to committed pro-lifers and pro-death forces to help develop their views. And with many pro-lifers willing to allow some abortions legislatively, it appears the public has followed their lead. As a result, we have lost ground with the public."[11]

The 1992 and 1996 presidential elections confirm that a pro-life strategy of compromise contributes to the institutionalization of the abortion ethic. Bill Clinton took the totally pro-abortion position. The "pro-life" candidates, George Bush and Bob Dole, backed by the establishment pro-life movement, supported legalized abortion in life of the mother, rape and incest cases. The Washington Post-ABC News, Gallup, election day exit polls and others indicate that those campaigns reinforced the trend toward public acceptance of legalized abortion. Only about twenty percent believe abortion should not be legal. "The public's attitude toward abortion largely lines up with President Clinton's phrase that abortions should be 'safe, legal and rare,' said [University of Maryland Professor] Elizabeth Adell Cook. Studies indicate an emerging consensus that 'it should be allowed under some circumstances but it isn't to be taken too lightly,'"[12] "In responses so paradoxical that they astound even experts like Dr. Cook, one third of the poll's respondents who said they considered abortion to be murder also agreed that abortion is sometimes the best course in a bad situation."[13]

Law is an educator. *Roe v. Wade* accelerated the dominance of an ethic in which the right to life is evaluated according to utilitarian norms. It would be unfair to blame this acceleration simply on the establishment pro-life movement. That movement, however, has abdicated its duty to affirm the absolute sanctity of innocent life. It has bought in to the pagan culture by itself treating the right to live as a negotiable political issue. It has sought piecemeal political victories at the price of strategic retreat. It has trivialized itself into a caricature of what it ought to be.

The political pro-life movement is not taken seriously, perhaps because it does not take its own rhetoric seriously. The advocates of the

[11]   Paul R. Dorr, *Rescue the Perishing Newsletter,* Jan. 1992.
[12]   *N.Y. Times,* Jan. 16, 1998, p. A1.
[13]   *Ibid.*

"practical" approach proclaim the sanctity of life. They urge support for limited abortions as the best we can get. They claim that we will go on, step by gradual step, to outlaw abortion totally. But it is fair to ask whether they ever will demand that abortion be totally prohibited by the law. And how can they persuade a legislator or anyone else to change sides and oppose abortion when they themselves lack enough confidence in their cause to insist that the right to life be protected as the inalienable right they profess it to be? Instead, the predictable reaction of legislators will be to propose additional exceptions, since the defenders of the "inalienable" right to life have already conceded that it is not inalienable. The allowance of even a life-of-the-mother exception could lead to negotiations for the addition of other appealing exceptions. Even if a bill were enacted with only the life-of-the-mother exception, that exception would be broadly interpreted. Thus, Dr. Michael Burnhill, a trustee of the National Abortion Federation, was asked, "Could you perform the abortions that you think, that you believe are medically necessary under a standard that calls it life-endangering?" He responded, "Yes."[14]

DON'T YOU WANT TO SAVE LIVES?

The most intimidating argument for the incremental approach is that we have a duty to save whatever lives we can: Why do you permit babies, whom you could save, to be killed just because you can't get a perfect law? Support for partial protection of the right to live can be morally justified, as Bishop Myers put it, "only if the legislator decides there is at that time no reasonable hope of enacting legislation which would protect equally all unborn children."[15] However, for at least two decades, the establishment pro-life movement has moved from reluctantly accepting exceptions to actively promoting them. It is fair to conclude that those compromise tactics have increased the toll of lives taken by abortion. The enactment, for example, of a requirement that an unmarried minor obtain parental consent before an abortion does decrease the number of abortions from those under a previously unrestricted law.[16] But a more reliable comparison would be between a situation, on the one hand, where the law was either wholly permissive or required parental consent, and, on the other, a situation where the pro-life movement was insisting that the law can never rightly allow the murder of the innocent. A law allowing abortion with parental consent tells the pregnant girl that killing her unborn child is qualitatively the same as getting

---

[14] MacNeil-Lehrer Report, Apr. 22, 1980.
[15] See Question 32.
[16] See *Wash. Times*, Aug. 9, 1998, p. A9, describing the operation in 1997 of Virginia's parental notification law.

one's ears pierced. And if all that is required is parental "notice," the message is that killing your baby is even less significant than getting your ears pierced.

An educational variant of Gresham's Law[17] operates here. The pro-life political climate is dominated by those who have convinced themselves that full protection cannot be enacted, although they have never really tried to achieve it. No one bothers seriously to promote bills that would restore full protection. Those who might do so are dissuaded by the argument that to do so would be divisive. So if Able introduces a bill to forbid some abortions and to allow others, support for that bill becomes the test of pro-life solidarity. If Baker introduces a no-exception prohibition of abortion and refuses to support Able's compromise bill, Baker is labeled as divisive. Able, however, is not required to support Baker's no-exception bill because everyone knows that it is impractical and visionary. Bad bills drive out the good, in an accelerating trend toward compromise. The uncompromising, no-exception position has not failed. It has never been tried. The proposal of exceptions is not necessarily immoral, but, in prudential terms it is inherently self-defeating. And stupid.

Nor can the incremental approach be justified to preserve unity within the pro-life movement. Unity is an important goal. But to insist on it as essential is to commit the pro-life movement to a progressive softening of its position. The insistence on unity usually comes from those who advocate incremental, compromise proposals. It tends to lower the pro-life position to a least common denominator. The futility of the pro-life movement against euthanasia stems at least partly from the concession by its "practical" leaders on abortion, that some innocent human life is negotiable after all. The pro-death movement has been a consistent winner against an opposition that qualifies its own position by conceding that there are some innocent human beings whom it will allow to be directly and intentionally killed. And the end is not in sight.

PARTIAL BIRTH ABORTION

The campaign over the past few years to ban Partial Birth Abortion (PBA) illustrates the point.[18] That campaign won a tactical victory by

---

[17] Gresham's law is the economic principle that "bad money drives out good." In the 1960s and 1970s, when dimes and quarters made of copper and nickel were put into circulation, the silver dimes and quarters disappeared from circulation because people hoarded them because of their intrinsic value. The only coins left in circulation were the cupro-nickel ones. See *McGraw Hill Encyclopedia of Economics* (2d.ed. 1994), 485.

[18] See *N.Y. Times*, Sept. 27, 1996, p. A12; Thomas L. Jipping, "Banning a Murderous Practice," *Wash. Times*, Nov. 2, 1995, p. A17.

raising awareness of the depravity of the abortion culture. But is likely to have the unintended effect of reinforcing that culture. The PBA, despite its gruesome character, is qualitatively no different from any other abortion method. Unfortunately, the focus of the campaign on the method of the PBA killing distracted attention from the reality that the law can never validly tolerate any abortion or any other intentional execution of the innocent. For example, the pamphlet distributed by the National Conference of Catholic Bishops headlined its first page: "4/5 Infanticide, 1/5 Abortion," and went on to say, "Why all the furor over partial birth abortion? Because unlike any other abortion, this procedure kills a living infant when she is almost fully delivered from her mother's womb. It's a painful, brutal procedure that's paving the way to open infanticide."[19] Abortion, however, is not wrong because it leads to infanticide. All abortion is wrong in itself. If it is not wrong, what is wrong with infanticide? While it was legitimate and tactically effective to describe the PBA as practically infanticide, that tactic invited a strategic defeat, reinforcing the abortion culture by focusing on the method of the murder rather than on the murder as such. And it provided a cover for politicians to claim pro-life support because they opposed PBAs despite their otherwise pro-abortion records.

In any civilized society, the issue must be *whether* innocent human beings may be intentionally and legally killed. Over the past two decades, however, the establishment pro-life leaders have sought to limit, but not wholly prohibit, abortion, thus framing the issue as *which* innocents may be killed. The campaign to prohibit partial-birth abortion is a further retreat. While it achieved a tactical success by raising consciousness of the reality of abortion, it corrupted the public discourse by framing the issue not in terms of *whether* and not even in terms of *which*, but in terms of *how* innocent human beings may be legally executed.

The effort to ban PBAs was also flawed in its allowance of the PBA to save the life of the mother. If the PBA is such a horrendous atrocity that it must be banned, why should it — or any other type of abortion — be allowed to save the life of the mother? Since when should any civilized society allow the intentional killing of an innocent non-aggressor even to save the life of the killer? If two people are on a one-man raft in the ocean, the law does not give one the right to throw the other overboard.[20]

---

[19] Nat'l. Conference of Catholic Bishops, *4/5 Infanticide, 1/5 Abortion* (undated).
[20] See U.S. v. Holmes, 26 Fed. Cas. 360 (no. 15, 383) (C.C.E.D. Pa., 1842); *Regina v. Dudley & Stephens*, 14 Q.B.D. 624, (1884). See Question 31.

These comments are not intended as a reflection on the proponents of the PBA ban. Given the moribund state of the establishment pro-life movement, the PBA campaign was a tactically effective attempt to jump-start the pro-life effort. And the public commitment of the Catholic bishops and their agencies to that effort was laudable. Nevertheless, the PBA effort is a testimony to the weakness rather than the strength of the pro-life movement.

An uncompromising affirmation of life as the gift of God is the only course that offers a hope to restore reverence for the sanctity of life, provided, of course, that primary recourse is placed on prayer, especially through the intercession of Mary, who is the Mother of Life.

35.   WHAT KINDS OF LEGISLATION SHOULD WE PROMOTE ON THE FEDERAL LEVEL?

As noted in Questions 32-34, it can be morally permissible to support or vote for a law that would tolerate the intentional killing of innocent human beings. The "no-exception" approach, on the other hand, is premised on the practical judgment that the incremental tactic has been, and will continue to be, counterproductive. Those who follow "no-exception," for example, would decline to vote for laws that provide funding for any abortions, laws that outlaw abortions subject to exceptions such as life of the mother, rape, incest, etc., or laws that equate abortion to getting one's ears pierced by allowing it for a minor provided she has parental consent, or the approval of a court, before she can legally kill her child. But the "no-exception" way is positive. It requires the promotion of measures to restore protection to innocent life and to build a social and moral climate in which that protection can endure.

There is no realistic possibility of restoring full legal protection for the right to life at this time. Pro-life insistence on that protection, however, is essential as a form of witness and education that can itself promote respect for the right to life. This Question suggests initiatives to promote that respect without condoning the execution of the innocent.[1] It might be objected that these initiatives are an exercise in futility. True, they might not — in most cases certainly will not — be enacted. But they seek to shift the public debate to *our* agenda. The objective is not merely to tinker with statutes. It is to educate, witness and convert.

Pro-life efforts should focus on three main objectives on the federal level:

1. The Paramount Human Life Amendment to the United States Constitution;

2. Repeal of Title X of the Public Health Service Act and all other enactments, federal and state, through which government finances and promotes birth control;

3. Increase of the personal exemption from taxable income.

---

[1] For information on drafting pro-life legislation on the federal and state levels, contact: Thomas More Center for Law and Justice, 24 Frank Lloyd Wright Dr., P.O. Box 422, Ann Arbor, MI 48106-0422, (734) 930-4400; American Center for Law and Justice, New Hope, KY 40052, (512) 549-5454; American Life League, P.O. Box 1350, Stafford, VA 22554, (540) 659-4171.

THE PARAMOUNT HUMAN LIFE AMENDMENT

The ultimate legal remedy for *Roe v. Wade* is a constitutional amendment affirming that, with respect to the right to life, all human beings are persons. The Paramount Human Life Amendment (PHLA), which has been repeatedly introduced in Congress, provides:

> The paramount right to life is vested in each human being from the moment of fertilization without regard to age, health or condition of dependency.[2]

As noted in Questions 3 and 4, it is likely that a restoration of personhood to the unborn child, with respect to the right to life and without exception, would oblige the states to forbid all abortions, including even those claimed necessary to save the life of the mother. The PHLA would restore to the unborn child, as a person, the same right to live enjoyed by his elder brother and his grandmother. The PHLA would require legislation to make it effective. But that is generally the case with rights protected under the Fourteenth Amendment and other constitutional provisions. The PHLA would mean that the unborn child would no longer be outside the protection of the law. For the state to punish homicides committed against some persons while exempting from punishment homicides committed against other persons would be to deny the equal protection of the laws.

Under the PHLA, the state legislature could determine how to punish abortion, just as it does with other crimes. The legislature or prosecutors could forego punishment of the mother in order to focus on the doctor. The PHLA would be no different in this respect from the pre-1973 abortion laws.

The PHLA guarantees personhood once life has begun. It would not restrict contraception. With respect to the intrauterine device and other abortifacients, the PHLA would authorize a state legislature to control them as far as practicable.

When Louise Brown, the first "test tube" baby, was born in 1978, the world acknowl edged that her life had begun at fertilization *in vitro*.[3] A common practice is to fertilize several eggs *in vitro*, let them mature for a time, select the best ones for use and throw the others away or save them for experimentation. The PHLA would guarantee the right to live of all human beings, even the smallest. It would permit — and implicitly

---

[2] For information, contact March for Life, P.O. Box 90300, Washington, D.C. 20090, (202) LIFE-377.
[3] See *Medical World News*, Dec. 12, 1983, p. 55; *N.Y. Times*, July 27, 1978, p. A1.

require — the states to regulate *in vitro* fertilization to protect that right. There should be no "throw away" human beings.

The Human Life Bill (HLB), various forms of which have been introduced in Congress since 1973, would use Congress' power to enforce the Fourteenth Amendment to define all human beings, from fertilization, as persons with respect to the right to life protected by the Constitution.[4] The Supreme Court's 1997 decision in *City of Boerne v. Flores*,[5] discussed in Question 9, indicates that the Court would not uphold a Human Life Bill. There is even less chance of enacting the HLB then there is of the PHLA. Still, the HLB should be included among pro-life proposals as a witness not only to the right to life but also to the pathetic state of Congressional power under the transformed Constitution.

REPEAL OF TITLE X

As noted in Question 17, government funding of birth control promotes the culture of death in the United States and abroad. It usually entails the coercion of conscience. And it has been used in a genocidal way on minority groups. Repeal of such provisions, starting with Title X, has to be a central element of a coherent pro-life agenda. This effort should also include the exclusion from federal employee health plans of coverage for abortifacients and contraceptives.[6]

INCREASE OF PERSONAL EXEMPTION FROM FEDERAL INCOME TAX

In 1948, the personal exemption of income from federal income tax began at $600. For 1998, the basic exemption was $2,700. If it were set at the same percentage of per capita income as it represented in 1948, it would now be at least $10,000 for each parent and each dependent child.[7] This is not a tax credit but an exemption of income. For a taxpayer in the 28% bracket, a $10,000 exemption would save $2,800 in taxes. The exemption should be increased so as to allow families to keep more of their own money so that, among other things, they can more ef-

---

[4] See *S. 158* (97th Cong., 1st Sess.), introduced in 1981 by Senator Jesse Helms (R.-NC). *S.158* provided that "for the purpose of enforcing the obligation of the States under the fourteenth amendment not to deprive persons of life without due process of law, each human life exists from conception, without regard to race, sex, age, health, defect, or condition of dependency, and for this purpose 'person' includes all human beings." An alternative wording of an HLB might provide, "With respect to the right to life guaranteed in the Constitution, every human being, subject to the jurisdiction of the United States or of any State, shall be deemed, from the moment of fertilization, to be a person and entitled to the right to life."

[5] 521 U.S. 507 (1997).

[6] See *Wash. Times,* July 6, 1998, p. A4.

[7] See discussion in Question 23.

fectively educate their children in the culture of life. Other adjustments can be made in the tax laws so as to ease the burden on families, but the increase in the personal exemption should be a priority.

Other measures could be proposed on the federal level, including effective prohibition of human cloning and research on human embryos;[8] and protection of Catholic and other hospitals against being compelled to admit to their staffs abortionists who perform abortion elsewhere.[9] Regardless of the prospects for adoption of these and other proposals that could be made, they should be advanced as a form of education and witness.

---

[8] Contact American Bioethics Advisory Committee, American Life League, P.O. Box 1350, Stafford, VA 22554, (540) 659-4171.
[9] See Charles E. Rice, "Catholic Hospitals and Abortionists," *The Wanderer*, Jan. 8, 1998, p. 4.

36. WHAT KINDS OF LEGISLATION SHOULD WE PROMOTE ON THE STATE LEVEL?

It would be a mistake to propose only legislation that the Supreme Court has already upheld or that it has indicated it would be likely to approve. Instead of going, hat in hand, back to the Court with a series of marginal restrictions on abortion, pro-life advocates should adopt, if only for educational purposes, an aggressive agenda centered on the restoration of full constitutional and legal protection to all human life.

ABORTION

1. *A statute making the performance of abortions a criminal offense, without exception.* This would be aimed at surgical abortions. As discussed in Question 31, a life-of-the-mother exception is neither necessary nor desirable. If such a provision were politically unavoidable, language along the following lines would appear to be morally and legally defensible:

> Provided, however, that the term, "abortion," shall not include the elimination of an ectopic or other extra-uterine pregnancy, a cancerous uterus, or similar pathological physical condition which itself imminently threatens to cause the death of the pregnant woman during that pregnancy, when that elimination is done with the specific intent only of treating that condition, even though such procedure unintentionally results in the unavoidable destruction of unborn human life.[1]

2. *Prohibition of the use of public funds or public facilities for the performance of any and all abortions, including the administration of abortifacients.* The Supreme Court has upheld similar legislation, although containing a life of the mother exception, with respect to surgical abortions.[2]

3. *Prohibition of prescription or distribution of substances or devices for abortifacient purposes.* This would be difficult to enforce, but it should be proposed.

4. *Disinvestment of state pension funds from, and prohibition of state contracts with, any company involved in the testing, production or distribution of abortifacient devices or pills.* Through the Sullivan Principles, devised by Rev. Leon Sullivan of Philadelphia, American corporations doing business in South Africa pledged to promote racial equality in their

---

[1] See Question 31.

[2] See *Harris v. McRae,* 448 U.S. 297 (1980); *Williams v. Zbaraz,* 448 U.S. 358 (1980); *Webster v. Reproductive Health Services,* 492 U.S. 490 (1989).

practices.[3] The MacBride Principles, devised by Irish statesman Sean MacBride, required disinvestment of pension funds in corporations practicing religious discrimination in Northern Ireland.[4] Pro-life shareholders should also press their corporations to forego contributions to, or investment in, entities promoting abortion or contraception. It makes no sense for a corporation to direct its contributions and investments toward the elimination of its own potential customers.[5]

5. *Prohibition of health insurance companies from compelling their insureds to pay for coverage for abortion or contraception, including sterilization.*[6]

6. *Exclusion from government employee health plans of coverage for abortifacients and contraceptives.*

7. *Requirement that complications from abortions and deaths caused by abortions be reported to the state even if the complication or death occurs years after an abortion.*

8. *Protection, as a matter of state law, of the right of persons, on public property, to exercise their freedoms of speech and association, guaranteed by the state constitution, to communicate with others in a non-obstructive manner and without trespassing on private property.* As discussed in Question 39, the Supreme Court, as a matter of federal constitutional law, has upheld severe restrictions on the speech rights of pro-life persons in the vicinity of abortuaries. A state, however, can afford greater protection in state law to a personal right than is afforded to that right by the United States Constitution.[7] There is no guarantee that a state law of this sort would be upheld. The Supreme Court might hold it invalid as an interference with the federally protected right to abortion. However, the law should be proposed for its educational value.

9. *Requirement that, at least 24 hours before a woman has an abortion, the abortionist must give her detailed information not only about the unborn child and the techniques of abortion, but also about any predictable risk factors that could cause her to have an adverse reaction to abortion. Failure to provide such information should be defined as malpractice subjecting*

---

[3] *N.Y. Times,* Sept. 9, 1985, p. A8.

[4] See *Insight,* May 4, 1987, p. 26.

[5] Contact Pro-Life Shareholders, P.O. Box 1812, Marshalltown, IA 50158.

[6] See *National Catholic Register,* Dec. 7-13, 1997, p. 19; for information, contact ValuSure Corp., 3707 W. Maple, Bloomfield, MI 48301, (810) 354-7232; Assn. for Family Finances in America, 2300 N. Street, N.W., Washington, DC 20037, (202) 663-9023.

[7] See Robert F. Utter, "Advancing State Constitutions in Court," *Trial,* Oct. 1991, 41; William J. Brennan, Jr., "The Bill of Rights: State Constitutions as Guardians of Individual Rights, "*N.Y. State Bar J.,* May 1987, 10.

the abortionist to tort liability for damages. In *Casey,* the Supreme Court upheld a Pennsylvania law requiring the provision of information about abortion to the woman.[8] The "Protection from High Risk and Coercive Abortion Act," pending in several state legislatures, requires the abortionist to
give comprehensive information to the mother about the risk to herself.[9]

PROTECTION OF THE RIGHTS OF CONSCIENCE

10. *A statutory conscience clause allowing police officers to refuse to arrest
those who, nonobstructively and without trespass or breach of the peace, exercise
their rights of speech and association in the vicinity of abortuaries.* When a police officer is required to arrest such a person he removes what may be the
only means of dissuading the mother from entering the abortuary and mur-
dering her child. The law should affirm the officer's right of conscience
where he can exercise that right without detriment to public safety. Such a
law would leave the legal status of abortion untouched while protecting the
right of conscientious objection.[10] It would not imply a general right of public officers to be selective in their obedience of orders. It would, rather, recognize the unique character of legalized abortion, which is the only situation
in which a public officer is required to protect, rather than arrest, the intentional killer of an innocent, nonaggressing human being.

11. *A statutory conscience clause allowing medical personnel to refuse
to take part in abortion or euthanasia procedures.*

12. *A statutory conscience clause allowing medical personnel to refuse
to take part in sterilization or other contraceptive procedures.[11]*

13. *A statutory conscience clause to guarantee the right of pharmacists
to refuse to dispense abortifacients or contraceptives.[12]*

MALPRACTICE REMEDIES

14. *Provision for the payment of reasonable attorneys' fees by defendants to plaintiffs who prevail in malpractice tort actions arising out of abortion, sterilization or contraception.[13]*

---

[8] See Question 4.
[9] For information contact Family Research Council, 801 G St. N.W., Washington,
D.C. (202) 393-2100.
[10] Contact National Federation of Officers for Life, 237 Audubon Dr., Slidell, LA
70458; National Cops for Life, P.O. Box 67, Cutchogue, N.Y. 11935; *Nat'l. Catholic
Register,* May 17- 23, 1998, p. 16.
[11] See *Wash. Times,* July 2, 1998, p. A8.
[12] See *Newsday,* May 18, 1998, p. A4. Contact Pharmacists for Life, P.O. Box 130,
Ingomar, PA 15127, (412) 487-8960.
[13] For information on malpractice claims against abortionists, contact Legal Action for
Women, P.O. Box 11061, Pensacola, FL 32524, (334) 962-3554; Life Dynamics,
Inc., P.O. Box 2226, Denton, TX 76202, (940) 380-8800.

15. *Extending the statute of limitations for medical malpractice involving abortion, sterilization and contraception, including a provision that the statute would not begin to run until the plaintiff's actual discovery of the injury.* This would make it more difficult for tortfeasors in those areas to escape their proper liability.

FETAL EXPERIMENTATION AND HOMICIDE

16. *Prohibition of fetal experimentation* which is not therapeutic, that is, which is not for the benefit of the child experimented upon, whether the child is in the womb or out of it.

17. *Prohibition of fetal homicide, i.e., killing an unborn child by causing injury or death to the mother.* Some state homicide laws are so interpreted.[14] Others should be changed to reflect the reality that the unborn child is as much a person as is his mother.

THE "RIGHT TO DIE"

18. *Prohibition of withholding or withdrawing artificially or naturally provided nutrition or hydration from any patient with the intent or known effect of causing death by starvation or dehydration.*

19. *Prohibition of administration of sedation or pain-killers to a patient with the specific intent to cause that patient to die.* As noted in Question 13, this, too, would be difficult to enforce. But it should be proposed.

20. *A statutory declaration of policy that suicide is contrary to the common good.* It is senseless, of course, to make suicide itself a crime. How would the law punish a successful suicide? Attempted suicide is apparently still a common law crime in several states but is no longer a statutory crime in any state.[15] The pro-life effort ought to press, at least, for legislative recognition that, despite the absence of criminal sanctions, the taking of one's own life is a social as well as a moral evil.

21. *Prohibition of assisting another person to commit suicide, including assistance by knowingly providing that person with the means to take his own life.*[16]

---

[14] See Murphy S. Klasing, "The Death of an Unborn Child: Jurisprudential Inconsistencies in Wrongful Death, Criminal Homicide, and Abortion Cases," 22 *Pepperdine L.Rev.* 933 (1995).

[15] H. Tristram Engelhardt, Jr., and Michele Malloy, "Suicide and Assisting Suicide: A Critique of Legal Sanctions," 36 *Southwestern L. J.* 1003, 1018 (1982); N.Y. State Task Force on Life and the Law, *When Death is Sought* (1994), xi.

[16] See Questions 5 and 13.

22.   *Prohibition of categorical exclusions by health care insurers of coverage on the basis of the age or disability of the patient.*[17] A decade ago, Daniel Callahan argued for the rationing of expensive health care according to "fixed categories" of patients:

> The combination of an aging society, constant technological progress, and unlimited need and demand will require firm limits. We have already begun to spend too much money on one age group (older persons) in comparison with the needs of other age groups; too much on many kinds of expensive high-technology treatments (e.g., neonate intensive care) in comparison with more efficacious spending of the same amount on other forms of care (e.g., prenatal care); and too much in general on expensive forms of individual curative treatment (e.g., organ transplants) than on more generally productive public health measures.

> [T]here are many possible forms of fixed categorical standards. . . . One would be to use an age limit on entitlements to. . . expensive, life-extending. . . care under the Medicare program. Congress. . . might declare that neither newly initiated dialysis nor bypass surgery would be reimbursed beyond the age of eighty-two. Another possibility would be. . . that reimbursement under the Medicaid program would not be provided for neonatal care for any baby below a fixed weight. A third possibility would be that both Medicare and Medicaid would refuse. . . reimbursement for medical care in an intensive care unit unless that unit had. . . firm admission standards based on high probabilities of good outcomes.[18]

Callahan and others have continued to advocate what he calls "a sustainable medicine," including rationing of health care and an emphasis on public health measures.[19]

Pressure for euthanasia comes from the monitoring of physicians' decisions by insurance company representatives, with cost-accounting tables and formulas possibly overriding the judgment of physicians and the welfare of patients. "Health insurers. . . are. . . moving toward 'managed care' . . . by way of HMOs and other systems in which decisions about medical care are taken out of the hands of patients and their phy-

---

[17] See *National Right to Life News,* Aug. 1, 1995, p. S-1.

[18] Daniel Callahan, "Rationing Health Care: Will It Be Necessary? Can It Be Done Without Age or Disability Discrimination?" 5 *Issues in Law and Medicine* 353, 361-62 (1989); see Daniel Callahan, *Setting Limits: Medical Goals in an Aging Society* (1987).

[19] Daniel Callahan, *False Hopes: Why America's Quest for Perfect Health Is a Recipe for Failure* (1998).

sicians and handed over to bureaucrats. These are. . . often life and death decisions, and so what is evolving is a system for rationing medical care, on the assumption that we simply do not have the resources to provide adequate care for everyone. As a result, these systems are becoming a force for euthanasia, voluntary and otherwise (mostly otherwise, I suspect)."[20]

As Wesley J. Smith, attorney for the International Anti-Euthanasia Task Force, observed:

> People who are elderly, disabled, prematurely born, or seriously ill have much to fear from the medical intelligentsia — those bioethicists and moral philosophers who have in recent years transformed medical ethics. . . . It was bioethicists and moral philosophers. . . who promulgated "Futile Care Theory," which allows doctors and health-insurance executives to deny not merely high-tech interventions but also such treatments as CPR and antibiotics to the profoundly disabled and people at the end of life. Even if the patient or the patient's family wants the care, what matters is the medical professional's assessment of the quality and worth of the patient's life. Little noticed by the mainstream media, Futile Care Theory is already being implemented in hospitals and nursing homes, both informally in clinical settings and formally through hospital protocols.[21]

In Vitro Fertilization

23.   *Prohibition of in-vitro fertilization.*   See Question 16.

Surrogate Motherhood

24.   *Prohibition of all surrogate motherhood contracts.* Surrogate motherhood is of two types. In one, the woman "carries in pregnancy an embryo to whose procreation she has contributed. . . her own ovum, fertilized through insemination with the sperm of a man other than her husband. She carries the pregnancy with a pledge to surrender the child once it is born to the party who commissioned or made the agreement for the pregnancy."[22] In the other type, which is a sort of rental of the womb, the woman "is genetically a stranger to the embryo [implanted in

---

[20] George Kendall, "How Not to Support the Death Industry," *The Wanderer,* June 7, 1990, p. 4; for information on pro-life insurance systems, contact Pro-Life Marketing Group, Box 2606, Southfield, MI 48037, (313) 357-7852.

[21] Wesley J. Smith, "Sick Transit: The Bioethics of Big Brother," *The Weekly Standard,* June 22, 1998, 31.

[22] Congregation for the Doctrine of the Faith, *Instruction on Bioethics* (1987), II, A, 3. See *In re Baby M,* 525 A. 2d 1128 (1987), aff'd, in part, rev'd. in part, 537 A.2d 1227 (N.J., 1988).

her uterus] because it has been obtained through the union of the gametes of 'donors.' She carries the pregnancy with a pledge to surrender the baby once it is born to the party who commissioned or made the agreement for the pregnancy."[23] The *Instruction on Bioethics* condemned surrogate motherhood of both types as "*contrary to the unity of marriage and to the dignity of the procreation of the human person.*"[24] Both types ought to be prohibited as a matter of public policy. Surrogate motherhood agreements, with or without the payment of money, treat the child as a non-person, as an item of property to be disposed of at the will of others without regard to his own interest.

THE FAMILY

25. *Declaration of policy that, for the common good, marriage ought to be permanent.*

26. *Enactment of restrictions on the availability of divorce.* As discussed in Questions 14 and 16, divorce is a symptom of the errors that have led to legalized abortion and euthanasia. A civil divorce is not an intrinsic evil in the same sense as is abortion because the civil divorce does not affect the reality of the marriage in the sight of God. Therefore an incremental approach is an appropriate strategy to restore respect for marriage and the family. The requirement of a substantial waiting period for divorce could be a useful first step. Also worth considering are proposals that would allow the choice of a "covenant marriage" which would be more difficult to terminate than an ordinary marriage.[25]

27. *Enactment of state income tax credits for mothers who care for their dependent, minor children at home.*

28. *A law that no surgical procedure or medical treatment, except in a serious emergency, may be provided to any unemancipated minor under 18 years of age without the consent of at least one parent.* This would not establish a consent requirement just for abortions. Rather, without mentioning abortion, it would vindicate parental rights with respect to all surgical and medical procedures, including provision of contraceptives.[26] The Supreme Court might not uphold such unrestricted legislation. But it would be advantageous to propose it at least for educational purposes.

---

[23] *Instruction on Bioethics*, II, A, 3.

[24] *Ibid.*; see Charles E. Rice, *50 Questions on the Natural Law* (2d ed., 1999), Question 49.

[25] See *Times-Picayune* (New Orleans, LA), Aug. 17, 1998, p. A1; Dr. Bob Christensen, *When You Say I Do, God Says I Will* (Covenant Marriages Ministry, 17301 W. Colfax, Golden, CO 80401, 1998).

[26] See proposal 35 in this Question.

HOMOSEXUAL ACTIVITY

29.   *Statutory definition that marriage can be contracted only by a man and a woman.*[27]

30.   *Statutory definition of the family to include only those related by blood, marriage or adoption.* The law should make it plain that George and Harry are not, and never could be, a family.

31.   *Declaration of policy that homosexual activity is harmful to the common good and that its encouragement is contrary to the public policy of the state.* This would be self-evident in any sane, coherent society.

32.   *Prohibition of adoption by, or awarding of custody of minor children to, any active homosexual.*[28]

SEX EDUCATION

33.   *Prohibition of explicit sex education in public schools.*[29]

CONTRACEPTION

34.   *Declaration of policy that contraception is a social evil, contrary to the common good.* A long process of reeducation may be necessary before the American people will be receptive to any reexamination of contraception. But a proposal such as this could promote public discussion. Don't bet the house and farm on the enactment of this one. But why not talk about it?

35.   *Prohibition of the distribution of contraceptive pills or devices to unmarried minors.*[30] Protestant lawmakers during the nineteenth century passed laws against the manufacture and distribution of contraceptives in the District of Columbia, the territories and numerous states. The experience of the past several decades has shown that those Protestant legislators were right. Contraception, unlike abortion, does not involve the

---

[27]   See Richard F. Duncan, "The Narrow and Shallow Bite of *Romer* and the Eminent Rationality of Dual-Gender Marriage," 6 *Wm. & Mary Bill of Rights J.* 1 (1997). The federal Defense of Marriage Act provides that, in the interpretation of federal statutes and regulations, "the word 'marriage' means only a legal union between one man and one woman as husband and wife, and the word 'spouse' refers only to a person of the opposite sex who is a husband or a wife." *Pub.L.* 104-199 (1996), 110 *Stat.* 2419, 28 U.S. § 1738C.
[28]   See *Family Research Report* (Family Research Institute, May-June 1998), 4.
[29]   See Question 24. See also, Kenneth D. Whitehead, "Do Sex Education and Access to Contraception Cut Down on Abortions?" *Crisis,* Jan. 1997, 37; Randy Engel, *Sex Education: The Final Plague* (Human Life International, Front Royal, VA 22630, 1990). Judith A. Reisman, *Kinsey: Crimes & Consequences* (1998).
[30]   See proposal 28 in this Question.

taking of life. Therefore, an incremental approach could be appropriate with respect to contraception. The *use* of contraceptives, as opposed to their distribution, should not be prohibited because of the intrusion into privacy that enforcement of such a law would require.[31]

36. *Disinvestment of state pension funds from any company involved in the testing, production, or sale of contraceptives.*

37. *Prohibition of the use of state funds or state facilities for the distribution of contraceptives.*[32] This would have immediate relevance to school-based clinics in public schools, but the prohibition should be worded broadly enough to prohibit all such use of state funds or facilities.

IN SUMMARY

It may seem frivolous to suggest legislative proposals of this sort. No one could seriously predict that many of them would be enacted. However, we ought to make the effort. The proposals at least could foster debate on *our* agenda. The list is not exhaustive. Other measures should be considered, for example, to facilitate adoption, to encourage and support the efforts of private social agencies to help economically disadvantaged mothers, married or not, who keep their babies and raise them, and to promote in various ways the revitalization of the family. The overall objective, however, is to shift public attention from marginal restrictions on surgical abortion to genuinely pro-life, pro-family proposals.[33]

We should introduce no-compromise bills, fight for them and vote against anything less. Surely we will lose at first, but we are losing now through our own acquiescence. When we lose we should come back and fight again and again without compromise. The objective is not the immediate enactment of legislation as such. Rather, the victory is in the educational effort, and in the witness, so long as we speak and live the Truth.

---

[31] See *Griswold v. Conn.*, 381 U.S. 479 (1965).

[32] For information, contact STOPP (Stop Planned Parenthood), 7 Hillview Circle, Poughkeepsie, NY 12603, (914) 485-6607.

[33] For texts and analyses of pro-life legislation on various subjects, contact Thomas More Center for Law and Justice, 24 Frank Lloyd Wright Dr., P.O. Box 422, Ann Arbor, MI 48106-0422, (734) 930-4400; American Center for Law and Justice, New Hope, KY 40052, (502) 549-5454.

37. WHAT ABOUT CANDIDATES? SHOULD WE EVER VOTE FOR ONE WHO IS PRO-ABORTION?

No. While a voter *could* morally vote for a pro-abortion candidate who is less objectionable on abortion than his opponent, he *should not.*

Bishop Myers, as noted in Question 33, explained how a voter, with a choice between two pro-abortion candidates, could be morally justified in voting for the less obnoxious one. That approach, however, has failed to work. Instead, the pro-life movement ought to adopt a more aggressive tactic. Pro-lifers could increase their political impact if they were single-issue voters, treating abortion as an absolutely disqualifying issue: Any candidate who believes that the law should treat any innocent human beings as nonpersons by tolerating their execution is unworthy to hold any public office, whether President of the United States or trustee of a mosquito abatement district. An incompetent has no claim on pro-life votes merely because of his pro-life stand. But those who favor legalized abortion should be opposed regardless of their talents or their stands on other issues. If necessary, pro-lifers should run an independent candidate if no pro-life alternative is offered by a major party. The campaign of that independent candidate could educate the public on the right to life. And if the pro-life candidate comes close to getting votes equal to the margin between the pro-abortion candidates, one of the major parties will be more likely to consider nominating a pro-life candidate the next time. We need to practice "punishment politics," to borrow the phrase coined a decade ago by Australian pro-life Senator John Martyr.[1]

The compromise tactic of voting for the less objectionable of two pro-abortion candidates is a tactic of incremental surrender. That approach in practice has mortgaged the pro-life effort to the interests and judgment of "the great human scourge of the twentieth century: the professional politician."[2] The politicians half-heartedly endorse marginal pro-life proposals in exchange for pro-life endorsement of their re-election campaigns. And pro-life activists give the politicians a veto power over the pro-life agenda by advancing only those proposals likely to get the approval of the politicians.

Solely concerned with re-election, the politicians know they can placate the pro-lifers with small-change rhetoric and guarded endorsements of peripheral bills without arousing the focused opposition of the pro-abortion camp. The "practical" pro-lifers are so devoted to politics as

---

[1] For information, contact Mrs. Margaret Tighe, Pro-Life Action Centre, 233 Brunswick Road, Brunswick, Victoria 3056, Australia.

[2] Paul Johnson, *Modern Times* (1985), 510.

"the art of the possible" that they risk becoming professional politicians themselves. As Solzhenitsyn asked, "Is it not true that professional politicians are boils on the neck of society that prevent it from turning its head and moving its arms?"[3] "For several decades we have been governed by alternating wings of a common political enterprise. In decisive respects, the national establishments of the Democratic and Republican parties act as if they were branches of One Party differing only in degree in their endorsement of high spending and taxes, acceptance of the anti-life culture as a permanent feature of American law, the expansion of federal power and control in disregard of constitutional limitations, the surrender of American sovereignty to international bureaucrats, and the imperial deployment and unjust use of American military and economic power to serve the interests, not of the American people, but of a New World Order at the service of an anti-life and moneyed elite."[4] The situation ought to prompt the emergence of a new party committed to moral and constitutional principle on pro-life and other issues.[5]

The political pro-life movement will be counterproductive until it stops playing politics and stands firm on the truth that the law can never validly tolerate the intentional killing of innocent human beings. Our only chance to succeed is through fidelity to the truth. But we should be faithful to the truth on this matter of life-and-death principle, whether it brings political success or not. We should be "faithful," wrote Charles Colson because "we are motivated not by a desire to make an impact on society but by obedience to God's Word and a desire to please him. When our goal becomes success rather than faithfulness, we lose the single-minded focus of obedience and any real power to be successful."[6]

---

[3] Aleksandr Solzhenitsyn, *The Gulag Archipelago, Part I* (1973), 391.

[4] Charles E. Rice, "Sen. Smith and a Third Party," *The Wanderer*, June 3, 1999, p. 4.

[5] For documentation and other information, contact Conservative Caucus, 9520 Bent Creek Lane, Vienna, VA 22182, (703) 281-6782.

[6] Charles Colson, "Living in the New Dark Ages," *Christianity Today,* Oct. 20, 1989, 30, 32. See Charles E. Rice, *No Exception,* (1990), 110.

38. WHY NOT KILL ABORTIONISTS?

In the moral sense, every abortionist, as the deliberate killer of an innocent human being, is a murderer. Why not blow away that murderer-for-hire as he walks from his car to the entrance of the abortuary? Abortionists are cowards. Otherwise they would not murder babies. If abortionists started dropping like flies, would not the abortion movement disappear for want of practitioners? These and other arguments are seriously made by some to justify the killing of abortionists. But what is wrong with those arguments?

THE LEGAL RIGHT TO RESCUE

If you were walking down the street and saw, through a living room window, a man strangling a child, you would have a legal and moral right to break down his door to intervene to save that child. You would have a legal and moral right to inflict injury and perhaps even death on the perpetrator if necessary. This necessity or justification defense is generally recognized in state and federal courts, but not in abortion cases. The unborn child is the only human being for whose benefit a lifesaving rescue cannot legally be attempted.[1] The Supreme Court defines the unborn child as a nonperson. The Court prevents interference by anybody with the killer of that child and makes that killing a constitutional right. If American law regarded the unborn child as a person, there would be no legalized abortuaries, and that child would be defended by public authorities rather than by private individuals.

The common law or statutory defense of necessity includes a privilege to use reasonable, and sometimes even lethal, force to defend others in some situations. The necessity defense, however, is not limited to the protection of persons; it authorizes the use of necessary and reasonable force for the protection of animals and other property as well as human beings. The Supreme Court could not change the reality that the unborn child, even though the Court defined him as a nonperson, is a human being. The result is a conflict of entitlements: the mother is entitled, by Court decree, to kill her child; other persons are entitled to protect a human being in danger, which the unborn child is. While no appellate court, state or federal, has upheld the necessity defense in the abortion context, it is not surprising that the legalized infliction of violence, in abortion, has caused some to respond in kind. This is so because *Roe v.*

---

[1] See Charles E. Rice and John P. Tuskey, "The Legality and Morality of Using Deadly Force to Protect Unborn Children from Abortionists," 5 *Regent U. L. Rev.* 83 (1995). See also, Charles E. Rice, "Issues Raised by the Abortion Rescue Movement," 23 *Suffolk L. Rev.* 15 (1989).

Wade has loosened the bonds of civil order by legalizing the intentional killing of the innocent.

Murder is Murder

The law cannot validly permit murder. Despite *Roe*, aboruaries, which are murder factories, have no moral right to exist. *Roe v. Wade* is an unjust law and therefore void. However, the fact that *Roe* is unjust does not mean that laws forbidding the killing of abortionists are unjust. Individuals have a right to defend themselves and others. "The act of self-defense can have a double effect: the preservation of one's own life; and the killing of the aggressor. . . . The one is intended, the other is not."[2] Note that the right to defend does not authorize the intentional killing of the aggressor. The intent must be to defend, rather than to kill.[3] The only situations in which anyone ever has the right intentionally to kill anyone are the just war, capital punishment, and a justified rebellion (or what the *Catechism* calls "armed *resistance* to oppression by political authority.)"[4] The just war and capital punishment are decreed by the state, which derives its authority from God.[5] Justified rebellion involves a rightful assumption by private persons of that authority of the state. Even in a justified war or rebellion, of course, the intentional killing of the innocent is never permitted.

But Why *Not* Kill the Abortionist?

So when, if ever, can one morally use force to save a child from abortion? Consider two cases. In the first, Able, an abortionist's assistant in the killing room, suddenly has a change of heart moments before the abortion begins. He has a moral right, and probably even a moral duty, to use reasonable force to defend the child. It is inconceivable, however, that lethal force would be the only way to stop the abortion. Lethal force would therefore not be justified there.

In the second case, Baker, an opponent of abortion, shoots the abortionist in the parking lot as he is approaching the building to do abortions a few minutes later. One difference between the cases is imminence. Able engages in the immediate defense of the child; he has no intent but to defend that child; he has no separate intent to harm or kill the abortionist. Baker, by contrast, is not in the heat of a physical struggle to save the child. He thinks, "I can get no closer than this. If I

---

[2] St. Thomas Aquinas, *ST,* II, II, Q. 64, 7; see Question 13. See also *CCC,* nos. 2263-68, 2321.

[3] *CCC,* no. 2263.

[4] *Ibid.,* no. 2243. See Questions 40 and 41.

[5] See *CCC,* nos. 2266-67, 2307-17.

do not stop him he will go in there and murder babies. So I will shoot him in the head." His purpose is to save children. But his intent in the act he performs that moment is to blow the abortionist's head off to achieve that purpose. Baker is performing an intrinsically evil act to achieve a good end.[6] He assumes the authority of God to decide when that person will face the final judgment of God. St. Thomas, quoting St. Augustine, said that "'A man who, without exercising public authority, kills an evildoer, shall be judged guilty of murder, and all the more, since he has dared to usurp a power which God has not given him.'"[7]

Some may argue that killing the baby killer in the parking lot is legitimate defense of the child because that is as close as Baker can get. But if Baker may kill the abortionist when he is not actually performing an abortion, why does he have to limit himself to the parking lot? Why can he not conclude that the only practicable way he can get a clear shot at him is to shoot him on the golf course? Or at the video store? St. Thomas speaks of the justified defender as one who "repels force."[8] The moral right to defend the child must be restricted to the immediate performance of the abortion. Even then it is practically inconceivable that lethal force would have to be used. Even if Baker somehow got himself into the killing room, he would have no more right than would Able to kill the abortionist.

The use of violence, whether lethal or non-lethal, against abortuaries and abortionists is unjustified also on several prudential grounds. It is not the most effective way to save the lives of unborn children threatened by abortion. It is counterproductive in that it distracts attention from the real, and spiritual, nature of the problem, and it diverts pro-life efforts away from more useful approaches. Moreover, it accelerates the disintegration of the civil order with predictably harmful impact on the common good. Violence should be utterly rejected as a pro-life tactic.

JUSTIFIED REBELLION?

Attacks on abortionists are a symptom of an unravelling of the civil order, which is directly traceable to *Roe v. Wade* and its sanction of the execution of the innocent. In her address on February 3, 1994, to the National Prayer Breakfast in Washington, Mother Teresa said that "the greatest destroyer of peace today is abortion, because it is a war against the child, a direct killing of the innocent child, murder by the mother

---

[6] See *CCC*, no. 1750.

[7] *ST*, II, II, Q. 64, art. 3.

[8] *ST*, II, II, Q. 64, art. 7, quoted in *CCC*, no. 2264.

herself. And if we accept that a mother can kill even her own child, how can we tell other people not to kill one another?"[9]

The intentional killing of an abortionist could be justified if it were incidental to a justified rebellion, which would itself be a just war, in which the abortionist was rightly regarded as a combatant and therefore a legitimate target. However, "Armed *resistance* to oppression by political authority" is not justified unless: 1) there is a grave, prolonged violation of fundamental rights; 2) every other means of redress has been exhausted; 3) resistance will not cause worse disorders; 4) there is reasonable hope of success; and 5) there is no reasonably foreseeable better solution.[10] No one can reasonably conclude, especially in light of numbers two through five of these criteria, that we are in an insurrectionary situation in the United States today such as to justify the intentional killing, as a combatant, of an abortionist who was not then attacking anyone. Despite the erosion of constitutional and legal protections, as described in Parts I and II of this book, no one can legitimately conclude that the disintegration of the American civic fabric precipitated by *Roe* has gone so far that armed rebellion is justified in whole or in part.

Rebellion, incidentally, is not something to be lightly sanctioned. The just war waged by a government has the limiting feature that it can be waged only by the duly constituted public authority. A rebellion, by contrast, is a do-it-yourself project. It involves an assumption of all or part of that public authority by private persons who themselves decide that they are justified in taking over the power of the state in whole or in part. And if one can so decide, so can another. As argued throughout Part III of this book, the solution to the culture of death will be found, not in violence but in the development of a culture of life, from the bottom up, through the conversion of the American people to life in Christ. A violent revolution would short circuit that conversion which is already in progress. To use force against the anti-life state would confront its strongest weapons with our weakest. In *Populorum Progressio,* Paul VI said that "a revolutionary uprising — save where there is manifest long-standing tyranny which would do great damage to fundamental personal rights and dangerous harm to the common good of the country — produces new injustices, throws more elements out of balance and brings on new disasters. Real evil should not be fought against at the cost of greater misery."[11]

---

[9] *Family Resources Center News,* May 1994, 13.
[10] See *CCC,* no. 2243.
[11] *Populorum Progressio* (1967), no. 31.

The divine prohibition of intentional and direct killing (apart from the just war, justified rebellion, and, in limited cases, capital punishment), is absolute. In *Veritatis Splendor,* John Paul II stated:

> The *negative precepts* of the natural law are universally valid. They oblige each and every individual, always and in every circumstance. It is a matter of prohibitions which forbid a given action *semper et pro semper,* without exception, because the choice of this kind of behavior is in no case compatible with the goodness of the will of the acting person, with his vocation to life with God and to communion with his neighbor. It is prohibited — to everyone and in every case — to violate these precepts. They oblige everyone, regardless of the cost, never to offend in anyone, beginning with oneself, the personal dignity common to all. . . . The Church has always taught that one may never choose kinds of behavior prohibited by the moral commandments expressed in negative form in the Old and New Testaments.[12]

NON-LETHAL FORCE?

Is the infliction of non-lethal injury or property damage on abortionists also prohibited absolutely? Instead of killing the abortionist, can you break his arms to prevent him from killing babies? Or can you destroy his property to put economic pressure on him to stop killing babies? If Baker intentionally wounded the abortionist in the driveway, for example, by shooting him in the arm, that act would still lack the imminence necessary for legitimate defense of others. It would therefore seem to be unjustified in principle. In response to the question, "Whether it is lawful for a private individual to kill a man who has sinned?", St. Thomas rejected the infliction of "harm" which is not sanctioned by public authority: "It is lawful for any private individual to do anything for the common good, provided it harm nobody: but if it be harmful to some other, it cannot be done except by virtue of the judgment of the person to whom it pertains to decide what is to be taken from the parts for the welfare of the whole."[13]

In any event, the infliction of even non-lethal injury, or of property damage, against abortionists and abortuaries, contributes to the loosening of civil order. It obscures the spiritual nature of the problem and it diverts attention from more useful approaches. The legitimacy of obstructive rescues, which involve no property damage or personal injury, will be discussed in Question 39.

---

[12] *VS,* no. 52.
[13] *ST,* II, II, Q. 64, art. 3.

VIOLENCE MAKES NO SENSE

If we attempt to combat the abortion movement with force, we oppose its strongest weapon, the coercive power of the state, with our weakest. The most effective on-site activity in defense of unborn children is prayer and counselling. That activity saves lives and it can be carried on day after day. By contrast, if an obstructive rescue occurs on Tuesday, its participants are in jail on Wednesday or otherwise entangled in legal proceedings which may keep them from pro-life activity for a considerable time. And if someone shoots the abortionist, the babies he would have killed that day will get a temporary reprieve and some might even be brought to term by their mothers. But a good purpose does not justify the use of an intrinsically evil means. And, as usually happens, another baby-killer will step forward to take the place of the executed abortionist. Even if coordinated attacks killed every abortionist in the country on the same day and even if that slaughter deterred others from stepping in to do abortions, and even if the abortion industry disappeared as a result, those killings would be unjustified. God put a mark on Cain to protect him because "God, who preferred the correction rather than the death of a sinner, did not desire that a homicide be punished by the exaction of another act of homicide."[14]

As the anti-life state increases its pressure against all forms of pro-life advocacy, we can expect some opponents of abortion to respond with violence. But the pro-life movement must reject all forms of violence against baby killers and their abortuaries.

What is wrong in the pro-life movement is not that we have not bombed or shot. What is wrong is that we have not spoken the truth and we have not prayed enough. For two decades, that movement has approached abortion as a legal and political problem. In a good-faith effort to save lives, the establishment leaders of that movement have proposed one compromise after another, affirming in their actions, despite their rhetoric, that the right to life is alienable — and therefore that the unborn child is a nonperson who, though innocent, may be executed in at least some cases. By permeating the public discourse with the message that even the pro-life leaders think that innocent life is negotiable, they have immeasurably increased the toll of innocent lives taken by abortion and now by euthanasia. The result is a climate of frustration among those who know by reason as well as by faith that we, and the law, can never validly tolerate the execution of the innocent. This climate is conducive to the emergence of some who convince themselves that murder

---

[14] *EV,* no. 9.

can be a solution. But the pro-death forces who dominate our government and media would like nothing more than to see the pro-life movement disintegrate in spasms of bombing and shooting. The media would portray that development as confirmation of the pro-death assumption that there is no objective morality and that the issue is reducible to the utilitarian exercise of power.

TRUTH AND PRAYER

Our strongest weapons are the truth and prayer.

The educational effort should put front and center the reality that the only coherent basis for affirming absolute rights in the human person is that he is an immortal creature made in the image and likeness of God, with a dignity which absolutely transcends the interests of the state.

Finally, and most important, the pro-life movement must put its primary reliance on prayer, especially through the intercession of Mary, who is the Mother of Life. Mary is the "Mother of each and every one of us, the Mother who obtains for us divine mercy."[15] The Rosary is a most powerful weapon for us here, with an appeal far beyond denominational lines. We must pray for our country, for the women who contemplate, or have committed, abortion, and especially for the abortionists and all who support them.

---

[15] *VS*, no. 119.

39. WHAT TACTICS, AT ABORTUARIES AND ELSEWHERE, ARE LEGAL AND EFFECTIVE WAYS OF SAVING LIVES?

Let's start with a good word for the Rescue movement, which used nonviolent tactics to obstruct abortuaries. While that movement has faded because of restrictive laws and injunctions, the rescues remind us of our duty to do something at the scene of the crime. However, the most effective on-site, life-saving tactic is the legal, peaceful prayer vigil with sidewalk counseling and referral to pregnancy help centers. Unlike rescues, these legal activities can be carried on continuously on sidewalks or other public property. Nevertheless, the nonviolent Rescue movement, as a sacrificial effort to awaken the American people from their tolerance of murder, earned respect.

I had the privilege of representing the Lambs of Christ, a group of nonviolent abortion rescuers founded by Fr. Norman Weslin, in their rescue in South Bend, Indiana, over Christmas in 1990. The police and other authorities acted with professionalism and restraint in their treatment of the rescuers at the scene and in prosecuting the case against them. The Lambs included students, grandmothers, priests, retired military combat veterans and women who themselves had had abortions. While they obstructed, non-violently, their primary weapons were prayer and love — for the abortionist as well as for the mother and her child. They condemned no one. They came and departed in peace. I regard them as probably the finest group of people that has ever visited South Bend.[1]

The abortion rescuers remind us of those who maintained the Underground Railroad in violation of the Fugitive Slave Act of 1793 and the fugitive slave provisions of the Compromise of 1850. In 1860, the United States District Court in Chicago convicted John Hossack of aiding the escape of Jim Gray, a fugitive slave. The court fined him $100 and imprisoned him for ten days. His speech before sentencing ought to make us uneasy in this era of legalized abortion:

> This law. . . is so obviously at variance with the law of that God. . .
> that the path of duty is plain to me. This law so plainly tramples upon
> the divine law, that it cannot be binding upon any human being under
> any circumstances to obey it. . . . This law is just as binding on me as
> was the law of Egypt to slaughter Hebrew children . . . .

---

[1] See *So. Bend Tribune,* Dec. 27, 1990, p. C1; Charles E. Rice, "The Lambs of Christ in South Bend," *The Wanderer,* Apr. 4, 1991, p. 6.

I am ready to die, if need be, for the oppressed of my race. But slavery must die; and when my country shall have passed through the terrible conflict which the destruction of slavery must cost, and when the history of the great struggle shall be candidly written, the rescuers of Jim Gray will be considered as having done honor to God, to humanity, and to themselves.[2]

WHAT DOES THE LAW ALLOW?

On-site activities at abortuaries are affected by recent laws and judicial decisions. The best short analysis of the current status of those activities is a booklet prepared by the American Center for Law and Justice and published by Catholics United for Life:

Is sidewalk counseling a constitutional right?
Yes. . . . The Supreme Court repeatedly has ruled that peaceful communication — such as spoken words, display of a sign, and leafletting — are all protected forms of free speech, especially in public places like sidewalks and parks.

What if somebody tells me to "shut up" or to go away?
The right to free speech in public places does not depend upon the consent of the listeners. . . . The Supreme Court has consistently ruled that speech cannot be censored simply because the speaker's message irritates or offends a listener. . . .

FACE
Does FACE outlaw sidewalk counseling?
The so-called Freedom of Access to Clinic Entrances (FACE) Act [enacted in 1994], does not prohibit sidewalk counseling. FACE makes it a federal offense when someone "by force or threat of force or by physical obstruction, intentionally injures, intimidates or interferes with" any person because that person is "obtaining or providing reproductive health services." FACE specifically exempts "any expressive conduct (including peaceful picketing or other peaceful demonstration) protected. . . by the First Amendment.". . . A sidewalk counselor who uses neither force, nor threats of force, nor physical obstruction, does not violate FACE.

RICO
Does RICO outlaw sidewalk counseling?
The federal Racketeer Influenced and Corrupt Organizations (RICO) statute targets "racketeering activity," which the statute defines to in-

---

[2] See Charles E. Rice, "Issues Raised by the Abortion Rescue Movement," 23 *Suffolk L. Rev.* 15, 30-31 (1989).

clude a variety of state felonies and federal crimes like murder, kidnapping, arson, and extortion. Abortion businesses have claimed that sit-ins and blockades are a form of "extortion," and some courts have upheld this misuse of RICO against Operation Rescue-style sit-ins. But peaceful sidewalk counseling is not "racketeering activity" and does not violate RICO.

Madsen
What about the Madsen *decision?*

In *Madsen v. Women's Health Center, Inc.,*[3] in 1994, the. . .Supreme Court reviewed a [lower] court injunction restricting pro-life activities. . . .:

1. The Court struck down a ban on "approaching any person seeking the services of the Clinic unless such person indicates a desire to communicate by approaching or inquiring of the [counselors]." This means a ban on sidewalk counseling is unconstitutional.

2. The Court struck down a ban on "observable images," rejecting the abortion businesses' attempt to prohibit "disagreeable" images such as graphic pictures or strongly worded messages on signs.

3. The Court upheld a "speech-free zone" on the public sidewalk adjacent to an abortuary but struck down a similar zone extending onto private property. The court reasoned that where protesters have repeatedly used public places to engage in unlawful obstruction of access, the protesters may be excluded from those places. Where the protesters have not blocked access, however, a "speech-free zone" is unconstitutional.

In sum, *Madsen* reaffirms that sidewalk counseling is a constitutional right but warns that those who persistently break the law may find themselves excluded from the sidewalk where they wish to counsel.

Schenck
What about the Schenck *decision?*

In *Schenck v. Pro-Choice Network of Western New York,*[4] the U.S. Supreme Court reviewed a court injunction restricting pro-life activities in the Buffalo, New York area. . . [T]he Court struck down "floating bubble zones" and upheld "fixed buffer zones."

1. "Floating bubbles" — The injunction had prohibited all "demonstrating" within 15 feet of people coming to or going from

---
[3] 512 U.S. 753 (1994).
[4] 519 U.S. 357 (1997).

abortuaries, with a limited exception for two sidewalk counselors. Because these zones "floated" along, with the person inside, there was practically no safe place to stand on the public sidewalk. The Supreme Court ruled that these "floating bubbles" burdened more speech than necessary.

2. "Fixed buffers" — The injunction also banned "demonstrating" within 15 feet of abortuary entrances and driveways. The Supreme Court upheld these restrictions because of evidence that pro-life misconduct in the Buffalo area was "indeed extraordinary," making a buffer zone necessary to safeguard "physical access." The Court rejected the idea that such buffer zones would be permitted simply to insulate pregnant women from undesired sidewalk counseling.

Schenck upholds the right to sidewalk counseling: "Leafletting and commenting on matters of public concern are classic forms of speech that lie at the heart of the First Amendment, and speech in public areas is at its most protected on public sidewalks, a prototypical example of a traditional public forum."[5] As in *Madsen,* the Court warned that those who persistently physically obstruct others may be excluded from "access zones." But unless and until a court creates such a zone, pro-life counselors remain free to use the public sidewalk. . . .

Sidewalk counseling remains a constitutional right. There is of course no guarantee that sidewalk counselors will never face harassing lawsuits or false charges. Nevertheless, the person who carefully obeys the law while sidewalk counseling can minimize the chance of legal problems while continuing to reach out to help mothers and their babies.[6]

In *Madsen,* the Supreme Court also struck down the prohibition on activities within 300 feet of the residences of clinic staff. In *Frisby v. Schultz,* in 1988, the court had upheld a law banning "focused picketing taking place solely in front of a particular residence."[7] In *Madsen,* the Court struck down the injunction against "picketing, demonstrating, or using sound amplification equipment within 300 feet of the residences of clinic staff." The Court said that the record "does not contain sufficient justification for this broad a ban on picketing; it appears that a limitation on the time, duration of picketing, and number of pickets outside a smaller zone could have accomplished the desired result."[8]

---

[5] 519 U.S. at 377.
[6] Walter M. Weber, *Sidewalk Counseling: Still a Constitutional Right* (Catholics United for Life, New Hope, KY 40052, 1998) (quoted with permission).
[7] 487 U.S. 474, 483 (1988).
[8] 512 U.S. at 774-75.

The *Madsen* ruling, however, upheld most aspects of the lower court injunction. That ruling illustrates the readiness of the Supreme Court to distort and disregard otherwise applicable precedents in order to facilitate the exercise of the right to abortion. As Justice Scalia stated in dissent:

> 'Today's decision. . . makes it painfully clear that no legal rule or doctrine is safe from ad hoc nullification by this court when an occasion for its application arises in a case involving state regulation of abortion.'. . . Today the ad hoc nullification machine claims its latest, greatest, and most surprising victim: the First Amendment. Because I believe that the judicial creation of a 36-foot zone in which only a particular group, which had broken no law, cannot exercise its rights of speech, assembly and association, and the judicial enactment of a noise prohibition, applicable to that group and that group alone, are profoundly at odds with our First Amendment precedents and traditions, I dissent.[9]

In April, 1998, a federal court jury found Joseph Scheidler, Andrew Scholberg, Timothy Murphy and the Pro-Life Action League civilly liable, in a class action brought by the National Organization for Women on behalf of two abortuaries, for violating the Racketeer Influenced and Corrupt Organizations Act, which had been enacted in 1970 to combat organized crime. The jury found that defendants had joined with others in a racketeering enterprise, the Pro-Life Action Network, which committed extortion, violence and other illegal acts against abortuaries and their customers. The jury awarded damages in the amount of $85,926. Under RICO, the judge would be expected to triple that amount and to award attorneys' fees to the plaintiffs. The judgment has not been entered by the trial court as of this writing.

In 1994, the Supreme Court had unanimously decided, in an earlier appeal in that case, *NOW v. Scheidler*,[10] that defendants could be liable under RICO even though their acts were not motivated by any purpose of economic gain for themselves. Section 1962(c) of RICO makes it unlawful "for any person. . . associated with any enterprise engaged in, or the activities of which affect, interstate or foreign commerce, to conduct or participate, directly or indirectly, in the conduct of such enterprise's affairs through a pattern of racketeering activity." "Section 1961(1)," said the Supreme Court, "defines 'pattern of racketeering activity' to include conduct that is 'chargeable' or 'indictable' under a host of state and

---

[9] 512 U.S. at 785, quoting dissent by Justices O'Connor and then-Justice Rehnquist in *Thornburg v. ACOG*, 476 U.S. 747, 814 (1986).
[10] 510 U.S. 257 (1994).

federal laws. RICO broadly defines 'enterprise' in § 1961(4) to 'includ[e] any individual, partnership, corporation, association, or other legal entity, and any union or group of individuals associated in fact although not a legal entity.' Nowhere in either § 1962(c) or the RICO definitions in § 1961 is there any indication that an economic motive is required."[11]

Plaintiffs alleged, said the Supreme Court, that defendants "were members of a nationwide conspiracy to shut down abortion clinics through a pattern of racketeering activity including extortion in violation of the *Hobbs Act*, 18 U.S.C. § 1951. Section 1951(b)(2) defines extortion as 'the obtaining of property from another, with his consent, induced by wrongful use of actual or threatened force, violence, or fear, or under color of official right.'" Plaintiffs "alleged that [defendants] conspired to use threatened or actual force, violence, or fear to induce clinic employees, doctors, and patients to give up their jobs, give up their economic right to practice medicine, and give up their right to obtain medical services at the clinics."[12]

Chief Justice Rehnquist, writing for the Supreme Court, noted that "the alleged extortion may not benefit the protesters financially but still may drain money from the economy by harming businesses such as the clinics. . . in this case."[13]

"[T]he occasion for Congress' [enactment of RICO]," said the Supreme Court, "was the perceived need to combat organized crime. But Congress for cogent reasons chose to enact a more general statute, one which, although it had organized crime as its focus, was not limited in application to organized crime. . . . Congress has not. . . required that an 'enterprise' in § 1962(c) have an economic motive. . . . We believe the statutory language is unambiguous and find in the. . . legislative history no such 'clearly expressed legislative intent to the contrary' that would warrant a different construction. . . . '[T]he fact that RICO has been applied in situations not expressly anticipated by Congress does not demonstrate ambiguity. It demonstrates breadth.'. . . We hold only that RICO contains no economic motive requirement."[14]

First Amendment concerns did not enter into the Supreme Court's 1994 decision. But Justice Souter emphasized that "nothing in the Court's opinion precludes a RICO defendant from raising the First Amendment in its defense in a particular case. Conduct alleged to

---

[11] 510 U.S. at 256-57.
[12] 510 U.S. at 253.
[13] 510 U.S. at 260.
[14] 510 U.S. at 260-62.

amount to *Hobbs Act* extortion, for example, or one of the other, somewhat elastic RICO predicate acts may turn out to be fully protected First Amendment activity, entitling the defendant to dismissal on that basis. . . . I think it prudent to notice that RICO actions could deter protected advocacy and to caution courts applying RICO to bear in mind the First Amendment interests that could be at stake."[15] The Supreme Court in 1994 remanded the case for the trial, which resulted in the 1998 verdict against defendants.[16] It is likely that the case will return to the Supreme Court on the First Amendment and other issues.

The activities of the *Scheidler* defendants at the aborturies were nonviolent and nonobstructive. If Joe Scheidler, one of the authentic heroes of the pro-life cause, can be subjected to crushing damages on the ground that his peaceable prayer and counseling activity on sidewalks constitutes extortion, then anti-nuclear, peace, AIDS, environmental and other peaceable activists should look for good lawyers. It would not even be enough for them to cease their protest activity thenceforth. They could have potential liability for their past activities.

The application of RICO to activities at aborturies remains uncertain.[17]

THE ALTERNATIVES

Pregnancy-help centers which provide pregnancy tests, counseling, and material as well as spiritual support, will continue to play an essential role in the pro-life effort. The pro-life enterprise is not about a political or legal debate. It is about education and conversion. And saving lives.[18] We cannot be satisfied merely with "polarized debate" on legal issues. We must insist on legal protection for the unborn child. But "the key ingredient that affects society's attitude toward abortion [is] the welfare of the woman involved. That is why the ministry of crisis pregnancy centers is so crucial. . . . These centers offer the woman in crisis the practical and compassionate assistance necessary to help her see that preg-

---

[15] 510 U.S. at 264-65.

[16] See *New York Times*, Feb. 3, 1999, p. A11, discussing the civil verdict of more than $107 million awarded against anti-abortion activists in a suit brought by Planned Parenthood and abortionists under RICO and FACE.

[17] See Comment, "Speech, Conduct and Regulation of Abortion Protest by Court Injunction," 34 *Gonzaga L. Rev.* 201 (1998-99).

[18] For information on pregnancy help centers, contact Nurturing Network, Franciscan University, Steubenville, OH 43952; Shield of Roses, P.O. Box 9053, Glendale, CA 91226; Pregnancy Problem Center East, 3200 Linwood Road, Cincinnati, OH 45226; see *Wash. Times,* April 6, 1998, p. A1; *Baltimore Sun,* April 6, 1998, p. B1; Philip F. Lawler, "Positive Alternatives," *Catholic World Report,* Jan. 1999, 49.

nancy is not the end of her life and that the future life of the child she carries within her is not without hope."[19]

To the extent permitted by the courts, peaceable prayer vigils, with nonobstructive offering of counseling, should be held at abortuaries. Even if the abortuary is situated behind a private parking lot so that close access to the mothers is not practicable, the prayer vigil should be held and help should be offered. The importance of this is underlined by the experience one college student related to this writer. She was pregnant and her boyfriend, in the finest tradition of the 1980s, talked her into having an abortion in another city. She entered the abortuary, filled out the papers, and waited her turn. Just as her name was called, the young woman suddenly pictured the little Franciscan nun (in a habit) who was standing on the sidewalk praying the Rosary as she entered the abortuary. She thought of that nun who was praying for her, and she immediately left the place. She had the baby, placed him for adoption, and successfully resumed her life. She left the abortuary without ever saying a word to that nun. And that nun probably went home and thought she hadn't done much that day. But God responds to prayer as he knows best.

The American Leviathan, of course, is hostile to the right to life. *Madsen* and other cases show that the law is a stacked deck here. The Supreme Court will distort settled legal principles to insulate abortionists from interference and even annoyance by pro-life advocates. It will probably become increasingly difficult to carry on peaceful, non-obstructive prayer and counseling efforts. Even if such activities are so restricted as to be impracticable, it must be remembered that the most effective weapon against abortion is prayer. That prayer can be effective whether at home, in a church or at the abortuary. As abortion becomes a private matter through pills and other early abortifacients, surgical abortion at abortuaries will have a decreasing share of the "market." Prayer vigils in churches or other places, Perpetual Eucharistic Adoration, and other forms of prayer will play a deservedly more central role in the pro-life effort as the need for on-site activity, or its legal permissibility, decreases.

---

[19]   Paul Swope, "Heart and Soul: A New Abortion Strategy," *Crisis*, March 1999, 33, 35; Mr. Swope is a director of The Caring Foundation (800) 705-9497, which promotes pro-life television as directed toward pregnant women who are "pro-choice."

D.   Related Issues

NOTE: These questions extend beyond the usual abortion, euthanasia and family issues. They are relevant to our subject, however, because each involves the dignity of the person in a special way relating to the power of the state over his mobility, his livelihood and even his life itself.

40.   CAN WE BE PRO-LIFE AND SUPPORT CAPITAL PUNISHMENT?

Paul VI's 1968 encyclical, *Humanae Vitae*, was too hard for many Catholics to swallow. They rejected that teaching, papal authority and, in many cases, the Church herself. The teaching of John Paul II and of the *Catechism* on the death penalty is proving to be the *Humanae Vitae* of many orthodox and politically conservative Catholics. The case of Karla Faye Tucker put the issue in focus.

Karla Faye Tucker should not have been executed.[1] On February 3, 1998, the 38 year-old Tucker was executed by injection after Texas Gov. George W. Bush refused to use his power to delay the execution for 30 days. In 1983, Tucker and her boyfriend, who later died in prison, were, in Tucker's words, "casing" a house so they could come back later and rob a motorcycle. They encountered the husband of Tucker's best friend and another woman and murdered them both. The victims were brutally axed, bludgeoned and stabbed to death. Tucker later said she enjoyed the violence, which left each of the victims with more than 20 stab wounds and the woman, Deborah Thornton, with a three-foot axe embedded in her chest by Tucker's boyfriend.

Tucker was from a broken family, raised by a drug-addicted mother. Karla Faye was using marijuana at age 8, heroin at 10, and was a prostitute at 13. Tucker's case drew worldwide attention because she was the first woman executed in Texas in over a century and because she "found Christ" in prison, through a conversion which made her "a different person." The conversion occurred when "I stole this Bible not realizing Bibles were given out free in jail, 'cause I'd never been there. . . . I started reading the Bible. I didn't know what I was reading and before I knew it, I was in the middle of my floor on my knees and I was just asking God to forgive me." Governor Bush was besieged by requests for clemency for Tucker from a wide range of sources, including Pope John Paul II, the European Parliament, and Pat Robertson, who himself generally favored the death penalty.

---

[1] This Question is an adaptation of Charles E. Rice, "Showdown in Texas: The Pope vs. the Culture of Death," *Catholic Dossier*, Sept.-Oct. 1998, 16.

"My religion says to forgive. Turn a cheek. I still cannot do it," said Richard Thornton, whose wife was killed by Tucker. "I don't believe her conversion," he said. "I don't believe her Christianity."[2] Deborah Thornton's brother, on the other hand, favored commutation of the sentence. Conversions on death row are common. But, according to Catholic teaching, the case for sparing Tucker does not depend on the genuinity of her conversion. Indeed, the case for sparing her would have been stronger if she had *not* converted. The Tucker case is a useful means to analyze the teaching of the Catholic Church on the subject in light of *Evangelium Vitae* and the *Catechism of the Catholic Church*. It may be helpful to review some basics.

The only situations in which anyone ever has the moral right intentionally to kill anyone are the just war, capital punishment and a justified rebellion (or what *The Catechism* calls 'armed *resistance* to oppression by political authority').[3] But no one *ever* has the right intentionally to kill the innocent.[4] Note that the right of personal self-defense does not include the right intentionally to kill: "'The act of self-defense can have a double effect: the preservation of one's own life, and the killing of the aggressor. . . . The one is intended, the other is not.'"[5] In self-defense or defense of others, the defender's intent must be to defend rather than to kill. The just war and capital punishment are decreed by the state, which derives its authority from God. A justified armed rebellion involves a rightful assumption by private persons of the authority of the state. The right to kill intentionally, therefore, can properly be asserted only by those responsible for the common good, that is, the state or those engaged in a justified rebellion. Private persons on their own authority *never* have the right intentionally to kill anyone.

The death penalty is legal in 38 states. A total of 3,549 inmates were on death row in the United States at the start of 1999, including 17 condemned under federal law. About 300 more are sentenced to death every year. In 1998, 68 persons were executed. To eliminate the backlog could require the execution of one person every day for about 60 years.[6]

Church teaching has traditionally regarded the decision whether to exercise the authority of the state to impose the death penalty as, in effect, a prudential judgment subject to a strong presumption against the use of that penalty.

---

[2] *Catholic World News, Catholic News Brief No. 6860*, Feb. 4, 1998.
[3] No. 2243. See Question 38.
[4] See *EV*, no. 57.
[5] *ST*, II, II, Q. 64, art.7. See *CCC*, no. 2263.
[6] For statistics, contact Death Penalty Information Center, 1320 18th Street N.W., Washington, D.C. 20036, (202) 293-6970.

Has the Church changed its affirmation of the authority of the state to impose the death penalty? Or has it restricted the conditions under which that authority may rightly be exercised? The answer is: No on the first, Yes on the second.

The *Catechism of the Catholic Church* was issued in 1992, *Evangelium Vitae* in 1995, and the final Latin text, with revisions, of the *Catechism* in 1997. It will be helpful to compare the final *Catechism* text with *Evangelium Vitae*. Three sections of the 1997 final text of the *Catechism* are relevant here:

> 2265. Legitimate defense can be not only a right but a grave duty for one who is responsible for the lives of others. *The defense of the common good requires that an unjust aggressor be rendered unable to cause harm.* For this reason, those who legitimately hold authority also have the right to use arms to repel aggressors against the civil community entrusted to their responsibility. (emphasis added)

Comment: While this paragraph does not mention the death penalty, it shows that rendering the aggressor harmless is an essential element of the defense of the common good.

> 2266. The efforts of the state to curb the spread of behavior harmful to people's rights and to the basic rules of civil society correspond to the requirement of safeguarding the common good. Legitimate public authority has the right and the duty to inflict punishment proportionate to the gravity of the offense. Punishment has the primary aim of redressing the disorder introduced by the offense. When it is willingly accepted by the guilty party, it assumes the value of expiation. *Punishment* then, in addition to defending public order and protecting people's safety, has a medicinal purpose: *as far as possible, it must contribute to the correction of the guilty party.* (emphasis added)

Comment: This paragraph does not refer to the death penalty. But it refers to the expiative "value" of punishment and its "medicinal purpose: as far as possible it must contribute to the correction of the guilty party."

> 2267. Assuming that the guilty party's identity and responsibility have been fully determined, the traditional teaching of the church does not exclude recourse to the death penalty, *if this is the only possible way of effectively defending human lives against the unjust aggressor.*
>
> If, however, non-lethal means are sufficient *to defend and protect people's safety from the aggressor,* authority will limit itself to such means, as these are more in keeping with the concrete conditions of

the common good and more in conformity with the dignity of the human person.

Today, in fact, as a consequence of the possibilities which the state has for effectively preventing crime, *by rendering one who has committed an offense incapable of doing harm — without definitively taking away from him the possibility of redeeming himself—* the cases in which the execution of the offender is an *absolute necessity* 'are *very rare, if not practically non-existent.'* (quoting *EV*, no. 56) (emphasis added)

Comment: This paragraph allows the death penalty only "if this is the only possible way of effectively defending human lives against the unjust aggressor," which is the only justification for the use of the death penalty. The criterion no longer includes a generalized protection of what the 1992 text of no. 2267 called "public order and the safety of persons," which could have justified the achievement of that goal by deterrence of others than this criminal from attacking the safety of persons, or by a retributive promotion of respect for law and justice. Rather, the sole criterion is now the protection of human lives *from this convicted criminal.*

Next, let us look at *Evangelium Vitae*, which was quoted in the 1997 text of the *Catechism*, no. 2267. It would be a mistake, however, to focus solely on no. 56, which is the section explicitly dealing at length with the death penalty.

Evangelium Vitae "is meant to be a *precise* and *vigorous reaffirmation of the value of human life and its inviolability,* and at the same time a pressing appeal addressed to each and every person, in the name of God: *respect, protect, love and serve life, every human life!"*[7] John Paul's reference to Cain and Abel is significant:

God, who is always merciful even when he punishes, '*put a mark on Cain,* lest any who came upon him should kill him' (Gen 4:15). He thus gave him a distinctive sign, not to condemn him to the hatred of others, but to protect and defend him from those wishing to kill him, even out of a desire to avenge Abel's death. *Not even a murderer loses his personal dignity,* and God himself pledges to guarantee this. . . . God, who preferred the correction rather than the death of a sinner, did not desire that a homicide be punished by the exaction of another act of homicide.[8]

---

[7] *EV*, no. 5.
[8] *Ibid.*, no. 9.

The Pope's teaching on the death penalty must be considered in the context of his insistence on the dignity of the human person and the importance of reform of the criminal:

> The blood of Christ, while it reveals the grandeur of the Father's love, shows how precious man is in God's eyes and how priceless the value of his life. . . .[9]

> Among the signs of hope we should also count. . . a *growing public opposition to the death penalty*, even when such a penalty is seen as a kind of 'legitimate defence' on the part of society. Modern society in fact has the means of effectively suppressing crime by rendering criminals harmless without definitively denying them the chance to reform. . . .[10]

> Life is always a good. . . . Man has been given *a sublime dignity*, based on the intimate bond which unites him to his Creator; in man there shines forth a reflection of God himself.[11]

The Texas Catholic Bishops had it right when they called, on October 21, 1997, for an end to capital punishment because the state was "usurping the sovereign dominion of God over human life."[12] This position echoes *Evangelium Vitae*, which essentially puts a challenge to the pretensions of the modern state:

> Man's life comes from God; it is his gift, his image and imprint, a sharing in his breath of life. *God* therefore *is the sole Lord of this life;* man cannot do with it as he wills."[13]

> With regard to things, but even more with regard to life man is not the absolute master and final judge, but rather — and this is where his incomparable greatness lies — he is the 'minister of God's plan.'[14]

Evangelium Vitae affirms the Church's teaching that the state has authority to impose the death penalty in some situations. But it mandates that a different and very much heavier burden of proof must be met before that authority can rightly be exercised. No. 56 of *Evangelium Vitae* states:

> This is the context in which to place the problem of the *death penalty*. On this matter there is a growing tendency, both in the Church and in

---

[9] *Ibid.*, no. 25.
[10] *Ibid.*, no. 27.
[11] *Ibid.*, no. 34.
[12] *Catholic World News, Catholic News Brief No. 6106,* Oct. 21, 1997.
[13] *EV*, no. 39.
[14] *Ibid.*, no. 52, quoting *Humanae Vitae*, no. 13.

civil society, to demand that it be applied in a very limited way or even that it be abolished completely. The problem must be viewed in the context of a system of penal justice ever more in line with human dignity and thus, in the end, with God's plan for man and society. The primary purpose of the punishment which society inflicts is "to redress the disorder caused by the offence." Public authority must redress the violation of personal and social rights by imposing on the offender an adequate punishment for the crime, as a condition for the offender to regain the exercise of his or her freedom. In this way authority also fulfills the purpose of defending public order and ensuring people's safety, while at the same time offering the offender an incentive and help to change his or her behaviour and be rehabilitated.

It is clear that, for these purposes to be achieved, *the nature and extent of the punishment* must be carefully evaluated and decided upon, and ought not go to the extreme of executing the offender except in cases of absolute necessity: in other words, when it would not be possible otherwise to defend society. Today however, as a result of steady improvements in the organization of the penal system, such cases are very rare, if not practically non-existent.

In any event, the principle set forth in the new *Catechism of the Catholic Church* remains valid: "If bloodless means are sufficient to defend human lives against an aggressor and to protect public order and the safety of persons, public authority must limit itself to such means, because they better correspond to the concrete conditions of the common good and are more in conformity to the dignity of the human person."[15]

The 1997 final version of the *Catechism* incorporates the teaching of *Evangelium Vitae* and makes it clear that the death penalty can be justified only if it is the only possible way to defend lives against this particular unjust aggressor.[16] Even under the new criterion of *Evangelium Vitae* and the *Catechism*, one could evidently still argue for the death penalty in very limited situations, such as that of a prisoner serving a life sentence who murders a guard or another inmate. Should he get another life sentence? Would it be consistent with his dignity not to kill him but to wall him up permanently in a cell, with food and wastes passed through an aperture and with no direct contact ever with any other human being? The death penalty could be argued to be absolutely necessary in such a case, although even there it is debatable. Other situations could

---

[15] *EV*, no. 56, quoting in the third paragraph the 1992 version of *CCC*, no. 2267, which was superseded by the 1997 final text of *CCC*.
[16] *CCC*, no. 2267.

be argued, such as a condition of unrest or rebellion in which the authorities would lack the physical means to keep a murderer securely imprisoned. Even those cases are debatable. In any event, the letter as well as the spirit of *Evangelium Vitae* and the *Catechism* should lead a Catholic to oppose a general death penalty statute in the United States, and to oppose the imposition of that penalty in practically every conceivable case.

In short, *Evangelium Vitae*'s allowance of the death penalty only "in cases of absolute necessity. . .when it would not be possible to defend society" refers not to some generalized protection of society by imposing retribution or by deterring other potential offenders. Rather it refers only to the protection of society *from this convicted criminal*. The final text of the *Catechism* makes it explicitly clear that a Catholic can no longer argue for the death penalty from an undifferentiated need to protect society or to promote the common good.

The criterion of *Evangelium Vitae* and the *Catechism*, incidentally, is more narrow than the justifications for the death penalty advanced by St. Thomas Aquinas, who said that "the common good is better than the particular good of one person. So, the particular good should be removed in order to preserve the common good. But the life of certain pestiferous men is an impediment to the common good which is the concord of human society. . . . Therefore, certain men must be removed by death from the society of men. . . . Therefore, the ruler of a state executes pestiferous men justly and sinlessly in order that the peace of the state may not be disrupted. . . . [I]f a man be dangerous and infectious to the community, on account of some sin, it is praiseworthy and advantageous that he be killed in order to safeguard the common good, since 'a little leaven corrupteth the whole lump' (I *Cor.* 5:6)."[17]

Before *Evangelium Vitae*, this writer and others argued for the use of the death penalty on grounds consistent with the position taken by St. Thomas Aquinas. The death penalty probably deters some premeditated homicides. Its abolition could put at risk innocent victims who might be murdered by persons who could have been executed or by persons who would have been deterred by the prospect of the death penalty. For some crimes, we argued, only the death penalty would fit the crime and restore the balance of justice which is required by the common good. Murder should be stigmatized as the crime of crimes. To punish it by imprisonment, a penalty qualitatively no different from that inflicted for

---

[17] *ST*, II, II, Q. 64, art. 2; see also *ST*, II, II, Q. 66, art. 6. See generally Brian Calvert, "Aquinas on Punishment and the Death Penalty," 37 *Amer. J. of Jurisprudence* 259 (1992).

embezzlement, is to devalue innocent life. Seen in this light, we argued, the death penalty uniquely promotes respect for innocent life. These and other arguments were legitimate and persuasive. However, John Paul has shown that these arguments are obsolete. He has raised the discussion to a new level in universal terms addressed to everyone regardless of creed.

The classic purposes of punishment are retribution, which is not revenge but the restoration of the balance of justice; deterrence of the criminal himself and others; and rehabilitation or reform of the criminal. *Evangelium Vitae*, in accord with the *Catechism*, affirms the retributive purpose by stating that the "primary purpose" of punishment is "to redress the disorder caused by the offence."[18] But those teachings do not accept "redress [of] disorder" as a justification for the death penalty. Capital punishment obviously deters the executed criminal from committing other crimes and it probably deters some others from committing capital crimes. *Evangelium Vitae* and the *Catechism*, however, exclude deterrence as a justification for the death penalty. With respect to rehabilitation, those teachings make the "reform"[19] of the criminal a nearly absolutized objective, permitting the death penalty only in cases of "absolute necessity" in which the state lacks the means of rendering an offender incapable of doing harm.[20] Only then can the state justify "taking away from him the possibility of redeeming himself."[21] Apart from such "very rare, if not practically non-existent,"[22] circumstances, John Paul seeks the protection of society through a "cultural transformation," building a "new culture of life."[23] "The first and fundamental step towards this cultural transformation consists in forming consciences with regard to the incomparable and inviolable worth of every human life."[24]

John Paul challenges the prevailing pagan culture of death on its basic premises. He insists that God — not the individual and not the state — is in charge of the ending as well as the beginning of human life. Because man is made in the image and likeness of God, all human life is sacred and all human persons have a sublime dignity that transcends the interest and power of the state. For these reasons, human life cannot be taken away except on God's terms. We are called, each of us, to choose the culture of life rather than the culture of death. Moreover, our "freedom. . .possesses an *inherently relational dimension*" because "God

---

[18] *EV*, no. 56.
[19] *Ibid.*, no. 27.
[20] *CCC*, no. 2267.
[21] *Ibid.*
[22] *Ibid.*
[23] *EV*, no. 95.
[24] *Ibid.*, no. 96.

entrusts us to one another."[25] Therefore, "every man is his 'brother's keeper.'"[26] Even if his brother, like Cain, is a murderer.

In our pagan culture, abortion, euthanasia and capital punishment all rest on a utilitarian base, or what John Paul described as "the criterion of efficiency, functionality and usefulness."[27] The death penalty is not intended by the state today as a protection for the sanctity of the innocent lives of potential victims. In a culture of death which allows the execution of the innocent unborn, the comatose and others, there is no sanctity of life. There is none because the inviolable sanctity of life depends on God, and the American state has declared its neutrality as to whether God even exists.[28] The result is an established militant secularism in which man lives out the contraceptive ethic to make himself, rather than God, the arbiter, employing utilitarian criteria, of the ending as well as the beginning of life. In this climate, the use of the death penalty can only aggrandize the power of the state, which recognizes no moral authority higher than itself.

Karla Faye Tucker's conversion was not the reason she should not have been executed. In light of the teaching of the Church, the case to spare her life could be said to be stronger if she had not been converted. As long as the criminal can be securely confined so as to be rendered "incapable of doing harm," the fact that he has *not* experienced a religious conversion is an additional reason *not* to take away from him "the possibility of redeeming himself."[29] The importance of the conversion of even one person was spelled out by St. Thomas Aquinas: "[T]he justification of the ungodly, which terminates at the eternal good of a share in the Godhead, is greater than the creation of heaven and earth, which terminates at the good of mutable nature. Hence, Augustine, after saying that 'for a just man to be made from a sinner is greater than to create heaven and earth,' adds, 'for heaven and earth shall pass away, but the justification of the ungodly shall endure'. . . The good of the universe is greater than the particular good of one, if we consider both in the same genus. But the good of grace in one is greater than the good of nature in the whole universe."[30]

If the death penalty is rejected, pursuant to *Evangelium Vitae* and the *Catechism*, one alternative could be life imprisonment without

---

[25] *Ibid.*, no. 19.

[26] *Ibid.*

[27] *Ibid.*, no. 23.

[28] See Question 10.

[29] *CCC,* no. 2267.

[30] *ST,* I-II, Q. 113, art. 9.

chance of parole. Or the life imprisonment without parole could be "hard time," under much more onerous conditions than those experienced by other prisoners. Or the sentence could be life imprisonment with possibility of parole, or a lengthy prescribed term of imprisonment. In any case — including those where the death penalty would be allowed under the teaching of the Church — the offender deserves punishment proportionate to the gravity of the offense.[31]

It might be objected that it makes little sense to argue for life imprisonment without parole as an alternative to the death penalty. A life sentence without parole permanently removes the criminal from society outside the walls. In significant respects, it is more onerous than the death penalty. Therefore, it might be argued, the death penalty should not be evaluated under criteria more stringent than those applicable to such a life sentence, including the generalized protection of society by the deterrence of others and the retributive promotion of respect for law and justice. On the contrary, the reason why Church teaching rejects that generalized protection of society as a justification for the death penalty is precisely because the death penalty decisively cuts off the criminal's "chance to reform."[32] Only for the absolutely necessary protection of others from that criminal can the promotion of the common good justify cutting off that "chance to reform."

It might be argued also that the greater includes the lesser and, since a murderer can merit eternal punishment for his sin, he ought to be held to merit the lesser punishment of bodily death. But this argument must yield to the imperative, as spelled out in *Evangelium Vitae* and the *Catechism*, of preserving that murderer's "possibility of redeeming himself" so as to avoid that eternal punishment and to gain the salvation which is in accord with his dignity as a creature made in the image and likeness of God. Even when the murderer has reformed, as Tucker did, he should not be executed. To say the least, to execute only those who reform would put a damper on the reform process. More important, the death penalty, except where absolutely necessary to protect others from that criminal, is inconsistent with the dignity of that criminal. "Not even a murderer loses his personal dignity."[33] "Non-lethal" punishment, when consistent with the protection of human lives from this criminal, serves the common good more than execution would, because the use of such means bears witness to "how precious man is in God's eyes and how priceless the value of his life."[34] "God," in his placing of the protective

---

[31] *CCC*, no. 2266.
[32] *EV*, no. 27.
[33] *Ibid.*, no. 9.
[34] *Ibid.*, no. 25.

mark on Cain, showed that he "did not desire that a homicide be punished by the exaction of another act of homicide."[35]

Jerry Falwell, in his interview with Jesse Jackson on CNN, February 8, 1998, opposed Tucker's execution but said, "I've always believed that there needed to be in the system capital punishment for the monsters of society like the Ted Bundys, the Timothy McVeighs, the John Wayne Gacys, etc." Jerry has it wrong. The state has no right to execute a person because he is a "monster" or because of the gravity of what he has done, but only has that right where that execution is absolutely necessary to protect other persons from that criminal. John Paul has it right. And so did Karla Faye Tucker when she said that what her supporters "were really speaking out for is the cause of Christ. I believe that they see what Jesus Christ has done in a life, the way he has transformed a life. And what they're speaking out for is saying, he's real. If he did this in this life, in this person who did something like that, he can do that in anybody's life."[36] And we should give him the chance.

---

[35] *Ibid.*, no. 9.
[36] CNN interview with Larry King, Jan. 31, 1998.

41. IF WE ARE PRO-LIFE, DON'T WE HAVE TO BE OPPOSED TO WAR? DOESN'T A CATHOLIC HAVE TO BE A PACIFIST?

How could anyone in his right mind *not* be opposed to war? But that does not mean that one has to be a pacifist.

UNIVERSAL PACIFISM

Peace and prudent reduction of armaments must be our goals. But there is no sound basis for a pacifist conclusion which would deny all legitimacy to the use of defensive force. The *Catechism* commends the witness offered by persons who renounce the use of violence:

> 2306.   Those who renounce violence. . . and,. . . to safeguard human rights, make use of those means of defense available to the weakest, bear witness to evangelical charity, provided they do so without harming the rights and obligations of other men and societies. They bear legitimate witness to the gravity of the physical and moral risks of recourse to violence, with all its destruction and death.

The only authority cited by this paragraph is Vatican II's *Pastoral Constitution on the Church in the Modern World*, which praises "all who forgo the use of violence to vindicate *their* rights."[1]

It can, of course, be a commendable "witness to evangelical charity" for one to renounce force in defending *himself.* A universal pacifist, however, who denies that force can ever be justified in defense of the common good, refuses to defend *others.* And he would deny to others their right to have the state provide what the *Catechism* calls "*legitimate defense by military force.*"[2] Note also that those who "renounce violence" are commended by the *Catechism* only "provided they do so without harming the rights and obligations of other men and societies."[3] Elsewhere, the *Catechism* noted that "Legitimate defense can be not only a right but a grave duty for one who is responsible for the lives of others. . . . [T]hose who legitimately hold authority also have the right to use arms to repel aggressors against the civil community entrusted to their responsibility."[4]

The universal pacifist denies any right of the state to use force to defend the common good. But the nobility of that position fades when it is realized that the pacifist would consign the helpless and innocent to

---

[1]   *Gaudium et Spes*, no. 78 (emphasis added).
[2]   *CCC*, no. 2309.
[3]   *Ibid*, no. 2306.
[4]   *Ibid.*, no. 2265; see also *CCC*, no. 2308.

death or servitude rather than recognize a right to come to their defense. Suppose that military force exercised by proper authority could have saved the innocent Cambodian people from the living hell of rule by the Khmer Rouge. Would it have been moral to use force as necessary to protect their freedom against the unjust aggressor? Or would Christian morality have required us to stand by, let those people die or disappear into slavery and salve our consciences later by sending food packages to such of them as might still be alive? Not only is universal pacifism not a dictate of Christianity. It can work an injustice on those to whom we owe a duty of defense.

An insight into the moral incongruity of universal pacifism is seen in the 1983 pastoral letter of the American Catholic bishops. The bishops say: "Nonviolent means of resistance to evil deserve much more study and consideration than they have thus far received. *There have been significant instances in which people have successfully resisted oppression without recourse to arms.* Nonviolence is not the way for the weak, the cowardly, or the impatient. Such movements have seldom gained headlines even though they have left their mark on history."[5] The bishops' disclosure of the examples where "people have successively resisted oppression without recourse to arms" is revealing: "The heroic Danes who would not turn Jews over to the Nazis and the Norwegians who would not teach Nazi propaganda in schools serve as inspiring examples in the history of non-violence."[6]

The common denominator, however, is that the Danes and Norwegians in World War II were conquered, subjugated people. The bishops continued: "Nonviolent resistance, like war, can take many forms depending upon the demands of a given situation. There is, for instance, organized popular defense instituted by government as part of its contingency planning. Citizens would be trained in the techniques of peaceable non-compliance and non-cooperation as a means of hindering an invading force or non-democratic government from imposing its will."

Such theorizing offers little more than a prescription for surrender followed by passive resistance. It ignores the human lives that would be lost by a failure to resist aggression. What the pacifist asserts is not merely his purpose to turn his own cheek, but also his willingness to turn the cheeks of his fellow citizens who rightly look to him for protection.

---

[5] Catholic Bishops of the United States, Pastoral 21, "The Challenge of Peace: God's Promise and Our Response," 13 *Origins* 1 (May 19, 1983) (emphasis added).
[6] *Ibid.*

This criticism of universal pacifists — that their adherence to principle disregards the lives of innocents whom they ought to defend — may appear similar to the charge leveled by incrementalists against "no-exception" pro-lifers. The charge is that they would rather adhere to their principle than save the lives of unborn children by incremental legislation. The two cases, however, are different. The universal pacifist rejects the teaching of the natural law and the Church that force can rightly be used in defense of the common good. The "no-exception" pro-lifer does not reject, but applies, the teaching that the human law can never validly tolerate the execution of the innocent. When he rejects the incremental strategy of piecemeal restriction of abortion, he does so on sound prudential grounds, including the reality that the incremental strategy increases the toll of lives lost by abortion. Moreover, his rejection of the incremental strategy is not an abdication of duty to the unborn. The "no-exception" approach includes the advocacy of legislative and other measures which are likely to save more lives than would the policy of incrementalism. Advocacy of a "no-exception" approach to abortion, therefore, does not require approval of a universal pacifism which denies absolutely the right to use force in defense of the common good. Granting the sincerity of those who hold to it, such a universal pacifism is objectively ignoble and unworkable.

Selective Pacifism

A selective pacifism involving a refusal to fight, not in all wars, but only in a particular unjust war, has much in common with a sound pro-life position on abortion. Both positions insist that the state is not god, whether the issue is killing in a war or killing in an abortuary. The just or unjust character of a war is more difficult to determine than is the unjust character of laws permitting abortion. And a presumption of validity has to be given to a decision of the state to use force to defend the common good. The use of such force can be legitimate, where the allowance of abortion can never be anything but unjust. Apart from the difficulty of making the decision that a given war is unjust, both the selective pacifist and the sound pro-lifer affirm the subordination of the state to the higher law. And they both act in accord with the natural law and the teaching of the Church.

We all should be selective pacifists, reserving the right to submit, with prudence, any act of the state, even a war, to the higher standard of the natural law and the law of God.

THE JUST WAR: A CONTRADICTION?

The theory of the just war, formulated by St. Augustine and developed by St. Thomas Aquinas and others, involves two concepts. First is *Jus ad Bellum*, determining when recourse to war is permissible. The second is *Jus in Bello*, determining the principles governing the conduct of the just war once it has begun.

JUS AD BELLUM

"In order for a war to be just," wrote Aquinas, "three things are necessary. *First,* the authority of the sovereign by whose command the war is to be waged. For it is not the business of a private individual to declare war, because he can seek for redress of his rights from the tribunal of his superior. Moreover, it is not the business of a private individual to summon together the people, which has to be done in wartime. . . . *Secondly,* a just cause is required, namely that those who are attacked should be attacked because they deserve it on account of some fault. . . . *Thirdly,* it is necessary that the belligerents should have a rightful intention, so that they intend the advancement of good, or the avoidance of evil."[7] The Catholic bishops of the United States specified the requirements for going to war:

1. *Just cause*

2. *Competent authority*

3. *Comparative justice,* i.e., "Which side is sufficiently 'right' in a dispute, and are the values at stake critical enough to override the presumption against war?"

4. *Right intention.* War must be intended only for reasons which constitute just cause and it must be waged with the goal of peace and reconciliation, "including avoiding unnecessarily destructive acts or imposing unreasonable conditions (e.g., unconditional surrender)."

5. War must be the *last resort.*

6. There must be a *reasonable "probability of success."* The Bishops note that this criterion prevents "irrational resort to force or hopeless resistance when the outcome of either will clearly be disproportionate or futile. The determination includes a recognition that at times defense of key values, even against great odds, may be a 'proportionate' witness."

---

[7] *ST,* II, II, Q. 40, art. 1 (emphasis added).

7.   *Proportionality*, i.e., "the damage to be inflicted and the costs incurred by war must be proportionate to the good expected by taking up arms."[8]

These concepts were incorporated into the *Catechism* which insists that "legitimate defense by military force" must be in response to grave and lasting damage inflicted by an aggressor, it must be the last resort, with reasonable prospects of success, and it must not cause greater evils than the evil to be eliminated.[9]

JUS IN BELLO

The two criteria that govern *Jus in Bello*, the manner of conducting a war, are "proportionality and discrimination."[10] Proportionality requires that the war itself must be for a proportionate good, and also that tactics and weapons used in that war must be proportionate to the situation. Discrimination "prohibits directly intended attacks on noncombatants and nonmilitary targets."[11] "Every act of war," said the Second Vatican Council, "directed to the indiscriminate destruction of whole cities or vast areas with their inhabitants is a crime against God and man, which merits firm and unequivocal condemnation."[12]

Cardinal John O'Connor expressed his doubt that the NATO attack on Serbia in 1999 was a "just war": "Does the massive bombing in which we are engaged meet the 'just war' teaching of the Catholic Church that 'the use of arms must not produce evils and disorders graver than the evil to be eliminated? Can we say with integrity that the kind of bombing in which we are apparently engaged includes only 'surgical strikes,' without serious danger of indiscriminate destruction, including the deaths of innocent human beings?"[13]

The intentional killing of innocent noncombatants can never be justified. Thus, the bombing of Dresden in February, 1945, was an abomination because the purpose was to kill numerous civilians by fire and thereby to terrorize the German population, inducing them to pressure their government into ending the war.[14] In this writer's view, the cases of Hiroshima and Nagasaki are comparable to Dresden, although it has been argued that the use of the atomic bomb was justified because it

---

[8]   Pastoral, 13 *Origins* at 10-11 (1983).
[9]   *CCC*, no. 2309.
[10] Pastoral, see 13 *Origins* at 11 (1983).
[11] *Ibid.* See also *CCC*, nos. 2312-13.
[12] *Gaudium et Spes*, no. 80. See *CCC*, nos. 2312-14.
[13] *The Wanderer*, May 13, 1999, p. 1. See also "Signs of the Times," *Chronicles*, June 1999, 24.
[14] See David Irving, *Apocalypse 1945: The Destruction of Dresden* (1995); Raymond H. Willcocks, *The Ethics of Bombing Dresden* (1998).

made unnecessary an invasion of Japan that would have cost many American and Japanese lives. The objective of shortening the war and thus saving lives on both sides, however, could not justify the intentional killing of noncombatants.

Note that the Second Vatican Council condemned acts of war "directed to the indiscriminate destruction of whole cities or vast areas with their inhabitants."[15] Under the principle of double effect, it could be morally justified to attack a military target of sufficient importance even though the attacker knows, but does not intend, that innocent civilians in the vicinity will be killed.[16] However, at some point one would have to conclude that the unintended loss of civilian lives is so disproportionate that the attack could not rightly be made. A further consideration is whether the risk of escalation to a nuclear war of total destruction is so great as to preclude any use of nuclear weapons. This risk of escalation is present in any conflict but it would be especially acute if nuclear weapons were used.

DOES THE "JUST WAR" THEORY STILL APPLY?

Not that there's anything intrinsically wrong with just war theory. It does provide the only middle ground between promiscuous pacifism (war is always a no-no) and totalistic crusading (kill them all; God will know His own). And, during the Cold War's chillier seasons, it did offer a useful alternative to the false dichotomy of better-red-than-dead vs. nuke-'em-till-they-glow. . . . But the real shortcoming is that, increasingly, just war theory no longer applies to realities. This began in World War II, when it became apparent that discriminating between civilians and combatants was no longer possible. Nuclear weapons and anti-colonial insurgencies further blurred the neat distinctions. . . . Most important, though, just war theory has nothing to say about "stateless Warfare," conflicts waged by subnational groups who may have access to weapons of mass destruction.[17]

Some observers speculate that "future war will increasingly be. . . waged outside the nation-state framework" due to "the nation state's loss of its monopoly on armed violence."[18] Whatever changes may occur in warfare patterns, they do not abrogate the right of those in authority to use force to repel aggressors against the community.[19] It may be difficult,

---

[15] *Gaudium et Spes*, no. 80.
[16] See Fr. Hardon's explanation of the double effect principle in Question 13.
[17] Philip Gold, "Scholarly Theory, Absent Reality," *Wash. Times,* Dec. 7, 1996, p. A13.
[18] See William S. Lind, Major John F. Schmitt, USMCR, and Col. Gary I. Wilson, USMCR, "Fourth Generation Warfare: Another Look," *Marine Corps Gazette,* Dec. 1994, 34, 37; see also, Martin van Creveld, *The Transformation of War* (1991), ch. 6.

however, to conclude that the use of force is justified when its purpose is something other than the traditional defense of the nation-state from overt and immediate attack. Harold O. J. Brown, for example, explained his reasons for concluding that the proposed bombing raids on Iraq in 1998 would not have been justified: "If bombing comes, there will be no declaration of war, and no real way of determining that the raids have forced Saddam's compliance, nor that he will continue to comply for any length of time even if he begins by submitting. Who will suffer? Iraqi soldiers and civilians, who, like victims of other terrorist attacks, will be exposed to death and destruction with little if any possibility of self defense. From the point of view of the attackers, it will be a justified, neat, 'surgical' way of forcing Saddam's compliance, treating his people as hostages. From the point of view of the victims, it will simply be murder. Do we have the moral right to send our aviators out to destroy and to kill? Killing in war is not murder, but killing in time of peace, with no declaration of war, to pressure a dictator into compliance with the demands of self-appointed international authorities certainly is. There might be a case for a just war against a nation that behaves as Hussein's Iraq does. But simply to kill people in an effort to 'send a message' is not moral because a United Nations resolution, or an alliance of English-speaking nations, approves it. Killing with premeditation is murder, whether done by a terrorist bomb or by a cruise missile."[20]

The state has authority to defend the common good in a just war. This does not mean that citizens should uncritically accept the decisions of government leaders to send their (and perhaps not the leaders') sons and daughters into harm's way.

---

[19] See *CCC*, no. 2265.
[20] *Religion & Society Report*, Apr. 1998, 1-4.

42. SHOULDN'T THE GOVERNMENT RECOGNIZE THE
RIGHT OF CONSCIENTIOUS OBJECTION TO MILITARY SERVICE?

Yes. It is not surprising, however, that the Church is cautious here. As Aquinas teaches, a just law is morally binding on the citizen.[1] In some circumstances, the state has a duty to defend the community by force. When Pope Paul VI addressed the United Nations in 1965, he made his dramatic plea for peace: "Never again war, never again war!" he said. "If you want to be brothers, let the arms fall from your hands. A person cannot love with offensive weapons in his hands." But he went on to say, "So long as man remains that weak, changeable, and even wicked being he often shows himself to be, defensive arms will, alas, be necessary."[2] The laws providing for that defense are therefore just laws and morally binding on the citizens.

THE DUTY TO DEFEND AND THE RIGHT TO OBJECT

How can the state defend if the citizens have no moral duty to assist in that defense? The citizen has a moral duty to participate in the just defense of the community. The state has the "right and duty to impose on citizens the *obligations necessary for* "*national defense*."[3] The state should make "equitable provision" for conscientious objectors.[4] Those objectors, however, are "obliged to serve. . . in some other way" than bearing arms.[5]

CAN YOU REFUSE TO SERVE?

The law of the United States allows exemption from military service for conscientious objectors only if their objection is to all war and not merely to the war in question.[6] But what if a war is unjust?

An unjust law, as Aquinas teaches, is "no law" and may not be morally binding.[7] If the state engages in an unjust war, the citizen may have no moral duty to serve and may even be under a moral duty not to serve. As the *Catechism* suggests, the state should make "equitable provision" for conscientious objectors, provided they "serve the human community in some other way."[8] If the law does not exempt the selective objector, at

---

[1] See *ST,* I, II, Q. 96, art. 4.
[2] 11 *The Pope Speaks* 47, 54-55 (1966).
[3] *CCC,* no. 2310.
[4] *Ibid.,* no. 2311.
[5] *Ibid.*
[6] See *Welsh v. U.S.,* 398 U.S. 333 (1970); *Gillette v. U.S.,* 401 U.S. 437 (1971).
[7] See *ST,* I, II, Q. 96, art. 4. See Question 2.
[8] *CCC,* no. 2311.

some point he (or she) may still have the right and even the duty to refuse to serve. Similarly, *Evangelium Vitae* affirmed the duty of conscientious objection in the context of abortion: "Abortion and euthanasia are. . . crimes which no human law can claim to legitimize. There is no obligation in conscience to obey such laws; instead there is a *grave and clear obligation to oppose them by conscientious objection.* From the very beginning of the Church, the apostolic preaching reminded Christians of their duty to obey legitimately constituted public authorities. . . but at the same time it firmly warned that 'we must obey God rather than men.'"[9]

The decision of the state to wage war, like its decisions on other matters, carries a presumption of validity. But, as John A. Hardon, S.J., notes, there can be a moral duty, in exceptional circumstances, to refuse to serve in an armed conflict whether or not a legal exemption is granted: "[D]uring a just war a citizen must aid his country to gain victory, but he may not voluntarily provide help if his nation's cause is evidently unjust. Moreover, those conscripted or in military service when war [begins] may, if they doubt the justice of the war, assume that their nation is right and so engage in the conflict. The reason is that they do not have complete knowledge of the facts to warrant making a contrary judgment."[10] Similar considerations apply to the potential draftee.

"Volunteers, on the other hand," continued Fr. Hardon, "should seriously investigate whether or not their country's cause is a just one. . . . He should make an honest effort to find out the merits of the situation and, if he cannot persuade himself that the war is licit, he must abstain from active military participation."[11]

It may be practically impossible for the state to exempt the selective conscientious objector without encouraging wholesale fraud. If such an exemption were enacted, a remarkable number of college students and others would suddenly develop scruples about the justice of the war to which they might be "invited." In his January 1, 1968 "Message for the Observance of a Day of Peace," Paul VI said:

> It is, therefore, to true Peace, to just and balanced Peace, that We invite men of wisdom and strength to dedicate this "Day.". . .[I]t is to be hoped that the exaltation of the ideal of peace may not favor the cowardice of those who fear it may be their duty to give their life for the

---

[9] *EV,* no. 73.
[10] John A. Hardon, S.J., *The Catholic Catechism* (1975), 349-50.
[11] *Ibid.*

service of their own country and of their own brothers, when these are engaged in the defense of justice and liberty, and who seek only a flight from their responsibility, from the risks that are necessarily involved in the accomplishment of great duties and generous exploits. *Peace is not pacifism;* it does not mask a base and slothful concept of life, but it proclaims the highest and most universal values of life: truth, justice, freedom, love.[12]

While the potential for abuse might prevent legal exemption, it should not obscure the reality that there can be a moral right, and even a duty, to refuse to serve in an unjust war.

A RESERVATION

The principles are clear. However, the situation in the United States is more complicated than it was three decades ago. With an adjudicated liar in the White House,[13] the government has embarked on foreign adventures of dubious relevance to the defense of the common good of the American people or of anyone else. That government, too, has sponsored since 1973 an extermination of the innocent that has produced a body count at least six times that of the Holocaust. At some point, a citizen will have to face the issue of whether his duty to avoid proximate and unjustified cooperation with evil[14] prevents his cooperation in the military adventures, other than evidently legitimate defense, of such a regime. So let us not be too quick to criticize the pacifist. We may have to share a cell with him someday.

---

[12] Pope Paul VI, "Pope's Message Proclaiming a Day of Peace," in *Day of Peace* (1968), 41, 44.

[13] *N.Y. Times,* Apr. 13, 1999, p. A1, reporting on the U.S. District Court order holding President Clinton in civil contempt for falsely testifying in the Paula Jones case.

[14] See Question 33.

43. How does immigration affect the life issues and the family?

Like Romans in ancient times, Americans are losing their country to immigration, and few seem to know it. . . . Peter Brimelow, himself an immigrant and. . . naturalized citizen [i]n his book, *Alien Nation,*. . . predicts that immigration is undermining social cohesiveness and has the United States on the road to breakup. Four separate regions are emerging: an Asian Pacific coast, an Hispanic southwest, a black and white southeast and northeast, and a white landlocked center. Among the culprits in the smashing of the once-fabled melting pot are the 1965 Immigration Act, uncontrolled illegal immigration, a continuous stream of immigrants without pause for assimilation, politically correct multiculturalism, which has redefined assimilation as "racist," support systems and race-based legal privileges for "protected minorities" that have made group identity more valuable than assimilation, and the denial of dangers posed by all of the above by experts and intellectuals across the political and ideological spectrum.

The 1965 Immigration Act abolished national origin as the basis for immigration. The national origin basis helped the melting pot to function by admitting people based on cultural ties. These are the very people whom the 1965 act discriminates against, and ever since then Europeans have been crowded out by Hispanics, Asians, and blacks.
— *Paul Craig Roberts*[1]

Americans of European origin are, indeed, losing their dominance in the United States. But this is because they have embraced the "race suicide" of the contraceptive ethic. White Americans have no intrinsic claim to superiority or dominance. When they refuse to reproduce themselves, others will rightly take their place. And Hispanics, especially, carry the potential to reinvigorate the Catholic faith in the United States.

The Need to Tighten Laws

This book is not a treatise on immigration law and policy. However, something must be done to restrict illegal immigration and to reform the system of legal immigration. "This country," said President Ronald Reagan, "has lost control of its borders. And no country can sustain that kind of position."[2] As Representative Lamar Smith (R-TX) put it in 1996:

[1] Paul Craig Roberts, "Alien Future," *Chronicles,* July 1995, 29.
[2] Peter Brimelow, *Alien Nation* (1995), 27.

Of course we are a nation of immigrants, and our generosity toward immigrants will continue. But our current immigration laws are broken and must be fixed. When 40 percent of the births in the public hospitals of our most-populous state, California, are to illegal aliens; when the number of illegal aliens entering our country every three years could populate a city the size of Boston or Dallas or San Francisco; when half of the 5 million illegal aliens in the U.S. today use fraudulent documents to illegally obtain jobs and welfare benefits, it's not a problem, it's a crisis. When immigrant husbands or wives and their young children are forced to wait 10 years to be united; when one-quarter of all federal prisoners are foreign-born; when one-quarter of legal immigrants are on welfare, it is not a problem, it's a crisis. The crisis must be faced and solved.

We must put the national interest first. This means both reducing illegal immigration and reforming legal immigration. For illegal immigration, it means increasing the number of Border Patrol agents and reducing the attraction of the twin magnets of easily available jobs and easy access to welfare benefits. For legal immigration, it means giving priority to uniting spouses and their children and discouraging immigrants from living off the taxpayer.[3]

IMMIGRATION TO REPLACE ABORTED AND CONTRACEPTED BABIES

We are not concerned here with the policy debate as to whether immigration, as it exists or might be reformed, is good for the economy.[4] One aspect of the immigration issue, however, does relate to the subject of this book. Peter Brimelow makes the "crucial point" that recent immigration is shifting the ethnic balance of the nation because "American Anglos" are not reproducing themselves: "*At the beginning of this century, the U.S. birthrate was much higher, as much as twice what it is now.* Now American Anglos are reproducing below replacement levels—generally defined as 2.1 children per woman. *So post-1965 Second Great Wave immigrants are having a proportionately much higher demographic impact on America than the pre-1925 First Great Wave.* Hence the steadily shifting ethnic balance."[5] Brimelow notes that the federal government "officially

---

[3] *Christian Science Monitor,* Mar. 7, 1996, p. 19. For a detailed analysis of the Immigration and Nationality Act of 1965, see Gabriel J. Chin, "The Civil Rights Revolution Comes to Immigration Law: A New Look at the Immigration and Nationality Act of 1965," 75 *N.C.L. Rev.* 273 (1996).

[4] See Ben Wattenberg, "The Easy Solution to the Social Security Crisis," *N.Y. Times Magazine,* June 22, 1997, 30, 30-31; James P. Smith and Barry Edmonston, eds., *The New Americans: Economic, Demographic and Fiscal Effects of Immigration* (1997).

[5] Brimelow, *Alien Nation,* 43.

projects an ethnic revolution in America: Specifically, it expects that American Whites will be on the point (53 percent) of becoming a minority by 2050."[6] "In 1990, only 8 percent of the 1.5 million legal immigrants, including amnestied illegals, came from Europe. (And a good few of those were individuals who were re-emigrating, having originally come from Asia or the Caribbean.)"[7]

With respect to the impending minority status of whites, Brimelow said, "There is no precedent for a sovereign country undergoing such a rapid and radical transformation of its ethnic character in the entire history of the world."[8] However, that transformation cannot be blamed simply on immigration.

Since 1970, the number of immigrants living in the United States has risen from 9.6 million to 26.3 million, "far outpacing the growth of the native-born population."[9] The 17 million increase in the number of immigrants, however, is less than half the number of those who would have been "native-born" if they had not been killed by surgical abortion during that period. We need legal immigrants, among other reasons, because the white, and increasingly the black, American middle and upper classes are contracepting and aborting themselves into oblivion. "College-educated white women have a [total fertility rate] of about 1.6 children per woman. It takes a 2.1 rate merely to keep a population constant over time. But college-educated black women have an even lower fertility rate than whites (1.5 children per woman)."[10] In this context, the proportionate increase among Hispanics is welcome news. The Hispanic population of the United States increased by more than one-third in the 1980s, compared to a 7% increase for the non-Hispanic population. Eighteen percent of the births in the United States are to Hispanic women. And "much of the increase in Hispanic-origin births is the result of high fertility rates among Mexican-Americans, particularly recent immigrants."[11] Reasonable control of immigration can be justified. But if the whites, and increasingly the blacks, are unwilling to reproduce themselves, they ought not complain at the erosion of their cultural dominance.

[A] naturally growing and youthful population can welcome and assimilate. . . newcomers far better than a nation of childless geriatrics.

---

[6] Ibid., 62.

[7] Ibid., 28.

[8] Ibid., 57.

[9] Wash. Post, Jan. 9, 1999, p. A1.

[10] Ben Wattenberg, "Demographics Good News for Future," Chattanooga Free Press, Aug. 11, 1997, p. A4.

[11] N.Y. Times, Feb. 13, 1998, p. A12.

University of Maryland economist Frank Levy points out that one in five Americans is now born in poverty — not because the poor have too many children, but because the wealthy and middle classes bear so few. . . .[12]

Immigration to the United States has surged in the last 20 years. . . . Yet. . . anti-immigration activists. . . remain. . . reticent about another . . . peril: depopulation. For while more and more people enter the country through admission at a visa office, fewer and fewer enter through birth in an American maternity ward. . . . [F]ertility in the United States has languished below replacement level since the early 1970's. This American birth dearth would be even more severe were it not for high. . . fertility among immigrants, especially Hispanics. . . . America must depend upon an influx of immigrants just to avoid population contraction. . . .

[H]istorian Franz Schurmann frankly admits, "America needs the South's babies." "American civilization wants sex, but does not want children," he explains. "America thrives on success and sex. But what about children? Immigrants bring in lots of babies and make even more." Unfortunately, concerns about the birth dearth can rarely be heard above the complaints about the costs of providing welfare, medical, and educational benefits to immigrants. . . .

However, in the furor over immigrants on welfare, Americans may be diverting their attention away from two issues of greater import: first, the impending crisis in government programs for the elderly; second, the ongoing damage inflicted by the welfare state on the family life of all recipients — native and immigrant. If the government programs for the elderly do survive, their. . . clients will have to accept cuts in. . . benefits or younger workers will have to submit to unprecedented taxation. A more potent formula for intergenerational strife would be difficult to devise. This intergenerational strife might be prevented if Americans ended their twenty-year retreat from child bearing. . . .

[E]conomic analyst. . . Ron K. Unz argues that "a country in which 22 percent of white children and 70 percent of black children are born out of wedlock need not look to immigrants as the source of social breakdown." "Our real enemy," Unz insists, is not the recent influx of immigrants, but rather "a welfare state that encourages individuals to destroy their own families." Unz believes it makes more sense to dismantle the welfare state than the Statue of Liberty. . . .

---

[12] Bryce J. Christensen, "Birth Dearth — The Other U.S. Deficit," *Houston Post,* June 10, 1987, p. 83.

[I]mmigrants with strong family ties may not seek rapid assimilation into a culture they perceive as a threat to those ties. And. . . much of modern American culture. . . subverts marriage and the family. . . .

For the sake of civic order and the rule of law, Americans must insist upon vigilant protection of our borders and upon strict enforcement of our immigration laws. But what will Americans have gained if we create tighter borders around a land in which public policies and perverse ideologies continue to destroy marriage and the family? If Americans cannot overcome threats from within, we can hardly hope to identify, much less repel, threats from without.[13]

THE RIGHT TO IMMIGRATE

The owner of any property is "a steward of Providence," with the task of making it fruitful and communicating its benefits to his family and to others.[14] This applies to the earth itself as well as to other goods: "The *right to private property*. . . does not do away with the original gift of the earth to the whole of mankind. The *universal destination of goods* remains primordial, even if. . . the common good requires respect for the right to private property and its exercise."[15]

In *Pacem in Terris,* Pope John XXIII said that, "among men's personal rights we must include his right to enter a country in which he hopes to be able to provide more fittingly for himself and his dependents."[16] To protect the common good of its own citizens, the state may impose conditions on the right to immigrate. Immigrants are obliged to respect the laws and heritage of the country they enter, and to help shoulder civic burdens in that country.[17]

A government has the duty to promote the common good of its own society and people. However, the exercise of that duty, pursuant to the principle of solidarity, "cannot be divorced from the common good of the entire human family."[18] The "universal common good" requires governments to try to alleviate the hardships of refugees throughout the world and to help migrants and their families.[19] Persons have a right to migrate which is based on their dignity as persons and on the universal

---

[13] Bryce Christensen, "Importing People: Why Modern America Needs but Resents Immigrants," 9 *The Family in America* 1, 1-7 (1995).

[14] *CCC,* no. 2404; see nos. 2401-06.

[15] *Ibid.,* no. 2403.

[16] *Pacem in Terris* (1963), no. 106.

[17] See *CCC,* no. 2241.

[18] *Pacem in Terris,* no. 98.

[19] See *CCC,* no. 1911.

destination of land as of other goods.[20] No community has a moral right absolutely to foreclose immigration. Its right to restrict immigration, and perhaps even to declare a moratorium on immigration, will depend on a balancing of its own common good against the needs of potential immigrants.

IMMIGRANTS, EVEN IF ILLEGAL, ARE PERSONS

In his message for World Migration Day in 1995, Pope John Paul said: "Today the phenomenon of illegal migrants has assumed considerable proportions. . . . His irregular legal status cannot allow the migrant to lose his dignity, since he is endowed with inalienable rights, which can neither be violated nor ignored. . . . Illegal immigration should be prevented, but it is also essential to combat vigorously the criminal activities which exploit illegal immigrants."[21]

Proposition 187, adopted by referendum in California in 1994, denied non-emergency services, including public health care and public education, to "illegals" and their children. Federal law, incidentally, denies some federal welfare benefits to illegal immigrants.[22] That result, on the state as well as the federal level, appears to be just, as long as government, at some level, continues to provide medical and other services in emergencies. However, the issue should not be framed only in terms of emergency or non-emergency services. The community at large, and Christians in particular, are under a moral duty to provide needed assistance to illegal immigrants whether or not it is a legally defined emergency. Under the principle of subsidiarity, the state should be the provider of last resort rather than the first. Catholic and other private charities have been so long on the government dole that they automatically react to problems by looking first to the government for help. The religious and other charities in California opposed Proposition 187. But there was no indication of a serious effort by the churches and other private charities to pick up the slack created by Proposition 187. Why did the Catholic Church not respond to Proposition 187 by saying, "We will take those children of 'illegals' into our schools," and launching a fund drive to raise the money to do it? Perhaps that strategy would not have worked. But to the extent that the churches and other private agencies could step in to provide needed "non-emergency" services that govern-

---

[20] See *CCC*, no. 2403.

[21] 41 *The Pope Speaks* 8 (1996).

[22] See Paul Meehan, "Combatting Restrictions on Immigrant Access to Public Benefits: A Human Rights Perspective," 11 *Georgetown Immigration Law J.* 389 (1997); *Note,* "Section 434 of the Welfare Act: Does the Federal Immigration Power Collide with the Tenth Amendment?," 63 *Brooklyn L. Rev.* 551 (1997).

ment would no longer provide, Proposition 187 was justified. While private agencies rather than the state ought to provide as far as possible for such needs, the fact is that immigrants, whether legal or illegal, do have valid claims on the community, including the state, and especially on the Church and its members. In the words of John Paul II:

> It is necessary to guard against. . . new forms of racism or xenophobic behavior, which. . . make these brothers and sisters of ours scapegoats for what may be difficult local situations. It is necessary to avoid. . . administrative regulations, meant to restrict the criterion of family membership, which result in unjustifiably forcing into an illegal situation people whose right to live with their family cannot be denied by any law. . . .

> In the Church no one is a stranger, and the Church is not foreign to anyone anywhere. . . . [T]he Church is the place where illegal immigrants are. . . accepted as brothers and sisters. It is the task of the. . . dioceses actively to ensure that these people, who are obliged to live outside the safety net of civil society, may find a sense of brotherhood in the Christian community. . . .

> Today, the illegal migrant comes before us like that "stranger" in whom Jesus asks to be recognized. To welcome him and to show him solidarity is a duty of hospitality and fidelity to Christian identity itself.[23]

On the practical level, John Paul said, "The first way to help these people is to listen to them. . . and whatever their legal status. . . to provide them with the necessary means of subsistence. [I]t is important to help illegal migrants to. . . obtain a residence permit. Social and charitable institutions can. . . contact. . . the authorities. . . to seek. . . solutions to various cases. This kind of effort should be made especially on behalf of those who, after a long stay, are so deeply rooted in the local society that returning to their country of origin would be. . . a form of reverse emigration, with serious consequences particularly for the children. When no solution is foreseen, these same institutions should direct those they are helping, perhaps also providing them with material assistance, either to seek acceptance in other countries, or to return to their own country."[24] On his 1999 visit to Mexico and the United States, John Paul released his apostolic exhortation, *Ecclesia in America*, The Church in America, in which he reflected on "America as a single entity, by rea-

---

[23] 41 *The Pope Speaks* 8-11 (1996).
[24] *Ibid.*, 9.

son of all that is common to the peoples of the continent."[25] "The Church in America," he said, "must be a vigilant advocate. . .against any unjust restriction on the natural right of individual persons to move freely within their own nations and from one nation to another. Attention must be called to the rights of migrants and their families and to respect for their human dignity, even in cases of non-legal immigration."[26]

We Americans of the last half of the twentieth century inherited a nation which, at the end of World War II, was the acknowledged leader of the world. But we have refused even to reproduce ourselves. We have no God-given right to hold this land in perpetuity. Nor do we have the right to exclude unjustifiably people of other backgrounds who share the right to the universal destination of the earth as of other goods. And maybe those sturdier people will teach a few home truths to the jaded whites (and prosperous blacks) who cannot bring themselves even to reproduce their own kind.

Cardinal Francis George described "the difference between Mexico City and St. Louis," in the spontaneity of the reception they gave to the Pope in his 1999 visits, as "a contrast between a culture of relationship and one of autonomy, a culture of communion in contrast to one of control."[27] "One of the great blessings to the North," said Archbishop Charles Chaput of Denver, "is the immigration of so many people from the South into our part of the Americas. In some ways, they may be the salvation of the Church in the United States, because they bring with them a spirit and a soul and a deep kind of faith that will, I think rekindle and re-enliven the faith of the churches of the North."[28]

---

[25] *EA*, no. 5.
[26] *Ibid.*, no. 65.
[27] 28 *Origins* 609, 612 (Feb. 18, 1999).
[28] *Inside the Vatican*, May 1998, 22, 23.

44.   WHAT IS THE ECONOMIC FOUNDATION OF THE
CULTURE OF LIFE?

"'[T]he human person. . . is. . . the principle, the subject and the end of all social institutions.'"[1] "Intimately linked to the *foundation,* which is man's dignity, are the *principle of solidarity* and the *principle of subsidiarity.*"[2] "The Church," however, "has no models to present for economic and political organization."[3]

THE PERSON, SOLIDARITY AND SUBSIDIARITY

"[T]he foundation on which all human rights rest is the dignity of the person."[4] That dignity flows from man's creation with an immortal destiny which transcends the state. Because man is created in the image of God, relation to others is intrinsic to his person as it is to the Persons of the Trinity. From this it follows that the civil order should foster solidarity among persons rather than the isolated individualism of the Enlightenment. "The awareness of communion with Christ and with our brothers and sisters. . . leads to the service of our neighbors in all their needs, material and spiritual, since the face of Christ shines forth in every human being. Solidarity is thus the fruit of the communion which is grounded in the mystery of the triune God, and in the Son of God who took flesh and died for all. . . . For the particular Churches of the American continent. . . a culture of solidarity needs to be promoted, capable of inspiring. . . initiatives in support of the poor and the outcast, especially refugees forced to leave their villages and lands in order to flee violence."[5] The solidarity urged by the Pope is shown "in the first place by the distribution of goods and remuneration for work. It also presupposes the effort for a more just social order."[6] It requires solidarity among the poor and workers, between rich and poor, between employers and employees and among nations and peoples.[7] This virtue of solidarity extends beyond material goods. In spreading the faith over the centuries, however, the Church has fostered material and social development as well as spiritual. "Seek first his kingdom and his righteousness, and all these things shall be yours as well."[8] "For two thousand years this senti-

---

[1]   *CCC,* no. 1881, quoting *Gaudium et Spes,* no. 25.
[2]   Congregation for the Doctrine of the Faith, *Instruction on Christian Freedom and Liberation* (1986), no. 73.
[3]   *CA,* no. 43.
[4]   *Ecclesia in America,* no. 57.
[5]   *EA,* no. 52.
[6]   *CCC,* no. 1940
[7]   See *CCC,* no. 1941.
[8]   Mt. 6:33.

ment has lived and endured in the soul of the Church, impelling souls then and now to the heroic charity of monastic farmers, liberators of slaves, healers of the sick, and messengers of faith, civilization, and science to all generations and all peoples for the sake of creating the social conditions capable of offering to everyone possible a life worthy of man and of a Christian."[9]

As a person with an eternal destiny, man cannot find his fulfillment in the state or in any temporal order. From this arises the principle of subsidiarity, which denies the claim of the state to total competence:

> Just as it is wrong to withdraw from the individual and commit to the community at large what private enterprise and industry can accomplish, so too, it is an injustice, a grave evil, and a disturbance of right order for a larger and higher organization to arrogate to itself functions which can be performed efficiently by smaller and lower bodies. This is a fundamental principle of social philosophy, unshaken and unchangeable, and it retains its full truth today. . . . The true aim of all social activity should be to help individual members of the social body, but never to destroy or absorb them.[10]

Society, therefore, should observe the principles of solidarity and subsidiarity, both of which derive from the dignity of the human person. The purpose of civil society and of human law is to promote the common good, which is "the sum total of social conditions which allow people, either as groups or as individuals, to reach their fulfillment more fully and more easily."[11] The common good has three essential components:

1. *Respect for the person*, including respect by the state for the rights of the person;

2. *Social well-being and development*, including the availability to each person of the means to lead a fulfilling life; and

3. *Peace*, including the security of its members in a just order of society.[12]

The common good is always focused on the good of persons. "The social order and its development must constantly yield to the good of the person, since the order of things must be subordinate to the order of

---

[9] Pius XII, *Discourse*, June 1, 1941; see *CCC*, no. 1942.
[10] Pope Pius XI, *Quadragesimo Anno* (1931), no. 79; see also *LF*, no. 16.
[11] *Gaudium et Spes*, no. 26.
[12] See *CCC*, nos. 1905-09.

persons and not the other way around."[13] The good of the person here includes his economic welfare. Moreover, "[e]xcessive economic and social disparity between individuals and peoples of the one human race is a source of scandal and militates against social justice, equity, human dignity, as well as social and international peace."[14]

IS THE FREE MARKET THE ANSWER?

John Paul II has acknowledged that "the free market is the most effective instrument for utilizing resources and responding to needs."[15] But he warned against "an 'idolatry of the market.'"[16] He endorsed "a society of free work, of enterprise and of participation [which] demands that the market be appropriately controlled by the forces of society and by the state so as to guarantee that the basic needs of the whole of society are satisfied. The Church acknowledges the legitimate role of profit as an indication that a business is functioning well. . . . [T]he purpose of a business firm is not simply to make a profit, but is. . . in its very existence as a community of persons. . . . Profit is a regulator of the life of a business, but it is not the only one; other human and moral factors must also be considered, which. . . are at least equally important for the life of a business."[17]

Centesimus Annus rejected not only socialism but also Western materialism. The Pope criticized "the affluent society or the consumer society. It seeks to defeat Marxism on the level of pure materialism by showing how a free-market society can achieve a greater satisfaction of material human needs than communism, while equally excluding spiritual values. . . . Insofar as it denies an autonomous existence and value to morality, law, culture and religion, it agrees with Marxism in the sense that it totally reduces man to the sphere of economics and the satisfaction of material needs."[18] The atheism that is the "first cause" of socialism's errors is "closely connected with the rationalism of the Enlightenment, which views human and social reality in a mechanistic way. Thus there is a denial of the supreme insight concerning man's true greatness, his transcendence in respect to earthly realities, the contradiction in his heart between the desire for the fullness of what is good and his own inability to attain it, and above all, the need for salvation."[19]

---

[13] *Gaudium et Spes*, no. 26; see *CCC*, no. 1912.
[14] *Gaudium et Spes*, no. 29; see *CCC*, nos. 1934-38.
[15] *CA*, no. 34.
[16] *Ibid.*, no. 40.
[17] *Ibid.*, no. 35.
[18] *Ibid.*, no. 19.
[19] *Ibid.*, no. 13.

John Paul asked whether, "after the failure of communism. . . capitalism should be the goal of the countries now making efforts to rebuild their economy and society?"[20]

> The answer is obviously complex. If by "capitalism" is meant an economic system which recognizes the fundamental and positive role of business, the market, private property and the resulting responsibility for the means of production as well as free human creativity in the economic sector, then the answer is certainly in the affirmative even though it would perhaps be more appropriate to speak of a "business economy," "market economy" or simply "free economy." But if by "capitalism" is meant a system in which freedom in the economic sector is not circumscribed within a strong juridical framework which places it at the service of human freedom in its totality and which sees it as a particular aspect of that freedom, the core of which is ethical and religious, then the reply is certainly negative.[21]

"Catholic social doctrine," John Paul has said, "is not a surrogate for capitalism." The "first principle" is that "[t]he center of the social order is man, considered in his inalienable dignity as a creature made 'in the image of God.' The value of society comes from the value of man, and not vice versa. . . . [M]an is. . . a relational being. Although his first and fundamental relationship is with God, relationships with his fellow men and women are also necessary and vital. Such an objective inter-dependence is raised to the dignity of a vocation, becoming a call to solidarity and love, in the image of. . . the inner life of the triune God.

"From this vision of man there flows a correct vision of society. Centered on the human person's ability to form relationships, society cannot be conceived as a shapeless mass which ends up being absorbed by the state, but must be recognized as a complex organism 'realized in various intermediary groups, beginning with the family and including economic, social, political and cultural groups which stem from human nature itself and have their own autonomy, always with a view to the common good.'"[22]

To Apply the Principles

The Pope then listed "the requirements" that are "essential in any policy of the state, economy and society":

---

[20] *Ibid.,* no. 42.

[21] *Ibid.,* no. 42.

[22] John Paul II, Address at the University of Latvia, Sept. 9, 1993, quoting *Centesimus Annus,* no. 13; 23 *Origins* 256, 257-58 (1993).

-The universal destination of goods, an expression of God's common gift and of the solidarity which must characterize human relations.

-The legitimacy of private property,. . . . an indispensable condition for the autonomy of the person and the family.

-The recognition of the importance of work, beginning with the dignity of the human subject who performs it, who can never be reduced to a commodity or a mere cog in the machinery of production.

-The promotion of human ecology, implying respect for every human person from conception to natural death. . . .

-A balanced concept of the state, which emphasizes its value and necessity, while protecting it from every totalitarian demand; a state conceived. . . as a service. . . for civil society. . .; a state based on law together with a social state which offers everyone the legal guarantees of an orderly existence and assures the most vulnerable the support they need in order not to succumb to the arrogance and indifference of the powerful.

-The value of democracy understood as participative management of the state through specific organs of representation and control in the service of the common good; a democracy which,. . . has in the first place a soul made up of the fundamental values without which it "easily turns into open or thinly disguised totalitarianism."[23]

THE "SOCIAL MORTGAGE"

The first of these requirements, "the universal destination of goods," is the basis for John Paul's conclusion that '[p]rivate property. . . is under a 'social mortgage.'"[24] The gap in material well-being between rich and poor nations, and between individuals within a nation, has drawn persistent criticism from John Paul: "[A]longside individuals and groups which are wealthy, surfeited, affluent and dominated by consumerism and pleasure-seeking, the human family also contains individuals and societies which go hungry."[25] "Side-by-side with the miseries of underdevelopment," noted John Paul, "we find. . . a form of *superdevelopment,* equally inadmissible. . . . This superdevelopment, which consists in an *excessive* availability of every kind of material goods for the benefit of cer-

---

[23] *Ibid.* (emphasis added).
[24] Pope John Paul II, *Sollicitudo Rei Socialis,* On Social Concerns (1987), no. 42; see *CCC,* no. 2403.
[25] *Dives in Misericordia,* Rich in Mercy (1980), no. 11.

tain social groups, easily makes people slaves of 'possession' and of immediate gratification, with no other horizon than the multiplication or continual replacement of the things already owned with others still better. This is the. . . civilization of 'consumption' or 'consumerism,' which involves so much 'throwing away' and 'waste.' An object. . . now superseded by something better is discarded, with no thought of its possible lasting value in itself nor of some other human being who is poorer. . . . One of the greatest injustices in the contemporary world consists precisely in this: that the ones who possess much are relatively *few* and those who possess almost nothing are *many*. It is the injustice of the poor distribution of the goods and services intended for all."[26]

So the bottom line is that the gap in wealth is itself a problem, even if the people at the low end are better off than they used to be.[27]

"It is not wrong to want to live better," wrote John Paul. "[W]hat is wrong is a style of life which is presumed to be better when it is directed toward 'having' rather than 'being' and which wants to have more not in order to be more, but in order to spend life in enjoyment as an end in itself. It is. . . necessary to create lifestyles in which the quest for truth, beauty, goodness and communion with others for the sake of common growth are the factors which determine consumer choices, savings and investments."[28] He criticized "consumerism," in which "people are ensnared in a web of false and superficial gratifications rather than being helped to experience their personhood in an authentic and concrete way."[29]

THE PRIMACY OF THE PERSON

The Pope rejected "the welfare state, dubbed the 'social assistance state'," as a violation of the principle of subsidiarity. "By intervening directly and depriving society of its responsibility, the social assistance state leads to a loss of human energies and an inordinate increase of public agencies which are dominated more by bureaucratic ways of thinking than by concern for serving their clients and which are accompanied by an enormous increase in spending. . . . [N]eeds are best understood and

---

[26] *Sollicitudo Rei Socialis*, no. 28.

[27] See discussion in Todd David Whitmore, "The Maximum Living Wage," *The Observer* (Univ. of Notre Dame), Mar. 19, 1999, p. 13; Michael Novak, "Catholic Social Thought, The Pope and Me," *The Observer*, Apr. 8, 1999, p. 11; Todd David Whitmore, "Catholic Social Teaching and a Response to Mr. Novak," *The Observer*, Apr. 27, 1999, p. 11; see also Michael Novak, "Capitalism Rightly Understood: The View of Christian Humanism," 17 *Faith and Reason* 317 (1991).

[28] *CA*, no. 36.

[29] *Ibid.*, no. 41.

satisfied by people who are closest to them and who act as neighbors to those in need."[30] In accord with subsidiarity, the Pope stressed the importance of the family and "other intermediate communities":

> In order to overcome today's widespread individualistic mentality, what is required is a concrete commitment to solidarity and charity, beginning in the family. . . . It can happen, however, that when a family does decide to live up fully to its vocation, it finds itself without the necessary support from the state and without sufficient resources. It is urgent. . . to promote. . . policies which have the family as their principal object,. . . providing. . . resources. . . both for bringing up children and for looking after the elderly so as to avoid distancing the latter from the family unit and in order to strengthen relations between generations.

> Apart from the family, other intermediate communities. . . give life to. . . networks of solidarity. . . preventing society from becoming an anonymous and impersonal mass. . . . The individual today is often suffocated between two poles represented by the state and the marketplace. At times it seems as though he exists only as a producer and consumer of goods or as an object of state administration. People lose sight of the fact that life in society has neither the market nor the state as its final purpose, since life itself has a unique value which the state and the market must serve.[31]

The Pope noted the Church's "preferential option for the poor, which. . . is not limited to material poverty, since it is well known that there are many other forms of poverty, especially in modern society- not only economic, but cultural and spiritual poverty as well."[32] He emphasized also "the legitimacy of workers' efforts to obtain full respect for their dignity and to gain broader areas of participation in the life of industrial enterprises. . . . A business cannot be considered only as a 'society of capital goods'; it is also a 'society of persons' in which people participate in different ways and with specific responsibilities. . . . To achieve these goals there is still need for a. . . workers' movement directed toward the liberation and promotion of the whole person."[33] "[L]ove for the poor," however, "must be preferential, but not exclusive;" the Pope urged increased "pastoral care for the leading sectors of society. . . insisting especially on the formation of consciences on the basis of the Church's social doctrine."[34]

---

[30] *Ibid.*, no. 48.

[31] *Ibid.*, no. 49.

[32] *Ibid.*, no. 57.

[33] *Ibid.*, no. 43. See Charles E. Rice, *50 Questions on The Natural Law* (2d ed. 1999), Questions 39, 40.

[34] *Ecclesia in America,* no. 67.

In his 1991 visit to a "favela," or shanty town, in Brazil, John Paul condemned "'ruthless capitalism,' whose prevailing characteristics are the unrestrained pursuit of profit, joined to a lack of respect for the primary value of work and the dignity of the worker. . . . [T]he church exhorts workers to practice solidarity in their 'struggle for social justice,'. . . to unite their efforts, avoiding gratuitous or ideological violence, to be open to reaching a settlement and determined to win job security, wages sufficient for a family life, a solution to their problems in shelter and education, and social security for old age, sickness and unemployment. . . . [T]he church reminds business people of their. . . responsibility to create in their companies true 'communities of work' where work itself occupies a 'central position' without ever being reduced 'to the level of a mere commodity.'"[35]

In sum, the Church's teaching on the economy is centered on the dignity and primacy of the human person. But it rejects materialism and the treatment of human beings as merely economic units.[36] So how does that help us to live the culture of life? We can agree on the abstract concepts. The more demanding task, however, is to translate them into a culture of "being" instead of one of "having." Whether we are talking about economic policy, abortion "rights" or family living, the decisive point will be the dignity of the human person. Made in the image and likeness of God, he is never to be treated as an object or as an unconsenting means to an end. If we follow that principle, it will keep us straight — on the economy as on other things.

---

[35] 21 *Origins* 342, 343 (1991).
[36] See *CCC*, nos. 2423-26.

45. WHAT DOES "GLOBAL FREE TRADE" HAVE TO DO WITH ALL THIS?

IS IT REALLY *FREE?*

"Global free trade" is relevant to this book because of its impact on persons and families. In principle, "free trade" tends to reduce the control of government over the economy. As Llewellyn Rockwell put it, the free-market conservatives of the "Old Right" in the 1930s and 1940s "took a strict laissez-faire attitude toward international trade. They loathed tariffs, and saw protectionism as a species of socialist planning."[1] However, the free trade at issue today is not the unfettered exchange of goods without government manipulation. Rather, "global free trade" today is imposed and enforced by regulations of a super-government of international bureaucrats, including the World Trade Organization which has authority to supersede United States laws regulating business. This point was made by Sir James Goldsmith, a businessman and member of the European Parliament. He described the World Trade Organization as "the organization which is supposed to. . . regulate international trade, and lead us to global economic integration. It is yet another international bureaucracy whose functionaries will be largely autonomous. They report to over 120 nations and therefore, in practice, to nobody. Each nation will have one vote out of 120. Thus, America and every European nation will be handing over ultimate control of its economy to an unelected, uncontrolled, group of international bureaucrats."[2]

Sir James argued for regional free trade areas among "nations with economies which are reasonably similar."[3] And he noted that "[d]uring the past few years, four billion people have suddenly entered the world economy. They include the populations of nations such as China, India, Vietnam, Bangladesh, and the countries that were part of the Soviet empire. . . . These populations are growing fast. . . . [T]hese new entrants into the world economy are in direct competition with workforces of developed countries."[4]

"The winners" in this new situation, argued Goldsmith, "will be. . . the companies who move their production offshore to low-cost areas; the companies who can pay lower salaries at home; and those who have capital to invest where labour is cheapest, and who, as a result, will re-

---

[1] *Wash. Times,* Mar. 10, 1996, p. B3.
[2] Sir James Goldsmith, *The Trap* (1994), 37-38.
[3] *Ibid.,* 40.
[4] *Ibid.,* 26-27.

ceive larger dividends. But they will be like the winners of a poker game on the *Titanic*. The wounds inflicted on their societies will be too deep, and brutal consequences could follow. . . .

"[O]ne of the characteristics of developing countries is that a small handful of people controls the. . . nation's resources. It is these people who own most of their nation's industrial, commercial and financial enterprises and who assemble the cheap labour which is used to manufacture products for the developed world. *Thus, it is the poor in the rich countries who will subsidize the rich in the poor countries*. This will have a deep impact on the social cohesion of nations."[5]

THE IMPACT ON PERSONS AND FAMILIES

"[E]conomic globalization," said John Paul II, "brings. . . efficiency and increased production and. . . can help to bring greater unity among peoples and make possible a better service to the human family. However, if globalization is ruled merely by the laws of the market applied to suit the powerful, the consequences cannot but be negative. . . . And what should we say about the cultural globalization produced by the power of the media? Everywhere the media impose new scales of values which are often arbitrary and. . . materialistic, in the face of which it is difficult to maintain a lively commitment to the values of the Gospel."[6]

Patrick J. Buchanan has criticized the "Global Economy" for its impact on American workers and their families:

As America's Industrial Revolution spawned a new elite, so, too, has the Global Economy. . . . [U]nencumbered by any national allegiance, [this elite] roams a Darwinian world of the borderless economy, where sentiment is folly and the fittest alone survive. In the eyes of this rootless transnational elite, men and women are not family, friends, neighbors, fellow citizens, but "consumers" and "factors of production." . . .[7]

The transnational corporation is a mutant of the old multinational. Unlike yesterday's IBM, which was a U.S. corporation with subsidiaries abroad, the new transnational has no country. . . .[8]

To transnational corporations, U.S. workers are expensive and troublesome, and the easy way to keep profits rising — and stock prices and executive stock options soaring is to shut down here and move production outside the United States. The social costs? As work-

---

[5] *Ibid.*, 36-37 (emphasis added).
[6] *Ecclesia in America*, no. 20.
[7] Patrick J. Buchanan, *The Great Betrayal* (1998), 97.
[8] *Ibid.*, 100.

ers' wages stagnated and fell, wives and mothers entered the job market in record numbers to maintain the family standard of living. *In 1960 fewer than one-fifth of women with children under the age of six were in the labor force; today almost two-thirds are.* No other modern nation has so many of its married women in the labor force. While this keeps median family income (which fell 5.8 percent between 1990 and 1995) from collapsing, the price is paid in falling birthrates and rising delinquency, in teenage drug abuse, alcohol abuse, promiscuity, illegitimacy, and abortions — and in the high divorce rate among working parents. The American family is paying a hellish price for the good things down at the mall. . . .[9]

. . . [R]eal wages are what they were during the presidency of Lyndon Johnson; wages in retail are what our grandparents used to earn. This wage stagnation has forced into the job market millions of wives and mothers who would prefer to stay at home, to have children or to raise their children, adding to the stress and strain of middle-class life. *In 1947, 30 percent of our population was employed, earning 44 percent of the GDP. Forty-four percent is employed now, but wages are only 34 percent of the GDP.* As Affluent America takes stride after stride into prosperity, Middle America remains on a treadmill.[10]

Some proponents of global free trade acknowledge its adverse impact on some workers and their families. In his critical review of Buchanan's book, Andrew J. Bacevich, of the Paul H. Nitze School of Advanced International Studies, admitted that "the much-celebrated process of creating a global economic order is leaving by the wayside a considerable number of American citizens. These are the castoffs for whom successive waves of consolidation, downsizing, and restructuring have meant the loss of jobs, status, and self-respect. Less visible than these unfortunates is a much larger number: those who seemingly manage to keep up, but who view the ongoing change in our everyday life with a deep and growing sense of unease. In a profound insight, Buchanan identifies the anguished and the left behind as 'the rooted people' — rooted, like the populists of old, in place and time, adhering to received truths, clinging to traditional folkways. The rooted people identify with what is familiar and close at hand. They value continuity over change. They are instinctively patriotic and nationalistic. They view with suspicion the outsider and the cosmopolitan. When it comes to translating grievances into political platforms, they are not articulate and may too easily fall prey to appeals to a utopian past."[11]

---

[9] *Ibid.*, 112-13.

[10] *Ibid.*, 282-83 (emphasis added); see also Wallace C. Peterson, *Silent Depression* (1994); Ravi Batra, *The Myth of Free Trade* (1993).

[11] *First Things*, Aug./Sept.1998, 48-49.

The "rooted people" tend to be oriented toward the person rather than profit. However, it is not only the displaced worker in Michigan who is the victim of "global free trade." In numerous underdeveloped countries the transnational employers can find a supply of workers whose exploitation can be translated into extraordinary profits:

> According to Cardinal George of Chicago, many Catholics are. . . influenced by Calvinism. . . . This religious thinking says that if you work hard, God will reward you materially. Better yet, material success is a sign of God's blessing. . . . Calvinism has worked for CEOs, including Catholic CEOs, many of whom receive millions of dollars in pay. . . but it does not work for most Hispanics and others from Third World countries. . . . Maria Elena, age 15, tried the CEO's Calvinism and capitalism where she worked sewing shirts for the GAP company in El Salvador. She wanted desperately to rise out of poverty and have a better life for her family. She worked hard, always over 60 hours a week, thought hard and even prayed hard, like the popular American children's story, "*The Little Engine that Could.*" In this children's book a little engine couldn't make it over a sharp incline, but kept thinking positively and repeating, "I think I can," "I think I can. . .," and finally made it.
>
> Maria Elena tried and tried to make it, never missing work, always arriving on time, always obeying her supervisor and only going to the bathroom once in the morning and once in the afternoon (she practiced pure Calvinism), but the company would not pay her enough to live on. Her family lived on the margin of human existence. She felt especially bad that the GAP company sold the shirt she made for $25.00, whereas she was paid $0.16 to make it.[12]

"Foreign companies operating factories in Mexico, most with corporate headquarters in the United States, routinely deny work to those who are pregnant or who might become pregnant.

"The factories, called *maquiladoras,* are usually located close to the border in cities like Tijuana, Ciudad Juárez, Chihuahua, Matamoros and Reynosai. International firms use cheap Mexican labor, do not have to pay duties on raw materials imported into Mexico, and get a huge tax break when the assembled products are shipped back to their home country. The Mexican government estimates that 2,600 maquiladoras employ nearly 874,000 Mexicans, more than half women. As of June 1997, there were 567 maquiladoras operating in Tijuana."[13] Such "cor-

---

[12] *Houston Catholic Worker,* Mar.-Apr. 1999, p. 1.
[13] *San Diego News Notes,* Apr. 1999, p. 1.

porations, the vast majority of which are U.S. owned, forced female applicants to undergo. . . pregnancy testing. . . to deny pregnant women work . . . . [F]emale employees are compelled to show their used sanitary napkins to verify nonpregnancy before they receive permanent contracts. . . . In violation of Mexican. . . law maquiladora operators. . . in one instance, retaliated against a woman who complained that pregnant co-workers were breathing in noxious fumes and fainting on the job by firing her. . . . These corporations see hiring pregnant workers as a drain on their resources and as having a potentially detrimental effect on production."[14]

IS NATIONALISM THE ANSWER?

In his criticism of the market, Buchanan quotes Wilhelm Roëpke, the economist who guided the West German recovery after World War II: "'The market is not everything. It must find its place in a higher order of things which is not ruled by supply and demand, free prices, and competition. It must be firmly contained within an all-embracing order of society in which the imperfections and harshness of economic freedom are corrected by law and in which man is not denied conditions of life appropriate to his nature.'"[15] The pivotal element in Buchanan's proposed solution, however, is nationalism. In arguing for "a new nationalism and humane economy," Buchanan says, "[w]e must put our own people first — black and white, Hispanic and Asian, immigrant and native-born. Because they belong to the American family, they have first claim on our compassion and concern; and it is un-American to force members of one's own family into a global hiring hall to compete against foreign workers who make five dollars a day."[16] "Enlightened nationalism" according to Buchanan, "is not some blind worship of the nation. . . that wishes to denigrate or dominate others. It is a passionate attachment to one's own country: its history, heroes, literature, traditions, culture, language, and faith."[17] By "economic nationalism [we] mean tax and trade policies that put America before the Global Economy, and the well-being of our own people before what is best for 'mankind.' Trade is not an end in itself; it is the means to an end, to a more just society and more self-reliant nation. Our trade and tax policies should be designed

---

[14] *Mexico: A Job or Your Rights?* (Human Rights Watch Report, 350 5ᵗʰ Ave., N.Y., NY 10118, Dec. 1998), 3, 11.

[15] Buchanan, *The Great Betrayal*, 288, quoting Wilhelm Roëpke, *A Humane Economy: The Social Framework of the Free Market* (1960), 331; see also Wilhelm Roëpke, *The Social Crisis of Our Times* (1992).

[16] Buchanan, *The Great Betrayal*, 297.

[17] *Ibid.*, 286-87.

to strengthen U.S. sovereignty and independence and should manifest a bias toward domestic, rather than foreign, commerce."[18]

That makes a lot of sense. But it would be unsound to absolutize the nation and to make a religion of nationalism, whether enlightened or otherwise. People do not exist for the nation. And the nation is not an end in itself. Nations, as Buchanan says, may outlast empires. But every nation on the earth will ultimately disappear. And each human being will live forever. The nation, the state and society exist for the good of the person. A government, of course, has the obligation to "promote the common good of civil society, its citizens and intermediate bodies."[19] However, a state or nation has no right to promote its own common good without due regard for the common good of all people everywhere: "The unity of the human family. . . implies a *universal common good.*"[20] "[O]rganizations of the international community. . . should. . . provide for the different needs of men; this will involve the sphere of social life to which belong questions of food, hygiene, education, employment,. . . a general need to promote the welfare of developing countries, to alleviate the miseries of refugees. . . and to assist migrants and their families."[21]

Nationalism makes moral sense only if it is defined and practiced with due regard for the universal common good as well as for the good of the citizens of the nation. That universal common good requires recognition of the dignity of all persons and the universal destination of goods as having been given by God for the benefit of all rather than for the disproportionate and exclusionary use of some. Opposed to that dignity of persons is the utilitarian individualism of the Enlightenment, which treats the human person as "economic man," whose worth is measured by his contribution to somebody's monetary bottom line. "Utilitarianism," said John Paul II, "is a civilization of production and of use, a civilization of things and not of persons, a civilization in which persons are used in the same way as things are used."[22]

CONCENTRATION OF POWER

The people with the green eyeshades and the sharp pencils believe that all that counts is efficiency, which must be sought no matter what its effect on families and communities. But the "bottom line" of the utilitarians is not really the bottom line at all. The ideologies of the libertarian free market and of global free trade enhance the arbitrary power of

---

[18] *Ibid.*, 288.
[19] *CCC*, no. 1910.
[20] *Ibid.*, no. 1911, quoting *Gaudium et Spes,* no. 84.
[21] *Gaudium et Spes,* no. 84.
[22] *LF*, no. 13.

transnational corporations and bureaucracies, for whom the human person is merely an interchangeable economic unit. One result is the economic and social burden imposed on "weaker" nations through "foreign debt," about which the Pope expressed his concern:

> Stronger nations must offer weaker ones opportunities for taking their place in international life, and the latter must learn how to use these opportunities by making the necessary efforts and sacrifices and by ensuring political and economic stability, the certainty of better prospects for the future, the improvement of workers' skills and the training of competent business leaders who are conscious of their responsibilities. . . .

> [T]he positive efforts which have been made along these lines are being affected by the. . . problem of the foreign debt of the poorer countries. The principle that debts must be paid is certainly just. However, it is not right to demand or expect payment when the effect would be the imposition of political choices leading to hunger and despair for entire peoples. It cannot be expected that the debts which have been contracted should be paid at the price of unbearable sacrifices. In such cases it is necessary to find. . . ways to lighten, defer or even cancel the debt compatible with the fundamental right of peoples to subsistence and progress."[23]

"More and more," said John Paul II, "in many countries of America, a system known as 'neoliberalism' prevails; based on a purely economic conception of man, this system considers profit and the law of the market as its only parameters, to the detriment of the dignity of and respect due to individuals and peoples."[24]

Perhaps we are living out the prophetic warning of Pope Pius XI, in *Quadragesimo Anno*, in 1931, that "immense power and despotic economic domination is concentrated in the hands of a few, and that those few are frequently not the owners, but only the trustees and directors of invested funds, who administer them at their good pleasure. . . . This power becomes particularly irresistible when exercised by those who, because they hold and control money, are able also to govern credit and determine its allotment. . . . This accumulation of power, the characteristic note of the modern economic order, is a natural result of limitless free competition which permits the survival of those only who are the strongest, which often means those who fight most relentlessly, who pay least heed to the dictates of conscience, ... Unbridled ambition for domina-

---

[23] *CA*, no. 35; see *Ecclesia in America*, nos. 55, 59.
[24] *EA*, no. 56.

tion has succeeded the desire for gain; the whole economic life has become hard, cruel and relentless in a ghastly measure. . . . As regards the relations of people among themselves, a double stream has issued forth from this one fountainhead: on the one hand, economic nationalism or even economic imperialism; on the other hand, a not less noxious and detestable internationalism or international imperialism in financial affairs, which holds that where a man's fortune is, there is his country."[25]

A sound evaluation of "global free trade" must be made in light of the Church's teaching that "economic freedom is only one element of human freedom. When it becomes autonomous, when man is seen more as a producer or consumer of goods than as a subject who produces and consumes in order to live, then economic freedom loses its necessary relationship to the human person and ends up by alienating and oppressing him."[26]

---

[25] Pope Pius XI, *Quadragesimo Anno* (1931), nos. 105-109.
[26] *CA*, no. 39.

46. CAN WE EVER HOPE TO RESTORE MORALITY IN GOVERNMENT?

"[A] new race of men is springing up to govern the nation," wrote Supreme Court Justice Joseph Story in 1818. "[T]hey are the hunters after popularity, men ambitious, not of the honour so much as of the profits of office, — the demagogues whose principles hang laxly upon them, and who follow not so much what is right, as what leads to a temporary vulgar applause. There is great, very great danger that these men will usurp so much of popular favor that they will rule the nation; and if so, we may yet live to see many of our best institutions crumble in the dust."[1]

What would Justice Story have said if he had seen the Clinton Administration? More to the point of this book, how can we restore morality in the economy, the family and the law if the nation is governed by "demagogues" who are even more practiced in the art of corruption than those feared by Justice Story?

"So many lawyers, so little truth."[2] This column heading sums up the "spinning" of truth by lawyers defending Bill Clinton against the charges that led to his impeachment. One casualty of the Clinton scandals was the very idea that truth and morality are objective. If the polls were right, the American people bought the "spin" that a lie is not wrong if it is "only about sex," adultery is immaterial if the adulterer's spouse tolerates it, the character of a public official (even a President) does not matter as long as he is "doing his job," etc.

In its final 1974 report, the Senate Watergate Committee said, "Hopefully, after the flood of Watergate revelations the country has witnessed, the public can now expect, at least for some years to come, a higher standard of conduct from its public officials and business and professional leaders."[3] The public got that "higher standard," but only for a few years. If the standards of conduct within the Beltway are lower than they were during the Watergate era, the reason may be that those standards reflect the cultural dominance, over the past two decades, of relativism. As *Boobus Americanus* tells the pollster, "I wouldn't act like that, but who am I to say it's wrong for him? It's private. And all politicians are like that anyway."[4] "As our society becomes more addictive and

---

[1] *Life and Letters of Joseph Story* (William W. Story, ed., 1851), 361.
[2] Mark Levin, "So Many Lawyers, So Little Truth," *Wash. Times,* Sept. 14, 1998, p. A19.
[3] *U.S. News & World Report,* July 22, 1974, 68.
[4] See discussion in Paul Craig Roberts, "Clinton's Consequences," *Wash. Times,* May 14, 1999, p. A17.

out-of-control," wrote Archbishop Elden Francis Curtiss of Omaha, "we will have to expect more leaders in the years ahead who, like Clinton, will exhibit these same characteristics."[5] Any moral rebound from the Clinton scandals will last no longer than the one after Watergate unless it is based on sound principles.

So how to restore morality in government? Let us mention only two things: the primacy of truth, and citizen responsibility. "In the political sphere," John Paul said, in words that every public official ought to memorize, "truthfulness. . . between those governing and those governed, openness in public administration, impartiality [and] the rejection of equivocal or illicit means. . . all these are principles. . . rooted in. . . the transcendent value of the person and the objective moral demands of the functioning of States. When these principles are not observed, the very basis of political coexistence is weakened and the life of society itself is gradually jeopardized. . . and doomed to decay." [6]

A respect for truth, however, can be restored to the political sphere only if it first takes root in the lives of citizens. In Question 18, we discussed the answers offered by the Church to the Enlightenment errors of secularism, relativism and individualism. We have to recover in our personal and family lives the conviction that "[t]he *negative precepts* of the natural law. . . oblige. . . always and in every circumstance. . . without exception. . . . [O]ne may never choose kinds of behavior prohibited by the moral commandments expressed in negative form in the Old and New Testaments."[7]

These precepts apply not only to sex but to business and politics. "The seventh commandment prohibits actions or enterprises which for any reason — selfish or ideological, commercial or totalitarian — lead to the *enslavement of human beings,* disregard for their personal dignity, buying or selling or exchanging them like merchandise. Reducing persons. . . to use-value or a source of profit is a sin against their dignity as persons and their fundamental rights." [8]

With respect to citizen responsibility, John Paul reminds us that "if there is no ultimate truth to guide and direct political activity, ideas and convictions can easily be manipulated for reasons of power."[9] As discussed in Question 37, voters should withhold support from politicians

---

[5] Archbiship Elden Francis Curtiss, "The Acquittal of President Clinton: The Basic Issues Remain Unresolved," *Celebrate Life*, July-Aug. 1999, 23.

[6] *VS*, no. 101.

[7] *Ibid.*, no. 52.

[8] *Ibid.*, no. 100.

[9] *Ibid.*, no.101.

who manipulate the truth in support of unjust laws. "Today," said the Catholic bishops of the United States, "Catholics risk cooperating in a false pluralism. . . . American Catholics have long sought to assimilate into U.S. cultural life. But in assimilating, we have too often been digested. We have been changed by our culture too much and we have *changed it not enough.*"[10] The bishops urged "our fellow citizens to *see beyond party politics, to analyze campaign rhetoric critically, and to choose their political leaders according to principle, not party affiliations or mere self-interest.*"[11]

How can we restore morality in government? The answer is simple. Not by sending to the Beltway new faces who share the relativist premises that infect our culture. That would be like changing the pins on a soiled diaper. Nor will the answer be found in arguments, however sound in themselves, for adherence to a natural morality. The "natural" man is a myth, fostered by Enlightenment errors. Man is a creature with a supernatural destiny. The solution to the moral problem today is therefore supernatural, of the spirit. It will not be found, however, by merely adding a second "supernatural" story to the flimsy one-level building that is the supposed "natural" man. Rather, the supernatural is like the steel framework that wholly defines a sound building, giving it form and durability. The supernatural should permeate all that we do. It is not merely an add-on, a bottle of Gatorade lowered down to us from on high to help us do the job by our own natural powers. Instead we first need, one by one, to commit ourselves totally, by the supernatural act of faith, to Christ who is the Truth. As John Paul said to 20,000 young people at the Kiel Center in St. Louis, "You belong to Christ, and He has called you by name. Your first responsibility is to get to know as much as you can about Him. . . . But you will get to know Him truly and personally only through prayer. . . . Through prayer you will learn to become the light of the world, because in prayer you become one with the source of our true light, Jesus Himself."[12]

The act of faith in Christ entails the gift of self to others in our daily work. "To follow Jesus involves. . . inviting everyone to communion with the Trinity and to communion among ourselves in a just and fraternal society."[13] This living of the act of faith is a form of witness that can transform society. In *Veritatis Splendor*, John Paul discussed at length the "numerous Saints who bore witness to and defended moral truth even to

---

[10] Catholic Bishops of the United States, *Living the Gospel of Life: A Challenge to American Catholics* (Nov. 19, 1998), no. 25; http://www.nccbuscc.org/prolife/gospel.htm.

[11] *Ibid.*, no. 34.

[12] *The Wanderer*, Feb. 4, 1999, p. 1.

[13] *EA*, no. 68.

the point of enduring martyrdom. . . . Although martyrdom represents the high point of the witness to moral truth, and one to which relatively few people are called, there is nonetheless a consistent witness which all Christians must daily be ready to make."[14] "This witness," he said, "makes an extraordinarily valuable contribution to warding off, in civil society and within the ecclesial communities themselves. . .the most dangerous crisis which can afflict man: the *confusion between good and evil*, which makes it impossible to build up and to preserve the moral order of individuals and communities."[15]

Building a new culture of life is not a government project. If it were, it would be a lost cause. "I'm from the government, I'm here to help you," is deservedly on the all-time myth list. Government is more an enemy than a friend to the effort to build the culture of life. But we have to be concerned about the level of morality in government because government, for good or ill, is an educator. We can restore morality to government only when we demand it of public officials, but we can coherently make that demand only if we live that morality ourselves. As the bishops said, "We get the public officials we deserve. Their virtue — or lack thereof — is a judgment not only on them, but on us."[16]

---

[14] *VS*, nos. 91, 93.
[15] *Ibid.*, no. 93.
[16] *Living the Gospel of Life*, no. 34.

E.   The Constitution: Is It Still There?

47.   WAS THERE SOME DEFICIENCY IN THE CONSTITUTION WHICH INVITED ITS COLLAPSE?

[T]his Constitution is likely to be well administered for a course of years, and can only end in despotism, as other forms have done before it, when the people shall become so corrupted as to need despotic government, being incapable of any other. — *Benjamin Franklin*[1]

THE CONSTITUTION: A GREAT WORK UNDONE

To blame the collapse of the American Republic on some defect in the Constitution would be a cheap shot. That document justified British statesman William Gladstone's estimate that "the American Constitution is, so far as I can see, the most wonderful work ever struck off at a given time by the brain and purpose of man."[2] It was, however, a work of "man" and not an infallible prescription issued on Mount Sinai. No paper constitution can guarantee the preservation of liberty when the foundational conditions of that preservation erode.

The founding generation was influenced by both Enlightenment and traditional natural law ideas.[3] The Constitution was a technical document, not a philosophical tract. Only in the Preamble did it recite the reasons why the Convention would "ordain and establish" it. The Constitution does not mention God. The Declaration of Independence, in contrast, affirms "the Supreme Judge of the world," "Divine Providence," the "Laws of Nature and of Nature's God" and the "Creator" as the source of "unalienable Rights." The Declaration is one of the four "organic laws" at the head of the laws of the United States, along with the Articles of Confederation, the Northwest Ordinance of 1787 and the Constitution. Although the Declaration is not enforceable as such in the courts, its principles ought to inform our understanding of the purpose of the Constitution and the limits of law.[4]

---

[1] Benjamin Franklin, "Speech in the Convention at the Conclusion of its Deliberations," *Writings,* 1139, 1140 (1987).

[2] William E. Gladstone, "Kin Beyond Sea," 127 *No. Am. Rev.* 179, 185 (1878).

[3] See generally Douglas W. Kmiec and Stephen B. Presser, *The History, Philosophy and Structure of the American Constitution* (1998).

[4] See Harry V. Jaffa, *Original Intent and the Framers of the Constitution: A Disputed Question* (1994), reviewed by Robert H. Bork in *National Review,* Feb. 7, 1994, 61; see also Douglas W. Kmiec, "Do We Still Hold These Truths?" *Chicago Tribune,* July 1, 1996, p. 11; Douglas W. Kmiec and Stephen B. Presser, *The History, Philosophy and Structure of the American Constitution* (1998), chap. 2.

The Declaration also says that governments derive "their just Powers from the Consent of the Governed." And the Preamble to the Constitution says, "WE THE PEOPLE of the United States. . . do ordain and establish this Constitution." However, as Edward S. Corwin said, "The attribution of supremacy to the Constitution on the ground solely of its rootage in popular will represents. . . a late outgrowth of American constitutional theory. Earlier the supremacy accorded to constitutions was ascribed less to their. . . source than to their. . . content, to their embodiment of. . . principles of right and justice which. . . were made by no human hands. . . . They are eternal and immutable."[5] In his remarks on receiving the credentials of Ambassador Lindy Boggs, Pope John Paul II elaborated on that idea:

> The founding fathers of the United States asserted their claim to freedom and independence on the basis of certain "self-evident" truths about the human person: truths which could be discerned in human nature, built into it by "nature's God.". . .
>
> The United States of America was founded on the conviction that an inalienable right to life was a self-evident moral truth, fidelity to which was a primary criterion of social justice. The moral history of your country is the story of. . . efforts to widen the circle of inclusion in society, so that all Americans might enjoy the protection of law, participate in the responsibilities of citizenship and have the opportunity to make a contribution to the common good. Whenever a certain category of people — the unborn or the sick and old — are excluded from that protection, a deadly anarchy subverts. . . justice. The credibility of the United States will depend on its promotion of a. . . culture of life, and on a. . . commitment to building a world in which the. . . most vulnerable are welcomed and protected.[6]

In Questions 6 through 10, we discussed the transformation of the Constitution from its original design. As Forrest McDonald put it, the Constitution was undone by circumstances, beyond the control of the Framers, which were germinating even at the time of the founding:

> [T]he Constitution marked the culmination of a tradition of civic humanism that dated back more than two millennia and of a common-law tradition that dated back many centuries. But the order from which it sprang was already crumbling, and soon it was to be destroyed by a host of minor currents and events and by three develop-

---

[5] Edward S. Corwin, "The 'Higher Law' Background of American Constitutional Law," 42 *Harv. L. Rev.* 149, 152 (1928).

[6] 27 *Origins* 486, 487-88 (1998).

ments of monumental force: the adoption of the Hamiltonian financial system, the French Revolution, and the enormous commercial expansion that accompanied the long succession of international wars that began in 1792. Together, these ushered in the Age of Liberalism, the Age of Capitalism and Democracy. The ensuing society of acquisitive individualists had neither room nor need of the kind of virtuous public servants who so abundantly graced the public councils during the Founding Era.[7]

THE NATURAL LAW

Perhaps the decisive factor in the undermining of the Constitution was the erosion of the popular conviction that the Constitution itself was subject to "the Laws of Nature and of Nature's God." In the early years, the judiciary appears generally to have accepted the idea that "natural law principles should be both embodied in and in control of the operation of the Constitution itself."[8] In *Calder v. Bull*,[9] Justice Samuel Chase endorsed the idea that courts should apply a sort of natural law, but Justice James Iredell rejected that idea. Chase said that if a state enacted an *ex post facto* law, it would be invalid even if it had not been prohibited by the Constitution of the United States or the constitution of that state: "There are certain vital principles in our free Republican governments, which will. . . over-rule an apparent and flagrant abuse of legislative power; as to authorize manifest injustice by positive law; or to take away that security for personal liberty, or private property, for the protection whereof the government was established. An *act* of the Legislature (for I cannot call it a law) contrary to the great first principles of the social compact, cannot be considered a rightful exercise of legislative authority."[10]

Justice Iredell responded: "If. . . the Legislature of the Union, or the Legislature of any member of the Union, shall pass a law, within the general scope of their constitutional power, the court cannot pronounce it to be void, merely because it is in their judgment contrary to the principles of natural justice. *The ideas of natural justice are regulated by no fixed standard: the ablest and the purest men have differed upon the subject*; and all that the court could properly say, in such an event, would be, that the Legislature (possessed of an equal right of opinion) had passed an act which, in the opinion of the judges, was inconsistent with the abstract principles of natural justice."[11]

---

[7] Forrest McDonald, *Novus Ordo Seculorum: The Intellectual Origins of the Constitution* (1985), 261-62, 291-92.

[8] Stephen B. Presser, *Recapturing the Constitution* (1994), 86.

[9] 3 U.S. 386 (1798).

[10] 3 U.S. at 387-89.

[11] 3 U.S. at 398-99 (emphasis added).

"[F]or Chase, it was an inherent principle of free republican governments that there could be no *ex post facto* criminal laws. Once the framers chose to erect a republic, that principle would have been operative whether or not the Constitution explicitly included such a principle in the text."[12] It was "Chase's views, not Iredell's, that were in the mainstream of late eighteenth-century American jurisprudence. It is surely significant that Iredell was alone on the Court in his express criticism of Chase on this point."[13]

In the long run, Iredell's rejection of natural law prevailed in American culture and law. His view is in line with the theory of the Protestant Reformation, that private judgment controls, with "no fixed standard." If Iredell is right, the natural law is indeterminate and relatively useless as a higher standard for law and a guide for human conduct. Suppose you think an *ex post facto* law, or abortion, or anything else, is wrong. Who are you to say? Even if we recognize that there is a natural law, how do we know for sure what it means?

RECOGNITION OF THE LAWGIVER

The natural law is knowable to reason. But the idea of a natural law disembodied from its source — its Lawgiver — is a myth. "The problem with natural law conceived apart from its supernatural end is that it perpetuates the myth of the modern liberal state as a religiously neutral institutional arrangement. . . . [W]hen natural law is not ordered to its supernatural end, it lacks the linguistic and conceptual resources needed to challenge existing configurations of political power from a perspective other than the realm of the 'political.'"[14]

Justice Iredell rightly posed the question: Whose natural law? Everything has a nature, built into it by its maker. The maker of your Chevrolet built a nature into it, so that it will run if you feed it gasoline, but not if you feed it sand. And that maker provided you with a manual to tell you exactly what you ought to do to make that Chevy work. The natural law, whether of cars or anything else, is the story of how things work. Our Maker built our nature into us and gave us a set of Manufacturer's directions, a manual, in the natural law and in the Ten Commandments, which are a specification of that natural law. So whose natural law? The Lawgiver's. How do we know what it means? Through reason and the Revelation given to us by that Lawgiver. The natural law

---

[12] Presser at 120.

[13] *Ibid.*, at 121.

[14] Michael J. Baxter, C.S.C., "Peter Maurin Blows the Dynamite," *Houston Catholic Worker*, Mar.-Apr. 1999, Special edition, pp. 1, 8.

is the law of God. And Christ is God. It should be no surprise that the Catholic tradition affirms that we can rely on the authoritative interpretations of that natural law by the Vicar of Christ. The question is not whether there is a pope, but rather how many. Everyone has a pope, an ultimate visible authority on moral questions. If that authority is not the real Pope, it will be one of the individual's own selection, whether Ann Landers, *The New York Times* or the individual himself.

The recognition by the people, including those in government, that a higher law sets boundaries to what the state may rightly do, is itself a brake on the enactment of unjust laws. That recognition, if the people implement it in their own lives, can also provide an incentive for the enactment of laws in accord with natural justice. But if the government is limited by a higher law — and is to remain so limited — there must be someone, outside the government and themselves, to whom the people are willing to look for morally authoritative interpretations of that natural law. If the state is its own conclusive interpreter of the natural law, it is not really subject to it at all. If the state claims to make only legal interpretations, leaving moral questions to the private realm, that in itself is taking a moral position: that law and morality are separated and that the state can act without regard to the moral law. Nor can the people themselves function effectively as the ultimate interpreter of the natural law. How do we know what the people really think? Someone must decide what is the majority view. And there is no necessary relation between the majority view and objective truth. An independent interpreter, who draws his moral authority from the Lawgiver, is needed if the natural law is to work. That is exactly what a pope is. In the nature of things, there can be only one.

As discussed in Question 49, the voluntary recognition by the people of the natural law and their acceptance of its morally authoritative interpreter would have nothing to do with any sort of union of church and state. Such a union would be bad for the church and bad for the state. The First Amendment forbade it on the federal level and the remaining established churches in the states disappeared by 1828. However, the rejection of any union of church and state does not require a separation of morality and religion from public life. In the free exercise of religion, protected by the First Amendment, the people have the right to bring their moral and religious views into the public arena and into the performance of their duties as public officials. "The right to religious liberty. . . ought to be acknowledged in the juridical order. . . in such a way that it constitutes a civil right."[15] It is illusory, however, to expect

---

[15] *CCC*, no. 2108.

that religious liberty will endure if the people, in their own lives, reject the law of God who is the Author of that liberty. If the people do not themselves recognize, and try to practice, objective justice, they will hardly be likely to insist upon its observance by government. The way will be clear for the ascendancy of legal positivism.[16]

The founders of the American Republic tried to keep it Christian without the Church.[17] The system worked for a time because the founders, in setting it up, spent the capital they had inherited from pre-Reformation Catholic Christendom. However, the Protestant domination of the founding and later generations isolated the new Republic from that living Christian tradition, including the role of the Pope, and ensured that the Republic would draw no further income directly from that source. The Republic was on its own. Private judgment was the rule with respect to the moral law. And it should not be surprising that the state would eventually follow the example of the people and would claim the right to exercise its own private judgment as to its own conduct. This proved especially true in the twentieth century as Enlightenment ideas took root in a culture disarmed by its lack of commitment to an ascertainable and objective standard of morality.

THE INDISPENSABILITY OF FAITH

Alexis de Tocqueville, the French observer who analyzed American society in the 1830s, emphasized the relation between faith among the people, including their recognition of religious authority, and the preservation of political freedom:

> General ideas respecting God and human nature are. . . the ideas above all others which it is most suitable to withdraw from. . . private judgment, and in which there is most to gain and least to lose by recognizing a principle of authority. . . . When there is no longer any principle of authority in religion, any more than in politics, men are speedily frightened at the aspect of this unbounded independence. The constant agitation of all surrounding things alarms and exhausts them. As everything is at sea in the sphere of the mind, they determine at least that the mechanism of society shall be firm and fixed; and, as they cannot resume their ancient belief, they assume a master.

> For my own part, I doubt whether man can ever support at the same time complete religious independence and entire political freedom.

---

[16] See Question 15.
[17] See Questions 10 and 49.

And I am inclined to think that, if faith be wanting in him, he must be subject; and if he be free, he must believe.[18]

In his farewell address, George Washington said: "Of all the dispositions and habits which lead to political prosperity, Religion and morality are indispensable supports. . . . And let us with caution indulge the supposition, that morality can be maintained without religion. Whatever may be conceded to the influence of refined education on minds of peculiar structure, reason and experience both forbid us to expect that National morality can prevail in exclusion of religious principle. 'Tis substantially true, that virtue or morality is a necessary spring of popular government. The rule indeed extends with more or less force to every species of free Government."[19] John Paul II made a similar point. "In the end, only a morality which acknowledges certain norms as valid always and for everyone, with no exception, can guarantee the ethical foundation of social coexistence, both on the national and international levels."[20]

The framers, of course, were not dealing with a Catholic society. And the Constitution, unlike the Declaration of Independence,[21] did not itself recognize any determinate moral authority higher than the government and the people. It may not be out of place to borrow here Thomas Babington Macaulay's remark, made in another context in 1857: "Your constitution is all sail and no anchor."[22] In any event, no alternative phrasing or structuring of the Constitution would have enabled it to survive the erosion of religious and moral conviction among the people, especially as that erosion occurred under the impact of Enlightenment ideas in the twentieth century.

Benjamin Franklin had it right. The American people, corrupted by Enlightenment ideas and government subsidies, let the Constitution die. The fault lies not with the Constitution, but with the elites and others who transformed the Constitution from its original design, and with us, the people who let them get away with it because we profited from that transformation.

---

[18] Alexis de Tocqueville, *Democracy in America,* Part II, Book One, no. 17. (Richard D. Heffner, ed., 1956), 151-52.

[19] *George Washington: A Collection* (W.B. Allen, ed., 1988), 521.

[20] *VS,* no. 97.

[21] See Question 49.

[22] Thomas Babington Macaulay, *The Selected Letters of Thomas Babington Macaulay* (Thomas Pinney, ed., 1974), 286.

48. SHOULD WE GIVE UP ON THE CONSTITUTION?

The Constitution. . . remains a. . . topic of Fourth of July oratory. We still have elections. . . . But despite the persistence of. . .republican forms, the reality is. . . a mass democracy in which elected officials are more and more irrelevant and corrupt as their powers. . . are usurped by bureaucratic elites that cannot be removed. . . . Why did the American Republic die, and why can't it be restored?

Once the sociology of liberty is destroyed, it cannot be restored. Once the institutions and habits of independent discipline have withered, they do not naturally blossom again. Most Americans today are content with the mega-state, the cult of consumption that a bureaucratized economy encourages, and the. . . diversions of the mass media. The only discontent most of us have with the mega-state is when we have to pay for somebody else to get more from it — in welfare, services, subsidies, tax breaks — than we get.

Democratic politics in the leviathan state is never about dismantling or reducing leviathan but always about forcing somebody else to pay for what we want from it. . . . [T]he engorgement of leviathan is accelerated by the twin engines of a bureaucratic elite intent on enlarging its own power and the mass voting blocs it feeds, just as eighteenth-century demogogues fed their mobs. Unlike a republic, mass democracy doesn't restrain power; democracy unleashes power. Except for a few right-wing eggheads, no one seriously contemplates restoring the republic; no one seriously wants to because no one has any material interest in it. Hence, the republic will not be restored. — *Samuel Francis*[1]

Should we give up on the Constitution? In terms of trying to restore it? Yes. But we can still use it to protect those who are building the culture of life.

The old Constitution, with its division and separation of powers and its checks and balances, is dead. There is no practical possibility of breathing life back into the corpse to restore it as it was. Some conservatives and others regard the Constitution as if it were written on tablets of stone instead of parchment and as if it came from Mount Sinai instead of Philadelphia. The framers of the Constitution deserve to be called statesmen rather than merely politicians. But, unlike the Framer of the Ten Commandments, they were fallible. Their work is entitled to respect but not to idolatry or religious veneration. We ought to acknowledge that it has failed the test of time and then go on to build something new

---

[1] Samuel Francis, *Revolution from the Middle* (1997), 82-83, 87.

out of the wreckage. In that building project, the constitutional forms can be useful. Proposals to require that every bill introduced in Congress must specify the constitutional provision that authorizes it can remind people of the need to restrain government even though such proposals have no real chance of enactment.[2] Also useful is a proposed constitutional amendment to limit the surrender of American sovereignty by providing that "a provision of a treaty which denies or abridges any right enumerated in this Constitution shall not be of any force or effect."[3] Another example is the effort to repeal the Sixteenth Amendment and substitute for the income tax a national retail sales tax, which would promote freedom for persons and families by eliminating the intrusive power of the Internal Revenue Service.[4] And the constitutional freedoms of speech and association can be used to shield the growing culture of life in some situations. The objective of these and other efforts should be, not to restore the Constitution to its original design, but to use the Constitution and the law as defensive mechanisms to put roadblocks in the way of the Leviathan State so as to keep that state off the backs of people who want to live an authentic culture of life. In any event, as far as the right to life is concerned, we have to recognize that, at least in the foreseeable future, we will not restore complete protection for that right in American law.

WITNESS

As we move into the new millennium, the pro-life effort will be an aspect of the "consistent witness which all Christians must daily be ready to make, even at the cost of suffering and grave sacrifice."[5] This book has sought to note some ways in which that witness might be made through political, legal and other activities. In particular, pro-life people should insist on "no exception" with respect to legal protection of the right to life. We will not succeed at this time in restoring that legal protection. But the witness involved in that insistence will educate consciences as to the sacredness of life. It will save more lives than will the incremental strategies of "pro-life" Beltway pragmatists.[6]

A restoration of respect for life, however, will come about only through the reconversion of the American people to the conviction that the right to life is inalienable precisely because each human being is

---

[2] See, for example, H.R. 292 (105th Cong., 1st Sess., 1997).
[3] H.J. Res. 83, (105th Cong., 1st Sess., 1997).
[4] Contact Americans for Fair Taxation, P.O. Box 27487, Houston, TX 77227, (713) 963- 9023.
[5] *VS*, no. 93.
[6] See Question 34.

made in the image and likeness of God. The most important contribution we can make to that reconversion is for each of us to bring the culture of life into the world through his actions as well as his words. There is too much real work to be done for us to waste time pursuing the phantom of formal restoration of the Constitution, and the nation, as they were. Neither the Constitution nor the nation should be the object of absolute loyalty. "Citizens should cultivate a generous and loyal spirit of patriotism, but without narrow-mindedness, so that they will always keep in mind the welfare of the whole human family formed into one by various kinds of links between races, peoples, and nations."[7] While "[t]he Christian faithful. . . should sincerely and actively foster love of country,"[8] the nation is not an absolute. Neither the Constitution nor the United States, as a nation, is eternal. This nation-state, as a sovereign political entity, will at some time cease to exist, maybe sooner rather than later. The end may come through military subjugation,[9] division into ethnic regions or otherwise. As one knowledgeable observer commented to this writer, "Bill Clinton is the instrument of divine judgment on the United States. After what we have approved or tolerated, we do not deserve to exist as a nation." Maybe so. Maybe not. What will count in the long run is whether we have committed our lives, not to a temporal entity but to eternal Truth.

In his 1838 address to the Young Men's Lyceum of Springfield, Illinois, Abraham Lincoln said: "[T]o the support of the Constitution and Laws, let every American pledge his life, his property, and his sacred honor. . . . Let reverence for the laws. . . be preached from the pulpit, proclaimed in legislative halls, and enforced in courts of justice. And, in short, let it become the *political religion* of the nation."[10] Like all civil or political religions, it did not last. It is time for the real thing, not in a document but in the lives of the American people.

---

[7] Vatican II, *Gaudium et Spes*, no. 75.

[8] Vatican II, *Ad Gentes, Decree on the Missionary Activity of the Church*, no. 15.

[9] See *N.Y. Times*, Apr. 28, 1999, p. A1, describing the Communist Chinese espionage "compromising virtually every nuclear weapon in the United States arsenal." See Bill Gertz, *Betrayal: How the Clinton Administration Undermined American Security* (1999); Edward Timperlake and William C. Triplett II, *Year of the Rat: How Bill Clinton Compromised U.S. Security for Chinese Cash* (1998).

[10] *Abraham Lincoln, His Speeches and Writings* (Roy P. Basler, ed., 1981), 76, 81 (emphasis added).

49. SHOULD THE GOVERNMENT OF THE UNITED STATES AFFIRM THAT THE DECLARATION OF INDEPENDENCE IS TRUE?

When in the Course of human events, it becomes necessary for one people to. . . assume. . . the separate and equal station to which *the Laws of Nature and of Nature's God* entitle them. . . .

We hold these truths to be self-evident, that all men are created equal, that they are endowed *by their Creator* with certain unalienable Rights. . .

We, therefore, the representatives of the United States of America,. . . appealing to *the Supreme Judge of the world* for the rectitude of our intentions, do. . . solemnly. . . declare that these United Colonies are, and of Right ought to be Free and Independent States. . . .

And for the support of this Declaration, with a firm reliance on the Protection of *Divine Providence,* we mutually pledge to each other our Lives, our Fortunes and our sacred Honor.[1]

A FALSE NEUTRALITY

As discussed in Question 10, the First Amendment excluded the federal government from establishing any religion or prohibiting the free exercise of religion. But the Constitution and the First Amendment did not preclude that government from affirming the truth of the Declaration of Independence by acknowledging God, praying to Him and encouraging belief in Him, all of which that government did until the 1960s. Today the Supreme Court requires government at all levels to maintain neutrality as to whether the Declaration's affirmations of God are true. This neutrality is inaccurately defended as an implementation of Thomas Jefferson's dictum that the Establishment Clause built "a wall of separation between church and state."[2] This "neutrality" prohibits any government official to assert as a fact either that God exists or that He does not exist. That official is required by the Court to say, in effect, that as far as the government is concerned, the existence or non-existence of God is unknowable. This is not silence about religion. It is agnosticism, the affirmation of a non-theistic belief which is contrary to the theistic affirmations of the Declaration. It is a repudiation of the birth certificate of the nation. It has brought the relentless removal of theistic references from public schools and other public activities.

---

[1] *Declaration of Independence* (emphasis added).
[2] See discussion in Charles E. Rice, *The Supreme Court and Public Prayer* (1964), 62-63.

SHOULD THERE BE A UNION OF CHURCH AND STATE?

The alternative to that spurious neutrality mandated by the Supreme Court is not some sort of union of church and state. Nor is such a union required or sought by the Catholic Church. As Vatican II, the *Catechism* and John Paul II make clear, the objective is preservation of "the right to religious freedom," rather than the extension of legal privilege to the Church. As discussed in Question 10, the Supreme Court's implicit adoption of secularism as the national religion diminishes that religious freedom.

RELIGIOUS FREEDOM AND THE PERSON

Dignitatis Humanae, the Vatican II *Declaration on Religious Liberty,* said:

> All men are bound to seek the truth, especially in what concerns God and his Church, and to embrace it and hold on to it as they come to know it. . . . Truth can impose itself on the mind of man only in virtue of its own truth; which wins over the mind with both gentleness and power. So while the religious freedom which men demand in fulfilling their obligation to worship God has to do with freedom from coercion in civil society, it leaves intact the traditional Catholic teaching on the moral duty of individuals and societies towards the true religion and the one Church of Christ. . . .

> [A]ll men should be immune from coercion on the part of individuals, social groups and every human power so that, within due limits, nobody is forced to act against his convictions nor is anyone to be restrained from acting in accordance with his convictions in religious matters in private or in public, alone or in associations with others. . . . [T]he right to religious freedom is based on the very dignity of the human person as known through the revealed word of God and by reason itself. This right of the human person to religious freedom must be given such recognition in the constitutional order of society as will make it a civil right. . . . [T]he right to religious freedom has its foundation not in the subjective attitude of the individual but in his very nature. For this reason the right to this immunity continues to exist even in those who do not live up to their obligation of seeking the truth and adhering to it. . . .

> If because of the circumstances of a particular people special civil recognition is given to one religious community in the constitutional organization of a State, the right of all citizens and religious communities to religious freedom must be recognized and respected as well. . . . [S]ince civil society has the right to protect itself against possible

abuses committed in the name of religious freedom the responsibility of providing such protection rests especially with the civil authority. However, this must not be done in an arbitrary manner or by the unfair practice of favoritism but in accordance with legal principles which are in conformity with the objective moral order. . . . [M]an's freedom should be given the fullest possible recognition and should not be curtailed except when and in so far as is necessary. . . .

The freedom of the Church is the fundamental principle governing relations between the Church and public authorities and the whole civil order. As the spiritual authority appointed by Christ the Lord with the duty, imposed by divine command, of going into the whole world and preaching the Gospel to every creature, the Church claims freedom for herself in human society and before every public authority. The Church also claims freedom for herself as a society of men with the right to live in civil society in accordance with the demands of the Christian faith. . . .

At the same time the Christian faithful, in common with the rest of men, have the civil right of freedom from interference in leading their lives according to their conscience. A harmony exists therefore between the freedom of the Church and that religious freedom which must be recognized as the right of all men and all communities and must be sanctioned by constitutional law.[3]

The *Catechism* affirmed these principles[4] and John Paul II has emphasized and expanded upon them. In his message to the 1995 Congress on Secularism and Religious Freedom, John Paul said that, "in defending religious freedom, the Church is not defending an institutional prerogative; she is defending the truth about the human person." He continued:

> The *Dogmatic Constitution on the Church* states: "While it must be recognized that the temporal sphere is governed by its own principles,. . .that ominous doctrine must rightly be rejected which attempts to build a society with no regard whatever for religion, and which attacks and destroys the religious liberty of its citizens."[5]. . . [A]nother form of limitation on religious freedom,. . . is more subtle than overt persecution. I am thinking here of the claim that a democratic society should relegate to the realm of private opinion its members' religious beliefs and the moral convictions which derive from faith. . . .

---

[3] *Dignitatis Humanae*, nos. 1, 2, 6, 7, 13.

[4] See *CCC*, nos. 2104-09.

[5] Vatican II, *Lumen Gentium*, Dogmatic Constitution on the Church, no. 36.

[I]f citizens are expected to leave aside their religious convictions when they take part in public life, does this not mean that society not only excludes the contribution of religion to its institutional life, but also promotes *a culture which re-defines man as less than what he is?*. . . Should citizens whose moral judgments are informed by their religious beliefs be less welcome to express their most deeply held convictions?. . . On their part, *religious believers must be deeply committed to the method of dialogue and persuasion.* . . .

[T]he Church today holds firmly to that basic tenet of the Declaration on Religious Freedom: "the truth cannot impose itself except by virtue of its own truth, which wins over the mind with both gentleness and power." The Church neither seeks nor desires to see any worldly power placed at the service of the truths she bears. She asks only to be allowed to address man in freedom; and she asks for all human beings the freedom to respond to the Gospel in the full measure of their humanity.[6]

BUT SHOULD THE STATE ACKNOWLEDGE GOD?

The Vatican II demand that religious freedom be recognized as a civil right "leaves intact the traditional Catholic teaching on the moral duty of individuals and societies towards the true religion and the one Church of Christ."[7] Since Vatican II, the Church has refrained from advancing any claim under that "traditional" teaching that the Church should be given special recognition in a Catholic nation or that the state is obliged to acknowledge God in an explicit way. The Catholic Church does not seek any union of Church and state but insists on the primacy of religious freedom which must be preserved even if "because of the circumstances of a particular people special civil recognition is given to one religious community."[8] But should the state even admit that God exists?

Previous papal statements insisted on the moral duty of the state to acknowledge God. Pope Leo XIII said that "Nature and reason, which command every individual devoutly to worship God in holiness, because we belong to Him and must return to Him, since from Him we came, bind also the civil community by a like law."[9] "[C]ivil society," Leo XIII later said, "must acknowledge God as its Founder and Parent, and must obey and reverence His power and authority."[10] In his 1925 encyclical instituting the feast of Christ the King, Pope Pius XI said, "[T]he empire

---

[6] See *Inside the Vatican,* Jan. 1996, 45.
[7] *Dignitatis Humanae,* no. 1.
[8] *Dignitatis Humanae,* no. 6; see *CCC,* no. 2107.
[9] Pope Leo XIII, *Immortale Dei* (1885), no. 6.
[10] *Libertas Praestantissimum* (1888), no. 21.

of our Redeemer embraces all men. . . . Nor is there any difference in this matter between the individual and the family or the State; for all men, whether collectively or individually, are under the dominion of Christ. . . . If, therefore, the rulers of nations wish to preserve their authority, to promote. . . the prosperity of their people, they will not neglect the public duty of reverence and obedience to the rule of Christ. . . . 'With God and Jesus Christ. . . excluded from political life, with authority derived not from God but from man, the very basis of that authority has been taken away. . . . The result is that human society is tottering to its fall, because it has no longer a secure and solid foundation.'. . . When once men recognize, both in private and in public life, that Christ is King, society will at last receive the great blessings of real liberty, well-ordered discipline, peace, and harmony."[11]

In effect, the state implicitly affirms the Truth who is Christ when it promotes the common good in accord with the moral law of which Christ is the norm, whether or not the state goes further to acknowledge God explicitly. On the other hand, it cannot be a proper function of any government to deny God or to deny that he is knowable.

While the Constitution contains no explicit acknowledgment of him, the American Founding was not neutral on the existence of God.[12] The First Amendment excluded the federal government from establishing a national sect or prohibiting the free exercise of religion. But when the Declaration of Independence acknowledged God, it reflected the fact that "the framers understood that the nation's civic morality and well-being depended upon a corporate or sovereign affirmation of God's existence, while leaving individuals free to worship and to come to understand God in their own uncoerced fashion."[13]

The government of the United States cannot be neutral on that corporate affirmation of God in its founding document. It must opt for theism by affirming the truth of the Declaration, or for non-theism by denying that truth or by saying, contrary to the Declaration, that it is unknowable to the people in their public capacity. The question is not whether the federal government will take a position on the Declaration's affirmations of God. The question is: which position will it take? It cannot be neutral.

So the answer to the question is: "Yes," the government of the United States should affirm that the Declaration of Independence is

---

[11] Pope Pius XI, *Quas Primas*, The Kingship of Christ (1925), Nos. 18-19, quoting *Ubi Arcano Dei Consilio*, encyclical of Pius XI, Dec. 23, 1922.
[12] See Question 10.
[13] Douglas W. Kmiec and Stephen B. Presser, *The American Constitutional Order: History, Cases and Philosophy* (1998), 171.

true. The nation was founded on that truth, which can be repudiated only by adopting, in effect, an alternative, non-theistic religion as the official national creed. This is exactly what the Supreme Court has done with the acquiescence of Congress and the executive branch.[14]

There would be no inconsistency between an explicit affirmation by government of the Declaration of Independence and the primacy of religious liberty. Nor would affirmation of the Declaration be the first step on a slippery slope toward an established church. Separation of church and state *is* part of the American arrangement and it is good. But separation of religion from public life is not part of that arrangement.[15] The law is an educator. When the child asks his teacher, "Is the Declaration of Independence true when it says I get my rights from God the Creator?," the teacher's response should be some variant of "You'd better believe it, kid. It's true." Nevertheless, it would be a mistake to suppose that morality can be restored merely by governmental affirmations of God. The value of such affirmations is mainly symbolic. While it will not of itself change hearts, the recognition by government that God is in charge can encourage people to open their minds and hearts to grace and ultimately to Christ.

The Church today does not even talk about the issue of whether the state should explicitly affirm Christ. Given the secular condition of states today, it would be futile to raise that question. Rather, the emphasis is rightly placed on the transformation of society by persons who are themselves transformed by faith in Christ so as to give of themselves to others. In this light the emphasis by the Church on religious freedom assumes critical importance. The purpose of the state is to promote the common good,[16] which is "the sum total of social conditions which allow people, either as groups or as individuals, to reach their fulfillment more fully and more easily."[17] But man "can fully discover his true self only in a sincere giving of himself."[18] To make that gift, man must be free. "[T]he full meaning of freedom [is] the gift of self *in service to God and one's brethren*."[19] And freedom is especially necessary for man to commit himself to God in the act of faith. "To be human, man's response to God by faith must be free. . . The act of faith is of its very nature a free act."[20] Religious freedom, therefore, is not only a civil right. It

---

[14] See Questions 9 and 10.
[15] See Questions 10 and 47.
[16] *CCC*, no. 1910.
[17] *Ibid.*, no. 1906.
[18] Vatican II, *Gaudium et Spes,* no. 24.
[19] *VS,* no. 87.
[20] *CCC,* no. 160, quoting *Dignitatis Humanae,* no. 10.

is an essential component of the common good which it is the very purpose of the state to promote. That is why the Church's emphasis on religious freedom is so important.

There is no realistic prospect today of getting the United States government to affirm the truth of the Declaration of Independence. While the effort to restore that affirmation should be made for its educational value, the main focus should be on promoting faith in Christ and on protecting religious liberty. We ought to use the Constitution and the language of the Declaration of Independence to keep the government off the backs of those who seek to live the culture of life.

PART IV:

THE FUTURE

50. ARE WE REALLY ON THE WINNING SIDE?

Yes. No doubt about it. "After the darkness, there came light. After the desolation, there came fruitfulness. The Church leapt out of the tomb, as she has done from the beginning."[1]

As noted in the first Question in this book, "One of John Paul's recurrent themes is that 'God is preparing a great springtime for Christianity, and we can already see its first signs.'" We cannot know *how* this will work out, but we can note some of those "first signs."

THE "CULTURE OF DEATH" CANNOT LAST

We have not yet seen the worst of the culture of death in the United States and elsewhere. As that culture approaches rock bottom, the utilitarian exploitation of the person will sink to a new level of compulsory abortion and euthanasia, genocidal suppression of nonwhites, delegitimization of the family and subordination of persons and families to the financial interests of the transnational architects of a world order founded on the treatment of the person as merely an economic object. The federal government, under the pretext of protecting the people, will assume greater powers over them. And that government has compromised the military ability of the United States to survive as an independent nation.

Suicide as a policy, though, whether personal or cultural, is necessarily short-lived. The culture of death has no future because it is contrary to nature. It can sustain itself only by repression of the basic inclinations of the human spirit. Already, it has generated the reaction that will overturn it. "Americans now place moral decline at the top of their list of items needing repair. . . . The fact that the proportion of the population expressing concern is at record levels. . . is. . . evidence that citizens are ready for countermeasures. Indeed. . . many citizens are already fighting back with new attitudes and behaviors."[2]

"A new phase in the history of freedom is opening up," said the Pope to American bishops on their 1998 *ad limina* visit to Rome. "The challenge is enormous," he continued, "but the time is right. For *other culture-forming forces are exhausted, implausible or lacking in intellectual resources* adequate to satisfy the human yearning for genuine liberation- even if those forces still manage to exercise a powerful attraction especially through the media. The great achievement of the council is to have

---

[1] Michael O'Brien, *Eclipse of the Sun* (1998), 851.
[2] Karl Zinsmeister, Stephen Moore, Karlyn Bowman, "Is America Turning a Corner?" *The American Enterprise*, Jan.-Feb. 1999, 36, 37.

positioned the Church to engage modernity with the truth about the human condition, given to us in Jesus Christ who is the answer to the question that is every human life."[3]

CHRIST IS THE ONLY ALTERNATIVE

In "The Drama of Atheist Humanism," Henri de Lubac, S.J. quoted Feodor Dostoevsky precisely on the point of this book: "[W]hen he is alone with himself, noting down his most serious reflections, Dostoevsky also said: 'We continually go astray if we have not Christ and His faith to guide us'; 'repudiate Christ, and the human mind can arrive at the most astounding conclusions.' Reflecting upon the West, which a strong party in his own country would have liked Russia to take as its model, he says: 'The West has lost Christ, and that is why it is dying; that is the only reason.'"[4]

The object here is not to restore "the West." We hope to see an authentic culture of life for all people in all places. And we *are* on the winning side. But the culture of life will not result from a conscious effort to build it for its own sake. It will come about when, one by one, we unite with Christ in the act of faith which involves the gift of self to God and to others. The Catholic Church provides the only coherent answer to the culture of death because the Church speaks for Christ, who is God. John Paul II reminds us that "conversion consists in commitment to the person of Jesus Christ, with all the theological and moral implications taught by the Magisterium of the Church."[5] "The Vicar of Christ is in fact 'the enduring principle of unity and the visible foundation' of the Church."[6]

This is choosing time. "[T]here are but two alternatives," said Cardinal Newman, "the way to Rome and the way to Atheism: Anglicanism is the halfway house on the one side, and Liberalism is the halfway house on the other."[7] A decade ago, Francis Canavan, S.J., wrote that "Christendom, the society in which Christianity could be taken for granted, has ended, has been coming to an end, in fact, for at least 300 years. With its final disappearance, we shall soon see no more merely nominal or post-Christian Catholics. The gap between Catholicism and the general culture will be so wide and so inescapably visible that we shall all

---

[3] 43 *The Pope Speaks* 238, 241 (1998) (emphasis added).
[4] Henri du Lubac, S.J., *The Drama of Atheist Humanism* (1963), 184; quoting Feodor Dostoevsky, *Notebooks* (1879), *Journal of an Author* (1873), and *Notebooks* (1871).
[5] *EA*, no. 53.
[6] *Ibid.*, no. 33, quoting Vatican I, *Pastor Aeternus*, Dogmatic Constitution on the Church of Christ.
[7] John Henry Cardinal Newman, *Apologia pro Vita Sua* (1924), 204.

have to take our stand on one or the other side of it."[8] That gap is far wider today than it was in 1990. And the necessity of choice is more imperative.

THE RISING GENERATION OF FAITH

In *Tertio Millennio Adveniente,* his Apostolic Letter for the Jubilee Year 2000, the Pope said, "The more the West is becoming estranged from its Christian roots, the more it is becoming missionary territory." He went on to say:

> The future of the world and the Church belongs to the younger generation, to those who, born in this century, will reach maturity in the next. . . . Christ expects great things from young people, as He did from the young man who asked Him: "What good deed must I do to have eternal life?". . .

> Young people, in every situation, in every region of the world, do not cease to put questions to Christ. They meet Him and they keep searching for Him in order to question Him further. If they succeed in following the road which He points out to them, they will have the joy of making their own contribution to His presence in the next century and in the centuries to come, until the end of time: "Jesus is the same yesterday, today and forever."[9]

A sign of the power of this "new evangelization" can be seen in John Paul's remarkable impact on youth.[10] "How could more than a million young people show up in Paris to meet Pope John Paul II, whose doctrine, according to the majority of mass media commentators, will soon be obsolete for citizens of the technocratic Third Millennium?. . . Perhaps in August 1997 Paris experienced a new 'French Revolution.' The anticlerical, 'enlightened' city of Voltaire and Diderot, the atheist, existentialist capital of Sartre, Mecca of free thinkers (and free livers), greeted a Catholic Pope, John Paul II, with unprecedented warmth and passion. The numbers which turned out to see and listen to the Holy Father increased beyond every expectation with each appearance. The Holy Father had not tried to sell anything– he had asked the world's youth only to give."[11]

---

[8] Francis Canavan, S.J., "Commentary," *Catholic Eye,* Feb. 20, 1990, p. 2.
[9] *Tertio Millenio Advenienti,* no. 58.
[10] See Brian O'Neel, "The Boom in Church Youth Programs," *Catholic World Report,* Oct. 1998, 46.
[11] *Inside the Vatican,* Oct. 1997, photo essay, pp. 3, 9.

The readiness of youth to give can be seen in the increasing vocations to the priesthood and religious life in orthodox dioceses, orders and congregations.[12] "There was a period of confusion and uncertainty after the Second Vatican Council," said Fr. Kevin Rhoades, rector of Mount Saint Mary's Seminary in Emmitsburg, Maryland. "But now we've had 20 years of a very strong pontificate. I think we're at a new era, and these [seminarians] represent it."[13]

In his 1979 address to high school students at Madison Square Garden in New York, John Paul II said, "we are convinced that only in Christ do we find real love, in the fullness of life. And so I invite you today to look to Christ. When you wonder about the mystery of yourself, look to Christ who gives you the meaning of life. When you wonder what it means to be a mature person, look to Christ who is the fullness of humanity. And when you wonder about your role in the future of the world and of the United States, look to Christ. Only in Christ will you fulfill your potential as an American citizen and as a citizen of the world community."[14]

The pagan, anti-life culture can offer young people nothing of the spirit. It can lead them only into a dead end of alienation, dissipation and self-absorption. It is no surprise that, in increasing numbers, they are following John Paul's invitation to "look to Christ" and to give of themselves.

THE NEW "MONASTERIES"?

The monastic movement founded by St. Benedict laid the foundations of a new Christian culture after the fall of the Roman Empire. Today, numerous small initiatives are laying the groundwork for the new culture of life. Home schools, independent religious or other private schools, and Catholic colleges and universities that have not prostituted themselves to the pagan culture, will provide the leaders of the future. Pregnancy-help centers and other life-saving initiatives practice the culture of life in the trenches. Authentic families are themselves the most important points of light in this developing culture of life. Other examples could be cited. The strength of these initiatives lies in their relative independence from the state. Pursuant to the principle of subsidiarity they get the job done at the local level. And they exemplify

---

[12] See *N.Y. Times*, Apr. 17, 1999, p. A10.
[13] Jennifer Egan, "Why a Priest," *N.Y. Times Magazine*, Apr. 4, 1999, 28, 32-33; see *Wash. Times*, Sept. 23, 1995, p. C4; Kenneth Baker, S.J., "Shortage of Vocations?" *Homiletic & Pastoral Review*, Jan. 1996, 80.
[14] *The Pope in America* (The Wanderer Press, 1979), 28.

solidarity because they help one another without looking first to the state. The center is the family.

"[T]he home is already, but must continue to be and grow in numbers to be the monastery of the new Dark Ages. Each family must be a monastery."[15] But each family must be more than a "monastery" in a ghetto-like isolation. Rather, the response to God in the act of faith is in the gift of self to God and to neighbors. In his family, in his work and other activities, each person is called in faith to be a witness. In his gift of self to others he communicates to them the reality that they themselves are a gift from Someone and ought to be a gift to others. As St. Thomas teaches, "the good. . . is by its nature diffusive."[16] The believer is not a reclusive ghetto resident but a witness, in his life, to the Truth. "'[T]he Church in America must speak increasingly of Jesus Christ, the human face of God and the divine face of man. It is this proclamation that. . . transforms hearts, in a word, converts. Christ must be proclaimed with joy and conviction, but above all by the witness of each one's life.'"[17]

"God the Father and Creator," wrote Fr. Samuel Tiesi, TOR, "wants to receive us as prodigal children who have come to our senses and returned to him, our loving father. As Pope John Paul explains in. . . *Tertio Millennio Adveniente*, 'The whole of the Christian life is like a great pilgrimage to the house of the Father, whose unconditional love for every human creature, and in particular for the 'prodigal son (cf. Lk 15:11-32), we discover anew each day. This pilgrimage takes place in the heart of each person, extends to the believing community and then reaches to the whole of humanity.' Simply put, Christianity is a family journey to our Father who is in heaven."[18]

THE POWER OF MARY

In *Redemptor Hominis,* his first encyclical, John Paul II concluded, "As I end this quasi-meditation with a fervent and humble call for prayer. . . I plead earnestly with Mary, heavenly Mother of the Church, that. . . she would deign to remain with us who make up the Church, the mystical body of her only son."[19] John Paul has reiterated his invocation of Mary in each of his encyclicals. In *Tertio Millennio Adveniente,* he said:

---

[15] Joseph Fessio, S.J., "The Family: Monastery of the New Dark Ages," *Catholic Dossier,* Nov.-Dec. 1998, 47, 53.
[16] *LF,* no. 14, quoting *ST* I, Q. 5, art. 4.
[17] *EA,* no. 67.
[18] Samuel Tiesi, TOR, *Loving Abba* (1999), 1-2.
[19] *Redemptor Hominis* (1979), 22.

I entrust this responsibility of the whole Church to the maternal intercession of Mary, mother of the Redeemer. She, the mother of fairest love, will be for Christians on the way to the Great Jubilee of the third millennium the star which safely guides their steps to the Lord. May the unassuming young woman of Nazareth, who 2,000 years ago offered to the world the incarnate Word, lead the men and women of the new millennium toward the one who is "the true light that enlightens every man" (Jn 1:9).[20]

"God has never made and formed but one enmity; but it is an irreconcilable one, which shall endure and grow even to the end. It is between Mary, His worthy Mother, and the devil — between the children and the servants of the Blessed Virgin, and the children and tools of Lucifer. The most terrible of all the enemies which God has set up against the devil is His holy Mother Mary."[21] Mary, of course, leads us to Christ. She is our supreme exemplar of a human person's "gift of self." Through her, and especially through our prayer of the Rosary, we can find the grace to help us live the culture of life and bring it to others through that gift of self which is the act of faith:

"Give me a million families with Rosaries in their hands, uplifted to Mary," said Joseph Cardinal Mindszenty in his last sermon before being imprisoned by the Communists in Hungary. "They will be a *military* power, not against other people, but for all mankind. . .for their welfare, their healing. . . We need a 'Rosary' of love. Let us therefore take the Rosary from family to family. With it in our hands, we shall conquer ourselves, convert sinners, do penance for our country, and will certainly attain the merciful, mild, and benevolent Heart of Mary."[22]

---

[20] *Tertio Millennio Adveniente,* no. 59.
[21] St. Louis de Montfort, *True Devotion to Mary* (1941), 30-31.
[22] *Mindszenty Report* (Cardinal Mindszenty Foundation, May, 1972) 1, 3-4.

INDEX

A

Abington Township School Dist. v. Schempp, 49-51, 64-65, 67

Abortion, 3-4, 8-21; Buckley Amendment, 233-34; cancerous uterus, 221-23; Cardinals, 1974 testimony of, 233-34; Catholic Church position on, 75-79, 225-27; conscience protection, 249; cooperation with, 229-31; definition of, 69-74, 137-38; early, 69-74; ectopic pregnancy, 221-23; exceptions, 221-24; fetal experimentation, 250; genocide by, 119-25; Hatch Amendment, 234; Human Life Bill, 245; incremental strategy, morality of, 225-27; incremental strategy, wisdom of, 233-42; legislation, federal, 243-46; legislation, state, 247-55; malpractice, 249-50; mother's health, 223; mother's life, 221-23; Mother Teresa on, 110; Paramount Human Life Amendment, 244-45; partial-birth abortion, 240-42; political candidates and, 257-58; prayer vigils, 273-74; pregnancy help centers, 273-74, 352; rape or incest, 223-24; rescues, 267-68; seamless garment, 234-35; states' rights approach, 235-40; statistics, 221; surgical, 69; tactics at abortuaries, 267-74; Title X, 245

Abortion, Procured, Declaration on, 226

Abortionists, killing of, 259-65

Adam and Eve, 159

Adarand Constructors v. Pena, 54

Ad Gentes, 337

Ad Tuendam Fidem, 138

Advance directives, 205-07

Africa, 105, 122, 247-48

AIDS, 173, 182, 211, 273

Alan Guttmacher Institute, 221

Albright, Madeleine, 119

Alexander, M.D., Leo, 30-31

Allgeyer v. La., 49

Altham, Elizabeth, 108

Ambach v. Norwick, 54

America magazine, 124-25

American Bioethics Advisory Commission, 115

American Center for Law and Justice, 255, 268-70

American College of Obstetricians and Gynecologists, 70

American Hospital Assn., 83

American Life League, 26-27, 110, 115, 119, 243

American Republic, 4, 35, 327-33

American Revolution, 221

Americans for Fair Taxation, 40, 336

Americans for Tax Reform Foundation, 40

Anderson, Carl A., 66

Angelou, Maya, 162

Anglican Church, 107-08, 350

Aquinas, St. Thomas, 8-9, 66, 75-76, 104-05, 129-30, 135, 183, 260-61, 263, 281-82, 283, 290, 295, 353

Argentina, 40

Arizona, 172

Articles of Confederation, 327

Atheism, 165, 173, 309, 350

Atheist, The American, 165

Assn. for Family Finances in America, 248

Atlanta, 221

Atomic bomb, 291-92

Augustine, St., 261, 283, 290

Australia, 257

Ave Maria Institute, 195

Ave Maria School of Law, 195

B

Baby M., In re, 252-53

Bacevich, Andrew J., 317

Baker, S.J., Kenneth, 352

Ball, William Bentley, 196-98

Bandow, Doug, 40

Bangladesh, 315

Barron v. Baltimore, 48

BATF, 42

Batra, Ravi, 317

Baugh, Robert R., 50

Baxter, C.S.C., Michael J., 330

Bell, William H., 162

Benedict, St., 352

Bentham, Jeremy, 90

Berger, Raoul, 48-49, 53

Berman, Harold, 90

Bertone, Archbishop Tarcisio, 138

Bettelheim, M.D., Bruno, 181

Bible, 136-37

Biden, Jr., Joseph R., 41

Bill of Rights, 14-15, 38, 47-53

Bill of Rights, English, 38

Bioethics, Instruction on, 116, 224-25, 252-53

Bishops, Catholic, U.S., Pro-life Committee of, 199-201, 205

Black Codes, 48-49

Blackstone, William, 48, 161

Blaine Amendment, 53

Blaine, James G., 53

Blake, Meredith, 120

Blakely, S.J., Paul L., 124-25

Blanshard, Paul, 159

Blessed Virgin, xiii, 143, 150, 188, 242, 265, 353-54

Bloom, Allan, 91

Bd. of Educ. v. Allen, 171

Body, theology of the, 149-50

Boggs, Lindy, 328

Bole, William, 218

Boles, Donald, E., 160-61

Bolling v. Sharpe, 53

Bond, James E., 47

Booker, Frank E., vii

Bork, Robert H., 47, 53, 327

Boston, 221

Boston College, 187, 196

Bouvia v. Superior Ct., 84, 205

Bowman, Karlyn, 349

Bozarth, G. Richard, 165

Bradley, Joseph P., 66-67

Brady Act, 44

Brazil, 121, 314

Brennan, William J., 64, 65, 248

Brimelow, Peter, 299-301

Bristow, Peter, 90

Brophy v. New England Sinai Hosp., 26, 85

Brown, Harold O.J., 293

Brown, Judie, 119

Bryce, Lord, 96

Buchanan, Patrick J., 37, 57, 122, 213, 316-20

Buckley, Sen. James L., 233-34

Buddhism, 64

Bundy, Ted, 285

Burnhill, Dr. Michael, 239

Burtchaell, C.S.C., James T., 185-86, 187, 194

Bush, George, 238

Bush, Gov. George W., 275

Busing, 57

Byrn v. N.Y. City Health & Hosp. Corp., 97-98

Byrne, M.D., Paul A., 29

C

Cairo Conference, 122-23

Calder v. Bull, 104, 329-30

California, 304-05

California Medical Assn., 221

California, Univ. of, 129

Callahan, Daniel, 251-52

Calvert, Brian, 281

Calvinism, 318

Camel, Joe, 211

Canavan, S.J., Francis, 89, 90, 350-51

Canon Law, 138, 184, 187, 196, 197, 219

Capitalism, 309-12, 328-29

Capital Punishment, 234, 275-85

Capitol Mall, 111, 225

Caplan, Dr., Arthur, 83, 86

Caring Foundation, The, 274

Carlson, Allan C., 66

Carroll, John Alexander, 35

Catechism of the Catholic Church, 7, 210, 219, 220, 260-62, 275-85, 287-93, 295, 303, 307-14, 320, 331, 340-45

Catholic Bishops of Maryland, 206-07

Catholic Bishops, Nat'l. Conf. of, 72, 125, 179-80, 222, 231, 233, 241

Catholic Bishops of Texas, 279

Catholic Bishops of the U.S., 233-35, 288-91, 325, 349-50

Catholic Health Facilities, Ethical and Religious Directives for, 222, 224

Catholic Physicians' Guilds, 29

Catholics and U.S. culture, 324-26

Catholics United for Life, 268-70

Centers for Disease Control, 211, 221

Centesimus Annus, 96, 121, 307, 309-10, 321-22

Cetrulo, Robert C., 207

Challenge of Peace: God's Promise and Our Response, The, 288-91

Chaput, Archbishop Charles, 111, 306

Charen, Mona, 12

Chase, Samuel, 104, 329-30

Checks and balances, 35, 38, 41

Chesterton, G.K., 107

Chin, Gabriel, 300

China, 315, 337

China, Communist, 337

Chinn, Rev. Harvey N., 129

Chodes, John, 162

Christ, Jesus, *passim*; and culture of life, 139-43; as only alternative, 350-53; as Truth, 325-26, 342-45; integrating faith & reason, 130-38; loss of, 350-51

Christendom College, 195

Christensen, Bryce, 301-03

Christensen, Dr. Bob, 253

Christian Education, Declaration on, 159, 169, 174

Christian Education of Youth, On the, 173-74

Christian Freedom and Liberation, Instruction on, 307

Christianity, *passim*; 61-67

Christianity Today, 107-08

Christmas, 61

Church of Jesus Christ of Latter-Day Saints v. U.S., 66-67

Church and state, union of, 339-45

Cincinnati, Ohio, 273

City of Boerne v. Flores, 58-59

Civil Rights Act of 1866, 48-49

Civil Rights Act of 1964, 43, 54

Civil Rights Restoration Act of 1987, 46

Civilization of love, 147-48

Civil War, 19-20, 163, 221

Clark, Mary K., 159

Clark Univ., 105

Cleburne v. Cleburne Living Center, Inc., 54

Clinton Administration, 323-24

Clinton, Bill, 40-42, 162, 238, 297, 323, 337

Cloning, 115-16

Cody, John Cardinal, 233-34

Cole, Leonard A., 72-73

College Board, 190-91

Collopy, Anne, 117-18

Colorado, 55, 129, 161

Colson, Charles, 258

Columbine High School, 161

Commandments, Ten, 51, 65-66, 136-38, 170, 335

Commerce Clause, 43-45

Common good, the, 308-09, 344-45

Condom, 124-25

Congregation for the Doctrine of the Faith, 116, 200, 224-25, 226, 252-53, 307

Congregation of Holy Cross, 191-92, 194-95

Congress of the U.S., 35-59, 82

Congress on Secularism and Religious Freedom, 341-42

Conn. v. Menillo, 17

Connecticut, 14, 17, 50-52, 79, 254-55

Connor, Rev. Robert A., vii, 136

Conroy, Matter of, 25, 84-85

Conscientious objection: to abortion and euthanasia, 249; military service, 295-97

Conservative Caucus, 258

Constitution, U.S., *passim*; 20, 35-67, 94-95, 102-06, 248; and natural law, 329-33; and recognition of God, 339-45; deficiency in, 327-34 restoration of, 335-37

Constitutional Convention of 1787, 35, 62

Constitutions, State, 248-49

Contraception: 10, 86-88, 107-25; and abortion, 112-13; and cloning, 115-16; and divorce, 114; and euthanasia, 113-14; and homosexual activity, 114-15; and in vitro fertilization, 115; and pornography, 114; and promiscuity, 114; and unitive and procreative aspects of sex, 108-09; as destroying self-donation, 109-110; legislation on, 254-55; man as arbiter in, 109; Pope John Paul II on abortion and, 113

Contraceptive ethic, 3-4

Contraceptive imperialism, 121-24

Cook, Elizabeth Adell, 238

Cook, M.D., Curtis R., 11

Cooperation, formal and material, 229-31

Corpus Christi, 37-38

Corwin, Edward S., 49-50, 328

Cost of Government Day, 40

Couple-to-Couple League, 110

Craig v. Boren, 54

Craig, Dr., Samuel A., 107-08

van Creveld, Martin, 292

Crime, federalization of, 41-43

Crosby, John F., 109

Cruzan v. Harmon, 27

Cruzan v. Director, Mo. Dept. of Health, 24-29, 83-88

Culliton, Joseph T., 78

Culpability, subjective, 7-9

Culture of death, passim; 3, 349-51

Culture of life, passim; xiii-xiv, 3-5, 139-43, 349-54

CURE, Ltd., 207

Curtiss, Archbishop Elden Francis, 323-24

Czechoslovakia, 95

D

D'Arcy, Most Rev., John M., 193

Daly, Cahal Cardinal, 107, 112

Daly, Erin, 17

Daniels, Jr., Mitchell E., 69

Darwinism, 4

Davidson College, 194

Death, brain, 29-30

Death, determination of, 29-30

Death penalty. See capital punishment.

Death with Dignity Act, Oregon, 24

Debt, foreign, 319-20

Declaration of Independence, 62, 65, 233, 327-28, 333, 339-45

Defense of Marriage Act, 254

DeGaulle, Charles, 69-70

Delaware, 11-12

Democracy, 104-06

Democratic Party, 258

Denmark, 288

Denver, 3, 129

Depression, the, 39

Desert Storm, 221

Dewey, Douglas, 171-72

Dewey, John, 164

Diamond, M.D., Eugene F., 29

Dies Domini, 218-20

Dignitatis Humanae, 340-45

Dives in Misericordia, 311

Divine law, 129-30

Doe v. Bolton, 15

Doe, Jane, Guardianship of, 26

Doerflinger, Richard, 115

Dole, Bob, 238

Donceel, S.J., Joseph F., 76

Dorland's Medical Dictionary, 70

Dorr, Paul R., 237-38

Dostoevsky, Feodor, 350

Double effect, principle of, 81-82, 221-23, 291-92

Douglas, James, 107

Dred Scott Case. See Scott v. Sandford.

Dresden, 291-92

Drummey, James J., 229

Due Process Clause, 18-19, 48-49

Duncan, Richard F., 254

E

Easter, 61

Easter, Sunday as weekly, 218

Ecclesia in America, 305-07, 313-14, 316, 321, 325, 351, 353

Economics, Church teaching on, 307-14

Edmonston, Barry, 300

Education, elementary and secondary: Catholic, 167-72, 173-74; enrollment statistics, 159; federal funding of, 40; home, 159-66, 352-53; private and public, 159-66; religious character of, 163-66; scholarships, privately funded, 172; secularism in public, 163-66; sex, see sex education; tax credits, 167-72; U.S. Dept. of Education, 162, 171; vouchers, 167-72. See Universities, Catholic.

Egan, Jennifer, 352

Egypt, 267

Eighteenth Amendment, 45

Eisenhower, Dwight D., 125

El Salvador, 318

Employment Division v. Smith, 58, 65

Engel, Randy, 254

Englehardt, Jr., H. Tristram, 250

Enlightenment, the, 89-96, 183-84, 327-28, 333

Ensoulment, 75-76

Equal Protection Clause, 47-49, 53-55

Establishment Clause, 49-51, 61-67, 75, 163-64, 168-69, 172, 217-18, 339-45

Ethical Culture, 64

European Parliament, 212-13, 275, 315

Euthanasia, 3-4, 81-88, 199-203; advance directives, 205-07; and contraception, 113-14; futile care theory, 251-52; legislation on, 250-52; nutrition and hydration, 200-03; rationing of care, 251-52

Evangelium Vitae, passim; 3, 132-43, 151, 199-200, 224-27, 229, 265, 275-85, 295-97

Evans, M. Stanton, 41, 95

Everson v. Bd. of Educ., 163

Ex Corde Ecclesiae, 183-98

F

Fairman, Charles, 52

Falwell, Jerry, 285

Familiaris Consortio, 109-10, 176

Family, and civil law, 151-57; *Charter of the Rights of the*, 151-57; legislation on, 253; nature and function of the, 145-50, 352-53. See *Letter to Families*.

Family of the Americas Foundation, 110

Family Planning Services and Population Research Act, 119-20

Family Research Council, 249

Faulk, Odie, 35

Fayette County, Ky, 61

Federal Council of Churches, 107

Federalist, The, 161

Fertility rate, 121-23

Fessio, S.J., Joseph, 353

Fetal experimentation, 250

Fides et Ratio (Faith and Reason), 5, 91-93, 130-38

Fifteenth Amendment, 47

Fifth Amendment, 43

First Amendment, 49-51, 61-67, 75, 163-64, 168, 172, 217-18, 272-73, 331-32, 339-45

Florida, school voucher program, 168

Food and Drug Administration, 72, 183, 193

Forbes, Jr., Malcolm S., 123

Ford, S.J., Norman, 76-78

Fordham Univ., 184, 195

Forstmann, Theodore, 172

Fort Wayne-South Bend, Diocese of, 193

Fortune Magazine, 190-91

Fost, M.D., Norman, 83

Fourteenth Amendment, 13-15, 17-19, 27, 47-59

France, 69-70, 328-29, 351

Francis, Samuel, 335

Franciscan Univ. of Steubenville, 195, 273

Franck, Matthew J., 57, 59

Franklin, Benjamin, 35, 327, 333

Free Exercise Clause, 61-67

Free trade. See global free trade.

Freedom of Access to Clinic Entrances Act (FACE), 268, 273

Freeman, Douglas Southall, 62

Frelinghuysen, Sen., 53

French Revolution, 328-29, 351

Freudianism, 4

Fugitive slave laws, 267-68

Fukuyama, Francis, 117

G

Gacy, John Wayne, 285

Gallup Poll, 238

Gannon, S.J., Robert I., 195-96

GAP Company, 318

Gaspari, Antonio, 119

Gaudium et Spes, 111, 287, 291-92, 307-09, 320, 337, 344

Gay Pride Parade, 211-12

Gay rights. See homosexuality.

General Welfare Clause, 43, 45-46, 57

Genetics & IVF Institute, 116

Genocide, 119-25

George, Francis Cardinal, 306, 318

George Washington Univ., 181

Gerber, Rudolph J., 76

Germany, 14, 20, 30-31, 69-70, 97-102, 104, 288

Germany, West, 319

Gertz, Bill, 337

Geyer, Georgie Anne, 121

"Gift of self," 344-45

Gillette v. U.S., 293

Gitlow v. N.Y., 49

Giuliani, Rudy, 212

Gladstone, William, 327

Glendon, Mary Ann, 235-36

GLND/SMC, 188-89

Global free trade, 315-22

God, *passim*; acknowledgment of by state, 339-45; the Father, 352-54. See also Christ, Jesus; Holy Spirit.

Gold, Philip, 292

Goldsmith, Sir James, 315-16

Good, Frederick L., 221

Goodman, Ellen, 12

Gordon, Dr. Hymie, 223

Goulden, Joe, 211

Graham v. Richardson, 54

Grand jury, 52

Gray, Jim, 267-68

Gray, Jr., William P., 50

Great Britain, 62

Gregorian Univ., 103-04

Grenier, Richard, 122, 162-63

Gresham's Law, 240

Grimes, M.D., David A., 70-71

Grisez, Germain, 73, 76, 166

Griswold v. Conn., 14-15, 52-53, 101-02, 254-55

Grossberg, Amy, 11-12

Grove City College v. Bell, 46

Gulfstream Aerospace, 172

Gun control, 44

Gun-Free School Zones Act, 44

Gustin, Kimberly J., 92

Guttmacher, Alan, 173

H

Hahn, Kimberly, 159

Hahn, Scott, 110

Hairston, Joe B., 171

Hale v. Everett, 52

Hall, O.P., Theodore, 78

Hamilton, Alexander, 161

Hardon, S.J., John A., 81-82, 222-23, 296

Hardwig, John, 87

Harris v. McRae, 247

Hartnett, Edward A., 57

Harvard Univ., 218, 235

Harvey, O.S.F.S., Rev. John F., 213

Hasson, Mary, 159

Havel, Vaclav, 95

Hayes, Rev. Edward J., 229

Hayes, Msgr. Paul J., 229

Health and Human Services, Dept. of, 71

Hellegers, M.D., Andre, 77

Hemingway, Dr. Les, 107, 116-17

Henkin, Louis, 52

Higgs, Robert, 39

Hilgers, M.D., Thomas, 77

Hill, Rev. Edward V., 120-21

Hinckley, John, 7

von Hippel, Ernst, 100-02

Hiroshima, 291-92

Hispanics, 299, 301-03, 305-06

Hitler, Adolf, 19
HMOs, 251-52
Hobbes, Thomas, 89
Hobbs Act, 272
Holmes, Oliver Wendell, 99-100
Holocaust, the, 105-06. See Germany; Nazis.
Holy Trinity Church v. U.S., 63
Holy Spirit, *passim*; 138
Home schools. See education.
Home School Legal Defense Assn., 159
Homosexual activity, 123-24, 209-10, 211-15
Homosexuality, 55, 209-10; and Catholic Church, 211-15; and contraception, 114-15; as disordered, 209-10; *CCC* on, 209-10; Courage, 213; discrimination, 213-15; Exodus, 213; Gay Pride Parade, 211-12; legislation on, 254; marriage and, 149, 211, 212-13, 254
Homosexual "marriage," 149, 211, 212-13, 254
Homosexual movement, 211-15
Homosexual Persons, Letter on the Pastoral Care of, 209-10, 214-15
Homosexuality, Nat'l. Assn. for Research and Therapy of (NARTH), 209, 213-14
Horace Mann League v. Bd. of Pub. Works, 184-85
Hossack, John, 267-68
Houston Ballet, 37
Hubbard, M.D., W.N., 71

Hubschman, Herbert, 218
Human Life Alliance of Minn., 207
Human Life Int'l., 173, 207, 222, 235
Human Rights Watch, 318-19
Humanae Vitae, 108-18, 119, 275
Hunter, Rev. Johnny, 120
Hussein, Saddam, 292-93

I
Idaho, 42
Illinois, 52
Immigration, 299-306
Immigration and Nationality Act of 1965, 299
Immortale Dei, 342
Impeachment, 41
Income tax, personal exemption from, 172, 245-46
Incorporation doctrine, 47-53, 57, 63-64
Indiana, 162
Individualism, 93-94, 96, 134-38, 147-49
Institute for Justice, 168
Int'l. Anti-Euthanasia Task Force, 252
Int'l. Catholic University, 195
Internal Revenue Service, 336
Iraq, 293
Iredell, James, 329-30
Irvine, Reed, 211
Irving, David, 291

J
Jackson v. Benson, 167-72
Jackson, Robert, 163

Jaffa, Harry V., 327
Japan, 105
Jay, John, 161
Jefferson, Thomas, 339
Jews, 14, 62-63, 64
Jipping, Thomas L., 240
Jobes, In re, 25, 26
Johnson, Paul, 257
Jones, Paula, 297
Joyce, Robert, 77
Jubilee, Great, 139
Jus ad Bellum, 290-91
Jus in Bello, 291-93
Justices of the Supreme Court of N.Y. v. U.S. ex rel. Murray, 52-53

K
Kamburowski, Michael, 40
Kass, Dr. Leon, 82
Kelly, R.N., Dorothy Ellen, 229
Kelsen, Hans, 97-101
Kemerer, Frank R., 171
Kendall, George, 251-52
Kennedy, Anthony M., 55
Kerrison, Ray, 211-12
Khan, Ghengis, 14
King, Dwight, vii
King, Larry, 285
Kinslow, Carmela, vii
Klasing, Murphy S., 250
Kmiec, Douglas, W., 41, 327, 343
Know-Nothing movement, 160-61
Koch, Ed, 211-12
Koppell v. Quill, 24
Korean War, 39
Koresh, David, 42

Kotterman v. Killian, 172
Kramer v. Union Free School Dist., 54
Krol, John Cardinal, 233-34
Ku Klux Klan, 120
Kuhse, Helga, 13-14

L
Lafayette College, 194
Laird, Bob and Gerry, 114
Lambeth Conference, 107-08
Lambs of Christ, 267
Lamm, Richard, 81
Land O'Lakes statement, 185, 194
Landers, Ann, 331
Lauerman, Keith, 171
Law as will, 105
Lawrance, In re, 26
Laws, unjust, 9, 101-06
Lawson, Gary, 41
Legal Action for Women, 249
Legislation, federal, proposed, 243-46
Legislation, state, proposed, 247-255
Leiter, Richard A., 205
Lejeune, Jerome, 77
Leo, John, 61, 105-06, 162
Lesbian activity, 123-24
Letter to Families, 108-09, 145-50, 151, 320, 353
Levin, Mark, 323
Liberalism, 350
Libertas Praestantissimum, 342
"Liberty interest," 17-18, 79
Lietzau, William K., 50
Life After Assault League, 224
Life Dynamics, Inc., 249

Life, Education & Resource Network (LEARN), 120
Life Issues Institute, 72
Lincoln, Abraham, 67, 162, 337
Lind, William S., 292
Little League, 217
Living the Gospel of Life: A Challenge to American Catholics, 231, 325, 326
Living Will, 205-07
Lochner v. N.Y., 49
Locke, John, 89
London Sunday Express, 107
Long Island, 121-22
Lopez Trujillo, Cardinal, 121
Lott, Trent, 40
Loudon High School, 61
Louisville, 221
Love, free, 148
Lubac, S.J., Henri de, 350
Lucey, S.J., Francis E., 99-100, 106
Lumen Gentium, 341-42
Lutz, David W., 189-90
Lynch v. Donnelly, 51
Lynch, Neil L., 85

M
Macaulay, Thomas Babington, 333
MacBride Principles, 247-48
MacBride, Sean, 247-48
Madison, James, 161
Madison Square Garden, 352
Madsen v. Women's Health Center, 18, 269-71
Magdalen College, 195

Maginot Line, 69
Magna Carta, 38
Mahometanism, 62-63
Malloy, C.S.C., Edward A., 189, 194, 196
Malloy, Michele, 250
Manhattan Theater Club, 37-38
Manichaeanism, 149-50
Mann, Horace, 160-61
Manning, Timothy Cardinal, 233-34
Maquiladoras, 318-19
Marbury v. Madison, 59
Marriage, covenant, 253
Marshner, William H., 78
Martyr, John, 257
Marxism, 4
Mary. See Blessed Virgin.
Maryland, 50, 64-65, 121, 184, 206-07, 217-18, 238, 352
Massachusetts, 50
Mazurek v. Armstrong, 17
McBrien, Rev. Richard, 186, 193
McClellan, Dr. James, 39-40, 58
McCloskey, Rev. C. John, 4
McCutchen, Peter B., 41
McDonald, Forrest, 328-29
McGuffey's Readers, 161-62
McHugh, Most Rev. James, 201-03
McIntyre, Michael J., 172
McLaughlin, S.J., Leo, 184-85
McVeigh, Timothy, 285
Mears, S.J., J. Gerard, 124-25
Medeiros, Humberto Cardinal, 233-34
Medicaid, 251
Medicare, 251

Meehan, Paul, 304

Meese, Edwin, III, 41-42, 54-55

Mellor, Chip, 168

Meltzer, Milton, 19-20

Mexico, 305-06, 318-19

Miles, Dr. Steven, 83

Mill, John Stuart, 90

Miller, Matthew, 190

Miller v. Johnson, 54

Milwaukee, 108, 167-72

Milwaukee, Archdiocese of, 169-72

Milwaukee Parental Choice Program, 167-72

Mindszenty, Joseph Cardinal, 354

Minnesota, Univ. of, 83

Missionaries to the Preborn, 108

Missouri v. Jenkins, 54

Missouri, 24-27, 54, 75

Monan, S.J., J. Donald, 196

Monasteries, the new, 352-53

Montfort, St. Louis de, 354

Moore, Stephen, 349

Mormons, 66-67

Mosher, Steven W., 121

Motherhood, surrogate, 252-53

Mt. St. Mary's Seminary, 352

Mount Sinai, 327, 335

Murphy, Edward J., vii

Murphy, Timothy, 271-73

Myers, Most Rev. John J., 201, 229-31, 239, 257

N

Nagasaki, 291-92

Nassau County, 121-22

Nath_____ M.D., Bernard, 221-2_

Nat'l. Abortion Federation, 239

Nat'l. Academy of Sciences, 122-23

Nat'l. Center for Health Statistics, 211

Nat'l. Assn. for Research and Therapy of Homosexuality (NARTH), 209, 213-14

Nat'l. Conf. of Catholic Bishops. See Catholic Bishops, Nat'l. Conf. of.

Nat'l. Cops for Life, 249

National Endowment for the Arts, 37-38, 40

Natl. Endowment for the Arts v. Finley, 37

Nat'l. Federation of Officers for Life, 249

Nat'l. Home Education Research Institute, 159

Natl. Right to Life Committee, 3, 117-18, 221, 234

Nationalism, 317, 319-20

NATO, 291

Natural Family Planning, 110-12

Natural law, 7-10, 99-106, 129-30; and U.S. Constitution, 102-04, 327-33

Navarro-Valls, Joaquin, 123-24

Nazis, 14, 20, 30-31, 69, 97-102, 104, 288

Nelson, Truman, 20

Neoliberalism, 321

Netherlands, 83-84

New Deal, 39

New England Journal of Medicine, 70-71

New Hampshire, 50, 52

New Jersey, 53, 84-85

Newman, John Henry Cardinal, 186, 350

New York, 24-27, 63, 81, 161, 211-12, 352

New York Times, 331

Nicolosi, Ph.D., Joseph, 213-14

Ninth Amendment, 38

Nitze School of Advanced International Studies, 317

Nixon, Richard M., 119

Noonan, Jr., John T., 76

Northwest Ordinance of 1787, 327

Norway, 288

Notre Dame Law School, vii,188

Notre Dame, Univ. of, 183-98

Novak, Michael, 312

NOW v. Scheidler, 271-73

Nuremberg Laws, 14

Nurturing Network, 273

O

Obligations of Catholics and the Rights of Unborn Children, The, 229-31

O'Boyle, Patrick Cardinal, 164

O'Brien, Michael, 349

O'Brien, S.J., F. William, 53

Obscenity, 52

Observer, Notre Dame, 189, 191, 194, 312

O'Connor, John Cardinal, 23, 217, 291

O'Connor, Sandra Day, 73-74. 271

O'Hair, Madalyn Murray, 173

"Old Right," 315

Ollie's Barbecue, 43

Olson, Walter, 44-45

O'Meara, Timothy, 189, 191

O'Neel, Brian, 351

Oregon, 24

O'Reilly, M.D., Sean, 181

P

Pacem in Terris, 303

Pacifism, Pope Paul VI on, 296-97

Pacifism, selective, 289-93

Pacifism, universal, 287-89

Pakaluk, Michael, 235

Parenthood, responsible, 146

Paris, Treaty of, 62

Parker, Star, 162

Partial-birth abortion, 240-41

Pastor Aeturnus, 350

Pastoral Constitution on the Church in the Modern World. See *Gaudium et Spes*.

Patrick, Robert M., 180

Peace, Message for the Observance of a Day of, 296-97

Pennsylvania, 17, 83, 162-63, 218

Pennsylvania, Univ. of, 83

Peoria, 201, 229

Perez v. U.S., 43

Person, dignity of the, 307-09, 312-14

Person, functional definition of, 105

Personalism, 147-49

Person as relation, 134-36

Personhood, constitutional, 12-15, 18-21, 28-29

Peterson, Brian, 11-12

Peterson, Wallace C., 317

Petition of Right of 1628, 38

Pharmacists for Life, 72, 249

Philadelphia, 247, 335

Pilate, Pontius, 20

Pilsudski, Marshal, 69

Pittsburgh, 61

Planned Parenthood, 73, 173, 221, 273

Planned Parenthood v. Casey, 17-20

Planned Parenthood v. Danforth, 67

Plawecki, Lois, vii

Pledge of Allegiance, 65

Pluralism, false, 324-25

Poland, 69

Pollock v. Farmer's Loan & Trust Co., 39

Pontifical Academy of Life, 224

Pontifical Council for the Family, 174-75

Pope John XXIII, 233, 303

Pope John Paul II, *passim*; and youth, 3-5, 325, 351; at Capitol Mall, 20; in Latvia, 310-11; in New York, 352; in Paris, 351; on: abortion, 224, 225-27, 229, 234; beginning of life, 76; capitalism, 310; contraception, 109-18; contraceptive imperialism, 121-24; culture of death, 3, 349-50; culture of life, 139-43; death penalty, 275-85; determination of death, 30; faith and reason, 129-38; family, 145-50, 151-57, 175; founding of the U.S., 328; globalization, 316-22; homosexual marriage, 213; immigration, 303-06; individualism, 93-94; Mary, 143, 150, 265, 353-54; millennium, 351; natural family planning, 109-12; negative precepts as absolutely binding, 263; neoliberalism, 321; person as relation, 134-36; political morality, 324-26; postmodernity, 93; prohibition of intentional killing of innocent, abortion and euthanasia, 136-38, 221-24; relativism and democracy, 96; secularism, 91; social teaching of, 307-22; springtime of Christianity, 4, 138, 349-50; Sunday, 217-20; theology of the body, 149-50; union of church and state, 340-45

Pope Leo XIII, 220, 342

Pope Paul VI, 108-18, 119, 150, 262, 275, 295, 296-97

Pope Paul VI Institute, 110

Pope Pius XI, 173-74, 308, 321-22, 342-43

Pope Pius XII, 223, 307-08

Population, aging, 86-88, 121-24

Population control, 121-24

Population Council, 72

Population, declining, 121-24

Populorum Progressio, 262

Pornography, 95, 114

Postivism, legal, 97-106

Postmodernity, 93

Poverty, 234

Power of attorney, durable, 205-07

Powers, balance of, 35, 38, 41

Powers, division of, 35, 38-43
Powers, separation of, 46
Pregnancy, definition of, 69-74
Pregnancy Problem Center East, 273
Presser, Stephen B., 41, 327, 329, 343
Preston, Samuel H., 87
Priesthood, vocations to the, 352
Princeton Univ., 13
Printz v. U.S., 44
Privacy, right of, 51-52, 79
Privileges or Immunities Clause, 48-49, 53
Prohibition, 39, 45
Pro-Life Action League, 271-73
Pro-Life Action Network, 271-73
Pro-Life Marketing Group, 252
Pro-Life Shareholders, 248
Proposition 187, 304-05
Protestantism, 160-66, 217, 254-55, 329-33
Provan, Charles D., 108
Provincetown, Mass., 211

Q
Quadragesimo Anno, 321-22
Quas Primas, 342-43
Quill, MD., Timothy, 82

R
Racketeer Influenced and Corrupt Organizations Act (RICO), 268-74
Radbruch, Gustav, 101-02
Rahner, Karl, 78
Ratzinger, Joseph Cardinal, 138
Raucher, Alan, 217

Rea-Luthin, Marianne, 70
Reagan, Ronald, 7, 299
Rebellion, justified, 261-63, 276
Redemptor Hominis, 353
Redemptoris Missio, 4
Rees, G. Joseph, 121
Reformation, Protestant, 330, 332
Regina v. Dudley and Stephens, 223, 241
Rehnquist, William, 18-19, 271, 272
Reisman, Judith A., 254
Relativism, 91-93, 95
Religion, incorporation doctrine and, 51-53, 63-67
Religion, governmental neutrality on, 63-67, 339-45
Religious Freedom Restoration Act, 58-59
Religious freedom, 58-59, 340-45
Rerum Novarum, 220
Republic, American. See American Republic.
Republican Party, 258
Reynolds v. Sims, 54
Rhoades, Kevin, 352
Rhode Island, 221
Rice, Charles E., xiv, 8, 15, 58-59, 62, 64-65, 100, 101, 105, 110, 115, 130, 136, 160, 163, 164-65, 183-97, 189, 191, 194, 252-53, 258, 259, 267-68, 275-85, 313, 339
Rice, Ellen, vii
Rice, Mary, vii
Rice, Patricia, vii
Right to die, 23-29, 250-52

Right to Life of Michigan Resource Center, 207

Roberts, Paul Craig, 299, 323

Robertson, Pat, 275

Rockville Centre, N.Y., 201

Rockwell, Llewellyn, 315

Roe v. Wade, 3, 11-31, 46, 52, 57, 64-65, 79, 233-34, 238, 259-60, 261-62

Roëpke, Wilhelm, 319

Roman Empire, 352

Romer v. Evans, 55

Rommen, Heinrich, 89, 101-02, 104

Roosevelt, Franklin D., 41

Rosary, the, 265, 274, 354

Rosenberger v. Rector of the Univ. of Va., 65

Rousseau, Jean Jacques, 89

RU-486, 72

Ruby Ridge, 42

Rutgers Univ., 72

S

Saenz v. Roe, 49

St. Ignatius Institute, 195

St. Louis, 306

St. Patrick's Cathedral, 211-12

San Francisco, Univ. of, 195

Sanders, Colonel, 14

Sanger, Margaret, 73

Sattler, C.S.S.R., H. Vernon, 178

Scalia, Antonin, 18-19, 54-55, 102-04, 271

Scalia, Rev. Paul, 145

Schaefer, Rev. Vernon J., 173, 181

Scheidler, Joseph, 271-73

Schenck v. Pro-Choice Network of Western New York, 18, 269-70

Schmitt, USMCR, Maj. John F., 292

Scholberg, Andrew, 271-73

Schools. See education.

Schor, Juliet, 218

Schulman, Dr. Joseph, 116

Schurmann, Franz, 302

Schwarz, Stephen, 77-78

Scientists for Life, 77

Scott v. Sandford, 13, 53

Secular Humanism, 64

Secularism, 61-67

Sekulow, Jay, 211

Self-defense, 276

Senate, U.S., 39, 233-34, 323

Senate, U.S., Subcommittee on Constitutional Amendments, 233-34

Senate, U.S., Watergate Committee, 323

Separation of School and State Alliance, 166

Serbia, 291

Seventeenth Amendment, 39, 49

Sex education, 147, 173-82, 254; and Catholic schools, 178-82; impracticality of, 180-82; NCCB on, 179-80; principles of, 173-78; secularized, 175-80; *The Truth and Meaning of Human Sexuality*, 174-80

Sex, safe, 147

Shalit, Wendy, 181

Shapiro v. Thompson, 54

Shivakumar, Dhananjai, 65

Sim, Dr. Myre, 181

Simon, Julian, 121-23

Simon, Robert L., 97

Singer, Peter, 13-14

Sinner, value of conversion of, 283

Sioux Falls, S.D., 237-38

Sisters of Life, 70

Sixteenth Amendment, 39-40, 49, 336

Slaughter-House Cases, 49, 53

Slavery, 19-20

Smith, James P., 300

Smith, Lamar, 299-300

Smith, Steven D., 50-51

Smith, William, 94-95

Smith, Msgr. William B., 119

Smoking, 211

Social teaching of the Church, 307-322

Solidarity, 307-09, 352

Sollicitudo Rei Socialis, 311

Solomon, Gerald B.H., 37, 40

Solzhenitsyn, Aleksandr, 89, 258

Sommers, Christina Hoff, 105

Sooner Catholic, The, 4-5, 121

South Africa, 247-48

South Bend, Ind., 267

South Carolina, 50

South Dakota, 237-38

Southern Baptist Theological Seminary, 217

Soviet Union, 315

Sowell, Thomas, 162-63

Spanish-American War, 39

Spencer, Robert, 92

Stalin, Josef, 14

Stanton, M.D., Joseph R., 31, 69-74

Steurle, C. Eugene, 172

Stevens, John Paul, 18-19, 28-29, 73-76, 170

Stone v. Graham, 66

STOPP (Stop Planned Parenthood), 255

Story, Joseph, 62-63, 323

Stromberg v. Calif., 49

Subsidiarity, 307-09, 352-53

Suffolk County, 121-22

Suicide, 23-29, 81-88, 113-14, 250, 349

Suicide, assisted, 23-29, 81-88

Sullivan, Rev. Leon, 247-48

Sunday, 217-20; as weekly Easter, 218

Supreme Court of the United States, 3-4, 11-29, 35, 37, 43-67, 69, 81-88, 102-04, 172, 217-18, 237, 247-49, 259-60, 267-74, 323, 339-40

Swope, Paul, 273-74

T

Tacelli, S.J., Ronald K., 77-78

Talbot, Margaret, 72

Taney, Roger B., 53

Taoism, 64

Tax Reform Foundation Americans for, 40

Tax Freedom Day, 40

Tax, income, 39-40; personal exemption from, 172, 245-46

Tenth Amendment, 38-40

Teresa, Mother, 110, 261-62

Tertio Millennio Adveniente, 138, 351, 353

Texas, 275-85

Thanksgiving, 61-62

Thirteenth Amendment, 19-20, 48
Thomas Aquinas College, 195
Thomas More Center for Law and Justice, 255
Thomas More College, 195
Thomas, Clarence, 18
Thornburg v. ACOG, 19, 29
Thornton, Deborah, 276
Thornton, Richard, 276
Tiesi, TOR, Samuel, 353
Tiger, Lionel, 117
Tighe, Margaret, 257
Timperlake, Edward, 337
Titanic, The, 167, 172
Title IX, 46
Title X, 119-20, 245
Tocqueville, Alexis de, 332-33
Topczenski, Jerry, 169
Torcaso, Roy, 64-65, 67
Torcaso v. Watkins, 64-65, 67
Transnational corporations, 316-17
Travel, right to, 49
Trewhella, Matt, 108
Trinity, The, 145, 307
Triplett, III, William C., 337
Trujillo, Alfonso Cardinal, 174-75
Tucker, Karla Faye, 275-85
Tuskey, John, 211, 259
Twinning, 76-78
Twitchell v. Pa., 52-53
Two Guys from Harrison-Allentown, Inc., 218

U

Ubi Arcano dei Consililo, 343
Underground Railroad, 267-68

United Nations, 121-24, 145, 293, 295
U.S. v. Butler, 46
U.S. v. Holmes, 223, 241
U.S. v. Lopez, 44
U.S. v. Virginia, 47, 54
United Steelworkers of America v. Weber, 54-55
Universities, Catholic, 183-98, 352; accreditation of by Church, 196-98; and Canon Law, 184, 187, 196, 197; and *Ex Corde Ecclesiae*, 183-88, 193, 197-98; correctives for, 195-98; Land O'Lakes statement on, 185, 194
Unz, Ron K., 302-03
Upjohn Company, 71
Utilitarianism, 148-49, 320-21, 349
Utter, Robert F., 248

V

ValuSure Corp., 248
Value of Life Committee, 70
Vacco v. Quill, 23-29, 81-88
Vatican I, 350
Vatican II, 111, 135-36, 159-60, 169, 175, 182, 184, 287, 291-92, 337, 339-45, 352
Veritatis Splendor, 104-05, 129-38, 197, 263, 265, 324-26, 336, 344
Vietnam, 315
Vietnam War, 39
Villalobos, P. Michael, 46
Virginia, 47, 54, 58, 61, 239
Virginia, ex parte, 58

Virginia Military Institute, 47, 54
Virginia, parental notice law, 239
Voegelin, Eric, 94

W

Wal-Mart, 172
Walton, John, 172
War, 234, 287-97
War, Catholic teaching on, 287-97
War, conscientious objection to, 295-97
War, just, 289-93
War power, constitutional, 41
Washington, D.C., 111
Washington, George, 62, 333
Washington Post, 107
Washington Post-ABC News Poll, 238
Washington v. Glucksberg, 17, 23-27, 83-88
Wattenberg, Ben, 300, 301
Weaver, Richard, 95
Weber, Walter M., 268-70
Webster v. Reproductive Health Services, 18-19, 28-29, 73-76, 247
Weigel, George, 235-36
Weimar Republic, 100
Welsh v. U.S., 389
Weslin, Rev. Norman, 267
West, Christopher, 150
West Orange, N.J., 61
Westmont College, 220
White, Byron, 18-19
White, M.D., Margaret, 108
Whitehead, Alfred North, 163
Whitehead, Barbara Dafoe, 173

Whitehead, Kenneth D., 178-80, 221, 254
Whitmore, Todd David, 312
Wickard v. Filburn, 43-44, 46
Will, George, 12, 47
Will, living, 205-07
Willadsen, Dr. Steve, 116
Willcocks, Raymond H., 291
Williams, Walter, 162
Williams v. Zbaraz, 247
Willke, M.D., John C., 72
Wilson, David C., 221
Wilson, USMCR, Col. Gary I., 292
Wilson, James Q., 129
Wilson, Jonathan, 220
Wisconsin, 83, 108, 167-72
Wisconsin, Univ. of, 83
World Trade Organization, 315
World War I, 39, 49
World War II, 39, 101, 102, 124-25, 162, 288, 291-92, 306
World Youth Day, 3, 129
Wrong, objective, 7-9

Y

Yugoslavia, 41

Z

Zinsmeister, Karl, 349
Zwick, Louise, 148
Zwick, Mark, 148